CW00918222

NIETZSCHE'S FREE SPIRIT WORKS

Between 1878 and 1882, Nietzsche published what he called "the free spirit works": *Human, All Too Human*; *Assorted Opinions and Maxims*; *The Wanderer and His Shadow*; *Daybreak*; and *The Gay Science*. Often approached as a mere assemblage of loosely connected aphorisms, these works are here reinterpreted as a coherent narrative of the steps Nietzsche takes in educating himself toward freedom that executes a dialectic between scientific truth-seeking and artistic life-affirmation. Matthew Meyer's new reading of these works not only provides a more convincing explanation of their content but also makes better sense of the relationship between them and Nietzsche's larger oeuvre. His argument shows how these texts can and should be read as a unified project even while they present multiple, in some cases conflicting, images of the free spirit. The book will appeal to anyone who is interested in Nietzsche's philosophy and especially to those puzzled about how to understand the peculiarities of the free spirit works.

MATTHEW MEYER is an associate professor of philosophy at The University of Scranton. He is the author of *Reading Nietzsche through the Ancients* (2014) and a co-editor of *Nietzsche's Metaphilosophy* (Cambridge).

NIETZSCHE'S FREE SPIRIT WORKS

A Dialectical Reading

MATTHEW MEYER

The University of Scranton

CAMBRIDGE
UNIVERSITY PRESS

CAMBRIDGE
UNIVERSITY PRESS

University Printing House, Cambridge CB2 8BS, United Kingdom

One Liberty Plaza, 20th Floor, New York, NY 10006, USA

477 Williamstown Road, Port Melbourne, VIC 3207, Australia

314–321, 3rd Floor, Plot 3, Splendor Forum, Jasola District Centre, New Delhi – 110025, India

79 Anson Road, #06–04/06, Singapore 079906

Cambridge University Press is part of the University of Cambridge.

It furthers the University's mission by disseminating knowledge in the pursuit of education, learning, and research at the highest international levels of excellence.

www.cambridge.org
Information on this title: www.cambridge.org/9781108474177
DOI: 10.1017/9781108564847

© Matthew Meyer 2019

First published 2019

Printed and bound in Great Britain by Clays Ltd, Elcograf S.p.A.

A catalogue record for this publication is available from the British Library.

Library of Congress Cataloging-in-Publication Data
NAMES: Meyer, Matthew, author.
TITLE: Nietzsche's free spirit works : a dialectical reading / Matthew Meyer, University of Scranton, Pennsylvania.
DESCRIPTION: 1 [edition]. | New York : Cambridge University Press, 2019. | Includes bibliographical references and index.
IDENTIFIERS: LCCN 2018050896 | ISBN 9781108474177 (hardback : alk. paper) | ISBN 9781108463904 (pbk. : alk. paper)
SUBJECTS: LCSH: Nietzsche, Friedrich Wilhelm, 1844–1900.
CLASSIFICATION: LCC B3317 .M55193 2019 | DDC 193–dc23
LC record available at https://lccn.loc.gov/2018050896

ISBN 978-1-108-47417-7 Hardback

To my loving wife and companion of nearly twenty years, Renata.

Contents

vii

Acknowledgments

This book is the result of a project that extends back to my time as a Master's student at Harvard University and my work at the University of Vienna as a Frederick Sheldon Fellow from Harvard University. It develops the argument of two previously published papers (Meyer 2004 and 2006) and expands on the ideas from my previous book (2014a). I am grateful to the various organizers, audiences, and venues at which I have been able to present my work, including the North American Nietzsche Society, the Friedrich Nietzsche Society, Nietzsche in the Northeast, and the Berliner Nietzsche Colloquium, and I would like to thank The University of Scranton for supporting my conference travel, a year-long sabbatical, and summer research with a faculty development grant.

I would also like to thank the various friends, colleagues, and conference participants who have offered their comments and feedback on this project over the years: Tom Bailey, Rebecca Bamford, Daniel Blue, Daniel Conway, Tsarina Doyle, Paul Franco, Robert Guay, Lawrence Hatab, Helmut Heit, Christopher Janaway, Scott Jenkins, Anthony Jensen, Peter Kail, Paul Katsafanas, Allison Merrick, Mark Migotti, John Richardson, Jordan Rodgers, Melanie Shepherd, Ivan Soll. I owe a special thanks to Paul Loeb for frequent discussions about Nietzsche and his feedback on this project. I also appreciate the feedback from the two anonymous reviewers who pushed me to organize my ideas better and express myself with greater clarity. Finally, Hilary Gaskin has been an impeccable editor and an excellent source of wisdom and guidance, and I would like to thank her and the entire staff at Cambridge University Press for shepherding this project from an idea to a manuscript and now a published book.

Abbreviations and Translations of Nietzsche's Published Works

The following is a list of abbreviations and the English translations I use for Nietzsche's works. Because the chronology of Nietzsche's texts is important for understanding the argument of this book, I have listed Nietzsche's works below in the order in which they were written. In most cases, the dates listed are dates of publication. Works marked by (*) are works that Nietzsche only distributed privately. Works marked by (**) are works that Nietzsche authorized for publication but were not published in his lifetime. Thus, the date next to these two types of works is the year in which the work was completed. "P" is the abbreviation for the preface to a given work (except for the preface to the 1886 edition of *The Birth of Tragedy*). Unless otherwise noted, translations of *Nachlass* notes from *Sämtliche Werke: Kritische Studienausgabe* (KSA) and Nietzsche's letters from *Sämtliche Briefe: Kritische Studienausgabe* (KSB) are my own. See the bibliography for information for KSA and KSB.

1872:   BT = *The Birth of Tragedy Out of the Spirit of Music*. In *The Birth of Tragedy and the Case of Wagner*, trans. W. Kaufmann, 15–151. New York: Vintage (1967). Republished in 1878 and then in 1886 with a new preface and title: *The Birth of Tragedy Or: Hellenism and Pessimism. New Edition with an Attempt at a Self-Criticism*. "Attempt" = "Attempt at a Self-Criticism" (1886).

1873:   DS = *David Strauss the Confessor and the Writer*. In *Untimely Meditations*, trans. R. J. Hollingdale, 1–55. Cambridge: Cambridge University Press (1983).

1874:   HL = *On the Uses and Disadvantages of History for Life*. In *Untimely Meditations*, trans. R. J. Hollingdale, 57–123. Cambridge: Cambridge University Press (1983).

ix

1874:   SE = *Schopenhauer as Educator*. In *Untimely Meditations*,
            trans. R. J. Hollingdale, 125–194. Cambridge: Cambridge
            University Press (1983).

1876:   RWB = *Richard Wagner in Bayreuth*. In *Untimely
            Meditations*, trans. R. J. Hollingdale, 195–254. Cambridge:
            Cambridge University Press (1983).

1878:   HH = *Human, All Too Human: A Book for Free Spirits*,
            trans. R. J. Hollingdale, 1–205. Cambridge: Cambridge
            University Press (1996). Republished as *Human,
            All Too Human I* in 1886 with an additional preface
            (= HH I P).

1879:   AOM = *Assorted Opinions and Maxims*. In *Human, All Too
            Human: A Book for Free Spirits*, trans. R. J. Hollingdale,
            215–299. Cambridge: Cambridge University Press (1996).
            Republished as part of *Human, All Too Human II* in
            1886 with an additional preface (= HH II P).

1880:   WS = *The Wanderer and His Shadow*. In *Human, All Too
            Human: A Book for Free Spirits*, trans. R. J. Hollingdale,
            301–395. Cambridge: Cambridge University Press (1996).
            Republished as part of *Human, All Too Human II* in 1886.

1881:   D = *Daybreak: Thoughts on the Prejudices of Morality*, trans.
            R. J. Hollingdale. Cambridge: Cambridge University Press
            (1982). Republished in 1887 with an additional preface.

1882:   IM = *Idylls from Messina*. Originally published in the
            Internationale Monatschrift. There is no English translation
            available.

1882:   GS = *The Gay Science*, trans. W. Kaufmann. New York:
            Random House (1974). Republished in 1887 with an
            additional preface, fifth chapter, and appendix of songs
            (JCR = "Joke, Cunning, and Revenge"; SPV = "Songs of
            Prince Vogelfrei").

1883–1885: Z (I–IV) = *Thus Spoke Zarathustra*. In *The Portable
            Nietzsche*, ed. and trans. W. Kaufmann, 109–439. New
            York: Viking Press (1954) (references include book number
            and an abbreviated section title). Z IV* was distributed only
            privately during Nietzsche's lifetime.

1886:   BGE = *Beyond Good and Evil*, trans. W. Kaufmann. New
            York: Random House (1989).

1887:   GM = *On the Genealogy of Morals*. In *On the Genealogy of
            Morals and Ecce Homo*, trans. W. Kaufmann, 13–163.

New York: Random House (1989) (references include essay number followed by section number).

1888:   CW = *The Case of Wagner*. In *The Birth of Tragedy and the Case of Wagner*, trans. W. Kaufmann, 153–192. New York: Vintage (1967).

1888:   TI = *Twilight of the Idols*. In *The Portable Nietzsche*, ed. and trans. W. Kaufmann, 463–564. New York: Viking Press (1954) (references include an abbreviated chapter title and section number).

1888**:   EH = *Ecce Homo*. In *On the Genealogy of Morals and Ecce Homo*, trans. W. Kaufmann, 215–335. New York: Random House (1989) (references include abbreviated chapter title and section number; in the section "Books," the section number is preceded by the abbreviation of the relevant book title).

1888**:   A = *The Antichrist*. In *The Portable Nietzsche*, ed. and trans. W. Kaufmann, 565–656. New York: Viking Press (1954).

1888*:   NCW = *Nietzsche contra Wagner*. In *The Portable Nietzsche*, ed. and trans. W. Kaufmann, 661–683. New York: Viking Press (1954).

1888**:   DD = *Dithyrambs of Dionysus*, trans. R. J. Hollingdale. London: Anvil Press Poetry (2001).

Unpublished Writings

The following are abbreviations for texts that Nietzsche neither published nor authorized for publication. The dates listed are dates of composition.

1872:   FEI = "On the Future of Our Educational Institutions." In *Anti-Education*, ed. P. Reitter and C. Wellmon, trans. D. Searls. New York: New York Review of Books (2016).

1873:   TL = "On Truth and Lies in a Nonmoral Sense." In *Philosophy and Truth: Selections from Nietzsche's Notebooks of the Early 1870's*, ed. and trans. D. Breazeale, 77–97. Atlantic Highlands, NJ: Humanities Press (1979).

1873:   PTAG = *Philosophy in the Tragic Age of the Greeks*, trans. M. Cowan. Washington, DC: Gateway (1962).

1872–1876:   PPP = *The Pre-Platonic Philosophers*, ed. and trans. G. Whitlock. Urbana, IL: University of Illinois Press (2001).

Introduction

CHAPTER I

Interpreting Nietzsche's Free Spirit Works

This is a book about what scholars have called Nietzsche's "middle period" or what Nietzsche calls the free spirit works: *Human, All Too Human* (1878), *Assorted Opinions and Maxims* (1879), *The Wanderer and His Shadow* (1880), *Daybreak* (1881), and *The Gay Science* (1882).[1] The primary aim of this book is to advocate for a paradigm shift in the way we interpret the free spirit works that may have consequences for how we understand Nietzsche's larger oeuvre. Whereas many scholars approach the free spirit works as collections of isolated aphorisms that express views the mature Nietzsche eventually rejects, I argue that these works are best understood as a consciously constructed dialectical *Bildungsroman* in which Nietzsche walks himself and his readers through a series of philosophical stages that begins with a quest for truth through the natural sciences in *Human* and culminates in the rebirth of tragedy in *Thus Spoke Zarathustra* (1883–1885). On this reading, the free spirit works do include ideas that Nietzsche eventually surpasses in his later publications. However, the steps he takes to reach what many consider his mature views are an essential part of telling the story of how he becomes a free spirit and eventually who he is.

The claim that the free spirit works are best understood as a consciously constructed dialectical *Bildungsroman* will surprise many. Although scholars are now paying more attention to Nietzsche's books, many still approach Nietzsche's published and unpublished writings as collections of independent thought experiments. For instance, so-called analytical readers of Nietzsche often follow Arthur Danto in trying to construct a set of coherent philosophical ideas from the seeming hodgepodge of

---

[1] Nietzsche republished each of these works in 1886 and 1887 with new prefaces. In so doing, he made *Assorted Opinions* and *The Wanderer* into the second volume of *Human*, and he added a fifth chapter to *The Gay Science*. Although a brief analysis of the fifth chapter of *The Gay Science* is included in this study, the primary focus of this study ends with the 1882 edition and so the first four chapters of *The Gay Science*.

statements Nietzsche puts forth in his writings. In contrast, so-called postmodern readers have been quick to argue that the fragmentary and contradictory character of Nietzsche's writings openly resists the analytic quest for coherence and systematicity and that his use of a variety of stylistic and literary techniques – including the aphoristic form of the free spirit works – shows that the meanings of his texts are fluid and thus allow for infinite interpretations.

Despite the potential role they may have played in shaping this image of Nietzsche's corpus, the fate of the free spirit works has been one of relative neglect. Although a small handful of books on the free spirit works have appeared in recent years in Anglo-American scholarship,[2] this pales in comparison with the attention lavished on a work such as *On the Genealogy of Morals*. At best, only *The Gay Science* has received the kind of attention that is comparable to Nietzsche's later works, and this is because many believe that *The Gay Science* transitions to Nietzsche's mature thinking.[3] Although *The Gay Science* does transition to Nietzsche's later works, the problem with this approach is that *The Gay Science* itself cannot be properly understood separately from the free spirit works that precede it.

The claim that the free spirit works constitute a dialectical *Bildungs-roman* implies that they must be understood as a single unit. This is because the claim is not that each free spirit work constitutes a separate *Bildungsroman*. Instead, it is that the five free spirit works, when taken together, constitute a *Bildungsroman*. This claim also implies that these works are about the education or the *Bildung* of the free spirit, and this implies that these works, as a *Roman*, tell a story about the education of the free spirit. Although there is no fictional hero that inhabits the free spirit works, the prefaces Nietzsche adds to these works in 1886–1887 indicate that there is an unfolding story in these texts about Nietzsche's own development as a free spirit that moves from sickness to health, immaturity to maturity, bondage to freedom. At the same time, Nietzsche presents his own education as the advancement of human culture, and so he endows these works with a world-historical dimension. Thus, the purpose of the free spirit project is not only to show how Nietzsche carries forward the banner of the Enlightenment by educating himself (HH 26), but also to

---

[2] See Abbey (2000), Franco (2011), and Ansell-Pearson (2018). There are, of course, other studies on individual works of the free spirit project such as Higgins (2000), Cohen (2010), and Langer (2010).

[3] Most recently, Jenkins (2018: 41). Also see Schacht (1983: xiii), Poellner (1995: 1), and Richardson (1996: 9).

advance human culture by inviting the reader to participate in this quest for freedom.

Despite the numerous differences between Nietzsche and Hegel, there is undoubtedly some resonance between this reading of Nietzsche's free spirit works and Hegel's *Phenomenology of Spirit*. Not only does Hegel attribute to philosophy and philosophical development a world-historical dimension, the *Phenomenology* itself has been labeled a *Bildungsroman* (Speight 2001: 12). Such a resemblance between Nietzsche and Hegel is strengthened by my claim that the free spirit works are best understood as a dialectical *Bildungsroman*. Specifically, Nietzsche moves from the rejection of art in the name of scientific truth seeking in *Human* to a project of self-creation and the aesthetic justification of existence at the end of *The Gay Science* in which the natural sciences are assigned an instrumental and so subordinate role. Thus, the free spirit works tell a dialectical story of how the privileging of science over art in Enlightenment thinking is eventually inverted and how the initial opposition between these two is then reconciled in what Nietzsche calls a gay science.

There is a second reason for thinking of the transformations that take place in the free spirit works as having a dialectical character of the Hegelian sort. In the *Genealogy*, Nietzsche gives an account of what he calls the *Selbstaufhebung* or the self-overcoming of the will to truth (GM III 27), and he links this event to the death of God. The death of God occurs in the third chapter of *The Gay Science* and so it is a central event in the free spirit works. In the following chapters, I argue that the free spirit works execute this *Selbstaufhebung* of the will to truth. Such a reading makes sense of the dialectical interplay between the natural sciences and art in these works. Whereas Nietzsche's commitment to the natural sciences in *Human* goes hand in hand with a will to truth that leads to a corresponding rejection of art, the death of God in *The Gay Science* represents the overcoming of the idea that truth has an absolute value, and the overcoming of this idea makes it possible for Nietzsche to re-embrace, in the final sections of *The Gay Science*, forms of art that he associates with falsification and lies.

In addition to evidence from Nietzsche's later writings that attests to the dialectical reading I propose, there is also contemporaneous evidence from Nietzsche's notes during this time showing that he thought of the death of God in terms of the self-overcoming of morality and the morality of truth, which I understand to be the idea that we have an obligation to pursue truth at all costs. We also know that Nietzsche was thinking in terms of a dialectical self-overcoming of the Socratic quest for truth and the eventual liberation of art as early as *The Birth of Tragedy* (1872). This not only shows that Nietzsche already had such a dynamic in mind before writing the free spirit works, it also suggests a certain continuity between Nietzsche's earliest writings and his free spirit works. Whereas Nietzsche describes a dialectical progression in *The Birth of Tragedy* in which the Socratic quest for truth bites itself in the tail and makes possible a rebirth of tragic art (BT 15), Nietzsche executes this dialectic in his free spirit works, one that culminates in the rebirth of tragedy in *Zarathustra*.

Perhaps the most controversial element of my thesis is that these works do not just happen to constitute a dialectical *Bildungsroman*. Instead, the claim is stronger: The free spirit works are best understood as having been consciously constructed to execute this dynamic. That is, we can best make sense of these works by holding that Nietzsche planned, with the release of *Human* in 1878, to publish a series of works in which the quest for truth initiated in *Human* would result in the self-overcoming of the will to truth and the eventual liberation of art. In what follows I devote much space to defending this aspect of my thesis, and although we have no set of notes from the time Nietzsche was composing *Human* that show he was planning such a progression, there are a number of features of the free spirit works that are best explained by this aspect of my dialectical reading. This, then, is why I think the free spirit works are *best understood* as a consciously constructed dialectical *Bildungsroman*.

This is all by way of introduction, and in the following sections of this first chapter, I show how my reading of the free spirit works can be situated within Nietzsche's larger corpus, go into more detail about my thesis, and explain why my reading provides a better understanding of the free spirit works than other approaches currently on offer in Anglo-American secondary literature. In the next chapter, I then develop three types of evidence that support the dialectical reading: *ex post* evidence from Nietzsche's later writings; *ex ante* evidence from Nietzsche's works prior to the free spirit project; and contemporaneous evidence gleaned from Nietzsche's notes and letters as he was working on the free spirit project as well as from the free spirit works themselves.

One of the pieces of *ex post* evidence for the dialectical reading is Zarathustra's first speech, "On the Three Metamorphoses." As I have argued elsewhere (Meyer 2006) and will further document here, the three metamorphoses that Zarathustra describes can be mapped onto the free spirit works, and I have titled the three sections of this book, each of which consists of two chapters, accordingly. The first part of this book, which provides a reading of *Human* and its two appendices, *Assorted Opinions* and

The Wanderer, is labeled "The Ascetic Camel." The second part, which provides an account of *Daybreak* and the first three chapters of *The Gay Science*, is called "The Dragon-Slaying Lion." Finally, the third part, which provides an account of the fourth and fifth chapters of *The Gay Science* and their potential relationship to Nietzsche's later writings, is called "The Dionysian Child."[4]

In Part I, and so Chapters 3 and 4, I begin with an account of the ascetic quest for truth that initiates the free spirit project in *Human*. Here, Nietzsche attaches the free spirit project to the Enlightenment and embraces an ethos of scientific inquiry that – in a manner reminiscent of Descartes' *Meditations* – enables him to liberate his mind from false beliefs. The program executed in *Human* is ascetic because it is based on the idea that truth has an absolute value – and so it is more valuable than life – and it strives for an objectivity that eliminates the all-too-human illusions – those created by metaphysics, morality, religion, and art – that have shaped our respective life-worlds. It can be associated with the camel because the truths Nietzsche *qua* free spirit discovers – most notably truths that destroy a metaphysical tradition that had hitherto given meaning to human existence – reveal that suffering is essential to life and so force the free spirit to bear the burden of these discoveries. *Human* can also be associated with the camel because the latter half of the text consists of Nietzsche detaching himself, *qua* free spirit, from personal relationships and society. Thus, like the camel, Nietzsche finds himself at the end of the work a wanderer alone in the desert of knowledge (HH 638).

In the two appendices to *Human*, Nietzsche *qua* free spirit takes some small steps to confront and even ameliorate this suffering and despair in ways that nevertheless accept the critique of metaphysics executed in *Human*, and in Chapter 4 I document these transitions in the free spirit project. In *Assorted Opinions*, Nietzsche sketches and even affirms forms of art that align with, rather than oppose, the Enlightenment project he initiated in *Human*. In *The Wanderer*, Nietzsche adopts an Epicurean indifference toward metaphysical questions and instead turns his attention to a series of life-preserving strategies that focus on basics such as food, clothing, and shelter. In both cases, Nietzsche is thinking about art and life in ways that accept the results of *Human* and yet provide glimpses of

---

[4] The application of these metamorphoses to the free spirit works does not amount to a separate thesis. Instead, it is – assuming the association is right – supposed to be a helpful way to think about the transformations in the free spirit works. Thus, my thesis can still be true even if I am wrong to make this association.

a full-fledged return to art and the affirmation of life at the end of *The Gay Science*.

At the end of *The Wanderer*, Nietzsche declares that the free spirit stands in the midst of removing the chains of morality, religion, and metaphysics and curing the sickness they have caused (WS 350), and in Part II (Chapters 5 and 6) I look at how Nietzsche endeavors to remove these chains by way of his lion-like attack on the prejudices of morality in subsequent stages of the free spirit project. This attack begins in *Daybreak* and continues into the first three chapters of *The Gay Science*. In *Daybreak*, Nietzsche sets out to liberate the free spirit from a morality of custom that demands obedience and a Christian morality that praises selfless compassion for others. In so doing, he begins to speak of the free spirit's heroism and passion for knowledge. It is this passionate, heroic condition that sets the stage for the killing of God and so the slaying of the dragon of all values in the third chapter of *The Gay Science*. The death of God and the elimination of his shadow is a significant moment in these works because it liberates the free spirit from the morality of truth and so makes possible a rebirth of the life-affirming arts associated with Dionysus in the final stages of the free spirit project and beyond.

In Part III (Chapters 7 and 8) I show how the final two chapters of *The Gay Science* transition to two art forms associated with Dionysus, tragedy and comedy. The original 1882 edition of *The Gay Science* consisted of only four chapters, and so the final aphorism, which bears the title, "*incipit tragoedia*" or "let the tragedy begin," of the 1882 edition introduces the character Zarathustra and provides the opening lines of Nietzsche's next work, *Thus Spoke Zarathustra* (GS 342). In contrast, the fifth chapter of *The Gay Science* was added to the 1887 edition of the work, and rather than transitioning to the tragedy of *Zarathustra*, there is reason to think – or so I suggest – that Nietzsche intends this second ending of *The Gay Science* to transition to the other mask of Dionysian theater, namely, comedy. This is because both the 1887 preface added to the work – the final preface of all the prefaces added to the free spirit works – and the final aphorisms of chapter five point not to "*incipit trageodia*" and so tragedy but rather to "*incipit parodia*" and so comedy (GS P 1). So understood, the 1887 edition of *The Gay Science* has a double ending that transitions to tragedy and comedy respectively.

Thus, what we find at the end of Nietzsche's dialectical *Bildungsroman* is not a rigorous system of theoretical philosophy, but rather the liberation of the "Dionysian" or "artistic" child and so the third of the three metamorphoses. Nietzsche had already given the figure of the child a central place in his philosophy as early as *The Birth of Tragedy* (BT 24) and *Philosophy in the Tragic Age of the Greeks* (PTAG 7), and so the free spirit works not only enact a dialectic between the quest for truth and the artistic affirmation of life that can already be found in *The Birth of Tragedy*, they also culminate in the emergence of a figure central to Nietzsche's earliest writings. The fact that Nietzsche returns at the end of the free spirit works to many of the positions he developed in his earliest writings is one good reason for reading the free spirit works as a consciously constructed dialectical *Bildungsroman*, and, as I explain in the next section, this approach can help make better sense of the relationship between Nietzsche's earliest writings and his later works.

The Free Spirit Works and Nietzsche's Oeuvre

Much of the scholarship over the past 50 years on Nietzsche in the Anglo-American context has been done with an eye to justifying his work to contemporary philosophers and the general public. Whereas Walter Kaufmann (1974) devoted his efforts to reaching the latter audience, disassociating Nietzsche from National Socialism in the Anglo-American context, more recent scholars have turned their attention to the former, endeavoring to show that Nietzsche has a number of theories that may be of interest to those working on contemporary philosophical issues. Although such work is important and can be philosophically fruitful, this approach puts aside various interpretive issues that surround Nietzsche's texts including, but not limited to, questions about their internal structure and the way in which they may or may not relate to each other.

This way of approaching Nietzsche's corpus has a long history and comes from diverse sources. In the German reception of Nietzsche, Martin Heidegger applied this method primarily to Nietzsche's unpublished notes or *Nachlass*, which, according to Heidegger, is the source of Nietzsche's true philosophy. In the Anglo-American reception, Danto began his work, *Nietzsche as Philosopher*, with the following statement:

> Nietzsche's books give the appearance of having been assembled rather than composed. They are made up, in the main, of short, pointed aphorisms, and of essays seldom more than a few pages long; each volume is more like a treasury of the author's selections than like a book in its own right. Any given aphorism or essay might as easily have been placed in one volume as in another without much affecting the unity or structure of either. And the books themselves, except for their chronological ordering, do not exhibit any special structure as a corpus. (1965: 19)

By adopting this understanding of Nietzsche's texts, Danto effectively frees the interpreter from having to investigate the internal structure of a given work and the potential role it might play within Nietzsche's larger oeuvre, and this paves the way for what he thinks is the real task of the interpreter: making up for Nietzsche's "lack of architectonic talent" by constructing coherent philosophical theories from the otherwise chaotic collection of aphorisms, essays, and verse (1965: 22). Thus, in the work of both Danto and Richard Schacht (1983), we are presented with a series of chapters dedicated to explaining Nietzsche's views on topics such as philosophy, truth, knowledge, and morality.

This approach also presupposes that the interpreter comes to Nietzsche's texts with a set of questions or topics that she finds interesting. That is, the questions brought to Nietzsche's texts are often taken from contemporary Anglo-American philosophy, and Nietzsche's writings are read through such concerns. It is this point that links the Danto approach to the interpretations of Nietzsche offered more recently by scholars such as Brian Leiter (2002) and Maudemarie Clark (1990) which, in contrast to the efforts of Danto and Schacht, focuses more on Nietzsche's published works. Because Leiter is primarily (but not exclusively) interested in understanding Nietzsche's view of morality, he develops a reading of Nietzsche by focusing on what is arguably Nietzsche's *Hauptwerk* on this topic, *On the Genealogy of Morals*. Because Clark is primarily (but not exclusively) interested in Nietzsche's views on truth, she begins her interpretation by using Nietzsche's early, unpublished essay "On Truth and Lies in a Nonmoral Sense" to generate a theoretical framework through which the rest of Nietzsche's published works and his development can be understood.[5]

Common to Danto and Schacht, on the one hand, and Clark and Leiter, on the other hand, is the view that our interests, not Nietzsche's, guide the selection of relevant passages and texts for interpretation. It is because *we* are interested in theories of morality that the *Genealogy* takes on such significance – Nietzsche himself has very little to say about the *Genealogy* in *Ecce Homo*. Similarly, it is because *we* are interested in Nietzsche's views on truth that "On Truth and Lies" takes on such significance, even though Nietzsche never published the work and rarely mentions it in his later writings. In this spirit, Clark (1990) has used the

---

[5] Clark's most recent study (co-authored with Dudrick [2012]) of *Beyond Good and Evil* further attests to her interest in focusing on Nietzsche's published texts.

issue of truth and the related concept of the thing in itself as the basis for her account of Nietzsche's development and eventual maturation. Here, however, one wonders why truth is the defining feature of Nietzsche's development: Why not his views on morality or art? Why not shifts in his style? Why not biographical details like his relationship to Wagner and his early retirement from the university?

Although there is nothing wrong with trying to decipher Nietzsche's views on issues of contemporary philosophical concern, we should guard against the tendency to assume that issues such as truth and morality are most significant to Nietzsche because they are most significant to us. In this respect, Bernard Reginster's *The Affirmation of Life: Nietzsche on Overcoming Nihilism* (2006) does a better job of identifying the issue or issues most important to Nietzsche and interpreting his project through this lens. Reginster argues that Nietzsche's battle with nihilism is central to his overall project, and this battle leads Nietzsche to develop strategies to affirm life in the face of meaningless suffering. In so doing, Reginster claims that the mature Nietzsche finds in art the means by which life can be affirmed and points to Dionysus, as opposed to the Crucified, as Nietzsche's symbol for the affirmation of life in his later writings (2006: Ch. 6).

Although Reginster identifies the guiding theme of Nietzsche's philosophy, it is surprising that his first chapter on nihilism largely relies on the "non-book" that the editors of the critical-historical edition of Nietzsche's works, Giorgio Colli and Mazzino Montinari, have rejected as illegitimate, namely *The Will to Power*. It is also surprising that Reginster only ends the first chapter by noting that many of the themes he finds important in Nietzsche's later writings are also foreshadowed in his first book, *The Birth of Tragedy* (2006: 51). Even though Nietzsche does not use the term "nihilism," the argument of *The Birth of Tragedy* is that modernity is confronted with the same pessimistic insights about the human condition through the philosophies of Kant and Schopenhauer that the ancient Greeks confronted in a mythical figure like Silenus, and the primary question we now face is whether we want to affirm a life characterized by chance and misery or whether we should deny such a life through strategies that range from Buddhistic meditation to suicide. Because he already wants to break with Schopenhauer in this work by avoiding the path of life-negation or nihilism, Nietzsche points, first, to Greek tragedy and, then, to what he claims is a revival of Greek tragedy in the operas of Richard Wagner as the primary means by which modern culture can affirm a life so understood.

So even though Reginster does not begin his work with an analysis of *The Birth of Tragedy*, it is nevertheless important that a major interpreter in Anglo-American scholarship has pointed back to the significance of Nietzsche's first work. This is because *The Birth of Tragedy* plays a relatively minor role in the interpretations offered by Danto (1965), Clark (1990), and Leiter (2002). Similarly, Jessica Berry (2011), who follows Clark by beginning her own interpretation of Nietzsche as an ancient skeptic with a close reading of "On Truth and Lies," says almost nothing about *The Birth of Tragedy* in a book on Nietzsche's relationship to ancient philosophy, and she continues this relative silence about *The Birth of Tragedy* even in the account she offers of Nietzsche's relationship to the ancient Greeks in the recently published *Oxford Handbook to Nietzsche* (2013).

Nevertheless, Berry does, in a concluding footnote to the latter essay, point to a passage from *Twilight of the Idols* in which Nietzsche emphasizes the importance of *The Birth of Tragedy* for his later project (2013: 103–104n.52): "And herewith I again touch that point from which I once went forth: *The Birth of Tragedy* was my first revaluation of all values. Herewith I again stand on the soil out of which my intention, my *ability* grows – I, the last disciple of the philosopher Dionysus – I, the teacher of the eternal recurrence" (TI "What I Owe" 5). This passage connects key features of Nietzsche's "mature" writings – the revaluation of values, the eternal recurrence, his discipleship to Dionysus – to *The Birth of Tragedy*. Given that it is Nietzsche's first work, that he republishes the work more than once over the course of his career (1878 and 1886), and that he refers back to the work at the end of his career, it seems that the only sensible place to start reading Nietzsche is *The Birth of Tragedy*.

Indeed, a case can be made that *The Birth of Tragedy* contains the basic framework for much of Nietzsche's later philosophy and so it is the *sine qua non* for understanding Nietzsche's larger project in at least three respects. First, it presents Nietzsche's belief that the pursuit of truth does not lead to happiness and human flourishing, but rather to the discovery of a tragic understanding of existence that is a potential source of despair. As we will see, such pessimism is a central theme of *Human*. Second, Nietzsche associates morality with the life-denying or nihilistic response to these insights, and much of his attack on morality in his later writings, including *Daybreak*, is designed to save us from this threat. Third, Nietzsche associates Dionysus and the arts performed in his honor with a life-affirming response to the pessimistic truths philosophy reveals, and Nietzsche's interest in Dionysian art can be used to explain both the claims he makes about art in his later works and his own activity as a Dionysian poet.

That Nietzsche conceived of himself as a Dionysian poet is made clear by the fact that he wrote his own *Dionysian Dithyrambs*. Moreover, there are reasons for interpreting *Zarathustra* as Nietzsche's own tragedy and so a replacement for the supposedly life-affirming operas of Wagner.[6] Even though he offers no systematic treatment of the work, Reginster (2006: 51–52) makes precisely this point: "Nietzsche initially believed that the Wagnerian musical drama would overcome modern nihilism, but, once he became disenchanted with Wagner, he offered instead his own *Thus Spoke Zarathustra*, a work explicitly devoted to determining the conditions of a new 'affirmation of life,' as the beginning (or rebirth) of a form of tragedy. Thus, in announcing the book, he declares: '*Incipit tragoedia*' (GS 342)."[7]

For these reasons, Reginster offers a better way of understanding Nietzsche's overall project because, unlike Danto, Schacht, Clark, and Leiter, he reads Nietzsche's works through what he thinks is Nietzsche's dominant concern: finding a life-affirming solution to the problem of meaningless suffering. However, I have also noted that by making this issue the centerpiece of Nietzsche's project, two texts that are often ignored by contemporary scholars, *The Birth of Tragedy* and *Zarathustra*, take on a significant role in his corpus.[8] Indeed, they are perhaps the two most important anchor points – along with *Schopenhauer as Educator* – of my reading of the free spirit works. Let me explain.

If we accept Nietzsche's claim in *Ecce Homo* that *Zarathustra* (1883–1885) is the work in which his concept of the Dionysian, first articulated in *The Birth of Tragedy* (1872), becomes a supreme deed (EH "Books" Z:6), we have to wonder what happens in the roughly ten years between the time Nietzsche first expresses his hopes for a rebirth of tragedy (1872) and the publication of his own tragedy (1883–1885). If Nietzsche was so enthusiastic about tragedy and eventually wrote a tragedy that he takes to be the greatest gift to humankind (EH P 4), why did he not just write his own tragedy immediately after publishing *The Birth of Tragedy*? To be sure, Nietzsche sketched some ideas for writing an Empedocles

---

[6] Hollinrake (1982: ix) claims that, "*Zarathustra* was planned as a whole and from the outset as a reply to Wagner."

[7] In Meyer (2002), I sketch an interpretive framework for reading *Zarathustra* as a tragedy. See Loeb (2010) for the most developed defense of this point. His book-length interpretation draws, in part, from a much earlier essay in which he identifies *Zarathustra* as a tragedy (1998). Higgins (1987: 103) also remarks: "it seems clear that Nietzsche intends that Zarathustra's tale be viewed as a tragedy."

[8] Katsafanas (2018) omits both of these works from the section on Nietzsche's "Major Works."

tragedy in 1870–1871.[9] However, *The Birth of Tragedy* itself reveals the reason why Nietzsche did not move beyond these mere sketches: Just as he identified Kant and Schopenhauer – and not himself – as the philosophers responsible for the rebirth of a tragic worldview, he looked to Wagner – and not himself – as the artist primarily responsible for the rebirth of tragedy.[10] In short, Nietzsche saw himself not as a leader in this cultural movement but rather as an intellectual auxiliary in a project that Schopenhauer and Wagner were supposed to realize.

Because it has a relatively clear structure and purpose, *The Birth of Tragedy* on its own challenges Danto's overly broad claim that *all* of Nietzsche's texts lack any order or purpose. Indeed, Nietzsche writes in his letters that *The Birth of Tragedy* is a kind of manifesto (KSB 3: 194) that expresses his most profound hopes and aspirations (KSB 3: 181), and once we get some sense of the purpose of the text, we can see how his other works from this period might relate to his greater hopes for a rebirth of tragedy. On the one hand, Nietzsche's unpublished writings such as "On Truth and Lies" and *Philosophy in the Tragic Age* are written as "companion pieces" to *The Birth of Tragedy* (KSB 4: 298), and they are designed as philosophical investigations that respectively liberate the artistic imagination from the tyrannical quest for truth and articulate a non-metaphysical vision of a tragic worldview through an interpretation of Heraclitus' philosophy. On the other hand, Nietzsche's *Untimely Meditations* bear some significant connections to the cultural project of *The Birth of Tragedy*. The two most obvious instances of this are Nietzsche's third and fourth meditations: *Schopenhauer as Educator* and *Richard Wagner in Bayreuth*. Whereas the former appeals to the philosophical hero of Nietzsche's first work, the latter largely rearticulates the significance Nietzsche attaches to tragedy and the tragic worldview and develops the connection Nietzsche sees between Wagnerian opera and ancient Greek tragedy.

If this rough sketch of Nietzsche's early period is right, then the works he publishes from 1873 to 1876 should be understood as largely developing the cultural project announced in *The Birth of Tragedy*, and so the reason Nietzsche did not write his own tragedy during this time is because he saw it as his role to promote, rather than accomplish, this cultural task.

---

[9] See, for instance, KSA 7: 5[118]. Hollinrake (1982: 5) claims that the model for an Empedocles tragedy can be found in Hölderlin.
[10] See KSB 5: 734 for evidence of this self-understanding. Also see Higgins (1987: Ch. 2) for a discussion of Nietzsche's understanding of tragedy in relation to a tragic worldview.

So understood, the remaining problem has to do with making sense of the works Nietzsche publishes in the period after 1876 and prior to the publication of his own tragedy with *Zarathustra* beginning in 1883. In short, the problem has to do with making sense of the five free spirit works that Nietzsche publishes from 1878 to 1882 in terms of their potential relationship to the rebirth of tragedy in *Zarathustra*.

The reason the free spirit works are much more difficult to explain in relation to his early and then later interest in the capacity of art to affirm life is that Nietzsche seems to reject the project of *The Birth of Tragedy* with the publication of *Human*. This is because *Human* presents us with a Nietzsche who embraces the cold and rigorous methods of the natural sciences and so rejects the imaginative, mythical, playful, and even deceptive world of art. Giving expression to this idea commonly found in the secondary literature, Paul Franco writes at the beginning of his study on Nietzsche's middle period: *Human* represents "Nietzsche's decisive break with his earlier philosophy and with the two figures who exercised the greatest influence on it, Arthur Schopenhauer and Richard Wagner" (2011: 1).[11]

To be sure, *Human* represents a break with both Schopenhauer and Wagner and so the central figures of *The Birth of Tragedy* and Nietzsche's final two *Untimely Meditations*. However, there is some question as to whether it represents "Nietzsche's decisive break with his earlier philosophy." One immediate problem with this understanding of the relationship between the cultural project of *The Birth of Tragedy* and *Human* is that Nietzsche returns, only four years later, to praising art in *The Gay Science* and writing his own tragedy in *Zarathustra*, and so if Nietzsche did abandon the project of *The Birth of Tragedy* with the publication of *Human*, he then decided to re-embrace the project only four years after the publication of *Human*. On a straightforward reading, the trajectory of the path Nietzsche takes in these texts can at best be described as "circular" (Young 1992: 1). At worst, Nietzsche looks confused, even schizophrenic, as he changes his mind about fundamental topics at least twice – in print! – in a mere six years.

The other problem with this reading is that Nietzsche introduces *Zarathustra* under the banner of "*incipit tragoedia*" in the final aphorism of the 1882 edition of the final free spirit work, *The Gay Science* (GS 342), and this indicates that Nietzsche wants to link at least one free spirit work

[11] See also Donnellan (1982: 9), Young (1992: 59). Lampert (2017: 3) calls it "an otherwise inexplicable break with the perspective of [Nietzsche's] first five books."

to his own tragedy. This difficulty is heightened by the fact that on the back cover to the 1882 edition of *The Gay Science* Nietzsche explains that *The Gay Science* is the final work in a series of works that begins with *Human* and falls under the rubric of the free spirit.[12] Taken together, Nietzsche has effectively created a chain of aphorisms in the free spirit works that links *Human*, which ostensibly rejects any interest in tragedy and art, to the publication of his own tragedy in *Zarathustra*.

The fact that Nietzsche presents *Zarathustra* as his own tragedy at the end of *The Gay Science* forces us to reconsider the relationship between the free spirit project and the rebirth of tragedy that largely animates Nietzsche's writings from the 1872 publication of *The Birth of Tragedy* to the inaugural festival in Bayreuth in 1876. If Nietzsche did reject his early project with the publication of *Human* only to return to the project prior to publishing *Zarathustra*, we are left with the task of positing a radical break – one in which Nietzsche decides to return to his earlier project of celebrating art as a means to life-affirmation – *within* the free spirit works that is similar to the radical break that *Human* seems to announce.

The problem is that there are a number of reasons for understanding the free spirit works as a single unit, and so it is difficult to find a point at which there is a clear break in the chain of aphorisms that constitute these texts. Because Nietzsche clearly understands *Assorted Opinions* (1879) and *The Wanderer* (1880) as appendices to *Human* (1878) and writes much of *The Gay Science* (1882) as a continuation of *Daybreak* (1881), the only possible breaking point in the free spirit project is between *The Wanderer* (1880) and *Daybreak* (1881). However, I argue in Chapter 2 that Nietzsche conceived of *Daybreak* as a continuation of *Human* and its two appendices both retrospectively and at the time of composition. If this is right, we are forced to ask whether *Human*, now understood as the first in a series of works that culminates in the tragedy of *Zarathustra*, breaks with the project of *The Birth of Tragedy* at all.

In *Ecce Homo*, Nietzsche claims that his final two untimely meditations on Schopenhauer and Wagner are actually about himself (EH "Books" UM:3), and although this is not how Nietzsche understood these works as he composed them, we can interpret Nietzsche's statement as saying that the cultural project he attributed to Schopenhauer

---

[12] See the Kaufmann translation of *The Gay Science* (1974: 30). Also see KSB 6: 256.

and Wagner at the time he composed these works is something he eventually decided to take over himself. If *Zarathustra* is Nietzsche's own tragedy, we can make sense of this claim by holding that Nietzsche takes over the role he assigned to Wagner in his earlier writings. So far so good: but what about Schopenhauer? In what sense does Nietzsche take over the role assigned to him?

Here we can begin to make sense of how *Human* might resonate with, rather than reject, the basic ideas of *The Birth of Tragedy*. Nietzsche assigns to philosophy and so philosophers like Kant and Schopenhauer an important role in the cultural project articulated in *The Birth of Tragedy*. According to Nietzsche, Kant and Schopenhauer are philosophers who embrace one important feature of the Socratic project: The belief that truth must be pursued at all costs. However, their uncompromising quest for truth destroys another essential feature of the Socratic project: optimism or the belief that the quest for truth will result in human flourishing and happiness. Kant and especially Schopenhauer do this by revealing a series of pessimistic or tragic truths that correspond to the description of the human condition that Nietzsche attributes to the mythical figure of Silenus in the opening stages of *The Birth of Tragedy* (BT 3). On the one hand, Nietzsche interprets Kant as denying the possibility of attaining the knowledge Socrates so ardently craved. On the other hand, Nietzsche attributes to Schopenhauer a genuine understanding of pessimistic truths that are a source of suffering for the knower. According to Nietzsche, now that modernity is again faced with such terrible truths, it will only be natural to turn to a musical tradition that runs from Bach and Beethoven up through Wagner for comfort and redemption (BT 19).

So understood, the argument of *The Birth of Tragedy* indicates that pessimistic philosophy is a necessary condition for the rebirth of tragedy. Applying this idea to Nietzsche's post-1876 works, it means that Nietzsche has to produce his own pessimistic philosophy as a necessary condition for the rebirth of tragedy in *Zarathustra*. On my reading, this is one important purpose of *Human*: under the banner of seeking truth at all costs, Nietzsche unpacks a tragic worldview that emphasizes the meaningless suffering of existence and so implicitly calls out for the life-affirming powers of art. Although it categorically rejects Schopenhauer's metaphysics, *Human* is nevertheless an exercise in pessimistic philosophy because it posits a tension between life and truth, and it does this by showing that life is saturated in illusions that make life meaningful and significant. This is why a number of the final aphorisms of the first book of

Human refer to the threat of *despair* that results from the removal of these illusions,[13] and as the free spirit works unfold, Nietzsche adopts a series of therapeutic strategies to respond to this threat, culminating in the tragedy in *Zarathustra*.

To be sure, the free spirit works are not simply about developing a tragic understanding of existence and thereby laying the foundation for the rebirth of tragic art. As Franco (2011) has emphasized, Nietzsche is also concerned about education or *Bildung*. Not only is this theme central to my claim that these works constitute a *Bildungsroman*, it establishes another line of continuity between Nietzsche's early writings and the free spirit project. As Daniel Blue (2016) explains, Nietzsche took a keen interest in self-cultivation at an early age, and this interest continued to develop with his hopes for a renewed culture through the art of Wagner. *Bildung* is the central theme of the public lectures Nietzsche delivered in 1872 under the title, "On the Future of Our Educational Institutions," and *Bildung* plays an important role in all four of the *Untimely Meditations*.

Of the four *Untimely Meditations*, none is more important in this respect than *Schopenhauer as Educator*. It articulates a vision for *Bildung* that Nietzsche thinks is necessary for the development of culture and ultimately the affirmation of life. Central to this project is the idea of becoming who one is, and this idea runs from Nietzsche's youth[14] through the free spirit works, and it not only appears in *Zarathustra* IV (Z IV: "The Honey Sacrifice"), it forms the subtitle for Nietzsche's autobiography, *Ecce Homo*. According to *Schopenhauer as Educator*, the first step in becoming who one is involves liberating oneself from everything foreign. This, then, prepares the soil for a positive project of giving laws to oneself and so becoming oneself. Although Nietzsche writes about the role that Schopenhauer can play in this process of education, the essay ultimately issues a call to educate oneself. Applied to the free spirit works, we can say that the break with Wagner in Bayreuth marked Nietzsche's decision to hear his own call and begin a project in which he would systematically liberate himself from the false beliefs he inherited from his upbringing and thereby prepare the ground for some further project of self-cultivation. In this sense, the free spirit project directly emerges from the ideas Nietzsche

---

[13] Reginster (2006: Ch. 4) makes despair central to his reading of Nietzsche, but does not point to the significant role it plays in the opening stages of *Human* and so the free spirit project.

[14] Blue (2016: 274–275) notes that Nietzsche used this as the motto for his prize-winning paper on Diogenes Laertius in 1867. He also explains that Nietzsche and Erwin Rohde erected a memorial at their "riverside refuge" in which they inscribed the motto, "*Genoi' hoios essi.*"

develops in *Schopenhauer as Educator* and contributes to his overarching project of becoming who he is.

Bringing these points together, the general picture that emerges regarding the relationship between Nietzsche's writings prior to the Bayreuth Festival in 1876 and his writings after Bayreuth is one in which Nietzsche decides to realize many of the ideas he sketches and often attributes to others in his earliest writings. Whereas he writes about the significance of tragedy in *The Birth of Tragedy* and *Richard Wagner in Bayreuth*, Nietzsche pens his own tragedy in *Zarathustra*. Whereas he discusses pessimistic or tragic philosophy in works like *The Birth of Tragedy* and *Philosophy in the Tragic Age*, he takes on the role of the pessimistic philosopher in a work like *Human*. Whereas he critiques the drive for truth and discusses how it should be restrained for the purposes of art and life in "On Truth and Lies" and other early *Nachlass* notes, he executes this very dynamic in the later stages of the free spirit works. Whereas he discusses the significance of education and educating oneself in "On the Future of our Educational Institutions" and *Schopenhauer as Educator*, Nietzsche becomes his own educator in the free spirit works. Whereas he sketches the ideal of a music-playing Socrates in *The Birth of Tragedy*, he becomes a music-playing Socrates in the progression that unfolds from *Human* to *Zarathustra* (Meyer 2004).

This reading of the free spirit works also has potential consequences for understanding Nietzsche's later writings. In Chapter 7, I sketch the connection between the fourth chapter of *The Gay Science* and the tragedy of *Zarathustra*. The concluding aphorisms of the 1882 edition of *The Gay Science* make clear that Nietzsche wants to link the two works together: Not only does *The Gay Science* end with the opening lines of *Zarathustra* under the title "*incipit tragoedia*" (GS 342), the penultimate aphorism introduces what Nietzsche calls the "fundamental conception" of *Zarathustra* in the eternal recurrence (EH "Books" Z:1; GS 341). So understood, we should not only read the free spirit works as a connected trilogy, but also read the tragedy of *Zarathustra* as resulting from the liberation of art in *The Gay Science* and as responding to the tragic worldview unpacked in *Human*.

The opening stages of *Beyond Good and Evil* can also be read in a new light given the dialectical reading of the free spirit. For instance, Nietzsche begins the work by raising questions about the will to truth and the value of truth. If Nietzsche has enacted, in the free spirit works, the *Selbstaufhebung* of the will to truth that he describes in the *Genealogy*, then the questions Nietzsche raises at the beginning of *Beyond Good and*

Evil can be understood as resulting from the events that take place in the free spirit works.

This reading of the free spirit works also sheds light on the potential relationship between Nietzsche's earlier critique of morality in a work like *Daybreak* and his more famous critique in the *Genealogy*. Although there is a sense in which the latter represents a more "mature" position than the former, we can also understand the differences between the two works in terms of the context in which they are written. Whereas *Daybreak* is written within Nietzsche's dialectic of the Enlightenment and so assesses morality according to the traditional standard of truth and falsity, the *Genealogy*, which follows *Beyond Good and Evil*, is written from a standpoint beyond the traditional standard of truth. As such, it provides an external critique of morality from the standpoint of life, and this is why the primary accusation Nietzsche levels against morality in the *Genealogy* is not that it is somehow false, but rather sick and degenerate.

Finally, once we read the free spirit works as a unified whole, we can speculate about potential connections between Nietzsche's post-*Zarathustra* writings and whether they also should be read in a more unified way. To be sure, the later works are fraught with more difficulties than the free spirit project, especially given the controversial status of Nietzsche's abandoned book project relating to the will to power. However, there are ways in which a work like *Beyond Good and Evil* is foreshadowing a philosophy of the future that may very well be found in his 1888 works. Indeed, I have argued that Nietzsche's 1888 writings constitute a Dionysian comedy in which Nietzsche presents himself as someone who has become who he is (Meyer 2012a), and, as I discuss in Chapter 8, there are important ways in which Nietzsche is already foreshadowing themes of comedy and laughter in *The Gay Science* and *Beyond Good and Evil* and so his prelude to a philosophy of the future. In short, it may be that *Beyond Good and Evil* initiates a series of works that culminate not in the tragedy of *Zarathustra*, but rather in a philosophy of the future that is the Dionysian comedy of Nietzsche's 1888 writings.

Taken together, we can see the way in which interpreting Nietzsche's free spirit works as a consciously constructed dialectical *Bildungsroman* has potential consequences for understanding his entire oeuvre. Although he did not think this way at the time of their composition, Nietzsche's pre-1877 writings come to function as seeds or inchoate blueprints for the writings he produces after breaking with Wagner in 1876. Indeed, it is because we have writings that discuss, in theory, the project that Nietzsche undertakes with *Human* that we can begin to speculate about Nietzsche having philosophical and literary intentions that project beyond *Human* itself even in the absence of any clear-cut evidence of such plans from the time he was composing the text. Similarly, once we understand the free spirit works as unfolding in a dialectical fashion such that each successive work builds on the insights of and responds to problems articulated in the previous works, we can begin to speculate as to whether he is also foreshadowing further projects in the free spirit works and whether his so-called mature writings consciously build upon the insights and positions developed in the free spirit works.

A Closer Look at the Thesis

In the opening sections of this chapter, I sketched the general thesis of this work and placed it in relation to the contemporary understanding of Nietzsche's oeuvre. In this section, I want to say more about my thesis before contrasting this interpretation with other approaches to the free spirit works currently on offer in the secondary literature. Specifically, I want to explain in more detail the four elements of my thesis: what it means for the free spirit works to be (1) best understood as a (2) consciously constructed (3) dialectical (4) *Bildungsroman*.

Before I explicate each of these elements, I want to begin with a point that I think is a helpful way of entering into this reading of the free spirit works. Implicit in my thesis is the claim that the free spirit works constitute a literary unit, and so they are best understood as a single work that Nietzsche publishes in installments. In this sense, I am arguing that we should understand the free spirit works in much the same way that we now understand *Zarathustra*, which scholars have also claimed is a *Bildungsroman*.[15] Nietzsche published *Zarathustra* in installments, and only later did he publish the first three books together as a single unit in 1887 (Hollinrake 1982: 1), distributing about 40 copies of the fourth part to a select group of readers (Montinari 2003: 83).[16] Now, however, we understand the individual books of *Zarathustra* as a literary unit (although there is much discussion about the relationship between the first three books and the fourth). On the reading I propose, we should think of the free spirit works in the same way. That is, we should think of them as a single

---

[15] See Loeb (2010: 1) for a general discussion of this point. Most notably, Gooding-Williams (2001: 28) compares *Zarathustra* to Hegel's *Phenomenology*, which he claims resembles a *Bildungsroman*.

[16] The fourth part was not made public until all four parts were published together in 1892.

work that Nietzsche originally published in installments and then later sought to unite.

There is a further feature of the compositional history of *Zarathustra* that is important for my purposes. Specifically, the first part of *Zarathustra* was not originally released as the first part of a larger project. Instead, what is now the first part of *Zarathustra* was originally presented as the entirety of *Zarathustra*. That is, there is no indication on the front cover or anywhere in the book that what becomes *Zarathustra* I was merely the first part of a larger work. Moreover, Brusotti (1997: 549) has noted that we do not have any evidence in the form of letters, sketches, or even preliminary titles during the composition of *Zarathustra* I (although see KSA 9: 11[197]) indicating that Nietzsche had plans for further parts. Thus, Brusotti concludes that Nietzsche had not yet made the decision to compose further parts, and so there is reason to think that Nietzsche considered, for a time, ending *Zarathustra* with a call for the *Uebermensch* to replace the dead God, thereby leaving any teaching of the eternal recurrence by the wayside.

Brusotti's claim is based on the assumption that if we do not have evidence of plans for subsequent parts at the time Nietzsche was composing the first part, then Nietzsche did not have such plans in mind. Brusotti argues that even though there is a clear coupling of *Zarathustra* and the eternal recurrence at the end of the 1882 edition of *The Gay Science*, Nietzsche temporarily abandons the idea that Zarathustra would be the teacher of the eternal recurrence (1997: 548–549). In my view, the absence of evidence for future plans – either in his notes or the publication itself – does not allow us to conclude that Nietzsche did not have such plans in mind. Instead, it simply means that we do not have evidence of such intentions.

However, there are at least three reasons for thinking Nietzsche did have a larger project in mind as he was writing *Zarathustra* I. First, it seems implausible that Nietzsche would couple the eternal recurrence with *Zarathustra* at the end of *The Gay Science*, then uncouple the two when working on *Zarathustra* I, and then recouple them only a few months later as he begins working on the final parts of *Zarathustra*. Second, Nietzsche begins writing the second part of *Zarathustra* almost immediately after the publication of *Zarathustra* I: *Zarathustra* I appears in April 1883, and he completes *Zarathustra* II in July 1883. Again, it seems implausible that Nietzsche would have decided within only a few months to transform what he intended to be a standalone book into the first part of a larger narrative. Finally, Nietzsche later claims that the eternal recurrence is the fundamental conception of *Zarathustra* (EH "Books" Z:8), an idea he formulated in 1881, and nowhere in his later writings does he indicate that *Zarathustra* I may have ultimately constituted the entirety of *Zarathustra*. Thus, if Brusotti is right, we must conclude that the later Nietzsche is not giving an honest account of the genesis and purpose of the work.

Of course, Brusotti *could be* right, and so it *could be* that Nietzsche is providing an over-simplified, even deceptive, account of the origins of *Zarathustra*. However, given that it is a lack of evidence that forms the basis for the position, my own view is that we should accept Nietzsche's retrospective account that the eternal recurrence is the fundamental conception of the work and hold that Nietzsche planned, from the start, to publish enough installments of *Zarathustra* so that Zarathustra could teach the idea. Such a reading avoids charging Nietzsche with an indecisiveness about his literary intentions, makes sense of the appearance of the eternal recurrence at the end of *The Gay Science* and so prior to *Zarathustra*, and adheres to a principle of interpretive charity in regard to an author's retrospective accounts of her own work.

The purpose of this discussion is to argue that we should understand the free spirit works in the same way that we now understand *Zarathustra*. Although one could consistently hold that neither the free spirit works nor *Zarathustra* was originally composed as a literary unit published in installments, my own view is that we should continue thinking of *Zarathustra* as a literary unit (problems with the fourth part notwithstanding) and attribute this same unity to the free spirit works. In both cases, we lack any clear-cut evidence in the form of plans for further parts from the time Nietzsche was composing the first part of each project. However, in both cases, we know that Nietzsche had already sketched ideas that appear in the later stages of each project prior to the start of the project, that he sets to work on subsequent parts of the project immediately after finishing the first part, that he at least attempts to publish the various installments of each project as a single unit upon completion, and that he retrospectively speaks of each installment as part of a larger whole.

The claim that we should understand the free spirit works as a single unit relies on the fact that Nietzsche planned to republish the free spirit works under a single title upon completing *The Gay Science* in 1882 (KSA 10: 1[13] and [14]), that he presents, on the backside of the front cover of the 1882 edition, *The Gay Science* as the final work of a free spirit project published in installments,[17] and that he eventually republishes these works

---

[17] See Kaufmann's translation (1974: 30).

in 1886–1887 with prefaces that effectively unite these works. However, Laurence Lampert has recently defended a claim about the publication history of *Human* that, if true, would undermine the unity I attribute to the free spirit works. Specifically, Lampert argues that after composing *Zarathustra*, Nietzsche wanted to buy back all the unsold copies of the first edition of *Human, All Too Human* to destroy them.[18] Nietzsche would then replace these copies with a new edition of *Human* that was significantly different from the first. According to Lampert, the mature Nietzsche believed that the first edition of *Human* was an "*erring* beginning" because it expressed his commitment to the "*optimism* of the modern Enlightenment" (2017: 7), and so in order to correct his mistake, Nietzsche's first inclination was to destroy the text.

According to Lampert, Nietzsche abandoned plans for an entirely new edition of *Human* once he came to believe that he could not destroy the unsold copies of the first edition (he was having difficulty buying these back from the publisher). Thus, Nietzsche developed a new plan. First, he would use the content for the new edition of *Human* to produce an entirely new book that is now *Beyond Good and Evil*. Second, Nietzsche eventually decided to republish the first edition of *Human* with a preface explaining the idiosyncrasies of the work, thereby allowing his friends to identify "its Enlightenment excesses" (2017: 148). Having written the preface in April 1886, he then learned he could get possession of the unsold copies of all his previous books from his publisher, and it was only at this point that Nietzsche decided to reread his previous books and write prefaces to all of them to "show how they collectively" inscribe "a coherent trajectory in his becoming what he was" (2017: 7).

There are, however, serious problems with Lampert's account. First, Nietzsche did not intend to destroy *Human* as such, which is what Lampert implies when he speaks of Nietzsche's "intention to destroy *Things Human All Too Human*" (2017: 5), but only *the unsold copies* of *the first edition*. Had Nietzsche succeeded in executing this plan, there would still be a book with the title, *Human, All Too Human*. Indeed, there would be two books with this same title in existence: the approximately 400 copies of the first edition of *Human* that were already sold, and a second edition of *Human* that would have entirely different contents – similar to the contents of what is now *Beyond Good and Evil*.

---

[18] Lampert (2017) follows D'Iorio (2016: 142n48 and 109) in translating the title as *Things Human All Too Human*, thereby creating a connection to Plato's claim in the *Republic* that human things are not worthy of great seriousness, a point to which Nietzsche refers in HH 628.

Even more problematic for Lampert's account is that the evidence we have suggests that the revisions Nietzsche was planning to make to *Human* consist of mere modifications – rather than a wholesale replacement – of the contents of the first edition.[19] Some of the proposed revisions to *Human* did include ideas we now find in *Beyond Good and Evil*. However, in one fragment that reveals these changes, we see that the revised version of *Human* would still have nine chapters with roughly the same titles (see KSA 11: 42[3]). Thus, one has the sense that the phrases listed in this fragment – many of which appear in *Beyond Good and Evil* – are potential additions to, rather than replacements for, the contents of the first edition of *Human*.[20] Moreover, we possess a *Handexemplar* or personal copy of *Human* to which Nietzsche was making revisions in the summer of 1885, and these revisions are modifications of the first edition of the text (see KSA 14: p. 116). In other words, they give no indication that Nietzsche wants to replace the contents of the first edition of *Human* with entirely new contents similar to those now found in *Beyond Good and Evil*. Finally, we know that Nietzsche was composing a preface for the new edition of *Human* during this time (late summer of 1885), and in one version of the preface, he quotes from the first edition of *Human* on three different occasions (KSA 11: 40[65]; see also KSA 11: 41[9]). This, of course, presupposes that the original contents of *Human* would still be part of the second edition.

The existence of these prefaces from the summer of 1885 further complicates Lampert's account. Lampert claims that Nietzsche decided to write the preface to what is now the second edition of *Human* in the spring of 1886, and it was only when Nietzsche got back the unsold copies of his books from his publisher that he decided to write prefaces to all his books. The *Nachlass*, however, shows that Nietzsche was working on prefaces to some of his previous books, including *Human*, well before this time and that concepts from these earlier drafts are central to the narrative Nietzsche tells in the published 1886 preface to *Human*. Thus, Nietzsche speaks of "the great liberation [*die grosse Loslösung*]" in both 1885 variants (KSA 11: 40[65] and 41[9]) and the 1886 published preface to *Human* (HH I P 3, 6, and 7), and he speaks of "years of convalescence" in both a

---

[19] If there is additional evidence, Lampert, to my knowledge, does not supply it.

[20] As D'Iorio (2016: 121f.) notes, Nietzsche refers to HH 628 in KSA 11: 42[3]. What this implies, of course, is that HH 628 from the first edition would have been part of the planned second edition of *Human*.

variant and the published preface (KSA 11: 41[9] and HH I P 4).[21]
Moreover, we know that Nietzsche was also working on prefaces to
other works such as his *Untimely Meditations* (KSA 11: 41[2]) and
Assorted Opinions (KSA 11: 40[63]) in the summer of 1885. Thus, there
are reasons to believe, *pace* Lampert, that Nietzsche was already thinking
of giving an account of his development in the summer of 1885, and so
the project of trying to unify his works through these prefaces did not
result from a failed attempt to eliminate the first edition of *Human*
in 1886.

According to the view I am defending here, Nietzsche's desire to
republish his previous works with new prefaces that stress their unity –
and in particular the unity of the free spirit works – stems from the simple
fact that he wrote the free spirit texts as a literary unit and he now wants to
make this more explicit to his readers. So understood, *Human* is not an
"erring beginning," but rather a natural beginning to a free spirit project
that is designed to tell the story of how the Enlightenment project
culminates in the tragedy of *Zarathustra*. This, then, is why neither the
preface to the first volume of the second edition of *Human*, which is about
the entire free spirit project, nor the preface to the second volume of
Human, which is about *Human* and its two appendices, speaks of an
"erring beginning." Instead, both prefaces present *Human* as a proper
beginning to the dialectic of the Enlightenment that Nietzsche executes
in these works.

For my purposes, the 1886–1887 prefaces are important not only
because they provide retrospective evidence for the unity Nietzsche attributes to the free spirit works, but also because they give an account of the
free spirit project that closely aligns with my claim that these works are best
understood as a *Bildungsroman*. To be sure, the notion of a *Bildungsroman*
is itself complicated and the subject of much scholarly debate, and so my
use of the term may create more difficulties than it resolves. However, my
purpose here is not to take a pre-existing understanding of the free spirit
works and show how these works, so understood, can be classified as a
Bildungsroman. If this were the case, it would be necessary to define the
term precisely and enter into relevant scholarly debates. Instead, my

---

[21] This shows that these are variants of the eventual preface to the second edition of *Human* published
in 1886 and not to the preface that Nietzsche wrote in June of 1885 and placed at the beginning of
Beyond Good and Evil. To my knowledge, there is no evidence to support Lampert's claim (2017:
158) that Nietzsche originally wrote the preface to *Beyond Good and Evil* as a preface to *Human, All
Too Human*.

interest in applying the term to the free spirit works is purely instrumental. That is, it is a means by which I introduce and defend a new way of reading the free spirit works. If it turns out that the use of the term *Bildungsroman* does not help the reader understand the approach I am defending here, then the term should simply be disregarded. In the end, the truth or falsity of my thesis depends on whether a narrative of self-education structures these works, and so if one insists that *Bildungsroman* means something other than a narrative of self-education, then I would be fine with replacing the term with the definition I am stipulating here so that my thesis amounts to the claim that the free spirit works are best understood as a consciously constructed dialectical narrative of self-education.

In a straightforward sense, the term *Bildungsroman* simply means a novel (*Roman*) of education in the sense of formation (*Bildung*). So defined, one can already see some difficulties with the application of this term to the free spirit works. Unlike novels, the free spirit works are not fiction, but present philosophical truth claims. Moreover, the free spirit works are written in aphorisms, not the continuous prose characteristic of most novels. Finally, there is no main character that inhabits a specific space or context and acts in relation to a cast of other characters. Thus, there are reasons for thinking that the free spirit works are not a *Roman*, and so there are reasons to resist the idea that these works should be understood as a *Bildungsroman*.

However, there is, or so I contend, a narrative or story that Nietzsche develops in these works, and so just as the ordering of events is essential to the narrative, so is the order of the individual aphorisms of each free spirit work as well as the order of the individual works that constitute the whole. Although there is no concrete hero who interacts with other characters, there is a hero of the free spirit works in both the abstract figure of the free spirit and a Nietzsche that identifies with this figure. The story of the free spirit develops within a particular setting or context, namely, modern European intellectual culture, and the story is about the education and formation of the aforementioned hero at both the cognitive and affective levels. It is in this sense that we can understand the free spirit works to be a *Bildungsroman*.

This understanding of the *Bildungsroman* largely conforms to the original use of the term. Although popularized by Wilhelm Dilthey (Boes 2006: 231), Karl Morgenstern was the first to use the term in the early 1820s. Understanding Goethe's *Wilhelm Meister's Apprenticeship* to be the first novel of the type, Morgenstern defined the term as follows:

It will justly bear the name *Bildungsroman* firstly and primarily on account of its thematic material, because it portrays the *Bildung* of the hero in its beginnings and growth to a certain stage of completeness; and also secondly because it is by virtue of this portrayal that it further the reader's *Bildung* to a much greater extent than any other kind of novel. (Swales 1978: 13)

According to Martin Swales, the *Bildungsroman* emerged from a context in which there was a particular *Humanitätsideal*. Education or *Bildung* was therefore a process (*Werden*) of development (*Entwicklung*) in which the individual makes progress toward this ideal. A *Bildungsroman* tells the story of how the individual goes through a process of *Bildung* that results in self-realization and inner wholeness (1978: 14–15).

In one sense, the process of *Bildung* on display in the free spirit works is just the *Bildung* of a particular type or character, namely, the free spirit. In another sense, both Nietzsche's initial notes for the free spirit project as well as his retrospective descriptions show that these works are about Nietzsche's own formation as a free spirit. Thus, Nietzsche writes the free spirit works primarily to record and even monumentalize his self-education as a free spirit, and this is why he repeatedly remarks in his letters that he is writing for himself. However, there is a secondary purpose that corresponds to the second half of Morgenstern's understanding of the *Bildungsroman*: by writing and publishing these works, Nietzsche is inviting readers to accompany him on this journey (he sometimes calls them fishhooks (KSA 11: 40[59] and 41[9])). Thus, by reading the free spirit works, we not only learn how Nietzsche becomes the free spirit he presents himself to be in the prefaces, but we are also invited to embrace his reflections as we proceed down our own path toward liberation and enlightenment.

By claiming that the free spirit works are best understood as a *Bildungsroman*, I am also arguing that these works unfold in stages toward a particular goal in which each stage is essential to the process. In this sense, I follow Dilthey's claim that in a *Bildungsroman*, "each of the stages has its own intrinsic value and is at the same time the basis for a higher stage" (Boes 2006: 232). Reading the free spirit works as a *Bildungsroman* therefore moves against two tendencies in the secondary literature. The first is to read these aphorisms out of context and in any order. Because these works are telling a story, we cannot simply exchange aphorisms from, say, *The Gay Science* with aphorisms from *The Wanderer*. The second tendency is for readers to focus on the end of the free spirit story. Interpreting the free spirit works as a *Bildungsroman*, however, means that it is necessary to read all of these works to understand any part of the project.

Another upshot of this reading is that in order to understand what a free spirit is, we cannot simply cull the various statements Nietzsche makes about the free spirit and assemble them into a coherent view.[22] Instead, to know what a free spirit is, we need to follow the dialectic that unfolds over these works between science and truth seeking, on the one hand, and art and life-affirmation, on the other. Appealing to statements from a work like *Human* to say what a free spirit is can be misleading because the free spirit evolves over the course of these works, and so the free spirit at the end of the project is different from the free spirit at the beginning. Furthermore, understanding what the free spirit is involves more than just grappling with the explicit statements Nietzsche makes about the free spirit. Instead, it involves following Nietzsche through the progression of these works and understanding how each book, each chapter, and even each aphorism contributes to the *Bildung* of the free spirit.

On the reading I present, what drives the development or movement of thought in the free spirit works are the inner tensions that characterize the initial stages of the project, and it is for this reason that I argue that the free spirit works are best understood as a particular type of *Bildungsroman*, namely, a dialectical one, and why I refer to my account as a dialectical reading. Like the term *Bildungsroman*, the meaning of "dialectical" is not always clear. The notion of dialectics can be traced back to ancient authors such as Plato and Aristotle. In modern philosophy, the term is not only central to Hegel's project,[23] but also appears in the title of a work that bears some similarities to the reading of the free spirit works I defend here, Horkheimer and Adorno's *Dialectic of Enlightenment*.[24] For my purposes, I understand dialectic to be a movement or process that emerges from tensions or contradictions between disparate ideas and results in the revision or transformation of one or more of the conflicting ideas. Thus, my understanding of dialectic is largely Hegelian.

Although I argue that there are dialectical transformations that take place even within a single work like *The Gay Science*, such transformations are most evident when we examine the changes that take place over the free spirit project as a whole. Specifically, I hold that these dialectical transformations result from an implicit tension that emerges from the free spirit's initial investigations in *Human* that is only resolved in the final

---

[22] See Reginster (2013) for an example of this methodology.
[23] Forster (1993: 134f.) highlights the pedagogical function of Hegel's dialectical method. So understood, the dialectical method goes hand in hand with the notion of *Bildung*.
[24] See Martin (2008) for a similar comparison.

stages of the project. As Nietzsche explains in his later writings, an uncompromising quest for truth presupposes that truth has an absolute value, and the idea that truth has an absolute value depends on the existence of a metaphysical world (GS 344). In other words, Nietzsche believes that the Socratic quest for truth only makes sense in a world in which some version of Platonic metaphysics is true. However, in *Human*, Nietzsche's initial commitment to the uncompromising quest for truth leads to the destruction of the metaphysical framework that justifies this quest. Thus, the position developed in *Human* is riddled with dialectical instability between a traditional commitment to truth and the rejection of the metaphysical tradition in the name of truth.

On the reading I offer, one of the primary purposes of the free spirit works is to show, in step-by-step fashion, how this tension is resolved, and so at the heart of my dialectical reading is the idea that Nietzsche executes what he later calls a "*Selbstaufhebung*" of the will to truth in these works (D P 4; GM III 27). The notion of an *Aufhebung* – poorly translated as "sublation" – is a central feature of Hegel's understanding of dialectics, and we can profitably appeal to the understanding of *Aufhebung* that scholars have attributed to Hegel to make sense of the *Selbstaufhebung* that I claim occurs in these works. Specifically, an *Aufhebung* is the process by which something is abolished, preserved, and elevated at the same time (Forster 1998: 282).[25] A *Selbstaufhebung* would therefore be a process by which something abolishes, preserves, and elevates itself. A *Selbstaufhebung* of the will to truth would then be a case in which the will to truth abolishes, preserves, and elevates itself. The will to truth abolishes itself because the free spirit recognizes through an uncompromising quest for truth that truth does not have an absolute value and so there is no obligation to pursue truth at all costs. The will to truth, however, preserves itself because this insight into the value of truth – as well as the lack of any corresponding obligation to pursue it at all costs – is the result of the will to truth and depends on the truths that this will has revealed. The will to truth is also elevated because the free spirit now knows the truth about the value of truth and so the will to truth, and so it can now raise the question of the value of this will.

The *Selbstaufhebung* of the will to truth occurs in the free spirit works with the death of God and the elimination of his shadow in the third chapter of *The Gay Science*, and this moment is central to the dialectical

---

[25] Danto (1988: 189) gives "*Selbstaufhebung*" a similar gloss: "to negate, to preserve, and to transcend – *all at once*."

transitions that take place between science and art in the free spirit works. The scientific ethos that Nietzsche adopts in *Human* is rooted in a will to truth and aims at what Horkheimer and Adorno call the "disenchantment of the world" and the "dissolution of myth" (1999: 1). Thus, this scientific ethos is opposed to the very force that Nietzsche originally identified as possessing a myth-making capacity: art. However, once the free spirit recognizes that the unconditional quest for truth is itself rooted in the mythical idea that truth has an absolute value, the justification for opposing the myth-making capacities of art is undermined. Consequently, the scientific quest for truth, when taken to its logical conclusion, makes possible a return to art, and it is here that the initial antithesis between science and art in *Human* is overcome. In short, the quest for truth initiated in *Human* makes possible Nietzsche's eventual turn to the mythical poetry of *Zarathustra*, and it is in this sense that I think the free spirit works have a dialectical character.

Thus far, I have endeavored to explain what I mean by "dialectical" and "*Bildungsroman*," and although there are important differences, notions of *Bildung* and dialectic can already be found in Franco's (2011) account of the free spirit works. What most differentiates my account from other accounts already on offer – including Franco's – is that I also think the free spirit works are best understood as having been constructed to tell this dialectical story. That is, I resist the idea that the free spirit works just happen to unfold in this dialectical manner. Because I expect that this feature of my thesis will cause the most controversy, I want to explain in some detail what I mean when I say that these works are best understood as having been *consciously constructed* as a dialectical *Bildungsroman*.

To begin, it should be obvious that I do not mean that Nietzsche had all the details of the project in mind when he completed *Human*. There are a number of instances in which Nietzsche changed his mind about important details as he composed these works. For instance, he changed the title of *Daybreak* from "The Ploughshare" to *Daybreak* just prior to publication. Similarly, Nietzsche originally composed the first three chapters of *The Gay Science* as the final chapters of *Daybreak* and only later decided to make the former a separate book. Nietzsche also made last-minute changes to the concluding aphorisms of *Human* (D'Iorio 2016: 107ff.) as well as the final aphorisms of the second and third chapters of *The Gay Science* (Brusotti 2016). Because we know that Nietzsche was changing his mind about these details at the last minute, my claim about Nietzsche consciously constructing these works must be limited to certain features of this project.

Of course, this raises the question: which features of the free spirit project should we think Nietzsche planned from the beginning? In response to this question, I want to stake out the most minimal position possible without making this aspect of my thesis vacuous. Thus, I present three – and only three – claims that are essential to my reading, and so if any one of these claims is shown to be false, then this aspect of my thesis will be false. First, when Nietzsche publishes *Human*, he believes that the *Bildungs*-project of the free spirit works will continue beyond *Human* itself. Second, when Nietzsche publishes *Human*, he believes that the free spirit project will result in some overcoming or restriction of the drive to truth that initially animates this project. Third, when Nietzsche publishes *Human*, he believes that the free spirit project will eventuate in a return to the kind of art he praised in his earliest works.[26]

There are two reasons for identifying these three – and only these three – claims as those to which Nietzsche is committed from the start. First, these three claims, taken together, are necessary and sufficient for a dialectical reading of these works. With only the first claim, we are left with a planned project for some sort of *Bildungsroman*, but not necessarily a dialectical one. The second and third claims provide the dialectical character. These three claims are sufficient because we do not need further elements to describe the most important dialectical transformation that takes place in these works, namely, the transition from the scientific ethos of *Human* to the celebration of art at the end of *The Gay Science*. Second, contrary to Lampert's claim that Nietzsche had no way of knowing at the beginning where the free spirit project would end (2017: 145), there are reasons for thinking that Nietzsche could have known that the free spirit works would execute these dialectical transformations. Not only did he sketch the idea

---

[26] By limiting myself to these three claims, I think I also escape the objection – posed by one anonymous reader – that there is textual evidence that speaks against my claim that Nietzsche consciously constructed these works as a dialectical *Bildungsroman*. It is true that passages from the 1886 preface to *Human* (HH I P 7) and *Ecce Homo* (EH "Clever" 9) indicate that there are features of this project of which Nietzsche is unaware – in particular an understanding of exactly *what* he is or *what* is driving him in this project – and so indicate that he did not consciously have in mind the precise details of how this project would end. However, these passages do not provide evidence that he could not have known that his *Bildungsprogramm* would unfold in a dialectical manner, which is my claim, or that he was not consciously pursuing some sort of educational task or *Aufgabe* in the free spirit works. If they did suggest the latter, they would be contradicted by what Nietzsche says elsewhere in his later writings – most notably KSB 7: 617 and KSB 8: 1014 – and even letters prior to and from the time of the free spirit works in which Nietzsche repeatedly speaks of pursuing his *task* (e.g., KSB 5: 521 and 772; KSB 6: 120 and 138). In short, Nietzsche may not have known exactly where this task will end, but there are reasons for thinking that he did consciously pursue a task – one outlined in *Schopenhauer as Educator* – even if he was driven by unconscious forces and so a mysterious "inner voice" (KSB 5: 523).

of a self-overcoming of the Socratic quest for truth in *The Birth of Tragedy* and his *Nachlass* from this time, Nietzsche also outlined a program of education in *Schopenhauer as Educator* that extends well beyond the project in *Human* of eliminating false beliefs. Although Nietzsche could have had more features of the free spirit project in mind at the time of publishing *Human* – such as the Epicurean interlude in *The Wanderer* or "the passion for knowledge" in *Daybreak* – the reason for focusing on just these three claims is because we have evidence that Nietzsche had been thinking in these terms prior to composing the free spirit works. In the case of the Epicurean interlude or the passion for knowledge, we have no such evidence, and so I make no corresponding claim.

The fact that Nietzsche had already sketched these ideas in his early works falsifies Lampert's claim that Nietzsche could not have known how the free spirit project would develop. However, it does not prove that Nietzsche was, in fact, thinking this way when he published *Human*. At this point, one might expect that I will prove the claim that Nietzsche has consciously constructed these works in this way. Although I do think I can prove a version of the first claim – that Nietzsche had plans to continue the free spirit project beyond *Human* at the time of publishing *Human* – I cannot prove that Nietzsche had plans to construct the free spirit works to execute a dialectic between science and art that eventuates in a self-overcoming of the will to truth. Although Nietzsche's retrospective descriptions of the free spirit works as well as his repeated claims to have followed the program of education outlined in *Schopenhauer as Educator* in his subsequent works provide important support for my claim, the veracity of Nietzsche's retrospective claims can always be questioned. Because of the lack of evidence from the time Nietzsche was composing *Human*, I will have to pursue a different strategy.

This brings me to the final feature of my thesis: The free spirit works are *best understood* as a consciously constructed dialectical *Bildungsroman*. Specifically, my strategy is not to prove the truth of this reading, but rather to show that this is the best way of making sense of these works. The strategy consists of three moves. First, I claim that there is no substantive evidence that falsifies the three claims identified above. Thus, the evidence we have neither confirms nor denies the truth of my claim that Nietzsche consciously constructed these works as a dialectical *Bildungsroman*. Second, I claim that there is no evidence that proves the truth of any of the alternative readings of the free spirit works. Instead, each alternative reading is based on inferences and assumptions about how to read and approach these texts, and there is even evidence that speaks strongly against some of these alternative approaches. Finally, I argue that among the approaches available in the secondary literature that the evidence does not falsify, the dialectical reading offers the best explanation of key features of the free spirit works.

As we will see, the central assumption of the most formidable alternative to the dialectical approach that I want to challenge is that the views Nietzsche expresses in these aphorisms are always the views that Nietzsche himself holds at the time of their publication. Although this is a natural assumption to make when approaching a philosophical text, there are instances – such as Plato's dialogues or Hegel's *Phenomenology* – in which we should question this assumption, and I think the free spirit works, when read with this assumption in place, pose enough problems to reject it. Thus, I argue that we should apply to all of the free spirit works the point that Robin Small extracts from an unused 1877 preface for *Human* "that the book's voice is not [Nietzsche's] own but that of an imagined free spirit, engaging in dramatic monologue" (Small 2016: 10–11; see KSA 8: 25[2]). That is, we need to distinguish between Nietzsche *qua* author, or the individual that writes these texts, and Nietzsche *qua* free spirit, or the individual that appears in these texts, and not assume that the views expressed by the latter necessarily belong to the former. By making this distinction, I think we can make sense of a number of puzzling features of these texts and thereby see why these works are best understood as a consciously constructed dialectical *Bildungsroman*.

Competing Approaches to the Free Spirit Works

Although the amount of Nietzsche scholarship is immense, there is relatively little secondary literature on the free spirit works in Anglo-American scholarship. As noted above, it is generally assumed that Nietzsche matures around 1882 with the publication of works like *The Gay Science* and *Zarathustra*, and so although there is some interest in his earliest works and the themes they introduce, *Human* and *Daybreak* have often been ignored.[27] Nevertheless, scholars have gradually increased the attention they have given to these works, and roughly three approaches have been developed over the past two decades. The first is what I call – for reasons explained below – the "Danto approach." The second is what I call the

---

[27] For instance, *The Oxford Handbook of Nietzsche* (Gemes and Richardson 2013) excludes any treatment of these works and so implies that *Human* and *Daybreak* are not considered to be "principal works."

"postmodern approach," and the third I have labeled the "developmental approach." I treat each of these approaches in turn and then contrast them with my own "dialectical approach," which is a shortened way of referring to my overall thesis that the free spirit works are best understood as a consciously constructed dialectical *Bildungsroman*.

Ruth Abbey's *Nietzsche's Middle Period* (2000) is the first major work in Anglo-American scholarship devoted primarily to the free spirit works, and she implicitly adopts what I call the Danto approach. As noted above, Danto understands Nietzsche's oeuvre to be a collection of statements on a variety of topics scattered throughout various works that have little order or purpose. Although Abbey herself does not use the appellation and does not explicitly deny any sort of order or purpose to the free spirit works, her interpretation can be associated with Danto's general approach because she treats, in practice, the free spirit works as a monolithic collection of aphorisms that can be used to reconstruct Nietzsche's middle-period views.

At times, Abbey acknowledges that Nietzsche's views change, develop, or even conflict within the free spirit writings. However, she sets for herself the general task of extracting passages from these works that allow her to construct Nietzsche's middle-period view on a particular topic so that it can be contrasted with the position of Nietzsche's mature writings. As a result, Abbey quickly moves from one free spirit work to another in developing Nietzsche's middle-period views. One extreme example of this can be found in her discussion on love and egoism. There, she refers to passages from all five free spirit works within a mere two paragraphs to attribute a middle-period view to Nietzsche (2000: 124–125). So even though she might not subscribe to the Danto approach in theory, she clearly does in practice.

There is no doubt that some of Nietzsche's views remain relatively consistent throughout the free spirit works, and so although there are problems with her approach, Abbey's larger project of contrasting Nietzsche's views during the middle period with his later writings is not entirely unjustified. Nevertheless, there are key topics that Nietzsche treats in the free spirit works on which his views change quite dramatically, and so it seems impossible to attribute to Nietzsche a single middle-period view on these subjects.

One topic that Abbey strangely, but perhaps wisely, avoids is Nietzsche's understanding of art during this period.[28] It is curious that she avoids the topic because art is a central concern for Nietzsche

---

[28] Large (2015: 70) also makes this point about Abbey's reading.

throughout his career and even during his middle period, and some of the views he expresses on the topic during this time contrast sharply with those of his later writings. However, it is perhaps wise that she avoids the topic because even a superficial comparison of the views he expresses in *Human* with those in *The Gay Science* shows that no single and static middle-period view can be extracted from these works. In the fourth section of *Human*, Nietzsche argues that art is the product of an immature age that now needs to be subordinated to the rigors of the natural sciences (HH 222). In *The Gay Science*, Nietzsche reverses his opinion, calling on us to become poets of our lives (GS 299) by subordinating scientific inquiry to the larger project of creating ourselves (GS 335).

Another central topic of the free spirit works that Abbey largely avoids is God and Nietzsche's different portrayals of the death of God. On the one hand, Nietzsche rejects a metaphysical entity such as God at the beginning of *Human* and he continues to reject metaphysical beliefs, as well as the "metaphysical need," throughout the remainder of the free spirit works. Nevertheless, the attitude Nietzsche expresses regarding his rejection of metaphysical entities like God undergoes significant transformation over the course of the free spirit works. In *Human*, Nietzsche counsels himself, *qua* free spirit, to have a "good temperament" in investigating such matters, one that hovers above customs and takes pleasure in the search for truth (HH 34). In *The Wanderer*, Nietzsche endorses an attitude of Epicurean or skeptical indifference toward metaphysical questions and so the death of God, first announced here, is met with shoulder-shrugging indifference (WS 84). In *The Gay Science*, however, Nietzsche then has a madman announce the death of God and the earth-shaking implications of this event (GS 125).

Because topics like art and the appropriate response to the death of God are central to Nietzsche's project, they challenge the approach Abbey adopts to the free spirit works and Danto's approach to Nietzsche's works more generally. If Nietzsche contradicts himself on such fundamental issues, we cannot simply brush such contradictions aside and continue to construct coherent theories from Nietzsche's various works while ignoring those statements in his oeuvre that might challenge a particular view attributed to him. Indeed, the frequent presence of such contradictions has led some, like Karl Jaspers, to claim that, "*self-contradiction* is the fundamental ingredient in Nietzsche's thought. For every single one of Nietzsche's judgments, one can also find an opposite" (1997: 10).

Jasper's claim is undoubtedly hyperbolic: are we really supposed to think Nietzsche contradicts himself on *every* point? Even the death of

God passages, in which Nietzsche expresses two different reactions to this event, both agree that God is, in some sense, "dead," and one would be hard pressed to find a passage in which Nietzsche declares that God is, in some sense, alive. Nevertheless, contradictions are present in Nietzsche's oeuvre, and they are particularly acute in the free spirit works. It is for this reason that one might conclude that Nietzsche is intentionally contradicting himself, and one might further speculate that he does this to undermine the guiding assumption of the Danto approach, namely, that Nietzsche's works contain a series of positions that can be brought together to form a coherent and systematic whole.

The denial of a coherent system lies at the heart of what I call the postmodern approach to the free spirit works and Nietzsche's larger corpus. The postmodern approach holds that Nietzsche consciously employs various devices in his works to rebel against a philosophical tradition of system builders by consciously creating obstacles for readers who seek to systematize his ideas. On this reading, contradictions are one way he does this, and so if we are to reject the postmodern approach to Nietzsche's writings, we must give a satisfactory explanation of why he contradicts himself on such important issues within such a short period of time.

Many readers who adopt the postmodern approach also argue that Nietzsche employs various literary and stylistic techniques to undermine attempts to systematize his works. Of particular importance for the free spirit works is Nietzsche's use of the aphorism. According to both Abbey and Franco, a number of French deconstructionist readers (Franco 2011: xiii) and, to a lesser extent, Alexander Nehamas (Abbey 2000: 157), have highlighted the way in which Nietzsche's use of the aphorism rebels against systematizing or totalizing readings. Whereas Jacques Derrida has suggested that "the totality of Nietzsche's texts, in some monstrous way, might well be of the type 'I have forgotten my umbrella'" (1979: 133), Sarah Kofman argues that "the aphorism, by its discontinuous character, disseminates meaning and appeals to the pluralism of interpretations and their renewal: only movement is immortal" (1993: 116).[29]

Although they would likely resist the postmodern moniker and there are elements of their projects that differ significantly from such an approach, Werner Stegmaier (2009) and Joel Westerdale (2013) have also argued that Nietzsche uses the aphorism as a means of rejecting philosophical systems

---

[29] David Allison's reading of *The Gay Science* can also be aligned with the postmodern approach (2001: Ch. 2).

and the systematization of his philosophy.[30] Specifically, Westerdale claims that, "the aphoristic volumes deliberately shun the formal conventions of academic writing, forgoing sustained argumentation in favor of an array of isolated texts ranging in length from a single sentence to several pages." Thus, the works of the middle period or free spirit do not erect an "edifice of sober argumentation leading to a unified conclusion." Instead, they provide "a compilation of discrete statements that the reader must interpret and assemble without any assurance of eventual resolution." In this way, the free spirit works are a "formal manifestation" of Nietzsche's later admonition to mistrust and avoid all systematic philosophy (TI "Maxims" 26) (2013: 1).

Westerdale's approach explicitly builds upon Stegmaier's methodological reflections on Nietzsche's writings (2013: 4). According to Stegmaier, Nietzsche's aphoristic books form the basis for "infinite philology." Infinite philology recognizes that "nothing is final" in Nietzsche's work, and Nietzsche "seems to have had no intention toward completion or finality" (2009: 13). Completion and finality are features of the systematic philosophy Nietzsche rejects, and the aphorism is the literary form Nietzsche adopts to engage in what Stegmaier calls "philosophizing temporarily." The aphorism allows Nietzsche to place his thoughts within "intellectual contexts" but "without a principle of development, and without results of development in an explicit, logical system." In short, the principal feature of the aphorism is a continued openness to new interpretive possibilities, and so the meaning of an aphorism is always "in flux" (2009: 14). Like Kofman, Stegmaier claims that aphorisms resemble Nietzsche's understanding of the world in that they allow for "infinite interpretations" (GS 374),[31] and so reading the aphorism becomes an exercise in "infinite philology" (2009: 14).

What is striking about readings that emphasize the importance of Nietzsche's style is that there is often little textual evidence to support the various claims made about it. Kofman claims that Nietzsche employs the aphorism to disseminate meaning, but she supplies no textual evidence from Nietzsche's writings to support her claim. Stegmaier does the same: Although he provides one of the most rigorous readings of Nietzsche's aphorisms in the fifth chapter of *The Gay Science* (2012), he provides little

---

[30] Westerdale (2013: 6) criticizes "postmodern" readings for claiming that Nietzsche's writings are beyond interpretation. He sees the aphorism as moving between naturalistic and postmodern readings (2013: 60).

[31] Donnellan (1982: 132) also connects the aphorism to Nietzsche's rejection of system as well as the belief that reality is fragmented and chaotic.

textual support for his assertion that Nietzsche adopts the aphorism to avoid any intimation of finality or completion. And although Westerdale is right that Nietzsche later warns against systematizers (TI "Maxims" 26), nowhere does Nietzsche explicitly link his use of the aphorism to his later rejection of philosophical systems of the traditional sort.

In my view, there is too little textual evidence – in the form of explicit statements from Nietzsche's published works, unpublished notes, and letters – to know for certain why he chose to use the aphoristic form in the free spirit works.[32] The only thing we know with some confidence is that Nietzsche read Paul Rée's 1875 *Psychological Observations* and that the aphoristic style Rée employs in the work likely had some influence on Nietzsche.[33] Franco claims that Nietzsche saw in Rée's use of the aphorism a "cold clarity" that could be used "in his struggle against the cloudy enchantments of romanticism" (2011: 13), and this can be connected to another point that Franco extracts from the preface of *Daybreak* (2011: xiii). There, Nietzsche explains that he wants to be read slowly and most of all to be "read *well*," and this means "looking cautiously before and aft, with reservations, with doors left open, with delicate eyes and fingers" (D P 5).

According to Franco, the reason Nietzsche needs to be read well is that the aphorism forces the reader "to fill in what is left unsaid and thereby to think along with the philosophical writer" (2011: 14). Direct support for this way of approaching the aphorism comes from two *Nachlass* notes. One is from 1885: "In aphorism books like mine, nothing but forbidden, lengthy things and thought-chains [*Gedanken-Ketten*] stand between and behind brief aphorisms" (KSA 11: 37[5]). The other is from 1876: "A maxim [*Sentenz*] is a link in a thought-chain [*Gedankenkette*]; it demands that the reader reproduce this chain through his own means; this means demanding very much" (KSA 8: 20[3]).[34] As Franco points out, Nietzsche also remarks here that not everyone will be able to meet this challenge, and so there is an implied elitism in the use of the aphorism. In this sense, Nietzsche's use of the aphorism could have its origin in the philosophy of Heraclitus, a name to which Nietzsche explicitly refers in the latter note (KSA 8: 20[3]).

---

[32] Some, such as Graham Parkes (1994: 116), have claimed that Nietzsche's eyesight forced him to write "in fragments scribbled down in between long bouts of walking or being bedridden."

[33] For a general account of Nietzsche's relationship with Rée, see Small (2005).

[34] Westerdale (2013: 24) claims that the maxim (*Sentenz*) is a species of the aphorism.

These two notes also provide a piece of evidence that directly challenges the underlying assumption of both the Danto and postmodern approaches: there is no coherent philosophy or principle of development hidden among or behind the aphorisms that the reader is supposed to find. Although Westerdale charges readers like Franco with simply assuming that there is a general coherence or principle of development underlying the free spirit aphorisms (2013: 3–4), Nietzsche's reference to a *Gedanken-Kette* in the aforementioned notes indicates that this is no mere assumption. In an 1882 drafted letter to Malwida von Meysenbug, Nietzsche claims that *The Gay Science* completes the "*Gedanken-Kette*" that stretches back to his time with her in Sorrento in 1876 (KSB 6: 264). The notion of a *Gedanken-Kette* or thought-chain suggests that these aphorisms present an ordered connection of ideas and that the task of the reader is to decipher these connections.

Another reason for thinking that there is a principle of development at work in the free spirit writings is that even a cursory reading of *Human* shows how Nietzsche sometimes makes the organization of the thought-chain of aphorisms readily detectible. In the first aphorism, Nietzsche commits himself to what he calls historical philosophy, and he claims that he will apply this approach to the various moral, religious, and aesthetic sensations as well as to cultural and social intercourse (HH 1). Nietzsche is referring here to the various chapter titles of the book and so he is effectively revealing the structure of the work. Moreover, Jonathan Cohen's (2010) analysis of *Human* shows that each chapter begins with introductory and concluding aphorisms that summarize the contents of each chapter. Of course, if Cohen is right, then the Danto and postmodern approaches must be wrong.

A similar claim can be made about the other free spirit works. Although a work like *Assorted Opinions* may lack a readily identifiable argumentative structure, Brusotti (1997: 21) has shown that this does not hold true for *Daybreak* or *The Gay Science*. As letters from the time make clear, Nietzsche wants to be sure that these works express something "whole." Indeed, there is a well-known aphorism from *Assorted Opinions* that speaks against both the Danto and postmodern approaches: "*The worst readers.* – The worst readers are those who behave like plundering troops: they take away a few things they can use, dirty and confound the remainder, and revile the whole" (AOM 137).

So understood, the idea that there is an underlying logic or coherence that links Nietzsche's aphorisms together is no mere assumption, and so the task of the reader is to try to reproduce, rather than create, these connections.[35] In keeping with this idea, Franco claims that the value of Nietzsche's *Nachlass* from this time – in addition to the critical apparatus that the Colli-Montinari edition of Nietzsche's works and letters supplies – is that it helps us "fix" the meanings of what would otherwise seem to be indeterminate aphorisms in the published works (2011: xiv).

Elsewhere, I have followed Reginster in adopting the "priority principle" in regard to the relationship between the published works and unpublished notes (Meyer 2014a: 17). The priority principle makes Nietzsche's published works (and the works he intended for publication) the primary object of interpretation. However, it also allows for the use of Nietzsche's notes, letters, and sources to help decipher the meaning of the published works. Because the priority principle is the way most other authors in the history of philosophy are treated, there is good reason to adopt the priority principle as a default approach to Nietzsche's works. Thus, the burden of proof falls on anyone who rejects the priority principle, either by elevating the *Nachlass* to the status of a published work, as Heidegger does, or by rejecting use of the *Nachlass* altogether, as Clark seems to do.[36]

Although there are good reasons to resist the underlying assumption of both the Danto and postmodern approaches, namely that there is no underlying coherence or principle of development to these aphorisms, we still need a strategy for confronting the contradictions found in the free spirit works. Here again, Franco's reading provides a possible solution by implicitly adopting what I call the developmental approach. According to Franco, "Nietzsche's thought undergoes tremendous development over the course of the middle period" (2011: xiv), and so the apparent contradictions found in these works can be largely explained by the fact that Nietzsche changes his mind as he composes each work.

On the surface, Franco's developmental approach appears quite similar to the dialectical approach. For instance, I largely agree with Franco's view – one also shared by Abbey (2000: 156) – that the free spirit works allow us to observe Nietzsche working through the implications of the

---

[35] Allison (2001: 76) seems to endorse the opposite view: The reader should give meaning and determinacy to otherwise indeterminate aphorisms by projecting his or her own desires and beliefs on to the text.

[36] Clark and Dudrick's (2012) reading of *Beyond Good Evil* suffers from the fact that they make almost no use of Nietzsche's drafts, notes, and sources for the text. In fact, they *never* refer to any *Nachlass* notes from the critical edition to develop their interpretation. However, one suspects that this methodology is not a mere oversight, but rather intentional: By ignoring these sources, the authors can fill in Nietzsche's open-ended aphorisms not with what Nietzsche intended to say but rather with what they want Nietzsche to say.

positions he adopts in a work like *Human* so as to arrive "at his mature philosophical position." In this sense, these are works in which "Nietzsche truly becomes Nietzsche" (2011: xiv).

However, the difference between the two approaches is crucial. According to the developmental approach, Nietzsche does not foresee the free spirit project undergoing any further development as he publishes each text. Instead, he simply pens a set of ideas in a work like *Human* and then decides to revise and even reject a number of these ideas in subsequent works, and he continues this process until he reaches positions that we now attribute to the mature Nietzsche. So understood, the free spirit works are similar to Kant's pre-critical writings. They reveal views that Nietzsche held for a time but then ultimately came to reject in favor of more mature and sophisticated views. In this way, we can see why readers interested in Nietzsche's philosophy would ignore the free spirit works prior to *The Gay Science*: They largely contain immature ideas that Nietzsche himself ultimately discarded.

In contrast, the dialectical reading claims that these writings are definitely not like Kant's pre-critical writings in that Nietzsche's goal is to tell the story of how he educates himself to become a free spirit, and so Nietzsche is best understood as knowing, at the time of writing a work like *Human*, that the free spirit will undergo further transformations and developments. In this sense, the free spirit works can be understood more like Descartes' *Meditations*, especially if they had been published in installments. Although Descartes the author knows where his meditations will lead, the meditator in the text is presented as having little idea where the quest for knowledge will go once everything is subjected to radical doubt. On my reading, the free spirit works are similar. Although Nietzsche the author has some sense of where the free spirit project is headed, Nietzsche presents himself in *Human* as a free-spirited investigator who has little idea that the quest for truth initiated in *Human* will drive him into the desert of knowledge only to undergo a *Selbstaufhebung* in subsequent works and culminate in a return to tragedy. Thus, just as each meditation is essential to Descartes' project, all the free spirit works are endowed with significance. In both cases, they are designed to lead the reader from a familiar and agreed upon starting point to new ideas that advance beyond anything the reader might currently accept.

The developmental approach is based on the default assumption – there is no explicit justification or proof for this assumption – that there is a direct correspondence between what Nietzsche publishes at a particular time and what Nietzsche believes at that time. Although there are good reasons for accepting this as the default assumption, there are a number of problems that result from this assumption upon closer examination of the free spirit works and their relationship to Nietzsche's larger oeuvre. The first set of concerns has to do with the rapidity with which Nietzsche is ostensibly changing his opinions in these texts. The second set of concerns has to do with Nietzsche's interest in republishing these works at later stages of his so-called development. The third set of concerns, related to the second, has to do with Nietzsche's intention to unite the contradictory views expressed in these works into a single literary unit. The final set of concerns has to do with the way in which Nietzsche returns to a number of positions in his later works that are already expressed in his earlier works.

In thinking about the periodization of Nietzsche's works, we need to keep in mind that his productive career takes place over a relatively short period of time from 1872 to 1888. We can compare this with Heidegger's activity that stretches over a half-century, and over such a long period of time, a thinker will naturally develop and change her mind about various views. To be sure, Nietzsche also changes his views on important issues over the course of his productive career. The problem, however, is that these changes happen so quickly during the free spirit works that it is hard to believe Nietzsche is revising views he considered to be his final judgment at the time of their publication. Specifically, Nietzsche publishes one free spirit work every year from 1878 to 1882, and in all cases, he begins writing a new free spirit work as soon as – if not before – the preceding free spirit work is released to the public.

The second point has to do with the publication history of the free spirit works. Specifically, Nietzsche republished each of these works in 1886–1887. If the free spirit works contain a set of ideas that Nietzsche comes to reject, then it is hard to understand why he would republish these ideas at the same time he is publishing his more mature views. This would be akin to Kant republishing some of his pre-critical writings at the same time he is releasing his critical writings. Thus, if the mature Nietzsche considered the views expressed in the free spirit works to be immature ideas he now rejects, it seems that he would, first, want to distance himself from such views by simply leaving them aside or second, if he did decide to republish them, he would at least give the reader a clear indication that he now rejects the views contained in these works. However, Nietzsche makes claims that directly contradict such an understanding. That is, he repeatedly emphasizes that his writings flow from ideas expressed in early works like *The Birth of Tragedy* (TI "What I Owe" 5) and *Schopenhauer as*

Educator (KSB 7: 617), and he claims that these works are all "evidence of *one* will, *one* health *one* soil, *one* sun" (GM P 2).

The third problem has to do with the fact that Nietzsche publishes contradictory ideas in works that he understands to be a single literary unit. For instance, Nietzsche originally composed *The Wanderer* as an appendix to *Human*, and then, in 1886, he republished these two works, along with *Assorted Opinions*, as a single unit. As I explain in Chapters 3 and 4, Nietzsche adopts contradictory views in these texts about the significance of both art and metaphysical speculations. Whereas *Human* focuses on metaphysical questions in the first four books, Nietzsche directs the free spirit's attention to the "closest things" – and so away from metaphysical speculation – in *The Wanderer*. This same logic can be applied to the free spirit works as a whole. Although he never publishes the free spirit works as a single, two-volume set, it is clear that Nietzsche, as early as 1882, conceived of the free spirit works stretching from *Human* to *The Gay Science* as a single unit. However, we have noted above that contradictory ideas about art and the death of God run throughout these works. This causes a problem for the developmental reading because it means that Nietzsche wants to combine, in a single project, supposedly immature views he rejects with revised views he now accepts. So understood, one wonders if the developmental reading solves the problem of contradictions in the free spirit works at all.

A final problem with the developmental reading is that there is a striking convergence between Nietzsche's thought in his pre- and post-free spirit works, and so it seems that Nietzsche is more "mature" in his pre-1877 writings than he is in the early phases of the free spirit project. To be sure, there is no explicit talk of an *Uebermensch*, the will to power, or the eternal recurrence in his earliest writings. However, Nietzsche does wrestle with a version of nihilism in *The Birth of Tragedy*, praises art as a means of affirming life in the same work, articulates a project of becoming who one is in *Schopenhauer as Educator*, develops an ontology of becoming in *Philosophy in the Tragic Age* and *Pre-Platonic Philosophers* that is central to his later works, sketches a version of perspectivism in the concept of horizons in *History for Life*, and develops a critique of the drive to truth in *The Birth of Tragedy*, "On Truth and Lies," and *History for Life* that is central to his post-*Zarathustra* works. If this is right, then it is impossible to speak of a gradual development in which Nietzsche moves from immature positions in his earliest works to mature positions in his later writings.

In contrast to the developmental approach, the dialectical approach can solve each of the aforementioned problems. According to the dialectical approach, the reason Nietzsche adopts a position in *Human* that is more "immature" than the views he articulates in both his early and later works is that he is consciously adopting views that characterize the Enlightenment only to show how such views, when taken to their logical conclusion, lead to positions he articulates in his first works and to which he returns in his mature writings. The positions Nietzsche expresses in the free spirit works change so quickly because the works are not meant to express his final views at a given time. Instead, the purpose is to tell a story in which the free spirit undergoes a dialectical process of self-education that culminates in the rebirth of tragedy. Indeed, it is the dialectical structure of the free spirit works that explains why they contain a series of contradictions when considered as a single literary unit and why Nietzsche wants to republish these works together upon their completion. Because these works tell the story of how he has educated himself to become a free spirit, they present positions that change over time and even contradict each other, and because the story is just as important as the conclusion, Nietzsche wants to republish all of these works together at a later date.

Although there is no smoking gun or clear-cut piece of evidence that proves the dialectical reading, there is no such proof for the alternative approaches. Instead, each approach is an inference to what is thought to be the best explanation for the contents of these texts, and so the question is which approach best explains the *explanandum*. As I have argued in this chapter, the presence of contradictions directly undermines the Danto approach to these works, and there is significant evidence that speaks against the common assumption of both the Danto and postmodern approaches that there is no order, coherence, and development in the aphorisms of the free spirit works. Thus, the only viable approaches remaining – barring an unknown fifth or even sixth alternative – are the developmental and dialectical, and I have argued that the dialectical approach best explains the various difficulties that emerge when it is assumed that Nietzsche is straightforwardly expressing in these texts the views he holds at a given time.

This, then, is one reason I think the dialectical reading is superior to the alternative approaches currently on offer in the secondary literature. That is, the dialectical approach is to be preferred as an inference to the best explanation of these texts. Nevertheless, this by no means proves the dialectical reading. Instead, it simply provides reasons to prefer it to the other approaches. This, however, is not to say that this is the only reason for preferring the dialectical approach, and in the next chapter, I unpack a variety of evidence that further supports the dialectical reading. Although the lack of evidence from the time Nietzsche was composing these texts entails that I cannot prove my interpretation, there is substantive evidence – especially if we accept the general veracity of Nietzsche's retrospective descriptions – that supports my approach.

However, before I turn to this evidence, I do feel obliged to say a final word about Keith Ansell-Pearson's recently released work on Nietzsche's "middle writings" (2018). To be sure, Ansell-Pearson offers a number of insights that adds to the growing literature on this topic, and his work does not easily fit within the taxonomy of readings I have developed here. On the one hand, he acknowledges developments in the free spirit writings, claiming to be the first to notice the shift that takes place from Nietzsche's commitment to "the positivist goal of science" in *Human* to an ethical project of seeking health and maturity in *The Wanderer* that is nevertheless consistent with the "naturalistic demystification" of *Human* (2018: 8).[37] In this sense, Ansell-Pearson's analysis has elements that align with Franco's developmental approach. On the other hand, Ansell-Pearson appeals to passages primarily – but not exclusively – from *The Wanderer* to argue that an "ethos of Epicurean enlightenment pervades Nietzsche's middle writings" (2018: 3). In this sense, Ansell-Pearson seems to share Abbey's assumption that the ideas found in one free spirit work represent Nietzsche's attitude or views during this entire middle period.

Again, there is much to learn from Ansell-Pearson's book, and so those interested in this period of Nietzsche's writings should consult it. However, Ansell-Pearson's attempt to characterize the entire free spirit project as Epicurean overlooks the developments that take place after *The Wanderer*. In my mind, it is hard to square the "passion for knowledge" that animates *Daybreak* with the contemplative calm of Epicurean *ataraxia*, and it is hard to square an Epicurean indifference toward metaphysical questions with the madman's portrayal of the death of God in *The Gay Science*. So although Ansell-Pearson rightly emphasizes the Epicureanism of *The Wanderer*, there are good reasons for resisting the idea that this characterizes the entire free spirit period.

However, it should also be noted that the dialectical reading questions whether Nietzsche himself was ever a committed Epicurean, even in *The Wanderer*. Whereas the developmental reading assumes that the free spirit works straightforwardly express Nietzsche's views at the time they are

---

[37] I have noted this transformation in Meyer (2006: 52f.). See also Brusotti (1997: 12ff.).

published, the dialectical reading distinguishes between Nietzsche *qua* author and Nietzsche *qua* free spirit. Thus, if we find views in the free spirit works — such as the asceticism of *Human* or the claim that art can only make life bearable in chapter two of *The Gay Science* — that conflict with Nietzsche's earlier and later positions, there is reason to think that Nietzsche is merely presenting these views at a particular stage in the education of the free spirit. Given that Nietzsche rejects post-Socratic philosophy in *The Birth of Tragedy* as superficial for its eudaimonistic tendencies (BT 15) and later opposes Epicurus to his own Dionysian pessimism in the fifth chapter of *The Gay Science* (GS 370), there is reason to think that Nietzsche *qua* author is no more committed to the Epicureanism of *The Wanderer* than Hegel is to a given shape of consciousness in *The Phenomenology of Spirit*.

CHAPTER 2

A Defense of the Dialectical Reading

In the final section of the previous chapter, I explained the different approaches to the free spirit works on offer in the secondary literature and detailed the problems facing each, and I concluded with some reasons why the dialectical approach explains various features of the free spirit works better than the alternatives. The purpose of this chapter is to detail the various types of evidence that provide further support for the dialectical approach. Although there is no explicit evidence in the form of a note or a sketch from the time of composition of *Human* showing that Nietzsche planned to write the free spirit works as a dialectical *Bildungsroman*, there are three types of evidence that can be gleaned from across Nietzsche's oeuvre that support this reading.

The first type of evidence is found in Nietzsche's writings after the publication of the free spirit works. Such *ex post* evidence comes in the form of Nietzsche's retrospective accounts of the free spirit works in *Ecce Homo* and the prefaces he adds to the 1886–1887 editions of these works. It also comes from his various accounts of the history of philosophy, the metamorphoses or transformations of the spirit, and the *Selbstaufhebung* of the will to truth that can all be mapped onto the free spirit works. Such evidence indicates that the aphorisms contained in these works are not isolated and fragmented. Instead, they tell a story that goes through various stages or transformations that move from the natural sciences to art, sickness to health, truth seeking to life-affirmation.

Although this *ex post* evidence supports both the developmental and dialectical approaches, there is *ex ante* evidence that comes from Nietzsche's writings prior to the free spirit works that tips the scales in favor of the dialectical approach. What the *ex ante* evidence shows is that Nietzsche had already formulated, in his earliest writings, a number of the ideas, including the *Selbstaufhebung* of the will to truth, that appear at more advanced stages of the free spirit works. Such evidence speaks against the developmental reading because it disrupts any smooth and linear developmental story in Nietzsche's writings. At the same time, it speaks in favor of the dialectical approach because these early writings show that it is possible for Nietzsche to have had these ideas in mind while composing *Human.*

The final type of evidence comes from the time Nietzsche was working on the free spirit project. This contemporaneous evidence is found in Nietzsche's accounts of the free spirit project in his notes and letters as well as the compositional and publication history of the free spirit works. Such evidence not only reveals the rapidity with which Nietzsche produced these works, it also shows that he originally conceived of these texts as monuments to a project of self-education rather than standard philosophical treatises that present ideas he then revises. What we also see in the compositional history of these texts is that a number of them were composed as continuations of each other as well as the way in which Nietzsche conceives of and presents the free spirit works as a unified entity immediately upon the completion of *The Gay Science.*

I conclude the chapter by discussing one final type of contemporaneous evidence: the analeptic and proleptic references that run throughout the free spirit works. In this chapter, I only discuss the nature and importance of, as well as the potential problems with, this sort of evidence. This discussion sets the stage for the dialectical reading of the free spirit works that I unpack in subsequent chapters, one that reveals how Nietzsche weaves analeptic and proleptic references into the dialectical narrative that unfolds in these works.

Ex Post Evidence

There is a significant amount of *ex post* evidence showing that Nietzsche understands the free spirit works as representing a process of development, and so there is a significant amount of evidence that speaks against both the Danto and postmodern approaches to these texts. Indeed, it seems that the only way someone could defend either the Danto or postmodern approaches in light of such evidence is by claiming that Nietzsche is retrospectively projecting this developmental framework onto the free spirit project. Although some have claimed this, little effort has been made to prove it, and given Nietzsche's multiple statements to the contrary, the burden of proof is on those who reject the veracity of Nietzsche's retro-spective claims.[1]

Perhaps the best place to begin is the retrospective account Nietzsche offers of the free spirit works in *Ecce Homo*. What *Ecce Homo* makes clear is that Nietzsche wants us to believe that *Zarathustra* represents the fulfill-ment of his original hopes for the rebirth of tragedy. Not only does he call *Zarathustra* the work in which his concept of the Dionysian became a supreme deed (EH "Books" Z: 6), he also claims that the "idea of Bayreuth" discussed in *The Birth of Tragedy* and *Richard Wagner in Bayreuth* was transformed into the "great noon" of *Zarathustra*. Thus, Nietzsche explains that wherever one sees a mention of Wagner in *Richard Wagner in Bayreuth*, it should be replaced with either Nietzsche or "Zara-thustra" (EH "Books" BT: 4).

Although there is nothing in his account of either *Human* or *Daybreak* in *Ecce Homo* that explicitly links these works to the rebirth of tragedy in *Zarathustra*, there are a number of passages suggesting that Nietzsche is taking over the project of a rebirth of tragedy even at the time he began working on *Human*. Nietzsche highlights how *Human* announces his break with Wagner. Thus, Nietzsche claims that the book has its begin-nings during the Bayreuth Festival in August of 1876, and the "profound alienation" he felt at the event was a precondition for the work. The memories he had of Wagner laying the foundation stone in 1872 – the occasion to which Nietzsche dedicated *The Birth of Tragedy* – were soon tarnished by Wagner's turn to everything "German" at the actual event (EH "Books" HH: 1). Such remarks suggest that Nietzsche was not so much disappointed with the "idea of Bayreuth." Instead, he was disap-pointed with the realities of the event itself.

Nietzsche claims that he was also frustrated with himself. That is, he was frustrated that his work up to that point had not contributed to his "task," which seems to mean the task of "becoming who he is," and thus he "felt ashamed of this *false* modesty" (EH "Books" HH: 3). To return to himself, he adopted the rigorous thinking of the free spirit Voltaire (EH "Books"

[1] Westerdale acknowledges Nietzsche's later emphasis on the coherency of his writings, but then claims that Nietzsche is merely making assertions – not arguments – about the unity of his works and that this is just "another part of a calculated self-portrayal" on Nietzsche's behalf. The problem with Westerdale's position is that he places the burden on Nietzsche to *prove* the claims he makes about the unity of his own works. Instead, the burden should be on someone who rejects Nietzsche's claims, and Westerdale makes little attempt to do this. Instead, he devotes most of his discussion to speculating on why Nietzsche would "present such a model of interpretation at this point in his career" (2013: 121). In my mind, the reason Nietzsche presents such a model of interpretation is because it largely reflects the way in which he composed these works.

HH: 1) and the *"hard psychologica"* – a phrase that recalls the work of Rée – of the "ploughshare," the title under which Nietzsche assembled a series of aphorisms in 1876 that eventually formed the basis for *Human* (KSA 8: 17[105]). The purpose of the critical and scientific attitude that Nietzsche adopts in the work is to cure himself of any commitment to higher ideals (EH "Books" HH: 5). Thus, he claims that in *Human*, "one error after another is coolly placed on ice; the idea is not refuted – it *freezes* to death" (EH "Books" HH: 1).

In *Ecce Homo*, Nietzsche presents *Human* as a work that is similar to the beginning of Descartes' *Meditations* in that he employs a strict method to purge his mind of any false beliefs. His remarks also indicate that this strict self-examination and self-denial is only the beginning of a larger process. Thus, Nietzsche claims that we should look to *The Wanderer* and *Daybreak* in order to comprehend the significance of his return to himself in *Human* (EH "Books" HH: 4). He then presents *Daybreak* as a "Yessaying" book (EH "Books" D: 1) that prepares for "a moment of the highest self-examination for humanity, a great noon" (EH "Books" D: 2) and marks the beginning of his "campaign against morality" and a "revaluation of values" (EH "Books" D: 1).

We know that Schopenhauer associated morality – and in particular the morality of "selflessness" that Nietzsche explicitly identifies as the target of his attack (EH "Books" D: 2) – with the "life-denying" solution to the problem of suffering, and we know that Nietzsche, as early as *The Birth of Tragedy*, identified art with the life-affirming solution to the problem of suffering. The transition from a critique of morality to a celebration of art is precisely how Nietzsche characterizes the movement from *Daybreak* to *The Gay Science* in *Ecce Homo*. Thus, the "yes-saying" spirit continues in *The Gay Science* now "in the highest degree," and he explains how this gay science emerged from the "depths," a likely reference to his condition as he was writing *Human* and its two appendices. Moreover, he highlights how *The Gay Science* points forward to both *Zarathustra* and even *Ecce Homo*. On the one hand, he emphasizes that the 1882 edition of *The Gay Science* ends with the first words of *Zarathustra*. On the other, he points to the end of the third book of *The Gay Science*, which includes "the granite words in which a destiny finds for the first time a formula for itself, for *all* time" (EH "Books" GS: 1). Although only implicit, Nietzsche is referring to the task of becoming who one is (GS 270) and so the subtitle of *Ecce Homo*.

Nietzsche also mentions two musical moments that occur prior to the composition of *Zarathustra*. First, he met with Heinrich Köselitz (Peter Gast) in Recoaro, Italy, in April of 1881 between the time he completed the manuscript for *Daybreak* in March and its publication in July (KSB 6: 109). Second, Nietzsche refers to the *Hymn to Life* that was composed with Lou Salomé in 1882, and he characterizes the hymn as a symptom of the "tragic" or "yes-saying" pathos that was alive in him to the "highest degree" at this time (EH "Books" Z: 1) (KSB 6: 301). So understood, Nietzsche is claiming that the birth of tragedy in *Zarathustra* emerged from a spirit of music that gradually took hold of him as the free spirit works came to completion, and so his account bears striking parallels to his argument about the origins and nature of tragedy in *The Birth of Tragedy Out of the Spirit of Music*.

The picture that emerges from *Ecce Homo* is one in which the free spirit works begin with a process of purification and self-denial in *Human* and then, after a critique of the prejudices of morality, gradually crescendo into music, poetry, and the rebirth of tragedy. The prefaces added to the 1886–1887 republications of the free spirit works provide further evidence that Nietzsche wants us to read these works as exhibiting a movement from what he calls a "sick" commitment to the ascetic pursuit of truth at all costs to a healthy and exuberant celebration of art and life in the later stages of these works. As Michael Ure writes about the preface to *The Gay Science*, "Nietzsche retrospectively frames the works spanning his middle period [. . .] as a therapeutic drama that charts a course from illness, through convalescence to recovery" (2008: 128).

Indeed, Nietzsche explains to his publisher in 1886 that although he had to remain silent at the time he was composing these works, he can now say with greater clarity what these works are about, and he emphasizes that these writings exhibit "a *continuous development*, which is not just his personal experience and fate." The purpose of the proposed prefaces is to make clear the necessity of this development (KSB 7: 730), and in a letter written roughly three weeks later, Nietzsche repeats this idea: "The essential point is that in order to have the preconditions for understanding Zarathustra [. . .] *all* of my previous writings must be seriously and earnestly understood; likewise the *necessity* of the succession of these writings and the development they reveal" (KSB 7: 740). Taken at face value, these statements speak decisively against the Danto, postmodern, and developmental approaches.

In the preface to the 1886 edition of *Human*, Nietzsche describes a "history of the great liberation" that is necessary for a free spirit who "will one day become ripe and sweet to the point of perfection." This great liberation begins with the "painful" process of breaking free from youthful reverences and duties, one that is "at the same time a sickness that can destroy the man who has it," and this process leads the free spirit into a "desert" of "solitude." However, Nietzsche also speaks of a "long road" that leads to a "tremendous overflowing" of "certainty and health" and "to that *mature* freedom of spirit" and "*great* health" that "grants to the free spirit the dangerous privilege of living *experimentally* and of being allowed to offer itself to adventure" (HH I P 4).

Nietzsche concludes the 1886 preface to *Human* by noting that "no psychologist or reader of signs will have a moment's difficulty in recognizing to what stage in the evolution just described the present book belongs (or has been *placed*)" (HH I P 8). Specifically, *Human* represents the work in which the free spirit is driven into the desert of intellectual sickness and despair. In the 1886 preface to *Assorted Opinions*, which is dedicated exclusively to explaining *Human* and its two appendices, Nietzsche speaks of the "inquisitive coldness of the psychologist who takes a host of painful things that lie *beneath* and *behind* him and identifies and as it were *impales* them with the point of a needle" (HH II P 1). He also speaks of the sickness that resulted from his decision to break with Wagner, taking sides against himself and "*for* everything painful and difficult," and, like a camel, burdening himself "*more heavily* than" he has "ever been burdened before" (HH II P 4).

At the same time, Nietzsche refers to the "art of *appearing* cheerful, objective, inquisitive, above all healthy and malicious," even though "a sufferer and self-denier speaks as though he were *not* a sufferer and self-denier" (HH II P 5). As we will see, this is precisely the attitude Nietzsche adopts in the text. Although he is revealing a series of truths that themselves are a potential cause for suffering and despair, Nietzsche nevertheless presents himself as the "theoretical man" who takes a great joy in scientific discovery and observation. It is in this latter sense that *Human* is a work of "optimism" (HH II P 5).

The very title of *Daybreak* suggests that the work marks a turning point toward a convalescence that overcomes the sickness of *Human* and its two appendices. Whereas Nietzsche suspends judgment about ultimate questions of value in *Human*, *Daybreak* begins the process of undermining the value judgments that can lead to a denial of life. The value judgments that undermine the value of life are moral judgments, and so Nietzsche commences in *Daybreak* "to undermine our *faith in morality*" (D P 2). The preface also makes clear that this process of undermining our "moral prejudices" is undertaken "*out of morality*," and so the undermining of morality in *Daybreak* is, in effect, "*die Selbstaufhebung der Moral*" or "*the self-sublimation of morality*" (D P 4).

The first three chapters of *The Gay Science* continue the process of undermining morality, one that culminates in the death of God and the elimination of his shadow (GS 125). The cheerful temperament of *Daybreak* also escalates in *The Gay Science*. This is implied by the fact that Nietzsche publishes his own poetry in *The Gay Science*, something largely absent from the previous free spirit works, and this is highlighted in the 1886 preface to the work. There, Nietzsche tells us that *The Gay Science* is written with "the gratitude of a convalescent," and the title of the book "signifies the saturnalia of a spirit who has patiently resisted a terrible, long pressure – patiently, severely, coldly, without submitting, but also without hope – and who is now all at once attacked by hope, the hope for health, and the *intoxication* of convalescence" (GS P 1). Although not explicit, the reference to a "terrible, long pressure" and a time "without hope" matches Nietzsche's description of *Human*, and so *The Gay Science* marks a move from the sickness of the initial stages of the free spirit to an overflowing health that transitions to the tragic art of *Zarathustra*.

The preface of *The Gay Science* ends on an important note. Nietzsche devotes the final section of the preface – and so the final section of *all* the prefaces – to contrasting the will to truth with a need for laughter and comedy. This section of the preface begins with the claim that the free spirit has emerged from a period of sickness as a "*newborn,*" and it then discusses the convalescent's need for a kind of art that involves mockery and cheerfulness. What is not needed, however, is a will to truth that desires truth at any price. According to Nietzsche, the will to truth is not only now considered bad taste, it is even "indecent," and it is indecent because the truth might be the Greek goddess Baubo (GS P 4).

This final section of the prefaces shows that Nietzsche associates the will to truth with the initial phases of the free spirit project and that the free spirit has now transcended this very will to truth, and this implies that the free spirit exhibits an unfolding relationship vis-à-vis the will to truth. Further support for this reading can be found in Nietzsche's notes and letters. In an 1887 letter to Meta von Salis, Nietzsche explains that the 1886–1887 prefaces that begin with *The Birth of Tragedy* and end with the *Genealogy* present what he calls an *Entwicklungsgeschichte* or a developmental history of philosophy (KSB 7: 908). In a *Nachlass* note from this same time, Nietzsche casts "the entire development of philosophy" as "a developmental history [*Entwicklungsgeschichte*] of the will to truth" in which the will to truth calls itself into question (KSA 12: 9[1]; see also KSA 13: 12 [1]). By combining these passages, we see that the free spirit works enact a developmental history of philosophy that culminates in the questioning and subsequent overcoming of the very will to truth that animates this developmental history.

There is further evidence that Nietzsche thinks of the free spirit works as enacting this developmental history of philosophy in which the will to truth calls itself into question. In "How the 'True World' Finally Became a Fable" from the *Twilight of the Idols*, Nietzsche identifies six stages in the history of philosophy that move from a longing for the true world to the overcoming of the distinction between the true and apparent world. Based on subtle hints in each of these stages, Clark (1990: Ch. 4) has argued that the final three stages of this development should be applied to Nietzsche's works. Stage four should be mapped onto Nietzsche's earliest publications up through *Human*. Stage five applies to Nietzsche's works from *Daybreak* to *Beyond Good and Evil*, and stage six applies to Nietzsche's mature period that begins with the *Genealogy* in 1887 (TI "Fable").

There are two problems with Clark's account. The first not only questions the way in which Clark applies these stages to Nietzsche's works but also provides evidence for the dialectical rather than the developmental reading of the free spirit works. Specifically, Nietzsche had already abandoned the distinction between the true and apparent world in the 1873 essay, *Philosophy in the Tragic Age*, as well as the related idea that the true world has any obligatory power in the 1873 essay, "On Truth and Lies." So understood, Nietzsche is already at stage six as early as 1873, and so it is mistaken to place, as Clark does, all of Nietzsche's early writings in stage four. However, Nietzsche does place the 1878 *Human* at stage four, and so there is no clear linear development in Nietzsche's works. Instead, Nietzsche is at stage six in 1873, retreats to stage four in 1878, and then returns to stage six in his later writings. This lack of a linear development undercuts the developmental reading.

One can also question Clark's view that Nietzsche wants to extend these developments all the way up to the 1887 *Genealogy*. First, Nietzsche wrote the *Genealogy* as a supplement to *Beyond Good and Evil* (KSB 8: 946), and so it would be surprising if he then came to believe that the *Genealogy*, which Clark thinks marks the beginning of stage six, constitutes some significant advance over *Beyond Good and Evil*, which Clark places in stage five. Second, Nietzsche refers to the title of the final aphorism of the 1882 edition of *The Gay Science*, "*incipit tragoedia*," in the final words of his account of stage six, "*INCIPIT ZARATHUSTRA*" (TI "Fable"). This is obvious evidence that stage six begins with the end of the free spirit works and the start of *Zarathustra*.

On my account, the last three stages Nietzsche identifies in "How the 'True World' Finally Became a Fable" should be mapped exclusively onto the free spirit works and *Zarathustra*.[2] Specifically, stage four and so "the cockcrow of positivism" should be applied to *Human* and its two appendices. Stage five should be applied to *Daybreak* and the first three chapters of *The Gay Science*. This means that stage five begins with the "breakfast" and "bright day" of *Daybreak* and concludes with the death of God and the elimination of his shadow, an event that "abolishes" the *obligatory* power of the "true" world and so marks an overcoming of the morality of truth. The purpose of the fourth chapter of *The Gay Science* is to transition to stage six, and Nietzsche's rejection of the appearance-reality distinction becomes a marker of his final works beginning with *Zarathustra* and the teaching of the eternal recurrence. So understood, the free spirit works enact – in quasi-Hegelian fashion – the last three stages of the developmental history of philosophy.

In an 1884 *Nachlass* note, Nietzsche also describes a progression of three stages that explicitly refers to the free spirit and implicitly to the free spirit project. The title of the note is "the path to wisdom," and the subtitle is "pointers on the overcoming of morality." Nietzsche describes the first stage as an "asceticism of the spirit" in which everything heavy is carried. The second stage is identified as "the free spirit," where all reverences are rejected, and so it is a time of independence and experimentation with opposite valuations. In the final phase, there is a great decision about whether one is fit for affirmation. Here, neither God nor man stands above the free spirit, and so the door is open for creative activity. It is also a time of innocence and great responsibility (KSA 11: 26[47]).

According to Brusotti (1997: 505ff.), the aforementioned reference to the "asceticism of the spirit" in the first phase of the note characterizes Nietzsche's work during *Human*, and Brusotti substantiates this claim by associating *Human* with the description of the camel in Zarathustra's first speech, "On the Three Metamorphoses" in *Zarathustra*.[3] The connection between the "asceticism of the spirit" and the camel can be seen in how the soul suffers from a hunger for truth and knowledge that ultimately leads to the desert. This is ascetic because it subjects life to the demands of truth and so requires a sacrifice of subjectivity and the development of the self. It can be linked to *Human* because this is the set of values Nietzsche adopts in the work, and the desert is where the free spirit finds itself – as a

---

[2] Mullin (2000: 385) also claims that Nietzsche speaks of stages of the free spirit.
[3] Nietzsche also refers to all of the free spirit works as a period of asceticism (KSB 6: 366 and 427).

wanderer – in the final aphorism of *Human* (HH 638). Presumably, this is why Nietzsche, in an 1880 letter to Malwida von Meysenbug, characterizes the past few years of his life as something comparable to that of any ascetic (KSB 6: 2).

In a previously published article (Meyer 2006), I have taken Brusotti's attempt to apply the three metamorphoses to *Human* a step further by arguing that Zarathustra's description of the lion and child can be applied to the other free spirit works in combination with *Zarathustra*.[4] This is because the lion described in the three metamorphoses – in contrast to the laughing lion that ends *Zarathustra* IV[5] – does battle with a "great dragon" that represents the "thou shalt" of all created values (Z I: "Three Metamorphoses"). References in the text to "lord and god" suggest that the dragon stands for God, and we know that the free spirit does battle with God and his shadow in *The Gay Science*. So understood, Nietzsche's efforts from *Daybreak*, which begins his attack on the "thou shalt" of moral prejudices, to the first three books of *The Gay Science*, which culminates in the death of God and the elimination of his shadow, can be understood in terms of a lion-like confrontation with the dragon of all hitherto created values.

The child is a crucial metaphor in Nietzsche's philosophy that dates back to his early reflections on tragedy and the philosophy of Heraclitus (Wohlfart 1991). In particular, the child affirms the cyclical process of nature by adopting a playful attitude toward creation and destruction. Indeed, it is the destructive aspect of tragedy – the destruction of the heroic individual – that is central to Nietzsche's understanding of Dionysian art, and Nietzsche claims that a childlike attitude results from a confrontation with death and destruction in tragedy (BT 16 and 24; TI "What I Owe" 4). In relation to Heraclitus' philosophy, Nietzsche argues that the childlike attitude is one in which nature is understood as play in necessity (PTAG 7), rather than, as Anaximander and Schopenhauer understood it, a process of sin and atonement (PTAG 4). In other words, the "innocence" of the child is related to the "innocence of becoming" (TI "Four Great Errors" 8), and the purpose of *Zarathustra*, Nietzsche's

---

[4] This is in contrast to Gooding-Williams (1990) and Loeb (2010: 106–107), who apply the three metamorphoses to *Zarathustra* itself. Large (1995: 163) applies the three metamorphoses to the free spirit works, and Franco (2011: 165) associates the free spirit with the lion.

[5] It is my view that the laughing lion mentioned at the end of *Zarathustra* IV is a reference to Köselitz's (Peter Gast's) comic operetta, *The Lion of Venice*. This is, in part, because the laughing lion is surrounded by doves, and as Loeb (2004: 135n.3) notes, this could be a reference to Venice and the Piazza di San Marco. If this is right, then the end of *Zarathustra* IV points to comedy.

tragedy, is to achieve this childlike innocence by teaching the eternal recurrence.

Brusotti's characterization of *Human* as an exercise in asceticism is supported by Nietzsche's account of asceticism at the end of the third essay of the *Genealogy*. There, Nietzsche links asceticism to modern science and what he calls the will to truth – both essential features of *Human*. Specifically, Nietzsche claims that modern science is not the true opponent of asceticism, but rather "*the latest and noblest form of it*" (GM III 23). The reason why scientists still practice the ascetic ideal is because they "still have faith in truth" (GM III 24). By this, Nietzsche does not mean a faith that there are truths. Instead, he means the faith in "the absolute value of *truth*" (GM III 24).

Nietzsche's account of the ascetic ideal in the *Genealogy* also provides evidence for understanding the free spirit works as executing a *Selbstaufhebung* or *Selbstüberwindung* of the will to truth. In the *Genealogy*, Nietzsche claims that just as "all great things bring about their own destruction through an act of *Selbstaufhebung*," Christian dogma and even Christian morality are now being destroyed by Christian morality (GM III 27), and the text shows that Nietzsche links this *Selbstaufhebung* of the will to truth to the works of the free spirit. First, Nietzsche refers to free spirits and free spiritedness in his description of this dynamic in the *Genealogy*: although some who are committed to the pursuit of truth at all costs think they are free spirits, Nietzsche claims they are not because they still have faith in truth (GM III 24). Second, Nietzsche's account in the *Genealogy* refers to two passages from the fifth chapter of *The Gay Science* (GS 344 and GS 357) that link the *Selbstaufhebung* of the will to truth to the death of God, and since the death of God is a central moment in the free spirit project, there is a clear connection between the free spirit works and the *Selbstaufhebung* of the will to truth.

Such an idea is also supported by passages from *Ecce Homo* and the preface to *Daybreak*. As noted above, Nietzsche refers to "the *Selbstaufhebung* of morality" in his later preface to *Daybreak* (D P 4), and since these prefaces explain the dynamics that take place in the free spirit works, Nietzsche wants us to understand the *Selbstaufhebung* of morality as taking place in these works. Although there is no mention of truth in the passage from *Daybreak*, Nietzsche employs the language of truth in a passage from *Ecce Homo* in which he discusses the self-overcoming of morality. Thus, Nietzsche writes: "The self-overcoming of morality, out of truthfulness; the self-overcoming of the moralist, into his opposite – into me – that is what the name Zarathustra means in my mouth" (EH "Destiny" 3). The claim here is that morality is overcome through truthfulness, and it is a self-overcoming because morality includes the morality of truth. Although there is no explicit attempt to apply this dynamic to the free spirit works, the passage implies it. This is because Nietzsche connects the self-overcoming of morality to the figure of Zarathustra, and since Zarathustra emerges at the end of the free spirit project, we can apply the self-overcoming of morality to these works.

Given the amount of *ex post* evidence that Nietzsche understands the free spirit works as a dialectical process that runs from *Human* to *Zarathustra*, there are good reasons to reject the Danto and postmodern approaches that deny there is any order or development in these texts. Although a defender of either of these approaches could argue that Nietzsche is retrospectively projecting a developmental picture onto these works that is not actually there, such a defense will have to respond to all of the evidence outlined so far in this chapter. However, Nietzsche's accounts in his later works do not distinguish between the developmental and dialectical approaches. After all, it could be that Nietzsche is describing the trajectory his thinking just happened to take in these works. Although I find this highly implausible, it is nevertheless possible. In my mind, the *ex ante* evidence tips the scales in favor of the dialectical reading, and it is to this evidence that I now turn.

Ex Ante Evidence

One of the most significant reasons for thinking that Nietzsche consciously constructed the free spirit works to execute a dialectical progression has to do with the contents of his writings prior to these works. On the one hand, Nietzsche takes positions in these early writings that often resemble the views expressed at the end of the free spirit progression. On the other, he articulates a variation of the *Selbstaufhebung* of the Socratic quest for truth as early as *The Birth of Tragedy* (1872) and he repeats variants of this idea in his notes in subsequent years.[6] So although we do not have any explicit evidence from the time Nietzsche was writing *Human* that he conceived of the work as the first stage of a larger project that would result in a *Selbstaufhebung* of the will to truth, we do have evidence that he had already been thinking in these terms prior to undertaking the project.

The Birth of Tragedy provides much of the conceptual framework for understanding the dynamic that unfolds over the course of the free spirit

---

[6] See Zittel (1995) for a study of this theme in Nietzsche's works.

project. The work is not simply an analysis of how Apollonian and Dionysian artistic drives gave rise to tragedy in ancient Greece.[7] Instead, the entire work describes a world-historical dynamic that posits an initial tension between ancient Greek poetry and Socratic philosophy that is then reconciled in nineteenth-century German philosophy and music (Meyer 2014b). This reconciliation is occurring, according to Nietzsche, because the heirs of the Socratic tradition, namely Kant and Schopenhauer, have rediscovered the worldview of the tragic Greeks, and so it is only natural that we moderns, now confronted with such insights, will desire a rebirth of Greek tragedy in the form of Wagnerian opera to affirm a world so understood (BT 19).

This general framework can be mapped onto the developments that take place over the course of the free spirit project. Although Nietzsche undoubtedly sought to liberate himself from his allegiance to Wagner by publishing *Human*, the work is also an exercise in the tragic or pessimistic philosophy that Nietzsche finds in Schopenhauer and, to a lesser extent, Kant. This is because it emphasizes the ineluctability of meaningless suffering and so raises the question that Nietzsche attributes to Silenus in *The Birth of Tragedy*: Is non-existence preferable to existence (BT 3)? Although this question is explicitly raised at the end of the first section of *Human*, Nietzsche refrains from answering it by adopting the "good temperament" of the scientific investigator in which he suspends judgment about the ultimate value of life (HH 34), and as the works of the free spirit progress, he turns to various strategies, such as Epicureanism and Stoicism, to stave off the potentially life-denying effect of these tragic insights.

The argument in *The Birth of Tragedy* implicitly follows Schopenhauer in associating morality with what Nietzsche later calls a "life-denying" response to the problem of suffering. However, Nietzsche breaks with Schopenhauer by finding in art a life-affirming response to this problem. Important for the free spirit works is the fact that Nietzsche immediately turns to a critique of moral prejudices in *Daybreak* that culminates in the liberation of art by the end of *The Gay Science*. The basic idea is that to affirm existence as described in *Human*, Nietzsche must eliminate the moral prejudices that would have him condemn existence for its amoral character, and this is what he does in *Daybreak*. Similarly, if Nietzsche is

---

[7] Unfortunately, Kaufmann's translation of *The Birth of Tragedy* has led many readers astray because he claims in a footnote to the end of section fifteen that "the book might well end at this point. [...] The discussion of the birth and death of tragedy is finished in the main, and the following celebration of the rebirth of tragedy weakens the book and was shortly regretted by Nietzsche himself" (1967: 98–99).

going to use art to affirm life, he must liberate art from the restraints that a moral commitment to truth places on it, and this is what he does in *The Gay Science*.

The most significant event that occurs in *The Gay Science* with regard to the liberation of art is the *Selbstaufhebung* of the will to truth and the related morality of truth, and Nietzsche describes a version of this dynamic in *The Birth of Tragedy*. Nietzsche sees in the Socratic project an inherent tension between a drive for truth that seeks to eliminate all illusions and what Nietzsche claims is the optimistic illusion that drives a Socratic project in which knowledge is presented as the panacea for human ills. Kant and Schopenhauer occupy the unique position of being "theoretical men" who pursue truth at all costs only to destroy the optimistic illusion that truth is accessible and a source of happiness (BT 19). With these insights, Nietzsche claims that the Socratic project bites itself in the tail and leads to its own destruction, and this makes possible and desirable the rebirth of tragic art (BT 15).

In *The Birth of Tragedy*, Nietzsche portrays the music-playing Socrates as a figure who symbolizes this transition from the quest for truth to the need for life-affirming art (BT 15). However, Nietzsche does not point to a single individual who embodies this ideal. Instead, he identifies Kant and Schopenhauer as German philosophers who have rearticulated Silenic wisdom in the form of concepts (BT 19). At the same time, he points to Bach, Beethoven, and then Wagner as German artists who have redis-covered a Dionysian music that will redeem a humanity now confronted with pessimistic philosophy (BT 19). However, this leaves open the possibility for a single individual to become the music-playing Socrates, and I have argued elsewhere that this is what Nietzsche does from *Human* to *Zarathustra* (Meyer 2004).

In one sense, there can be little doubt that *Human* is an exercise in tragic philosophy. Rather than reaching the heights of bliss through the truths it reveals, Nietzsche is forced to confront the specters of despair, destruction, and suicide at the end of the first book. Nevertheless, some might worry about drawing a connection between *The Birth of Tragedy* and *Human* because the latter rejects the metaphysical principles of the former. Import-ant here is the unpublished work that Nietzsche composed just after *The Birth of Tragedy*: *Philosophy in the Tragic Age* (1873).[8] There, Nietzsche

---

[8] As I explain in Meyer (2014a: Ch. 3.4), Nietzsche's lectures on ancient philosophy from the 1870s now printed in *Pre-Platonic Philosophers* are also important for understanding this transition and how Nietzsche finds in contemporary science support for the Heraclitean view.

identifies Heraclitus as the philosopher of the tragic age of the Greeks, and he finds in Heraclitus' thought an anti-metaphysical understanding of reality that rejects the metaphysical principles he borrowed from Schopenhauer in his first work. In short, Nietzsche's turn to Heraclitus in *Philosophy in the Tragic Age* – a turn anticipated by the reference to the Heraclitean child in the penultimate section of *The Birth of Tragedy* (BT 24) – allows him to rethink his tragic worldview in anti-metaphysical terms, and as I have argued elsewhere (Meyer 2014a: Ch. 3), the anti-metaphysical thrust of *Human* is, at the same time, a revival of fundamental Heraclitean principles that Nietzsche associates with the tragic age of the ancient Greeks.

Nietzsche wrote *Philosophy in the Tragic Age* as a companion piece to *The Birth of Tragedy* (KSB 4: 298), and it provides evidence that Nietzsche is, in his thinking, already at stage six (TI "Fable") at this point in his career. Nietzsche credits Heraclitus with overcoming the appearance-reality distinction essential to stage six and so with making the so-called true world into a fable (PTAG 5). Moreover, "How the 'True World' Finally Became a Fable" is immediately preceded by the section "'Reason' in Philosophy" in *Twilight of the Idols*, and much of "'Reason' in Philosophy" is a recapitulation of the ideas that animate the central chapters of *Philosophy in the Tragic Age*. In the former, Nietzsche praises Heraclitus and his notion of becoming and critiques Parmenides for employing *a priori* reasoning to invent a concept of being that Nietzsche rejects (TI "Reason"), and this repeats the argument of the central chapters of *Philosophy in the Tragic Age*.

Nietzsche's early commitment to principles that are at stage six is not only articulated in the unpublished *Philosophy in the Tragic Age*, but can also be found in his 1874 essay, *On the Uses and Disadvantages of History for Life*. Nietzsche begins the essay by arguing that forgetting is a necessary protection against losing oneself in the Heraclitean "stream of becoming" (HL 1).[9] Because this Heraclitean "doctrine of sovereign becoming" is "true but deadly" (HL 9), Nietzsche argues that we should not pursue history as a truth-seeking science. Instead, we should think of history as an

---

[9] Jensen (2016: 23) claims that Nietzsche cannot be a Heraclitean in *History for Life* because Nietzsche claimed in "On Truth and Lies" that we can never reach the "thing-in-itself." The problem with Jensen's argument is, first, that there is no evidence in *History for Life* itself of Nietzsche's commitment to the position of "On Truth and Lies," and, second, the Heraclitean commitments Nietzsche exhibits in *History for Life* suggest that he is now following the argument of *Philosophy in the Tragic Age* in which he jettisons the idea of an inaccessible thing in itself in his treatment of Heraclitus' philosophy.

art form (HL 7) that can enhance life by creating horizons or limited worldviews that allow culture to flourish. The parallel between the argument here and Nietzsche's introduction of life-promoting perspectives in *Beyond Good and Evil* is readily evident, and so again there is reason for thinking that Nietzsche is already at stage six in writings that pre-date the free spirit works. If this is right, then any straightforward developmental picture of Nietzsche's thought becomes highly problematic.

Just as we find a description of the *Selbstaufhebung* of the Socratic project in *The Birth of Tragedy*, we also find Nietzsche critiquing the moral nature of the truth drive in the 1873 essay, "On Truth and Lies." According to the developmental reading, Nietzsche must be understood as only first coming to recognize in *The Gay Science* (1882) that the quest for truth animating *Human* is part of the moral prejudices that he begins to critique in *Daybreak*. However, in "On Truth and Lies," Nietzsche had already argued that the desire for truth is neither moral nor unconditional: it is not moral because it derives from non-moral impulses for security and order; it is not unconditional because we despise only those lies that have negative consequences. On the dialectical reading, "On Truth and Lies" provides an initial sketch for an idea that becomes a central feature of the free spirit project.

Nietzsche's other point in the essay is that once we see the desire for truth as one non-obligating drive among others, we are free to create artistic metaphors that do not aim at truth (TL 2). In this sense, the critique of the morality of truth results in the liberation of art, and this theme runs throughout Nietzsche's *Nachlass* from this time. As John Richardson has pointed out, Nietzsche penned a series of notes for a planned book called *The Philosopher*, and the central theme of the text is the need to restrain the knowledge drive (*Erkenntnisstrieb*) for the purposes of life. Here, Richardson refers to notes in which Nietzsche sketches the very self-critique or self-overcoming that he executes in the free spirit works (1996: 255–256). In one note, Nietzsche writes: "The drive for knowledge, when it reaches its limits, turns against itself in order to proceed now to a critique of knowledge. Knowledge in the service of the best life. One must *will illusion* itself – that is what is tragic" (KSA 7: 19 [35]).

Thus far, I have explained how Nietzsche's early texts indicate he is already at stage six in the progression outlined in "How the 'True World' Finally Became a Fable" from *Twilight of the Idols*, and I have shown that he has more than one account of what he later calls the *Selbstaufhebung* of the will to truth in these early works. However, there is more to my reading of the free spirit works than their dialectical nature. I also argue that they should be read as a *Bildungsroman* in which Nietzsche consciously undertakes the task of educating himself into becoming a free spirit and eventually who he is, and the stress that Nietzsche places on *Bildung* is nowhere more evident than in his 1874 *Schopenhauer as Educator*.

In *Ecce Homo*, Nietzsche claims that *Schopenhauer as Educator* inscribes "[his] innermost history, [his] *becoming*" (EH "Books" UM: 3) and the essay provides "inestimable information" about his concept of the philosopher. Nietzsche also claims that the title of the essay should not be "Schopenhauer as Educator" but "Nietzsche as Educator" (EH "Books" UM: 3). So just as works including *The Birth of Tragedy* and *Richard Wagner in Bayreuth* provide blueprints for the *Selbstaufhebung* of the will to truth and Nietzsche's own activity as a tragic poet in *Zarathustra*, Nietzsche wants us to understand *Schopenhauer as Educator* as a work that became a blueprint for his eventual task of becoming who he is.

The emphasis Nietzsche places on *Schopenhauer as Educator* in *Ecce Homo* is repeated throughout his later letters. In August of 1885, Nietzsche writes in an unsent letter: "My 'Untimelys' mean promises for me: what they are for others, I do not know. [. . .] Perhaps a person will come who discovers that from *Human, All Too Human* onwards I have done nothing other than fulfill my promises" (KSB 7: 617). In a letter only one year earlier, Nietzsche writes: "I have lived how I sketched it out for myself (namely in *Schopenhauer as Educator*)" (KSB 6: 524), and in 1883, he writes to Köselitz that everything from *Human* to the "overman" was already promised in *Schopenhauer as Educator* (KSB 6: 405). In a letter from 1882, Nietzsche encourages Erwin Rohde to read his essay on Schopenhauer because "there are a few pages in there that hold the key" to understanding the significance of *The Gay Science* and the way in which he has "*kept his word*" (KSB 6: 345). Finally, in 1888, Nietzsche explains to Georg Brandes in reference to *Schopenhauer as Educator* that, "essentially the schema is contained therein according to which I have since lived: it is a strict promise" (KSB 8: 1014). In sum, Nietzsche repeatedly claims in his letters from 1882 to 1888 that *Schopenhauer as Educator* contains the blueprints for his later activity and that this is no mere coincidence, but rather a program he consciously executed in his subsequent works.

There are a number of themes in *Schopenhauer as Educator* central to the free spirit project: liberation, education, self-knowledge, and self-legislation.

The theme that stands out most in both *Schopenhauer as Educator* and the free spirit works – one that can be traced back to Pindar's *Second Pythian* ode – is that of becoming who one is. Nietzsche connects this idea to the production of culture and genius in the form of the philosopher, artist, and saint, and he argues that the opinions and customs of the herd are the primary obstacle to the promotion of culture and genius. Thus, if one wants to promote culture and become who one is, one must first be liberated from "the chains of fear and convention," and Nietzsche claims that culture just is this liberation: "the removal of all the weeds, rubble and vermin that want to attack the tender buds of the plant" (SE 1). The parallel to Nietzsche's description of *Human* in *Ecce Homo* cannot be overlooked. Indeed, *Schopenhauer as Educator* is the first published work in which Nietzsche employs the term "ploughshare" (SE 3), and so the central idea of the free spirit project has its origins in this essay.

The rest of *Schopenhauer as Educator* indicates that there is more to culture than simply liberating oneself from the forces that inhibit cultural production. Instead, liberation from conventions is the first step in a process that culminates in self-legislation, self-knowledge, genius, wholeness, and redemption. These themes all emerge in the final stages of the free spirit works and even continue into Nietzsche's final writings. In the fourth and final book of the 1882 edition of *The Gay Science*, Nietzsche openly calls on free spirits to become who they are by giving laws to themselves (GS 335). Of course, the subtitle of *Ecce Homo* is "How One Becomes What One Is," and Nietzsche refers, in *Ecce Homo*, back to the final aphorisms of the third book of *The Gay Science* and so the theme of becoming who one is (GS 270).

Schopenhauer as Educator also makes clear that "no one can construct the bridge upon which precisely you must cross the stream of life, no one but you yourself alone" (SE 1). So construed, Nietzsche's flight from Bayreuth only two years later might have been just as much about his frustration with Wagner for failing to live up to the ideals of *Richard Wagner in Bayreuth* (KSA 8: 27[80]) as it was a frustration with himself for failing to follow the educational program outlined in *Schopenhauer as Educator*. Thus, there is reason to think that when Nietzsche broke with Wagner, he not only began to develop a philosophical project that would culminate in his own tragedy, but also that he would set for himself the task of becoming who he is. As I argue in the next section, Nietzsche's notes and letters from this time provide support for this understanding of this crucial period in his life.

Contemporaneous Evidence

In the final section of this chapter, I look at the biographical events that led to Nietzsche's turn to the free spirit project, the compositional history of these works, and the understanding of these works that Nietzsche presents in his notes and letters from the time of their composition. Part of the reason for doing this is to provide an account of how the free spirit project emerged in relation to Nietzsche's life and his other publications. At the same time, I develop this account with an eye to providing further evidence for the dialectical reading of the free spirit works.

Perhaps the best place to start is where the last section left off: The publication of *Schopenhauer as Educator* in October of 1874. Although he did not publish anything the following year, Nietzsche produced substantive notes for a planned untimely meditation under the title of "We Philologists" in 1875 (KSA 8: 2[Title]). Like *Schopenhauer as Educator*, the notes from "We Philologists" continue Nietzsche's reflections from his 1872 lectures on the future of educational institutions. Although some have argued that Nietzsche announces his break with any hopes for a rebirth of ancient culture,[10] the thrust of these notes is that we can indeed hope for a rebirth of ancient culture in the work of Goethe, Schopenhauer, and Wagner by approaching the ancients properly (KSA 8: 3[70]).

That Nietzsche had not, at this time, abandoned his hopes for a rebirth of ancient culture is shown by what would become his final untimely meditation, *Richard Wagner in Bayreuth*, published in July of 1876 just before the inaugural Bayreuth Festival. There, Nietzsche not only compares Germans such as Kant, Schopenhauer, and Wagner to ancient Greek figures like the Eleactics, Empedocles, and Aeschylus, respectively, he also argues that the only hope for culture is our *"retention of the sense for the tragic"* (WB 4). Thus, Nietzsche has hardly abandoned – at least publicly – the position he first articulated in *The Birth of Tragedy*: that Richard Wagner will lead German culture in the quest to recover, revive, and even surpass the cultural achievements of antiquity.

At the same time, there are signs that Nietzsche is looking to shed his role as a mere underling or surrogate for realizing this project. After an extended stay on Lake Geneva in the spring of 1876 in which he often spoke with the feminist Malwida von Meysenbug and read her book, *Memoirs of an Idealist* (KSB 5: 518), Nietzsche writes four different letters

---

[10] See Strong (1975: 136) and Acampora (2013a: 34). For a more detailed response to these claims, see Meyer (2014a: Ch. 1.7).

explaining that he feels more confident about pursuing his "task" (KSB 5: 521) and that he needs to remain true to himself (KSB 5: 520). In response to one of these letters, Meysenbug encourages Nietzsche to take a leave of absence from the university for the next academic year and to stay with her in Italy. On May 11, Nietzsche writes back that he is driven by an "inner voice" to pursue this path (KSB 5: 523), and in a letter about two weeks later to Carl von Gersdorf, Nietzsche writes: "All of my hopes and plans for an eventual spiritual freedom and for tireless progress are again in bloom; my trust in myself, I mean in my better self, fills me with courage" (KSB 5: 529). Nietzsche's request for a leave of absence from the university was eventually approved, and so his plans to devote the next academic year to himself, his writing, and his quest for spiritual freedom are already set prior to the Bayreuth Festival in August of 1876.

Such letters lend credence to Nietzsche's later claim that Bayreuth was just as much about his frustration with himself for not pursuing the project of *Schopenhauer as Educator* as it was with his frustration with Wagner for failing to fulfill his hopes for a rebirth of tragedy. These letters also indicate that Nietzsche already had a project of self-education in mind prior to going to Bayreuth, and we know that Nietzsche penned a series of notes in May of 1876 that refer to "liberation" (KSA 8: 16[4]), "path to liberation" (KSA 8: 16[5]), "path to spiritual freedom" (KSA 8: 16[8]), "path to freedom" (KSA 8: 16[9]), and "free spirit" (KSA 8: 16[11]).[11] In July, Nietzsche then writes Rohde both to congratulate Rohde on deciding to plan a family but also to explain that life has a different plan for him. To express this idea, Nietzsche includes a short poem in which he casts himself as "a wanderer through the night" (KSB 5: 542; see KSA 8: 17[31]).

We also know that when he fled from Bayreuth in August of 1876 to Klingenbrunn, he sketched notes for a work that formed the basis for *Human*. The first mention of a variant of the title of *Human* appears in what looks to be the first in a list of chapter titles (KSA 8: 17[72]), and the same title appears again in what is likely a list of chapter titles for a book planned under the title of "The Ploughshare" (KSA 8: 17[104] and [105]). He then dictated a number of the notes he wrote while in Klingenbrunn to Köselitz and had them compiled into a short book of 176 aphorisms under the title "The Ploughshare," and the work included section titles such as "Path to Spiritual Freedom," "Human and All Too Human," and "Continuation of 'Human and All Too Human'" (see KSA 8: 18).

---

[11] These notes are found in a pocket diary with dates next to each note (N II 1).

The unpublished text, "The Ploughshare," is a transitional work in which Nietzsche moves from what was his project of writing untimely meditations to what will become his free spirit project. On the one hand, Nietzsche conceives of "The Ploughshare" as the fifth of the *Untimely Meditations* (KSB 5: 562) and it continues a number of themes central to *Schopenhauer as Educator*. Moreover, it is bereft of the full-scale critique of metaphysics that Nietzsche executes in the opening chapters of *Human* and instead focuses on themes that are central to Nietzsche's characterization of the free spirit in the fifth chapter of *Human*. On the other hand, Nietzsche is now writing in aphorisms, and as the opening and closing indicate, the purpose of the text is to plough the ground to create a path toward spiritual freedom for both the reader and the author (KSA 8: 18[2] and 18[62]). Indeed, the notion of the ploughshare suggests that the ground is being overturned for some further project, and as Lampert has noted, the initial draft of the final aphorism concludes with a line that made this point explicitly: "Behind the ploughshare walks the seed-sower" (2017: 131f.).

That Nietzsche planned to continue his project of self-education after "The Ploughshare" – and so the aphorisms that he wrote in Klingenbrunn and then dictated just prior to leaving for Sorrento – is evidenced by the way in which he conceived of the community that he would soon join in Sorrento. In September, Nietzsche explains in a letter to Reinhart von Seydlitz that the community forming there with Meysenbug, Rée, and his former pupil, Albert Brenner, is a "monastery for free spirits," and Nietzsche describes this monastery with a phrase that recalls *Schopenhauer as Educator*: "the school of the educator," which is a place "where the educators educate themselves" (KSB 5: 554).[12] During his stay in Sorrento, Nietzsche also sketches in his notes what he calls the "ten commandments of the free spirit." These include everything from commands to avoid women, children, politics, and fame to preferring exile as a means by which the free spirit can speak the truth (KSA 8: 19[77]), and these are not merely abstract ideas, but rather commandments Nietzsche applies to himself.

We know very little about why Nietzsche never proceeded with plans to publish "The Ploughshare" as a fifth *Untimely Meditation*. All we know is that sometime during his stay in Sorrento he decided to abandon the idea of publishing any more meditations – he announces

---

[12] See D'Iorio (2016: 37–43) for more on "the monastery of free spirits" in Sorrento. See also Treiber (1992).

this to his publisher in February 1877 (KSB 5: 593) – and instead expand "The Ploughshare" into what is now *Human*. In so doing, he seems to have made two decisions that will become crucial for the free spirit project as a whole. First, he decides to couple his quest for freedom with a critique of metaphysics as it applies to morality, religion, and art (see KSA 8: 19[20]). As we will see, this will establish the dialectical tension between the rejection of metaphysics in *Human* and the quest for truth that characterizes the free spirit at this early stage. Second, he abandons the general idea in the *Untimely Meditations* of writing against his age. Perhaps due to his readings of Voltaire as well as his association with Rée (KSB 5: 573), Nietzsche decides to present himself as a proponent of Enlightenment science and so embrace the ideas of the age, and as we will see in subsequent free spirit works, this shift allows Nietzsche to execute an internal critique of the Enlightenment so as to return to the untimely positions he developed in his *Untimely Meditations*.

Although he breaks with the untimely stance of the *Untimely Meditations*, Nietzsche nevertheless sees himself in *Human* as executing the educational program outlined in *Schopenhauer as Educator*. That Nietzsche thinks of *Human* as a work in which he has replaced Schopenhauer as educator with Nietzsche as educator is evidenced by his 1878 correspondence with Mathilde Maier just after the publication of *Human*. In the second of two pieces of correspondence, Nietzsche explains to Maier that he went to Bayreuth in the summer of 1876 because he saw in Wagner a representative of a higher ideal. However, his commitment to this ideal was the source of his disappointment with the reality of Bayreuth (KSB 5: 741; see also KSA 8: 30[1]). In the first piece of correspondence, Nietzsche explains that he had merely honored and idolized philosophers prior to the publication of *Human*. Now, however, he has decided to devote his life to the pursuit of wisdom and so become a philosopher himself (KSB 5: 734; see also KSB 5: 729). In this sense, the "crisis" of *Human* – a term used in both the letter and *Ecce Homo* (EH "Books" HH: 1) – marks Nietzsche's decision to become a philosopher and so his own educator.

The first correspondence with Maier also substantiates my claim that Nietzsche understood *Human* to be part of a larger project at the time he composed the text. Although it comes just after, rather than before, the publication of *Human*, Nietzsche refers in the letter to a two-part plan for a project that extends over a number of years and largely matches what he undertakes in his subsequent works. Because it is important evidence for my reading and some have translated it differently,[13] it is worth quoting the relevant portion of the letter:

> In the Bayreuth summer it became clear to me: I fled after the first performances I attended, off into the mountains, and there, in a small village in the forest, the first sketches came into being, approximately one third of my book, at that time under the title "The Ploughshare." Following the wishes of my sister, I then returned to Bayreuth and now had the inner composure to bear what is difficult to bear – and remaining *silent*, in front of everyone! – *Now* I am shaking off what does not belong to me: people, as friends and enemies, habits, comforts, books; I am going to live in solitude for years to come until I may again (and then probably must) associate with people, mature and complete as a philosopher of *life*.[14]

We see from the letter that Nietzsche plans to continue living in solitude for some years, and the purpose of this solitude is to cast off anything that does not belong to him. Again, the language closely corresponds to the language of *Schopenhauer as Educator* and the idea of eliminating everything foreign to one's true needs. However, Nietzsche then sketches a second phase of his activity. Once he is mature (*ausgereift*) and complete (*fertig*), he will be permitted – even obligated – to associate with others as a "philosopher of *life*." Although he provides no specifics, Nietzsche's plan to return as a "philosopher of life" after years of solitude matches the trajectory that his works take from *Human* to his post-*Zarathustra* writings (KSB 5: 734).

Nietzsche continues to present the free spirit project as an exercise in self-education in his notes and letters until the publication of *The Gay Science* in 1882. As Salomé notes at the beginning of her book, "'*mihi ipsi scripsi*' is a recurrent cry in Nietzsche's letters after the completion of a work" (1988: 4). Although we only have evidence of this "recurrent" cry upon the completion of *The Gay Science* (KSB 6: 238 and 267), it is nevertheless a theme that can be traced back to a note (KSA 8: 2[2]) and a letter from 1875 (KSB 5: 488) and one that Nietzsche articulates in *Assorted Opinions* under the title "*sibi scribere*." There, Nietzsche claims that the "sensible author writes for no other posterity than his own, that is

---

[13] Lampert (2017: 138) mistranslates the letter in the past tense, so that it reads as a project Nietzsche completed with the publication of *Human* rather than as a plan that stretches beyond *Human*. When Nietzsche speaks of living in solitude, he uses the present tense to indicate a future purpose. Thus, Nietzsche is not writing as a "philosopher of *life*" in *Human*. Instead, he plans to do so in the future.

[14] My translation. See Middleton (1996: 168) for an alternative translation that is nevertheless consistent with my claim that Nietzsche is speaking of a project that is not yet complete.

to say for his old age, so that then too he will be able to take pleasure in himself" (AOM 167).

Brusotti has elaborated on the idea of *sibi scribere* by connecting it to other motifs in Nietzsche's letters and notes during this time (1997: 18–21). Specifically, Brusotti points to a note from 1880 in which Nietzsche explains that he is writing the free spirit works to create a series of *Denkmäler* or monuments of a particular time or condition (KSA 9: 7 [90]). Brusotti also points to a letter from March 1881 – just after the completion of *Daybreak* – in which Nietzsche claims that because thoughts are quickly forgotten it is necessary to "monumentalize" one's "entire life" even if such a project is a piece of conceit (KSB 6: 97).

That Nietzsche's primary intention in the free spirit works is to write for himself – and only secondarily for his readers – is echoed in his assertions that he is not a "writer [*Schriftsteller*]," a term used in the title of his polemic against David Friedrich Strauss in 1873. In a letter composed after the appearance of *Human* in 1878, Nietzsche asks his publisher Schmeitzner whether he thinks of him as a *Schriftsteller* (KSB 5: 722). In 1881, he asks his sister the same question (KSB 6: 116), and in another letter two years later, Nietzsche explains that he trembles that others might consider him a *Schriftsteller* (KSB 6: 470).

Around the time of the first letter to his sister, Nietzsche composes a note in which he connects his denial of being a *Schriftsteller* to the task of self-education and becoming who one is: "Become more and more the one who you are – the teacher and educator of yourself! You are not a *Schriftsteller*, you only write for yourself! In this way you preserve the memory of your good moments and find their connections, the golden chain of yourself! So you prepare yourself for the time in which you must speak" (KSA 9: 11[297]). Here, Nietzsche claims that he is not a *Schriftsteller* because he writes only for himself, and he writes only for himself because he is the teacher and educator of himself. As the opening line of the note indicates, this project of self-education is bound up with becoming more and more who one is, and so it is evidence that Nietzsche is consciously pursuing the project of *Schopenhauer as Educator* in a way that both preserves the "golden chain" of himself and prepares him for the time in which he must speak (language that recalls the 1878 letter to Maier).

Nietzsche's remarks in his letters and *Nachlass* from this period indicate that the free spirit works have a much different character and purpose than the standard philosophical treatise. His primary intention is not to communicate a set of philosophical views to a larger readership that he then revises with each subsequent publication. Instead, they are meant to monumentalize and so preserve the educational path he is traveling as a free spirit, and so they function as a memento of each successive stage of his quest to become who he is. Such remarks therefore provide substantive evidence that Nietzsche understood these works at the time he was composing them as his own *Bildungsroman*.

The notes from this time also provide evidence for the dialectical character of these works. That is, they provide evidence that Nietzsche is executing a *Selbstaufhebung* of morality and the related will to truth.[15] Nietzsche frequently refers to notions of the self-overcoming, self-defeat, and even the suicide of morality in his notes from the time he was publishing *The Gay Science* in 1882. In one fragment, Nietzsche writes: "Morals die by morality" (KSA 10: 1[76]); in another, "God has killed God" (KSA 10: 1[75]). In yet another note entitled, "That, which is coming," Nietzsche refers to a *Selbstbesiegung* or a self-defeat of morality (KSA 10: 2[6]), and in a subsequent fragment with the same title, he explains that although the first consequence of morality is the denial of life, the final consequence of morality is the denial of morality itself (KSA 10: 2 [5]).[16]

In another set of notes from 1882, Nietzsche refers to the moral character of the free spirit project (KSA 10: 6[1]), and although the asceticism that characterizes the early stages of the free spirit is an attempt to live without morality (KSA 10: 6[1]), Nietzsche notes that asceticism itself is still a form of morality (KSA 10: 6[2]). Since the free spirit uses asceticism to free itself from morality, it must employ this morality to overcome the morality of asceticism, and elsewhere Nietzsche claims that the free spirit accomplishes just this: "Through the free spirit, morality is driven to its extreme and *overcome*" (KSA 10: 4[16]).

In another note he wrote in 1881 as he began working on *The Gay Science*, Nietzsche explicitly links what he calls the *Selbstmord* or suicide of morality to both truth and honesty. The note begins with the rhetorical question: "what will happen after the end of morality? Oh you curious ones!" Nietzsche answers as follows: "All action required by morality has been required by reason of a deficient knowledge of human beings and a much deeper and graver prejudice. Once one has demonstrated this deficiency and this fabrication, one destroys the moral obligation for this and that action. There is no doubt! And indeed this is because morality

---

[15] See Brusotti (1997: Ch. 5.1.1) for a discussion of such evidence. See also Franco (2011: 105).

[16] Siemens and Hay (2015: 120–126) also appeal to a number of these aphorisms to explain how Nietzsche effects a self-overcoming of the morality of honesty (*Redlichkeit*).

itself demands truth [*Wahrheit*] and honesty [*Redlichkeit*] and thereby places the rope around the neck with which it can be – must be – strangled: the suicide [*Selbstmord*] of morality is its own final moral demand" (KSA 9: 15[15]).

Taken together, these notes show that, first, Nietzsche is thinking of a self-overcoming of morality associated with both truth and honesty during the time he is writing *The Gay Science* and, second, that this idea is associated with the death of God and the elimination of his shadow. As I argue in Chapter 6, we can locate this idea of a *Selbstaufhebung* of morality through the death of God in the 1882 edition of *The Gay Science* in the aphorism "*Homo Poeta*," in which Nietzsche declares that all gods have been killed for the sake of morality (GS 153). Of course, Nietzsche does not make any explicit claim that the free spirit works have been designed to execute this dialectical *Selbstaufhebung*. However, once we understand the works of the free spirit as a single literary unit, we can see how the overcoming of the morality of truth in *The Gay Science* is a *Selbstaufhebung* of this morality precisely because the free spirit project begins with the ascetic quest for truth in *Human*.

Because reading the free spirit works as a single unit is so important for understanding the dialectical nature of the project, I want to conclude this section by turning to the compositional history of these texts. Here, I stress three points that attest to the unity of these works. First, Nietzsche begins working on the next book in the free spirit progression at roughly the same time he publishes the preceding book. In this way, the compositional history of the free spirit works parallels the compositional history of *Zarathustra*. Second, Nietzsche writes a number of these books as continuations of a previous work in the series, and so a number of these works are already linked together by how they were composed. Finally, we know that Nietzsche conceived of *The Gay Science* as completing a unified project that stretches back to 1876.

After spending much of the 1876–1877 academic year in his "monastery" for free spirits in Sorrento, Nietzsche returned to lecture at Basel for the winter semester of 1877–1878. At the same time, he was working to complete the manuscript of *Human*, which he sent to his publisher in December of 1877 but did not want to have published until the centenary of Voltaire's death on May 30, 1878 (KSB 5: 673).[17] Nietzsche's return to the university did not last long. As early as October of 1877, he informs

[17] Nietzsche also considered publishing the book pseudonymously as Bernhard Cron (KSB 5: 676), but his publisher, Schmeitzner, rejected the suggestion (Schaberg 1995: 59; see also Small 2005:

the president that his stay in Sorrento did not improve his health (KSB 5: 670). In February 1878, Nietzsche writes the president again to ask to be relieved of his teaching duties at a local high school (KSB 5: 680), and he submits his final letter of resignation from the university in May 1879 (KSB 5: 846).

Despite his bad health, Nietzsche sets to work on what were initially conceived of and eventually became the two appendices of *Human*: *Assorted Opinions* and *The Wanderer*. Nietzsche composes much of *Assorted Opinions* in the summer of 1878 immediately following the publication of *Human* in May (KSB 5: 801). He sends the manuscript to the publisher at the end of December (KSB 5: 789), and it is published in March of the following year (KSB 5: 810). At the time of publication, Nietzsche understands *Assorted Opinions* as an appendix to *Human*. Not only does he refer to it as such in a letter to his publisher, he even considers continuing the pagination and numbering of the aphorisms from *Human* (KSB 5: 774).

Only six months after the publication of *Assorted Opinions*, Nietzsche sends Köselitz the manuscript of *The Wanderer* for proofreading, and in December 1879, Nietzsche requests that the publisher send free copies to friends (KSB 5: 915). The book is made public shortly thereafter with an official publication date of 1880. Again, Nietzsche refers to *The Wanderer* as a second supplement (KSB 5: 890) and appendix to *Human* in his letters from this time (KSB 5: 915). What this means is that even at the time he was composing these works, he understood them to be a continuous literary project.

If there is a break in Nietzsche's writings during the free spirit period, it is between *The Wanderer* and *Daybreak*. The title of *Daybreak* – which Nietzsche adopted only later in the editing process at the suggestion of Köselitz (KSB 6: 80) – indicates both a shift in the tenor of the free spirit project and so suggests the beginning of something new. In a series of letters from the first half of 1881, Nietzsche characterizes *Daybreak* as "a *decisive* book" (KSB 6: 102) and "more a fate than a book" (KSB 6: 85), and he claims that his name will one day be associated with it (KSB 6: 92).

There is a slight break between Nietzsche's completion of *The Wanderer* in September 1879 and the eventual publication of *Daybreak* in July 1881, and there are some letters from the time he completed *The Wanderer* in which Nietzsche seems to imply that he did not plan to write any further

29f.). This would cause a problem for my reading if Nietzsche had planned to keep his authorship a secret. However, we have no reason to think he had such plans.

books. As Brusotti has noted, Nietzsche writes to Köselitz – in the same letter that he sends the manuscript to *The Wanderer* – that he feels like the oldest man insofar as he has accomplished his life's work (KSB 5: 880). Moreover, Nietzsche details plans for a *"Winterkur-Programm"* that includes maximum rest from his constant inner work and so a "recovery from himself" (KSB 5: 884), and he claims he is going to cultivate an Epicurean garden in Naumburg (KSB 5: 870 and 899). Finally, Nietzsche repeats his claim that he is finished with his life's work in a January 1880 letter to Meysenbug just as *The Wanderer* was being distributed to the public (KSB 6: 2). Taken together, Nietzsche is writing as if *The Wanderer* is his last work and therefore that he plans to end his career as an Epicurean.

One problem with this understanding is that, between the letters he sent to Köselitz (September 1879) and Meysenbug (January 1880), Nietzsche writes to his publisher in November asking for a copy of Herbert Spencer's *Data of Ethics* (KSB 5: 921). As Franco has noted, Spencer's book becomes essential material for *Daybreak* (2011: 59), and this suggests that Nietzsche is already thinking about *Daybreak* before he writes Meysenbug in January of 1880. Furthermore, we know that Nietzsche begins working on *Daybreak* in the early months of 1880, and so around the time he tells Meysenbug he has completed his life's work. Finally, the last aphorism of *The Wanderer* states that the free spirit stands "in the midst" of the task of removing the chains of metaphysical errors and the sickness they have caused (WS 350). This suggests that when Nietzsche completed *The Wanderer*, he had further developments of the free spirit project in mind. Thus, what Nietzsche writes in the aforementioned letters to Köselitz and Meysenbug conflicts with what Nietzsche implies at the end of *The Wanderer* and what he is doing during the time he writes these letters. In short, there are good reasons for thinking that Nietzsche did not plan to end his productive career as an Epicurean.

Despite the short break between *The Wanderer* and *Daybreak*, we know that just as Nietzsche composed his works from *Human* to *The Wanderer* as a continuous unit, Nietzsche wrote *Daybreak* and the opening chapters of the 1882 edition of *The Gay Science* as parts of a single unit. He also wants us to understand both these works as a preparation for *Zarathustra*. Nietzsche makes this point in two 1884 letters in which he claims that both *Daybreak* and *The Gay Science* are commentaries and introductions to *Zarathustra*: "In reading through *Daybreak* and *Gay Science*, I found by the way that there is almost no line that cannot serve as an introduction, preparation, and commentary to the aforementioned *Zarathustra*. It is a fact that I made the commentary before the text" (KSB 6: 504; also see KSB 6: 510).[18]

The retrospective connection that Nietzsche wants to establish between *Daybreak* and *The Gay Science*, on the one hand, and *Zarathustra*, on the other, can be substantiated with details regarding the composition of these texts. Specifically, Nietzsche "discovered" the idea of the eternal recurrence – "the fundamental conception" of *Zarathustra* (EH "Books" Z: 1) – in August 1881 only one month after the publication of *Daybreak* and a full year before the publication of *The Gay Science* (KSA 9: 11[141]). This means that Nietzsche wrote *The Gay Science* with the eternal recurrence already in view. Furthermore, we find the first reference to the name Zarathustra and even a short version of the lines that then appear in both *The Gay Science* (GS 342) and the beginning of *Zarathustra* in the same notebook from the summer of 1881 (KSA 9: 11[195]). We also know that Nietzsche initially had Zarathustra, not the madman, proclaiming the death of God in the third chapter of *The Gay Science* (KSA 14: pp. 256–257), and in another 1881 notebook entry, we find the title of what becomes the final aphorism of the 1882 edition of *The Gay Science*, "*incipit tragoedia*" (KSA 9: 12[223]).

When Nietzsche began working on what would become *The Gay Science* in December 1881, he initially thought of it as a "continuation of *Daybreak*" (KSA 15: p. 118). Thus, he tells Köselitz in January 1882 that he has finished what were supposed to be books six, seven, and eight of *Daybreak*. However, he also notes that he has yet to finish what he foresees as books nine and ten of *Daybreak*. This is because he is not yet ready for the fundamental thoughts – presumably a reference to the eternal recurrence – that he wants to communicate in these books (KSB 6: 190; see also KSB 6: 192).

Soon thereafter, Nietzsche leaves for Messina in April, and he composes his *Idylls from Messina* while there, which is another sign – along with his musical rendezvous with Köselitz in Recoaro in the spring of 1881 – of his return to music and poetry during this time. After meeting Salomé in Rome at the end of April, Nietzsche eventually goes back to Naumburg. In June, he completes what is now a separate book known as *The Gay Science*. He receives the first copies in August while in Tautenberg with Salomé (KSB 6: 282), and the work is made public in September (Schaberg 1995: 85).

---

[18] Salaquarda (1997: 169–170) claims that a reading of these texts supports Nietzsche's retrospective assertion.

The compositional history of *The Gay Science* shows that the fourth book, "Sanctus Januarius," is special and contains ideas that go beyond those expressed in the first three books that were originally penned as a continuation of *Daybreak*. Nietzsche needed time to finish what turned out to be the last book of the 1882 edition of *The Gay Science* because it expresses the eternal recurrence (GS 341). As noted above, the eternal recurrence is the central concept of *Zarathustra*, and it appears in the penultimate aphorism of the 1882 edition of *The Gay Science* (GS 341), just prior to the introduction of *Zarathustra* as a tragedy in the following aphorism (GS 342). Based on the compositional history as well as the placement of these two aphorisms at the end of the book, it is clear that Nietzsche both understands and wants his readers to understand the tragedy of *Zarathustra* as flowing from *The Gay Science* and so the larger free spirit project.

What emerges from this picture is a chain of related works from *Daybreak* to *Zarathustra* that is similar to the chain of works that Nietzsche pens from *Human* to *The Wanderer*. Whereas the first three chapters of *The Gay Science* are a continuation of *Daybreak*, the 1882 edition of *The Gay Science* ends by transitioning to the tragedy of *Zarathustra*. Thus, the question remaining is whether we can extend these connections all the way back to the publication of *Human* in 1878. For my purposes, it is important that there is substantive evidence indicating that just as he wants us to understand each of the installments of *Zarathustra* as belonging to a single work or project, Nietzsche wants us to understand his works from *Human* to *The Gay Science* as belonging to a single project called the free spirit.

On the backside of the front cover of the 1882 edition of *The Gay Science*[19] and in an 1882 letter addressed to Salomé (KSB 6: 251), Nietzsche writes that *The Gay Science* concludes a series of works that are part of a single free spirit project that began with *Human*. Furthermore, we know that as Nietzsche was putting the finishing touches on *The Gay Science* in the summer of 1882, he was planning to publish a two-volume set of the free spirit works under titles such as "Vademecum. Vadetecum" and "The Ploughshare" (KSA 10: 1[13] and [14]). Finally, a number of letters from the latter half of 1882 indicate that Nietzsche thinks of *The Gay Science* as completing a project that began when he left Bayreuth in 1876 (KSB 6: 255, 256, 267, 272, and 366). Thus, he writes to Salomé that *The Gay Science* marks the completion of his "work of 6 years

---

[19] See Kaufmann's translation (1974: 30).

(1876–1882)" and his entire "*Freigeisterei*" (KSB 6: 256), and he writes in a drafted letter to Meysenbug that he has completed a "chain of thought [*Gedanken-Kette*]" that began roughly during his time with her in Sorrento in 1876 (KSB 6: 264).

Although such evidence falls within the timeframe of the free spirit project, it still might be argued that Nietzsche is retrospectively imposing a unity onto these texts that initially was not there and so contend that Nietzsche did not originally intend *Daybreak* and *The Gay Science* to be continuations of *Human* and its two appendices. Here, however, we need to recall one piece of evidence that indirectly establishes such a connection. It was remarked above that Nietzsche began his notes on the free spirit project in 1876 under the title of the "ploughshare" (KSA 8: 18[1]; also see KSA 8: 17[105]). Important here is that "The Ploughshare" was both the original title of *Daybreak* (KSA 9: 9[Title]) and a possible title for the two-volume edition of the free spirit works that Nietzsche wanted to publish in 1882 (KSA 10: 1 [14]). So although Nietzsche never used the title for any of the free spirit works, the ploughshare creates a thread that runs from Nietzsche's 1876 notes for *Human* to his draft for *Daybreak* up through the completion of *The Gay Science* in 1882. As such, Nietzsche's repeated use of the ploughshare from 1876 to 1882 effectively binds these works together as a literary unit.

What the compositional history of these works therefore shows is that there are good reasons to accept Nietzsche's 1882 claim that *The Gay Science* marks the conclusion of a free spirit project that stretches back to 1876 and so that we should understand the free spirit works as a single unit published in installments. This is important because once it is agreed that Nietzsche thinks of these works as a single unit, there are good reasons for favoring the dialectical approach over the developmental. This is because the dialectical approach best explains how Nietzsche can present multiple and even conflicting images of the free spirit over the course of these works and still consider these works to constitute a unified project.

A Concluding Remark on Analeptic and Proleptic References

The point of these first two chapters has been to develop and defend my dialectical approach to the free spirit works. In the first chapter, I developed my approach to Nietzsche's works more generally and explained the problems with the various approaches to the free spirit works currently on offer in the secondary literature and why the dialectical approach can better respond to these difficulties. In this chapter, I have provided a defense of the dialectical approach by highlighting a variety of evidence taken from all stages of Nietzsche's career. However, I have said very little about the contents of the free spirit works.

In subsequent chapters, I unpack my dialectical reading of the free spirit works in detail. Although these chapters are devoted to explaining the transitions that take place in these works through the dialectical framework I have established here, I will, along the way, highlight one further type of evidence that reinforces the dialectical approach. Specifically, I point to the numerous analeptic and proleptic references in the free spirit works. Although proleptic references are more important than analeptic references for my argument because they indicate that Nietzsche is thinking about future stages in the free spirit progression at the time he is composing a given work and thereby provide evidence for my claim that Nietzsche is consciously constructing these works as a dialectical *Bildungsroman*, it is necessary to proceed cautiously when attributing proleptic references to an author. Whereas analeptic references point back to past events that are already determined at the time such references are written, proleptic references point forward to a future that is still open to change, and so it is necessary to guard against the tendency to read such passages as clear references to a future work. After all, it is possible for an author to create retrospectively what looks to be a proleptic reference by referring back to an idea or concept in a previous work that was, in fact, never intended to be a harbinger of some future work.

Here are just two examples of why it is necessary to be cautious in dealing with what appear to be proleptic references. The final aphorism of *Human* concludes with the free spirit seeking "the *philosophy of the morning*" (HH 638). Here, one might jump to the conclusion that this is a clear proleptic reference to the next principal work in the free spirit progression, *Daybreak*. The problem is that the original title for *Daybreak* was "The Ploughshare," and so although one can still make the case that *Daybreak* represents a "philosophy of the morning" even if the work had been titled "The Ploughshare," the prolepticism of the final aphorism of *Human* would have been much less obvious.

Similarly, there are number of potentially proleptic references to *Ecce Homo* in *The Gay Science*: Nietzsche refers twice to the project of becoming who one is (GS 270 and 335); the title of the penultimate poem in "Joke, Cunning, and Revenge" is "Ecce Homo;" and the original version of the final aphorism of the second chapter ended with "ecce homo" (KSA 14: p. 253). Such passages seem to point to Nietzsche's 1888 autobiography, *Ecce Homo*. But here again, we can only read these as proleptic references if we can be sure that Nietzsche already knew, at this time, he was going to write a work called *Ecce Homo* with a subtitle of "How One Becomes Who One Is." This, however, is something we do not know for sure, and so we can only speculate as to whether Nietzsche wanted to indicate to the reader that some future work bearing this title or theme will be forthcoming or whether he chose this title at some later date and so retrospectively created these inter-textual references. For these reasons, I will speak of "potentially proleptic" references rather than "proleptic" references in cases where we cannot be certain that Nietzsche intended a reference to be proleptic.

Nevertheless, there is at least one clear proleptic reference in the free spirit works. Specifically, the 1882 edition of *The Gay Science* ends with roughly the same words that begin his next work, *Zarathustra* (GS 342), and since we also know that Nietzsche had already sketched plans for *Zarathustra* prior to writing *The Gay Science*, we can be certain that the 1882 edition of *The Gay Science* ends with a proleptic reference to *Zarathustra*. This means we know that Nietzsche consciously constructed *The Gay Science* with a future work in view, and because we know of one instance in which he is doing this, it encourages us to look for additional proleptic references and allows us to infer from such references that he consciously constructed other free spirit works with subsequent developments in the free spirit project already in view.

Looking for proleptic references in the free spirit works is also supported by a number of Nietzsche's letters from this time. In a January 1882 letter to Ida Overbeck, Nietzsche claims that *Daybreak* contains the foundation for a future project that is higher, more difficult, and more dreadful (KSB 6: 188), and so we should read the work looking for intimations of such a project. In another letter from this same month, Nietzsche explains to Köselitz that *Daybreak* is full of unarticulated thoughts and that he sees here and there "hidden doors that lead further and often very far" (KSB 6: 191). Finally, Nietzsche writes to Salomé in 1882 that he prefers to keep his plans a secret, and he concludes the letter by quoting Pindar's "become who you are" (KSB 6: 239). Although not explicit, the letter suggests that Nietzsche is working out some plan to become who he is, and so we have reason to look to his free spirit works for hints of a task that continues beyond these works.

When we combine this evidence with Nietzsche's emphasis on the unity of the free spirit project from 1876 to 1882, we have reason to look for both analeptic and proleptic references throughout these works. Although we need to exercise caution, such references – especially those that foreshadow future developments of some larger project – can serve as additional support for the claim that Nietzsche has consciously constructed these works as a dialectical *Bildungsroman*. In the following chapters, I therefore develop a reading of the free spirit works that emphasizes, where possible, these connections. In so doing, I hope to reproduce the chain of thought that Nietzsche has created with these aphorisms, one that begins with the ancient philosophical problem of opposites and ends with the beginning of his own tragedy in *Thus Spoke Zarathustra*.

PART I

The Ascetic Camel

CHAPTER 3

For the Love of Truth
Human, All Too Human

Perhaps one of the best ways of seeing why the free spirit works call out for the dialectical approach is to think about the highly idiosyncratic nature of *Human, All Too Human* in relation to Nietzsche's larger oeuvre. On the one hand, the stress on the natural sciences at the expense of art marks a striking departure from a work like *The Birth of Tragedy*. On the other, the work is an exercise in the very asceticism that Nietzsche later criticizes in the *Genealogy*. In other words, the general ethos of *Human* conflicts with Nietzsche's earlier and later writings, and it is this puzzling feature of the work that highlights the need for the kind of explanation the dialectical approach has to offer.[1]

The standard explanations for the abrupt shift in both the style and content of Nietzsche's writings are largely biographical.[2] In particular, two important features of Nietzsche's life at this juncture are often emphasized. The first is Nietzsche's break with Wagner. The idea is that Nietzsche wants to make public what he experienced when he fled Bayreuth in 1876, and there could be no better way to announce his break with Wagner than to publish a book praising science and condemning art. Such a reading is evidenced by the fact that Nietzsche originally mentioned Wagner by name in chapter 4, but then, at a very late stage in the editing process, decided to remove it. The second explanation is the friendship Nietzsche developed with Paul Rée while staying with him in Sorrento in 1876. The aphoristic style and tenor of *Human* certainly resembles Rée's anonymously published *Psychological Observations*, and in the second chapter of *Human* Nietzsche explicitly refers to Rée's other work, *On the Origin of the*

---

[1] Lampert (2017: 9) finds the work so puzzling that he is driven to the conclusion that the later Nietzsche must have dismissed the work as an "erring beginning." As I explained in Chapter 1, I think Lampert is mistaken.

[2] Cohen (2010: 51–57) discusses these explanations and rejects them as "uncharitable, insufficient, ambiguous, or even non-sequiturs."

Moral Sensations, which Rée wrote in Sorrento with Nietzsche (Small 2005: Ch. 4).

To be sure, these influences are present in the work, and there is no doubt that part of Nietzsche's task in *Human* is to announce his break with Wagner. However, if the content and style of *Human* are wholly explained in biographical terms, then the work can largely be ignored in the way that many scholars have done. On this reading, *Human* is a work in which Nietzsche is not really Nietzsche. On the one hand, he is under the influence of Rée and so producing ideas that are not truly his own. Once the influence of Rée subsides, Nietzsche can finally become Nietzsche, and this is why Nietzsche eventually criticizes Rée in his later writings (GM P 4). On the other hand, Nietzsche can be said to have adopted idiosyncratic ideas about the relationship between science and art simply to provoke Wagner and announce his break with his former "master." Once this mission is accomplished, Nietzsche can again adopt a more critical attitude toward science and reaffirm the importance of art. Thus, *Human* can be detached from Nietzsche's later philosophical projects and left to those interested in his biography.

The most obvious problem with this explanation is that Nietzsche later insists that *Human* belongs to a larger free spirit project, and so it conflicts with Nietzsche's later self-understanding. Although Nietzsche can be wrong about the nature of his works and their relationship to each other, the burden of proof falls on those who reject an author's retrospective descriptions. Such an understanding of *Human* also fails to make sense of why Nietzsche would then republish the work in 1886. If Nietzsche's primary purpose was to announce his break with Wagner, there would be little reason to republish the work some three years after Wagner's death. Similarly, Nietzsche explicitly denies any significant influence that Rée had on the work. As Robin Small (2005: 32) explains, Erwin Rohde privately criticized Nietzsche upon the publication of *Human* for being too much under Rée's influence, and Nietzsche responded by insisting that Rée did not have the slightest influence on the conception of philosophy presented in *Human* (KSB 5: 727).[3]

According to the dialectical reading, *Human* is an indispensable work in Nietzsche's corpus because it marks the beginning of a project that extends

---

[3] Nietzsche seems to be referring to Rohde in *Ecce Homo* when he explains that certain readers, such as "the typical German professor," were hopeless precisely because they surmised such an influence (EH "Books" HH:1). I also think Cohen (2010: 53) is correct to claim that Nietzsche was attracted to Rée because of a prior shift in his own thinking (in contrast to the claim that Rée caused the shift in Nietzsche's thinking).

through *The Gay Science* and *Zarathustra*. Although Nietzsche will leave behind a number of the positions he adopts in the work, it effectively lays the foundation for views that dialectically unfold as the free spirit works progress. He lays this foundation by taking a few steps back in the history of philosophy and presenting himself as an advocate of Enlightenment science and rationality. In so doing, he can now advance "the developmental history of philosophy" (KSA 12: 9[1]) through the process of self-education that he undertakes in the free spirit works and so carry forward the banner of the Enlightenment (HH 26).[4]

That Nietzsche attaches *Human* and so the free spirit project to the Enlightenment is made clear by the references in the text to figures such as Voltaire and Descartes. Nietzsche waited until May 1878 to have the text published on the centenary of Voltaire's death, and he made his allegiance to Voltaire clear on the title page of the book with the words: "Dedicated to the Memory of Voltaire for the Commemoration of his Death on May 30, 1778" (KSB 5: 673). The 1878 edition also included a short text on the back of the title page that implicitly refers to Voltaire as "one of the great liberators of the spirit" (KSA 2: p. 10).[5]

In addition to the dedication to Voltaire, Nietzsche quotes at length from Descartes in the section, "In Place of a Preface." As Robert Rethy (1976: 293) points out, the passage comes from part three of Descartes' *Discourse*, part of which reads as follows: "For my part nothing appeared better than to remain steadfast to my plans, which means: when I devoted the entire period of life to cultivating my reason and pursuing the path of truth in the way that I had set before me" (KSA 2: p. 11).[6] Based on this passage, Rethy claims that Nietzsche is philosophizing in the tradition of Descartes. However, he also notes that Nietzsche's goal is to deepen and even radicalize the Cartesian project (1976: 294).[7]

The passage that Nietzsche quotes from Descartes is significant in at least three further respects. First, it justifies the comparison I made in the first chapter between Descartes' *Meditations* and the free spirit works. Like the *Meditations*, *Human* invites the reader to join the free spirit in a

---

[4] Just as Martin (2008: 88) claims that, "sections 15 to 18 of *Die Geburt der Tragödie* anticipate in almost every essential Horkheimer and Adorno's diagnoses in *Dialektik der Aufklärung*," I think that the free spirit project bears interesting resemblances to Horkheimer and Adorno's work. Salaquarda (1997: 173) also explains Nietzsche's attempt to connect his free spirit project to the Enlightenment and to radicalize it.

[5] My translation. This is not included in Hollingdale (1996).

[6] My translation. This is not included in Hollingdale (1996).

[7] See Kirkland (2009: 32–33) for similar claims.

spiritual exercise of epistemic purification, and just as Descartes razes the foundations of belief in search of something rock solid, Nietzsche tills the soil with "the ploughshare" to clear his mind of false belief. Second, Nietzsche adopts a method for investigation in *Human* that resembles the method in Descartes' *Meditations*. Whereas Descartes turns to radical doubt, Nietzsche turns to the sober methods of the natural sciences to reveal the anthropomorphic and anthropocentric nature of many commonly held beliefs. Finally, the desire to identify and eliminate false beliefs from one's thinking presupposes that the discovery of truth is of the utmost importance, and both *Human* and Descartes' project exhibit a commitment to what Nietzsche later calls the ascetic ideal.[8]

Although the priority Nietzsche places on truth and the search for truth distinguishes *Human* from his earlier works, it is important not to underestimate, as Franco does (2011: 1), the important role that the quest for truth plays in Nietzsche's earliest works and so not to overstate the break that *Human* represents with Nietzsche's previous writings. Nietzsche turns to art in these earliest works because of what he thinks the quest for truth has discovered, namely, Dionysian wisdom in the form of concepts (BT 19). In my view, Nietzsche discovers these same kinds of truths in *Human*, and this is why the free spirit is quickly confronted with the problem of *despair* in the first chapter of the text. So understood, *Human* does not represent a complete break with Nietzsche's earlier works. Instead, it lays the foundation for the tragic or pessimistic philosophy essential to Nietzsche's earliest works and his later project.

Franco also underestimates the role that science plays in Nietzsche's earliest writings. Although art is superior to the natural sciences in those texts, Nietzsche nevertheless exhibits an increasing interest in the natural sciences during this time. Even though the purpose of "On Truth and Lies" is to liberate our creative capacities from the prison of concepts, Nietzsche nevertheless draws on research in the natural sciences on the nature of perception to make claims about our inability to know things in themselves (Scheibenberger 2016: 12–13). As I have explained elsewhere (Meyer 2014a: Ch. 3.3), Nietzsche took a keen interest in the natural sciences just after publishing *The Birth of Tragedy* in 1872, and he began to weave this research into his lectures on the pre-Platonic philosophers during this time to highlight the parallels between the pre-Platonics and contemporary scientific thought. Most notably, Nietzsche claims that the

---

[8] Sommer (2016: 252) explains that Nietzsche borrowed the terminus "the will to truth [*Der Wille zur Wahrheit*]" from Kuno Fischer's volume on Descartes in his *Geschichte der neuern Philosophie*.

natural sciences agree with Heraclitus' philosophy because their main proposition is that "all things flow" (PPP: p. 60).

As I discuss in this chapter, the connection Nietzsche establishes between the natural sciences and pre-Platonic philosophers is important because the being-becoming distinction central to Nietzsche's account of pre-Platonic philosophy in *Philosophy in the Tragic Age* is also central to the opening chapter of *Human*. In particular, it has been shown that the problem of opposites that begins *Human* is a problem that Nietzsche uses to separate Heraclitus' philosophy of becoming from Parmenides' philosophy of being (Heller 1972; Glatzeder 2000; Meyer 2014a). By taking sides on the problem of opposites at the beginning of *Human* and combining what he calls historical philosophy with the natural sciences, Nietzsche is effectively presenting the ideas he finds in pre-Platonic philosophy as his own, and in this sense *Human* is both continuous with his previous works – the ideas remain roughly the same – and yet marks a break with his previous writings – Nietzsche is now presenting himself as a philosopher with his own philosophy (KSB 5: 734).

The early Nietzsche associates the Heraclitean worldview with art in general and tragedy in particular. In *The Birth of Tragedy*, Nietzsche claims that the cycle of creation and destruction exhibited in tragedy creates a playful attitude toward existence captured in the image of the Heraclitean child (BT 24), and Nietzsche repeats this idea in *Philosophy in the Tragic Age* by associating Heraclitus' philosophy with the artist and the child (PTAG 7). So understood, the scientific principles Nietzsche adopts in *Human* go hand in hand with a worldview that the early Nietzsche associates with art and tragedy, and so although art and tragedy are seemingly rejected in *Human*, it is no coincidence that the chain of thought Nietzsche initiates in *Human* concludes with the beginning of a tragedy in *Zarathustra*, the goal of which is to achieve a childlike relationship to reality through the teaching of the eternal recurrence.

Also notable is the way in which Nietzsche methodically and systematically develops this thought chain as the aphorisms unfold in *Human*. As Cohen (2010) has shown, almost all of the chapters begin with some opening reflections and end with specific conclusions that are often programmatic in nature, and each of the chapters build on each other and lead to the conclusion of the book as a whole. Chapter 2 announces the free spirit's rejection of metaphysics, and chapters 2 through 4 simply apply the rejection of metaphysics to the areas of morality, religion, and art, respectively. Chapter 5 functions as an interlude in which Nietzsche reflects on the nature of the free spirit and champions the continuation of the free spirit project. Chapters 6 through 8 then proceed to liberate the free spirit from traditional commitments to family, friends, and society, and chapter 9 concludes the work with the free spirit alone in the desert of knowledge. In this sense, Cohen is right to claim that *Human* exhibits a "dialectical flow" that takes "the reader from a certain starting point to a certain conclusion" (2010: 193).

In the following sections, I highlight the dialectical flow of *Human* by examining the contents of the individual chapters in greater detail. However, my treatment of *Human* in this chapter is by no means exhaustive. Instead, I simply emphasize those features of the text that advance the narrative of what I claim is the first part of Nietzsche's dialectical *Bildungsroman* and so those features that are important for understanding later stages of the free spirit works. In this sense, I am simply providing a rough framework for interpreting *Human* in relation to Nietzsche's larger free spirit project.

Chapter 1: Of First and Last Things

Despite the relative lack of attention to *Human* in the secondary literature, there has nevertheless been a fair amount of energy spent interpreting the first chapter of the book. Specifically, two German scholars, Peter Heller (1972) and Britta Glatzeder (2000), have devoted monographs to understanding the contents of this chapter, and I have also dedicated a chapter in my recent work to elaborating on these ideas (Meyer 2014a). This attention is well deserved. This is because the section lays the foundations not only for the ideas developed in the following chapters of *Human*, but also for a number of ideas that re-appear in important works such as *The Gay Science* and *Beyond Good and Evil*.

The title of the first chapter is "Of First and Last Things." It indicates that Nietzsche is concerned with fundamental issues in ontology and epistemology and questions of ultimate meaning and significance. The question that Nietzsche thinks has ultimate significance is the problem of opposites: "how can something originate from its opposite?" (HH 1). Unfortunately, this question is nothing but cryptic to most contemporary readers, so much so that many scholars have simply ignored the issue and the implications it may have for understanding Nietzsche's larger project. From the aphorism itself, we know that Nietzsche thinks there are two answers to the question. On the one hand, there is a metaphysical philosophy which claims that opposites can be strictly separated and is committed to the existence of things in themselves. On the other hand, there is a historical philosophy that "can no longer be separated from natural science" (HH 1). It denies the existence of absolute opposites, and, as subsequent aphorisms of *Human* indicate, entails the rejection of things in themselves.

Elsewhere (Meyer 2014a: Ch. 3), I have followed Heller and Glatzeder in tracing the problem of opposites back to Nietzsche's reflections in *Philosophy in the Tragic Age.*[9] There are multiple reasons for doing so. First, Nietzsche claims that, "almost all the problems of philosophy once again pose the same form as they did two thousand years ago" (HH 1), and this makes it clear that Nietzsche has ancient philosophy in mind. Second, the problem Nietzsche raises has links to Heraclitus' philosophy because the denial of the strict separation of opposites that Nietzsche associates with historical philosophy recalls Heraclitus' unity of opposites doctrine. Third, the problem of opposites is central to *Philosophy in the Tragic Age.* There, Nietzsche points to Parmenides' strict separation of opposites as a moment in Greek philosophy that led to the invention of "being" (and so metaphysics) and a corresponding rejection of Heraclitean becoming (and so naturalism) (PTAG 9).[10]

Heller and Glatzeder have solidified the link between the opening section of *Human* and Nietzsche's reflections on pre-Socratic philosophy in *Philosophy in the Tragic Age* by turning to Nietzsche's 1888 revision of the first aphorism. The revision makes explicit what I think is implicit in the original version by showing that Nietzsche's historical philosophy is a "philosophy of becoming" that rejects notions of an "in itself" and "being" that are central to metaphysical philosophy (KSA 14: p. 119). Although he does not name Heraclitus and Parmenides, Nietzsche's explicit talk of "being" and "becoming" suggests that he has these two historical figures in mind. Moreover, the revised aphorism also shows that the being-becoming distinction central to interpretations of Nietzsche like that of Richardson (1996: Chs. 1 and 2) is not just something in the late *Nachlass,* but placed at the beginning of *Human* and so the free spirit trilogy.

The position adopted in this first aphorism is both theoretically and textually foundational for *Human* and arguably for the rest of Nietzsche's free spirit project. It is theoretically foundational because it commits

---

[9] That Nietzsche had continued interest in this work is indicated by his sister's claim that he tried to complete it just after finishing *The Wanderer* in 1879 (Förster-Nietzsche 1915: 73).

[10] That Nietzsche had Heraclitus on his mind when he began his work on *Human* is documented by the account that Ludwig von Scheffler provides of Nietzsche's lectures on pre-Platonic philosophy in the summer semester of 1876. There, Nietzsche put special emphasis on Heraclitus and ended the lecture with what he thought was the essence of Heraclitus' philosophy: "I sought myself!" (Gilman and Parent 1984: 73).

Nietzsche to a relational ontology or holism that eliminates things in themselves and so implies the denial of metaphysical entities such as God. It is textually foundational because it sets in motion a series of aphorisms that lead directly to a purge of metaphysics from morality, religion, and art in subsequent chapters in *Human*, and this destruction of the metaphysical tradition leads to a series of strategies in the free spirit project that are designed to deal with the loss of orientation and the sense of *despair* that the repudiation of metaphysics initially engenders. In this sense, the stance Nietzsche takes with respect to the problem of opposites is about as significant for the free spirit project as the *cogito* is for Descartes' *Meditations*, and so interpreting Nietzsche's works without an awareness of the significance of this problem is similar to interpreting Descartes' *Meditations* without an awareness of the *cogito*.

As noted above, Nietzsche links his historical philosophy to "chemistry" and so the "natural sciences," and his interest in the natural sciences not only has to do with their results – as the nineteenth aphorism makes clear – but also, and perhaps more importantly, their methods. In particular, Nietzsche praises the way in which the natural sciences reveal cold, hard, and even unpleasant truths. This is made clear in the third aphorism, "Estimation of Unpretentious Truths," in which Nietzsche distinguishes between "unpretentious truths which have been discovered by means of rigorous method" and "errors handed down by metaphysical and artistic ages and men, which blind us and make us happy." Here, Nietzsche associates the former with a higher form of culture, while denigrating the latter's occupation with "the symbolic" as "a mark of lower culture" (HH 3). Nietzsche claims in the next aphorism that there is little association between meaning and truth. To think that there is in matters of art, morality, and religion is to think like an astrologer (HH 4).

What we see here is a distinction between a genuine search for truth and what Nietzsche refers to as the "errors" that give meaning and value to existence. In terms of *The Birth of Tragedy*, Nietzsche is distinguishing between two key elements of the Socratic project that he thinks stand in tension with each other and eventually lead to its self-destruction. On the one hand, there is an uncompromising drive for truth that animates the free spirit project at this stage. On the other, there is the optimistic myth that the truth will provide meaning and happiness. In *The Birth of Tragedy*, Nietzsche claims that the Socratic project begins to self-destruct when the former reveals the falsity of the latter (BT 15).

In the early stages of *Human*, Nietzsche is beginning to enact this very dynamic by highlighting this tension. Evidence for such a reading can be found in his explicit references to optimism in the sixth aphorism and "Socratic schools" in the seventh. In the former, Nietzsche understands philosophers' interest in metaphysical explanations in terms of their desire to make the value of knowledge appear as great as possible, and he contrasts the philosophers' inflated sense of the value of knowledge with a science that "seeks knowledge and nothing further" (HH 6). According to Nietzsche, this inflated sense of the value of knowledge is the real "mischief-maker in science" because it demands that the truths the natural sciences discover should also make us happy. This causes mischief not only because it prevents the natural sciences from proceeding in an objective manner, but also because some of the truths the natural sciences reveal pose a threat to our desire for meaning and happiness (HH 7).

In some passages, Nietzsche's attack on metaphysics is merely a skepticism about metaphysical claims that renders metaphysical explanations superfluous. In one much-discussed passage, Nietzsche acknowledges that the possibility of a metaphysical world cannot be disputed (HH 9),[11] and so he urges us, in another passage, to "accept the validity of the skeptical point of departure" (HH 21). On the one hand, he claims that "the *scientific demonstration* of the existence of any kind of metaphysical world is already so *difficult* that mankind will never again be free of a mistrust of it," and once this mistrust is aroused, it will have the same effect as refuting metaphysical principles. In either case, no one will have the right to believe in metaphysics (HH 21). On the other hand, he argues that once we reveal the poor methods that led to religious and metaphysical systems and provide naturalistic accounts of the origin of religion, art, and morality without reference to metaphysical principles, we will no longer have any interest in such questions (HH 10).

In other aphorisms, Nietzsche adopts a more aggressive stance toward metaphysics. Just as his 1888 reworking of the first aphorism speaks of an absolute rejection of the concept of being in favor of the most radical philosophy of becoming (KSA 14: p. 119), Nietzsche chides past philosophers for their lack of a historical sense and a related belief in an *aeterna veritas*. According to Nietzsche, everything has become and so there are "*no eternal facts*, just as there are no eternal truths" (HH 2). In the sixteenth aphorism, Nietzsche addresses the appearance-reality distinction,

---

[11] Clark (1990: 97) uses this passage to claim that Nietzsche remains agnostic about transcendent truth. Berry (2004: 501) also appeals to the passage to argue that Nietzsche adopts a skeptical, rather than a dogmatic, denial of "purely metaphysical posits." As I explain in subsequent paragraphs, there are a number of passages (HH 16, 19 and 25) that conflict with these agnostic or skeptical readings.

arguing that although they have debated whether the realm of becoming comes from the realm of being, philosophers have generally overlooked the fact that the world of appearance has "*become*" and "is indeed still fully in the course of *becoming.*" According to Nietzsche, once we complete a "*history of the genesis of thought*" through the labors of science – a theme that Nietzsche develops two sections later (HH 18) – we will recognize the erroneousness of metaphysical thinking and so see the thing in itself as "worthy of Homeric laughter" (HH 16).[12]

These aphorisms show that Nietzsche understands the world in terms of becoming. What is not clear, however, is how we should understand the concept of becoming. In these aphorisms alone, the view seems to be that everything that has come to be will eventually pass away and thus there are no eternal facts (HH 2). Other aphorisms from the first chapter of *Human* suggest an even more radical understanding of becoming, one that denies the existence of things altogether (metaphysical, scientific, and common-sense). Hints of this more radical view appear in Nietzsche's critique of logic and language in the eleventh aphorism. There, Nietzsche rejects the idea – one that underlies a work like Aristotle's *Categories* – that the structures of language parallel the ontological structure of nature. Nietzsche then goes on to claim that "*logic* too depends on presuppositions with which nothing in the real world corresponds, for example on the presupposition that there are identical things, that the same thing is identical at different points of time" (HH 11).

To avoid misunderstanding, it needs to be emphasized that Nietzsche is not critiquing the process by which we draw logical inferences or even the structure of grammar *per se*. Instead, he is critiquing the assumption that there is an isomorphism between logical and grammatical structures and the structure of the world. As Nietzsche's critique of Parmenides in *Philosophy in the Tragic Age* shows, it was this presumed isomorphism between thinking and being that led Nietzsche's Parmenides to hold that there are things or beings in nature that correspond to the logical principle of identity, A=A, even though such entities are nowhere to be found in the sensible world (PTAG 10). In *Human*, Nietzsche is leveling the same attack against identical things. However, it is not clear from the eleventh aphorism whether Nietzsche is simply rejecting the existence of two or more qualitatively identical things – in which case this has little to do with logic – or whether he is rejecting the existence of self-identical things – a

---

[12] See Riccardi (2009: Ch. 4) for a detailed analysis of this aphorism and the way in which Nietzsche is responding to both Schopenhauer and Afrikan Spir.

move that would indeed question the relationship between logic and the world (HH 11).

Although the eleventh aphorism is ambiguous in this respect, the nineteenth aphorism is much less so. The aphorism is about number, and so it follows upon Nietzsche's critique of mathematics in the eleventh aphorism. It is less ambiguous about the denial of self-identical things because Nietzsche explicitly claims in this section that there are no things: "The assumption of plurality always presupposes the existence of *something* that occurs more than once: but precisely here error already holds sway, here already we are fabricating beings, unities which do not exist" (HH 19). For many readers, this will seem like an utterly bizarre claim: How can one possibly deny the existence of things? The answer has to do with Nietzsche's commitment to the natural sciences and his belief that the natural sciences provide us with a radically different – and superior – picture of reality than commonsense observation. Whereas commonsense suggests that the world is populated by individuated objects, Nietzsche claims that the natural sciences have followed the path of reducing "everything thing-like (material) in motion" (HH 19).[13] As we will see, it is this divide between the manifest and scientific images that underlies Nietzsche's belief that falsification is a necessary feature of human existence (Meyer 2012b).

Commentators like Glatzeder (2000: 53) and Cohen (2010: 229) have noted that the twentieth aphorism marks a distinct break in the first chapter. In the first 19 sections, Nietzsche lays out his fundamental methods and commitments, and he proceeds to attack metaphysical beliefs on the basis of these. The nineteenth aphorism concludes this part of the first chapter because it makes explicit the idea implicit in the first aphorism: The natural sciences have undermined the belief in metaphysical, commonsense, and scientific things by reducing everything to motions and so provide support for a philosophy of becoming. In the twentieth aphorism, Nietzsche takes a few steps back to assess the cultural and existential significance of metaphysical beliefs now that the free spirit has exposed their all-too-human origins (HH 20). So understood, the aphorisms of the first chapter are not a collection of randomly placed thought experiments. Instead, they unfold in such a way that later aphorisms are based on and respond to the claims presented in previous aphorisms.

In the final aphorisms of the chapter, Nietzsche highlights the potentially "tragic" consequences of his philosophical investigations in two

---

[13] For more on this, see Meyer (2014a: Ch. 3).

senses. First, his investigations are tragic because they reveal that life is essentially characterized by meaningless suffering. Let's call this factual pessimism. Second, his investigations are potentially tragic because they tempt the free spirit to reject life as something not worth living. Let's call this evaluative pessimism. Somewhat similar to the argument of *The Birth of Tragedy*, Nietzsche emphasizes the harsh nature of truth (factual pessimism) while trying to avert or overcome a negation of life (evaluative pessimism). However, in contrast to *The Birth of Tragedy*, Nietzsche does not endorse a full-blown affirmation of life in the face of tragic truth by calling for a rebirth of tragic art. Instead, he turns to a strategy of suspending judgment on the question of the value of life, a strategy consistent with the scientific ethos of *Human*.

Indications that Nietzsche endorses a suspension of judgment regarding the value of life at this stage in the free spirit project can be found in his remarks on pessimism and optimism in the twenty-eighth aphorism. Specifically, Nietzsche argues that we cannot apply the categories of good and evil to the world because these are anthropomorphic projections: "the world is neither good nor evil, let alone the best of all or the worst of all worlds" and "these concepts 'good' and 'evil' possess meaning only when applied to men" (HH 28). Nietzsche continues this line of thinking in the very next aphorism. Although we believed that art and religion, by giving us a feeling of depth and profundity, get us closer to "the true nature of the world and to a knowledge of it," this is only done through science.[14] Because it is "*error* that has made mankind so profound, tender, inventive," "anyone who unveiled to us the nature of the world would produce for all of us the most unpleasant disappointment." Thus, the consequence of Nietzsche's scientism seems to be one of "logical world-denial." However, Nietzsche also notes that such a philosophy can "be united with a practical world-affirmation just as easily as its opposite" (HH 29).

Nietzsche's point here is that there is no necessary connection between the world that science reveals and the attitude we should adopt about a world so understood. Indeed, such evaluations are rejected as unscientific. At the same time, Nietzsche emphasizes that the initial and even natural response to these insights is one of disappointment and even despair.

---

[14] As Clark (1998: 54) notes, Nietzsche is making a distinction within the empirical world between a world revealed by science and a (commonsense) world of our practical concerns, and HH 29 "is a major passage for the claim that science gives us knowledge of the 'true nature of the world'." Although I agree with much of Clark's reading of *Human* in the essay, I am surprised that she does not extend Nietzsche's error theory about value to include an error theory about commonsense things, a point Nietzsche makes in HH 19.

Thus, he tells the reader in HH 31 that the recognition that the "illogical is a necessity for mankind, and that much good proceeds from the illogical" is something that "can reduce a thinker to despair" (HH 31). In the next aphorism, Nietzsche claims that "we are from the very beginning illogical and thus unjust beings *and can recognize this*: this is one of the greatest and most irresolvable discords of existence" (HH 32). The following aphorism begins with the claim that "every belief in the value and dignity of life rests on false thinking," and Nietzsche argues that if we really did see existence as a whole and the sufferings inherent therein, we "would have to despair of the value of life" (HH 33).

The final aphorism of a given chapter in *Human* often provides a concluding statement as to what the chapter is about, and the final aphorism of the first chapter is paradigmatic in this sense. Based on what has been said in the previous aphorisms, Nietzsche opens the final aphorism by wondering whether this philosophy might not become a tragedy and whether death would be preferable: "Is all that remains a mode of thought whose outcome on a personal level is despair and on a theoretical level a philosophy of destruction?" (HH 34). The original version of the aphorism is even stronger. It begins with the claim that "my philosophy will become tragedy," and so it can be called "a preparation for a tragic philosophy" (KSA 14: p. 125).

The parallel between the philosophy unpacked here and the argument of *The Birth of Tragedy* cannot be overlooked. Nietzsche has just revealed a series of "deadly" truths, and so he seems to be confronting himself and his readers with the question Silenus poses in his first work: To be or not to be (BT 3). At the same time, there is a potentially proleptic reference at the end of the penultimate aphorism of the chapter. Nietzsche claims that *poets* are the only ones capable of knowing "how to console themselves" in light of these insights (HH 33). The idea is that despite his rejection of the life-affirming potential of art at this stage of the free spirit, Nietzsche nevertheless acknowledges that art can offer consolation to those who have pierced through the illusions of life, and so he may be foreshadowing his return to poetry at later stages of the free spirit works and beyond.

The problem is that the free spirit cannot turn to art at this stage because of its ascetic commitment to truth and science. So rather than turning to art, Nietzsche claims that how one responds to the sort of "tragic" knowledge on offer in *Human* (factual pessimism) depends largely on one's "temperament" (HH 34). Although it might lead to a philosophy of destruction (evaluative pessimism), a different reaction is possible. Specifically, Nietzsche thinks that by continuing to pursue knowledge in the way he has in this first chapter, the free spirit could "live among men and with oneself as in *nature,* without praising, blaming, contending, gazing contentedly, as though at a spectacle" (HH 34). In short, the free spirit can suspend judgment about the value of life. This, however, requires what Nietzsche calls a good temperament, "a firm, mild and at bottom cheerful soul" (HH 34). Here, the free spirit forgoes "almost everything upon which other men place value" and hovers over "men, customs, laws and the traditional valuations of things," taking joy in this condition.[15]

At the end of the first chapter of *Human,* Nietzsche is adopting an attitude similar to the theoretical man described in the latter half of *The Birth of Tragedy,* an individual who "finds the highest object of this pleasure in the process of an ever-happy uncovering that succeeds through his own efforts" (BT 15). The difference in *Human* is that Nietzsche does not share the theoretical man's optimistic belief that he "can correct the world by knowledge" and "guide life by science" (BT 18). Instead, Nietzsche adopts the values of the theoretical man only to show how this delightful process of uncovering the truth leads to the destruction of the optimistic myth that originally fueled such a project. In subsequent chapters of *Human,* Nietzsche continues to delight in revealing the illusions of morality, religion, and art. At the same time, the results of this process will eventually force Nietzsche to confront and even abandon the general ethos of the theoretical man and the "good temperament" attributed to the free spirit in the first chapter of *Human.*

Chapters 2–4: The Purge of Metaphysics

We can see from an analysis of the first chapter of *Human* that Nietzsche's aphorisms are a series of interrelated reflections that culminate in certain conclusions. The same holds true for each of the following three chapters on morality, religion, and art. Specifically, these three chapters are bound together by Nietzsche's program of replacing metaphysical explanations in each of these areas with naturalistic explanations of these same phenomena, and so they are based on Nietzsche's rejection of metaphysics in the first chapter. In this regard, the opening four chapters of *Human* suggest that Nietzsche's aphorisms are composed and structured in a way that few recognize.

---

[15] Although he is right to identify Stoical influences in the free spirit works, I disagree with Ure (2008: 126) that Nietzsche is describing "the realization of a cheerful Stoicism" in this passage.

To recall, a centerpiece of Nietzsche's tragic philosophy is the disjunction between truth and life, and Nietzsche begins the second chapter, "On the History of the Moral Sensations," by highlighting this very tension. In addition to praising Rée's *Psychological Observations*, Nietzsche turns to "La Rochefoucauld and the other French masters of psychical examination" to highlight the distinction between life-promoting errors about human nature and "knowledge of the truth" (HH 36).[16] Although he considers the advantages and disadvantages of each approach – Plutarch's heroes are held up as the counterexample to La Rochefoucauld – Nietzsche ultimately concludes that, "mankind can no longer be spared the cruel sight of the moral dissecting table and its knives and forceps" (HH 37). Whereas the older philosophy has typically evaded such investigations, the new science Nietzsche is promoting demands an account of the origins of moral sensations. This is because past philosophers, like Schopenhauer, have erected entire systems of false beliefs based on their misunderstanding of ethics (HH 37). Specifically, such thinkers have failed to recognize the truth that Rée's other work, *On the Origin of the Moral Sensations*, articulates: moral man "'stands no closer to the intelligible (metaphysical) world than does physical man'." It is this proposition, Nietzsche claims, that allows us to take an axe to the metaphysical need central to Schopenhauer's philosophy (HH 37).[17]

Nietzsche not only seeks to eliminate metaphysical speculations from the analysis of morality, he also presents positive claims that can be considered part of his tragic philosophy. In the second chapter, Nietzsche attacks what he calls "the fable of intelligible freedom" and asserts a fatalism in which "all the actions of man are determined by necessity" (HH 39). The view espoused here provides evidence for Leiter's claim that Nietzsche is a fatalist or someone who holds that "the basic character of each individual's life is fixed in advance in virtue of an individual's nature, that is, the largely immutable physiological and psychological facts that make the person who he is" (2001: 283). Although Leiter distinguishes the kind of fatalism he attributes to Nietzsche from classical fatalism (2001:

---

[16] To be sure, the French moralists play a greater role in Nietzsche's reflections than I can acknowledge here. For substantive reflections on this topic, see Donnellan (1982), Pippin (2010), and Abbey (2015).

[17] Nietzsche quotes from this passage at the end of his account of *Human* in *Ecce Homo*. In so doing, he comments that the "future" in which an axe will be taken to the metaphysical need is his own "revaluation of values" that happens in 1890 (EH "Books" HH:6). So understood, Nietzsche is interpreting the vague reference to "some future time" in the aphorism as a proleptic reference to his future works, and although this does not prove that Nietzsche initially understood the aphorism in this way, it does show that he, in 1888, wants us to interpret it as such.

288f.), there are good reasons for thinking that Nietzsche's fatalism, broadly construed, can be linked to the fatalism of tragedy and so understood as an essential feature of his tragic worldview.

Another feature that emerges in Nietzsche's analysis of intelligible freedom is that he understands the "truths" he is articulating to be something that most of us would rather not hear. Thus, he claims that it is "clear as daylight" that "no one is accountable for his deeds, no one for his nature." However, we retreat from such truths because we fear their consequences (HH 39). Nietzsche continues to articulate these true but unsavory ideas in the next aphorism, claiming that morality is simply a lie we tell ourselves to transcend our animal natures (HH 40). He then notes that the cruelty of past ages is still embedded within us (HH 41) and that the unfortunate who ask for pity do so in order to take pleasure in their power to hurt the fortunate (HH 50). Similarly, he claims that there is no inherent value to telling the truth (HH 54), and many of the actions we believe to be unegoistic are actually rooted in a concern for the self (HH 49 and 57). This includes justice – here Nietzsche refers to Thucydides' Melian dialogue (HH 92) – and rights (HH 93). Finally, he claims that it would be cruel if we had a right to take a man from death (HH 88), and he casts hope as an evil that "protracts the torment of men" (HH 71).

The second chapter concludes with a series of aphorisms that again stress the "total unaccountability" of humans for their actions. Nietzsche claims that recognizing this truth requires one to give up the idea that punishment is about justice and desert. Because we have no choice in how we act, we deserve neither praise nor blame for our actions. Thus, punishment is merely a means by which future behaviors are encouraged or deterred (HH 105). In the next aphorism, Nietzsche compares human actions to a waterfall. Although there might seem to be a tremendous amount of "capriciousness and freedom of the will" in a waterfall, everything is actually subject to a strict necessity such that an omniscient individual could calculate each action and its consequences in advance (HH 106).

The themes of naturalism, pessimism, and the complete unaccountability of human beings for their actions are all summarized in the final aphorism of the chapter. It begins with the claim that "the complete unaccountability of man for his actions and his nature is the bitterest draught the man of knowledge has to swallow if he has been accustomed to seeing in accountability and duty the patent of his humanity." Morality does not make us more dignified, and moral actions are certainly not worthy of Kantian respect. Instead, noble actions are merely the products of "the chemical processes and strife of elements" that determine the fate of human beings, and so praising such actions is akin to praising a plant for being a plant. Thus, Nietzsche concludes that we may "no longer praise, no longer censure, for it is absurd to praise and censure nature and necessity" (HH 107).

Nevertheless, Nietzsche does not see anything inherently depressing in such considerations. Instead, it will only be bitter for those who are used to finding their dignity in the supposedly moral nature of the human being. For such individuals – and here Nietzsche has his contemporaries in mind – these insights will be painful. However, Nietzsche also claims in the latter half of the aphorism that this pain is the pain of liberation, and this liberation is the beginning of something new. Thus, Nietzsche claims that the free spirit is moving culture from "*a moral to a knowing mankind,*" and one comforting insight that such knowledge provides is that everything is not only necessity but also innocence. If error and egoism are necessary for the advancement of culture, the insight into their necessity liberates the free spirit from the sense of guilt that accompanies these aspects of existence (HH 107).

In chapter 3, Nietzsche continues to press the theme of "complete unaccountability" as he explores "the religious life." In religious terms, our complete unaccountability translates into "the feeling of complete sinlessness," and although Jesus attained this feeling by conceiving of himself as the son of God, Nietzsche concludes the chapter by asserting that we can also attain this feeling through scientific study (HH 144). At the same time, he continues to emphasize the "tragic" nature of the knowledge he presents in a way that parallels the wisdom of Silenus in *The Birth of Tragedy*. Thus, Nietzsche couples his critique of Christianity with a moderate praise and admiration for Greek religion, and so there are significant ways in which Nietzsche is developing central themes of his first work now through the "rigors" of the scientific method and so without the baggage of Schopenhauer's metaphysics.

Nietzsche begins the chapter by casting religion as a means by which we re-interpret suffering into something we can tolerate or even celebrate (HH 108), and the theme of suffering is also found in the second aphorism. Here, Nietzsche repeats the claim – already announced in HH 25 – that we can no longer believe in "a God who desires that we do good, is the guardian and witness of every action, every moment, every thought, who loves us and in every misfortune wants what is best for us." Although we want to believe in these truths, "such truths do not exist." The "tragedy" of the situation is that "the development of humanity" has caused us to become so sensitive that we need such comforting beliefs, and yet the "rigorous methods of acquiring truth" prevents us from accepting such beliefs. For this reason, there "arises the danger that man may" – almost in Oedipus-like fashion – "bleed to death from knowledge of the truth" (HH 109).

Thus, Nietzsche insists that we face the sort of ugly truths that Schopenhauer's pessimism brought to light. However, Nietzsche also wants to avoid their deadly consequences. Here, Nietzsche suggests a bit of frivolity as a temporary antidote to the deadly nature of this knowledge. At the same time, he insists that anything, even a bit of melancholy, is better than "incurably dirtying one's intellectual conscience" by returning to Christianity. If one wants to be "an educator of mankind," and Nietzsche seems to fashion himself as such, then one must endure the painful agonies that result from the pursuit of truth (HH 109).

Although the reflections in *Human* fall within a tradition of factual pessimism that Schopenhauer articulates in his writings, Nietzsche nevertheless appeals to the natural sciences to attack what Schopenhauer calls the "need for metaphysics." For Schopenhauer, the metaphysical need is something peculiar to humans, and it arises from the wonder we feel at existence and the recognition of our own finitude. Although Schopenhauer, like Nietzsche, is an atheist, he nevertheless stresses the importance of metaphysics. This is because metaphysics is a necessary condition for morality, and this is why he insists that all "righteous and good men" have as their credo: "I believe in a system of metaphysics." For Schopenhauer, metaphysics is the means by which humans can escape the will to live that drives the natural world, and so it provides the necessary foundation for Schopenhauer's life-denying morality (1966: Vol. II, Ch. 17).[18]

If the dialectical reading of the free spirit works is right, then Nietzsche still has a keen interest in mapping out a life affirming response to the tragic insights he is unpacking in *Human*, and since Schopenhauer grounds his morality of life-denial in the need for metaphysics, we should not be surprised to find Nietzsche attacking the metaphysical need in the text. Indeed, we find references to the metaphysical need in each of the first four chapters of the work: In the first chapter, Nietzsche criticizes Schopenhauer for turning away from the scientific aspects of his system to satisfy the metaphysical need (HH 26); in the second chapter, he speaks of taking an "axe" to the metaphysical need (HH 37); and in the fourth

---

[18] Nietzsche explicitly refers to the "moral metaphysical purpose" that Schopenhauer attributes to the life of humans in a variant to HH 2 (KSA 8: 23[19]).

chapter, he critically notes the way in which the need for art is often tied to the metaphysical need (HH 153).

In the current chapter, Nietzsche attacks philosophers for having philosophized within a religious tradition and so inherited the "metaphysical need" (HH 110). The larger point of the aphorism is to argue that, contrary to Schopenhauer, there is no "truth in religion." Here again, Nietzsche appeals to the principles of the Enlightenment to reject Schopenhauer's claim that religions express truth *sensu allegorico*. According to Nietzsche, "*a religion has never yet, either directly or indirectly, either as dogma or as parable, contained a truth.*" This is because "every religion was born out of fear and need," not the rigorous methods of science that Nietzsche now champions as a free spirit. Like Bacon – but contrary to Aristotle's *endoxic* method – Nietzsche's commitment to the scientific method leads him to reject the view that the pervasive belief in God provides evidence for God's existence. According to Nietzsche, the consensus of mankind is nothing more than "a piece of folly" (HH 110).

Similar to the analysis of morality in chapter 2, Nietzsche now turns to psychological analysis to explain how religions emerged from fear, need, and error. Specifically, he claims that sin came into the world through a series of errors that have made humans appear much worse than they really are (HH 124). In another aphorism, he argues that "all the visions, terrors, states of exhaustion and rapture experienced by the saint are familiar pathological conditions which, on the basis of rooted religious and psychological errors, he only *interprets* quite differently, that is to say not as illness" (HH 126). Similarly, he provides a psychological explanation of the Christian need for redemption. It begins with a general discontent with oneself, and it reaches fever pitch by comparing oneself to a God that performs only selfless acts. Now standing before such a selfless God, one longs to be redeemed from a selfish and sinful self (HH 132).

As Nietzsche notes in the next aphorism, this spiritual discontent and corresponding longing for redemption results from "a succession of errors of reason." The reason why the human condition seems so dark is only because humans have constructed a standard for ethical behavior that no human could attain. According to Nietzsche, humans can only act in ways that have some mix of egoism. The problem is that they have set before themselves a God who only engages in unselfish acts, and this creates in human beings the "pang of conscience." However, once one recognizes that this conception of God is due to error and that there is an "unconditional necessity of all actions," the feeling of self-contempt and the related desire for redemption disappears (HH 134). In short, once one understands human psychology properly, "one ceases to be a Christian" (HH 135).

Nietzsche returns to the Christian idea of original sin toward the end of the chapter. His account begins with the ascetic's battle against sensuality. According to Nietzsche, such impulses are turned into demons, and these demons then cast suspicion and a sense of guilt on sexuality as such, so much so that even having children is accompanied by a bad conscience. This, then, becomes the root of the idea that "every man is conceived and born in sin," and so forms the basis for Calderon's lines that echo the wisdom of Silenus in *The Birth of Tragedy*: "the greatest guilt of man is that he was born." As he does throughout the chapter, Nietzsche quickly contrasts the Christian view with the ancient Greek view. According to Nietzsche, Empedocles knew nothing "of the disgraceful, diabolical, sinful in erotic things," and he even saw in Aphrodite a great counterforce to strife (HH 141).

Nietzsche's point is not simply to contrast the ancient Greeks with the Christians. Instead, it is to highlight the falsity of the Christian doctrine of sin and praise the ancient Greeks as a healthier alternative, and in this sense, Nietzsche's ideas here are again in line with his earliest writings. Thus, Nietzsche claims, "this suffering from the natural in the reality of things is completely groundless: it is only the consequences of opinions *about* things." Nietzsche claims that designating the natural as bad is an artifice used by religions and metaphysicians to cast suspicion on our natures and put us in need of a metaphysical redemption from our natural selves. The intention of such teachings is not to make humans "more moral," but to make them "feel *as sinful as possible*" (HH 141).

The chapter concludes with an analysis of the saint that foreshadows Nietzsche's critique of ascetic ideals in the third essay of the *Genealogy*. Although there is no talk of an all-pervasive will to power, Nietzsche explains the life of the saint in terms of "the lust for power" and "the feeling of power" (HH 142). On the one hand, Nietzsche claims that the saint is not motivated by a calling that comes from a metaphysical world. Instead, he rejoices in creating a spiritual drama within himself. On the other hand, the saint's extreme form of self-denial leads others to believe that his way of life must have a supersensuous origin. Indeed, the saint is also convinced of this. Thus, the saint lacks self-knowledge, and so the "perverse and pathological" aspects of the saint's nature are "concealed from his own sight just as it was from that of his spectators" (HH 143).

The upshot of Nietzsche's analysis is that just as we live in an age that "no longer believes in God," we can no longer believe in saints. By "believe in saints," Nietzsche means that we should no longer think that saints have tapped into some metaphysical reality and so provide us with a model according to which we should fashion our own lives. Nietzsche's mention of thinkers who do not believe in God but still believe in saints (HH 143) is a clear reference to Schopenhauer, and so even though Schopenhauer is only explicitly mentioned near the beginning of the chapter, Nietzsche's attack on religion and religious ideas is clearly an attack on Schopenhauer's theory of morality and religion. In the next chapter on art, Nietzsche continues his attack on Schopenhauer's theories, but, at the same time, he will also be setting his sights on a second target: Wagner.

Chapter 4 continues Nietzsche's project of naturalizing the metaphysical elements of morality, religion, and now art. Here, he launches a two-pronged attack on the idea, first, that art, like religion, can elevate the spectator into a supersensuous realm and, second, that artists produce their works in moments of inspiration that come from a metaphysical realm. The chapter begins by repeating the idea that begins the work as a whole. Although many think that great works of art have a miraculous origin in things in themselves, a scientific study of how a work of art comes to be can counter this illusion. Specifically, it can show that artworks largely trade in the sphere of deception and prey on the intellectual uncleanliness of the spectators (HH 145).

In the second aphorism of the section, Nietzsche's remarks show that his commitment to truth as a marker of culture informs and even animates his critique of art. Thus, Nietzsche refers to the artist's weaker sense of "morality" in "regard to knowledge of truths." This reference to a morality of truth that the artist fails to follow will be important for further stages of the free spirit project, as Nietzsche's return to art in *The Gay Science* will go hand in hand with a critique of this very morality. Here, however, Nietzsche claims that the artist rejects the sober methods that the free spirit embraces because the artist "does not wish to be deprived of the glittering, profound interpretations of life." Although the artist appears "to be fighting on behalf of the greater dignity and significance of man," the artist really wants to maintain the methods by which his art can be most effective: "the fantastic, mythical, uncertain, extreme, the sense for the symbolical, the over-estimation of the person, the belief in something miraculous in genius." In short, the artist rejects the morality of truth because it would put an end to his success (HH 146).

Nietzsche's characterization of art and the artist has clear parallels to his critique of religion and religious leaders, and he makes this point of comparison explicit in subsequent aphorisms. Specifically, he claims that art takes over the very sphere religion inhabits, and so "art raises its head where religions relax their hold" (HH 150). This has happened with the emergence of the Enlightenment. This is because the Enlightenment's commitment to truth and rigorous thinking "undermined the dogmas of religion and inspired a fundamental distrust in them." Nevertheless, the various feelings that religious worship once excited need to find their outlet somewhere, and this is where art – and also politics – has taken over (HH 150). Thus, art becomes the new religion, and although Nietzsche cele- brated some version of this idea in *The Birth of Tragedy* and conceived of the Bayreuth Festival in roughly these terms, the stance Nietzsche takes here is that both religion and art are opposed to the strict methods of the free spirit's quest for truth and knowledge.

Nietzsche extends his reflections on art by again mentioning the "meta- physical need" so essential to Schopenhauer's philosophy. Nietzsche acknowledges the difficulty the free spirit has in bidding the metaphysical need "a final farewell," and art makes this all the more difficult. This is because art can "easily set the metaphysical strings [...] vibrating in sympathy." Nietzsche's example is Beethoven's Ninth Symphony, which can make us feel like we are "hovering above the earth in a dome of stars with the dream of *immortality*" in our hearts. Here, one begins to believe that art can lead us back to religion and metaphysics, and so art constitutes a great challenge to the "intellectual probity" of the free spirit (HH 153).

Nietzsche not only critiques the effect that art can have on the specta- tors, but also the very idea that artists are inspired by a metaphysical beyond that elevates them into the realm of genius. Thus, he writes: "Artists have an interest in the existence of a belief in the sudden occur- rence of ideas, in so-called inspirations; as though the idea of a work of art, a poem, the basic proposition of a philosophy flashed down from heaven like a ray of divine grace." In reality, the critical faculty and power of judgment are very much at work in so-called products of inspiration. We know this, Nietzsche claims, from Beethoven's notebooks, and he argues that "all the great artists have been great workers, inexhaustible not only in invention but also in rejecting, sifting, transforming, ordering" (HH 157).

Nietzsche's discussion of artistic creation largely follows the distinction Plato makes in the *Ion* between art as a craft or *techné* and art as a product of inspiration, and Nietzsche's argument in *Human*, in contrast to both his appeal to the "musical mood" in *The Birth of Tragedy* (BT 5) and his later claim in *Ecce Homo* to have been divinely inspired while writing *Zarathus- tra* (EH "Books" Z:3), is that art is clearly a *techné*. Consequently, claims of the so-called artistic genius to be (divinely) inspired in a way that others are not must be looked upon with suspicion, and Nietzsche argues that the cult of genius actually springs from our own vanity: so that we do not feel disappointed with our own artistic incapacity, we conceive of artists like Raphael or Shakespeare as miraculous appearances. However, "the activity of the genius seems in no way fundamentally different from the activity of the inventor of machines, the scholar of astronomy or history, the master of tactics" (HH 162). Just as these crafts can be learned and perfected through hard work, artistic production can be, too. Thus, Nietzsche claims that all geniuses were "serious" and "efficient" workmen (HH 163).

It is also interesting to consider Nietzsche's remarks about "writers" and the apparent distinction he draws between a "writer" [*Schriftsteller*] and an author [*Autor*]. In the previous chapter, it was noted that Nietzsche insists in his letters that he is *not* a writer because he writes primarily for himself (KSA 9: 11[297]). In *Human*, Nietzsche implies both a distinction and establishes a hierarchy between author and writer: "the best author will be he who is ashamed to become a writer" (HH 192). This is followed by Nietzsche's claim that writers should be treated like "malefactors" who will only receive pardon in rare cases (HH 193). In contrast, Nietzsche speaks of a happy author "who as an old man can say that all of the life-engendering, strengthening, elevating, enlightening thought and feeling that was in him lives on in his writings, and that he himself is now nothing but grey ashes, while the fire has everywhere been rescued and borne forward" (HH 208). Although the link is by no means clear, this description of an author preserving his best moments through his writings corresponds to Nietzsche's later claim that the purpose of the free spirit works is to monumentalize his life and thought (KSA 9: 7[90]).

At the end of the chapter, Nietzsche's attacks on the aesthetics of Schopenhauer and Wagner become more direct. In the aphorism "Music," Nietzsche rejects Schopenhauer's claim that music is the highest of the arts because it is a direct expression of the will. Nietzsche claims that music is not "the *immediate* language of feeling" and that "it does not speak of the 'will' or of the 'thing in itself.'" Indeed, no music, in itself, "is profound or significant." Instead, the intellect introduces the significance of sounds (HH 215).

Nietzsche never explicitly mentions Wagner in his critique of art in the published version of *Human*. However, he explicitly refers to Wagner in drafts to HH 220 and HH 221. In the latter, Nietzsche discusses the relationship between art and constraint in music and poetry. Nietzsche initially placed Wagner's name at the end of a process in which fetters, originally required for the evolution of art, have finally been removed (KSA

14: p. 137). Although this seems to be praise for Wagner's achievement, Nietzsche raises concerns about the direction this is taking modern art. Specifically, the removal of the unreasonable fetters of Franco-Hellenic art has led to the belief that all fetters are unreasonable, and this, Nietzsche argues, is moving modern art toward "its *dissolution*." In this way, what might be understood as art's "birth and becoming" in the music of Wagner is actually a "going down to destruction" (HH 221).

In the other aphorism in which Wagner's name appears in the original drafts (KSA 14: p. 137), Nietzsche returns to his critique of art and its connection to metaphysics and religion. Here again, Nietzsche acknowledges the "profound sorrow" he feels in admitting that artists are "the glorifiers of the religious and philosophical errors of mankind, and they could not have been so without believing in the absolute truth of these errors" (HH 220). Once the belief in these errors subsides, this sort of art will perish, and this art includes not only the paintings of Raphael and Gothic cathedrals, but also Wagner's music. This is because they all presuppose a cosmic and "metaphysical significance in the objects of art" (HH 220). However, given the critique of metaphysics in *Human*, Wagner's art must now be deemed a thing of the past.

This is the message of the final two aphorisms of the chapter, "What is Left of Art" and "Evening Twilight of Art." In the former, Nietzsche speculates about how metaphysics might make art significant. However, he then asserts that such metaphysical propositions are false. Given this knowledge, Nietzsche asks about the significance of art, and the answer he gives is that art remains significant in that it teaches us that life is good and that human life is a piece of nature. Nevertheless, this idea has now been absorbed into the quest for knowledge, and so Nietzsche concludes the aphorism with the claim that "the scientific man is the further evolution of the artistic" (HH 222).

In the final aphorism, Nietzsche returns to a theme that he touched upon earlier in the chapter. Art is a product of a youthful humanity, and as culture matures through the labors of the free spirit, "the artist will soon be regarded as a glorious relic" (HH 223). Although this represents the view of a free spirit dedicated to the quest for knowledge, this is a view that undergoes significant alteration as the free spirit project unfolds. As I discuss in the next chapter, Nietzsche offers a number of reflections on art in *Assorted Opinions* that resuscitate some of its significance and so anticipate later developments in the free spirit project. What will never return in Nietzsche's writings is any attempt to ground the significance of art in metaphysics. This is something he did in *The Birth of Tragedy*, and it is something Nietzsche will never do again.

Chapter 5: An Interlude for Free Spirits

This cursory analysis of the first four chapters shows that Nietzsche has designed *Human* to develop a systematic attack on traditional metaphysics that eliminates the remnants of such a tradition from morality, religion, and art. This attack is driven by a desire for knowledge that liberates the free spirit from false beliefs. In this sense, the opening chapters of *Human* have a function similar to the opening of Descartes' *Meditations*: Nietzsche is seeking to free his mind from the shackles of false belief through rigorous inquiry and, like the *Meditations*, subsequent steps in the project build upon and so presuppose the results of these opening stages.

Although some of the aphorisms were the first Nietzsche penned during his time in Klingbrunnen and the chapter was originally planned to be the first (KSA 8: 17[105]), chapter 5, "Tokens of Higher and Lower Culture," functions much like an interlude. On the one hand, it provides a series of meta-reflections on the nature of the free spirit and makes a clear statement about the free spirit's continued commitment to the project of self-cultivation and so *Bildung*. On the other hand, it is also a transitional chapter in that Nietzsche shifts from liberating the free spirit from the metaphysical tradition to liberating the free spirit from customs and social obligations that might inhibit the quest for knowledge. In this sense, chapter 5 paves the way for Nietzsche's reflections on the free spirit's role in society, attitude toward family life, and relationship to the state in chapters 6, 7, and 8, respectively.

Nietzsche begins the chapter by pitting the free spirit against the demands of the community. For a community to flourish, Nietzsche claims that it needs, first, to share certain indisputable or self-evident truths and, second, to subordinate individuals to customs by having individuals internalize these principles. In contrast, the free spirit questions such principles and so resists obedience to the community. Although such free spirits weaken and even pose a threat to the community, Nietzsche claims that these individuals are ultimately responsible for "*spiritual progress.*" Customary ways of acting produce narrower minds and constitute an "inherited stupidity." Thus, the free spirit's initial harm to the community may actually benefit the community in the long run (HH 224).

In the following aphorism, Nietzsche provides a more precise definition of the free spirit and its relationship to the larger community. In one sense, a free spirit is often someone who thinks differently from the norms defined by one's country, class, profession, or religion, and this type of free spirit is often reproached. The free spirit is seen as someone interested in either shocking cultural norms or engaging in behavior deemed immoral. Although these motivations might be at work, the principles the free spirit adopts may be truer than those held by fettered spirits, and it is the truth of the opinions – not the motivations behind them – that ultimately matters. Still, the free spirit could be wrong, and so it is not always the case that being a free spirit means knowing the truth. Nevertheless, Nietzsche claims that the free spirit does have truth on her side in that she embraces inquiry and so demands reasons for beliefs rather than mere faith (HH 225).

Nietzsche's reflections on reason, faith, and belief continue in the following aphorisms in which he separates free and fettered spirits based on how they justify beliefs. The fettered spirit either does not raise the issue of justification or justifies such beliefs by appealing to habit or custom. Thus, a fettered spirit is someone who simply accepts the principles of a country or religion because she was born into that country or religion, and if there is any attempt to justify such beliefs, it consists of *post hoc* rationalizations (HH 226). In the following aphorism, Nietzsche explains that fettered spirits often hold customary beliefs to be true because it is advantageous to do so. Here again, the fettered spirit shows little interest in the truth of a belief independently of the advantages it might bring. Thus, they do not attempt to justify their beliefs with reasons. Indeed, they even resist the demand for such reasons, and in this respect they differ most from the free spirit (HH 227).[19]

Just as Nietzsche is concerned about the effects of custom on belief formation, he is also concerned about the effects of custom on individual character. Here, Nietzsche claims that the community has an interest in suppressing individuality. It wants to build "strength of character," and this is done by narrowing the choices available to the individual, requiring repeated action, and reinforcing such actions through praise. Education is therefore the means by which the individual becomes fettered to the community. In the end, the community does not want a new and unique individual like the free spirit, but rather the *repetition* of a type already

---

[19] Reginster (2013) emphasizes these aphorisms – HH 225, 226, and 227 – in discussing the nature of the free spirit. Although the free spirit is undoubtedly motivated by the spirit of inquiry and open to going wherever it may lead, the free spirit develops as this project unfolds and so the free spirit is, at the end of this process, more than just a figure open to the spirit of inquiry.

familiar and useful to the community (HH 228). Thus, the community opposes the guiding task of *Schopenhauer as Educator* – a text to which Nietzsche explicitly refers in this chapter (HH 252) – of becoming who one is, which, as Nietzsche tells us, consists in discharging what one is "in works and actions" (HH 264).

In addition to distinguishing the free from the fettered spirit, Nietzsche also returns to the topics of science and the pursuit of knowledge and the role that these play in the *Bildung* of the free spirit. In one respect, the chapter reaffirms the call, in the first chapter, to "bear the banner of the Enlightenment [. . .] further onward" (HH 26). Indeed, Nietzsche claims that there is now no going back given the results of the first four chapters: "we *cannot* return to the old, we *have* burned our boats; all that remains is for us to be brave, let happen what may. – Let us only *go forward*" (HH 248). In another respect, Nietzsche suggests that the free spirit's unequivocal commitment to science is receding. In the aphorism "Youthful Charm of Science," Nietzsche writes that the interest in searching for the truth is still much greater than living in error. However, the charm of this search is in decline, and one day, truth might become, in Nietzsche's words, "a scowling old woman" (HH 257).

In a well-known aphorism, "Future of Science," Nietzsche develops this theme in some detail. He is concerned that the advance of science will result in a twofold loss of pleasure. First, the process of scientific discovery causes the greatest joy; simply learning the results of science, however, is far less enjoyable. Thus, the more science discovers, the less enjoyable it becomes. Second, the discoveries of science deprive us of the pleasures associated with the consolations of metaphysics, religion, and art. In this way, science destroys the pleasures that make life worth living. To remedy this, Nietzsche proposes that we develop a "double-brain" with "two brain-ventricles": One chamber is for the "perceptions of science"; the other is "for those of non-science." This, Nietzsche claims, is a demand of health. On the one hand, the non-science chamber must be a power source heated with passion, prejudice, and illusion. On the other hand, the science chamber must regulate these passions so that the system as a whole does not overheat. If this double chamber is not developed, Nietzsche claims that the waning pleasure in truth will eventually result in a return to a barbaric rejection of science (HH 251).

It is worth noting the slight contrast between the position Nietzsche articulates in this aphorism and the stance he takes at the end of the first chapter. This difference suggests that the dialectical structure of the free spirit project is already animating a text like *Human*. In the first chapter,

Nietzsche claims that the free spirit will adopt a "good temperament" in response to the potentially life-denying effects of the truths he has discovered (HH 34). This "good temperament" is one in which the negative effects of any discovery will be overridden by the pleasure one takes in the process of scientific discovery and the joy of observing the world. In contrast, Nietzsche now claims that this pleasure in scientific discovery is now waning, and so some room needs to be made for passion, prejudice, and illusion for the sake of health. Thus, the free spirit must develop a split persona: a scientific side that searches for truth and a protected area in which life can be motivated by passion and error. As we will see, Nietzsche continues to develop this dialectical relationship between life and truth as the free spirit works unfold, and he will take another step beyond the position adopted here as early as *The Wanderer*.

Toward the end of the chapter, Nietzsche devotes a number of aphorisms to a topic that will reoccur in the free spirit works: the status of *vita contemplativa* and its relationship to the life of action. Here, Nietzsche explains how the emphasis on work and industry has spread like an epidemic – it is worse in America than in Europe – such that it even drives the scholar (HH 282). This means that the *otium* or *scholé* necessary for the contemplative life has declined (HH 284). Consequently, there is little time for independence of thought and the development of oneself as a unique individual. Independence of thought requires caution and so time, and this is precisely what scholars do not have (HH 282). Similarly, those who pursue the active life have little time to become themselves. Instead, they simply adopt a role as a businessman or statesmen, and they deflect any questions about the purpose and meaning of what they are doing (HH 283). Thus, there is something noble about leisure (HH 284), and Nietzsche claims that the person who does not have two-thirds of his day to himself is a slave (HH 283).

In the penultimate aphorism of chapter 5, Nietzsche explicates the conditions that the free spirit requires to achieve such freedom. Because they live for the sake of knowledge alone, free spirits will be content with "a minor office or an income that just enables them to live," and they will expend as little energy as possible on affairs having to do with society or the state. This is also true of personal relations: free spirits want "to become involved with the world of affection and blindness only insofar as it is necessary for acquiring knowledge" (HH 291). Thus, in the final aphorism, Nietzsche calls upon the free spirit to go "forward on the path of wisdom with a bold step and full of confidence!" (HH 292).

Chapters 6–8: The Liberation from Society

One cannot miss the programmatic nature of the final aphorisms of chapter 5. On the one hand, they provide a summary statement of what the free spirit is at this juncture and a statement about what the free spirit must do in order to continue the pursuit of knowledge into old age. It should also be obvious that Nietzsche continues this program in the remaining chapters of *Human* by detaching the free spirit from the various social obligations that inhibit the quest for knowledge. Thus, rather than consisting of a collection of random thought experiments or fragmented, indeterminate, and unrelated aphorisms, *Human* is telling a story of the free spirit's dual quest for truth and liberation.

It is not easy to decipher the underlying message of Nietzsche's reflections in chapter 6 from the first aphorisms alone. However, the point of "Man in Society" comes into view in the final aphorism. There, Nietzsche declares that there are no genuine friends in the sense that all friendship is based on "error and deception" (HH 376). Much of the chapter is about the difficulty or even impossibility of forming genuine relationships with human beings based on mutual understanding. Thus, Nietzsche begins the chapter by remarking that presumably free spirits need to practice "benevolent dissimulation" because they can often see through the dissimulations of others (HH 293).

Themes of concealment, appearance, vanity, conceit, fear, miscommunication, offense, and false judgment run throughout the chapter. In the second aphorism, we are told that we prefer copies to originals in both paintings and people (HH 294). Later, Nietzsche explains that vanity is behind the decision to reveal and conceal one's vices; in both cases, it is vanity "seeking its advantage" (HH 313). Similarly, Nietzsche points out that two vain persons in conversation do not get to know each other because each is focused on the impression he or she will make (HH 338). In another aphorism, he explains that the relatives of someone who commits suicide often begrudge the deceased for the damage it does to their reputation (HH 322). A few sections later, Nietzsche tells us that people secretly rejoice when they perform a heroic deed in front of others who are unwilling to do the same thing (HH 325). He also explains why conceited people deceive themselves and others about the extent to which they have been honored so that it corresponds to what they think they deserve (HH 341). In the penultimate aphorism, Nietzsche claims that we cannot reliably hope for any sort of posthumous fame. Values and opinions are continually changing, and so we cannot predict whether one's deeds or person will be valued in the future (HH 375).

Friendship is also a recurrent theme in the chapter, and it goes to the core of what Nietzsche means by "man in society." In the second aphorism in which friendship is mentioned, Nietzsche strikes a somewhat pessimistic chord: "There will be few who, when they are in want of matter for conversation, do not reveal the more secret affairs of their friends" (HH 327). In another aphorism, Nietzsche claims that even our closest friends judge us falsely, but then also wonders if they would still be our friends if they knew us well (HH 352). Elsewhere, he is baffled that the ancient Greeks understood relatives as close friends (HH 365). Although Nietzsche speaks positively of what he calls the "talent for friendship," he concludes with the claim: "Friends, there are no friends!" (HH 376).

Similar to the other chapters, the final aphorism functions as a summary of the contents of the preceding aphorisms. Thus, the aphorism begins by asking us to reflect on how feelings and opinions are divided even among our closest acquaintances and "how manifold are the occasions for misunderstanding, for hostility and rupture." Because of this, we must conclude that all friendships rest on uncertain ground and recognize just "how isolated each man is!" This pessimistic truth does cause "bitterness," but we can, according to Nietzsche, be comforted by the fact that the opinions of others necessarily proceed from the character, occupation, talent, and environment of others – a point Nietzsche makes only five aphorisms earlier (HH 371). Once we recognize this, we can be comfortable with friendships founded on error and deception. Friendship cannot be otherwise, and although there are no true friends, there are also no true enemies (HH 376).

Just as the purpose of chapter 6 is to detach the free spirit from friends and society more generally, the purpose of chapter 7 is to articulate the free spirit's attitude toward marriage and family. The chapter contains aphorisms that will undoubtedly offend the sensibilities of contemporary readers, and even the title, "Woman and Child," indicates that Nietzsche implicitly thinks of the free spirit project as something that only males will pursue, even though he composed much of the work while staying with Malwida von Meysenbug, a leading feminist of the day.[20] The basic idea is

---

[20] For more on the role of Meysenbug during this time and Nietzsche's relationship to women, see Young (2013). As Abbey (2000: 107) notes, Nietzsche's views on women are, however, more nuanced in the free spirit works than in his later writings. She also argues that, "women can be considered as candidates for free spirithood" (108).

that in order to pursue truth and knowledge in a way that is unfettered by custom, the free spirit needs to detach himself from love, marriage, and family. Thus, the chapter ends with Nietzsche's paraphrasing of Socrates' line from Plato's *Phaedo*: "O Criton, do tell someone to take those women away" (HH 437).

The chapter begins on a more optimistic note. Nietzsche claims, first, that a perfect woman is a higher type of being than a perfect man (HH 377) and, second, that a good marriage is founded on the aforementioned talent for friendship (HH 378). He also advises one to think of marriage as a long conversation (HH 406) and discusses a higher conception of marriage, endorsed by "free-thinking women," as a "soul-friendship" (HH 424).[21] At the same time, skepticism about love and marriage can be found in these same aphorisms. In the last of the aforementioned aphorisms, Nietzsche claims that this conception of marriage would require concubines because one woman could not be both friend and lover. Thus, Nietzsche concludes: we should not idealize the institution of marriage (HH 424).

Toward the end of the chapter, Nietzsche becomes increasingly negative about the institution of marriage and even the role of women in relationship to the free spirit project. For instance, Nietzsche claims that marriage can cause the spiritual retrogression of the man (HH 421). Because a happy marriage spins a spider web of habit, it will not be conducive to a free spirit who is continually changing (HH 427). Nietzsche also claims that living with someone too closely can cause the soul to become tattered and worn (HH 428). In marriage, women will tend to "work against the heroic impulse in the heart of the free spirit" (HH 431), and Socrates would not have married Xantippe had he known this (HH 433). For these reasons, the free spirit "must prefer *to fly alone*" (HH 426). Thus, Nietzsche concludes the section with the claim that in matters of "the most universal knowledge" and "in the affairs of the highest philosophical kind all married men are suspect" (HH 436).

Just as Nietzsche divorces himself from both friends and family, he also distances himself from political life in chapter 8, "A Glance at the State." The chapter begins with an extended section in which Nietzsche both disparages modern democratic aspirations and carves out space for the free

---

[21] Based on Young's (2010: 216–217) account of Nietzsche's proposal to Mathilde Trampedach, one wonders if this is what Nietzsche had envisaged for himself.

spirit to operate independently of political life. Thus, Nietzsche opens with a lament about the "demagogic character" of a contemporary politics that appeals to the masses. Nietzsche's point, however, is not to reject the democratic project wholesale. Instead, he simply resists the idea that everyone must be subordinate to the demands of politics. Thus, he writes: "a few must first of all be allowed, now more than ever, to refrain from politics and to step a little aside" (HH 438).

Many of Nietzsche's reflections are designed to undermine the idea that modern humanity can find salvation in some utopian political scheme. He does so by questioning modern political equality, socialist ideals, and the desire to eliminate war. Similar to the final chapter of *Beyond Good and Evil*, Nietzsche claims in the second aphorism of the chapter that higher culture requires a two-tiered society that gives the upper classes enough leisure to pursue cultural goals (HH 439). Similarly, Nietzsche claims that mere vanity drives the modern quest to eliminate slavery. The modern worker is much worse off than the slave and so the elimination of slavery has made things worse (HH 457). Elsewhere, Nietzsche argues that socialists who highlight the injustice of private property are no better in terms of justice than their predecessors (HH 452) because greed, rather than justice, drives socialist demands for equality (HH 451). Nietzsche also contends that satisfying the desire for an "age of happiness" through political revolution is impossible. At best, humans can hope for "*happy moments*" (HH 471). Indeed, Nietzsche rejects any hopes for perpetual peace among humans. As the title of one aphorism makes clear, he thinks war is "indispensable" (HH 477).

Toward the end of the chapter, Nietzsche again emphasizes the need to establish boundaries on the state to create space for the free spirit to pursue his private projects. Nietzsche's primary complaint against socialism is therefore that it "aspires to the annihilation of the individual" by making the individual a useful organ of the community. In contrast to the socialist's call for "*as much state as possible*," the free spirit responds with a call for "*as little state as possible*" (HH 373). In the penultimate aphorism, Nietzsche addresses the real cost of what he calls "grand politics": It is not the expense of war but the fact that so many talented people have to devote their energies to political matters. Because this leads to "spiritual impoverishment," Nietzsche wonders whether sacrificing "the more spiritual plants and growths" to the state is really worth it (HH 481). The final aphorism implies that it is not: "public opinions – private indolence" (HH 482).

Chapter 9: The Philosophical Wanderer

The final chapter, "Man Alone with Himself," functions as the conclusion to the entire work and so the positions it expresses are a result of the preceding chapters. The chapter has more aphorisms than any other and provides a restatement of the values most central to the free spirit project at this stage. It begins with some pithy maxims on truth, knowledge, and conviction, and Nietzsche returns to these topics toward the end of the chapter. In the final aphorism, Nietzsche presents himself as a homeless wanderer in a desert of knowledge who seeks the *"philosophy of the morning"* (HH 638).

Recalling a central theme of chapter 5, the first aphorism takes aim at convictions. Like Descartes' *Meditations* and even Plato's *Euthyphro*, the free spirit's quest for truth places it in direct opposition to ungrounded belief. Nietzsche's point here is simple: "convictions are more dangerous enemies of truth than lies" (HH 483). Nietzsche also continues to emphasize that certain truths will not always be pleasing or useful. Thus, we should question a thinker for presenting truths that please rather than criticizing him for presenting ideas that are hard to accept (HH 484). Indeed, a deeper comprehension of a thing and its origins is often unpleasant, and this is why few stay faithful to something once it is understood (HH 489). Nevertheless, Nietzsche claims that *"the one thing needful"* is to have "either a cheerful disposition by nature or a *disposition made cheerful by art and knowledge"* (HH 486).

This cheerful disposition toward knowledge is often contrasted with a passionate disposition toward convictions and ideals. Thus, Nietzsche writes of the way in which all idealists are deluded in two senses: First, they believe that the causes they serve are more important than all other causes, and, second, they deny that for their ideal to prosper, it requires the "same evil-smelling manure as all other human undertakings" (HH 490). Elsewhere, Nietzsche emphasizes the blinding effects that working for specific ideals can have. Just as we need to convince ourselves that our profession is more important than any other to work at it our whole lives (HH 492), "anyone who works in service of an idea [. . .] will cease to examine the idea itself" (HH 511). Not only is there too little time, one has a vested interest in not questioning ideas to which one is already committed to realizing (HH 511).

Although the free spirit is committed to truth and knowledge, Nietzsche nevertheless acknowledges – again, similar to the first chapter – the way in which error plays a central role in human culture and survival. For

instance, he drives a wedge between truth and human flourishing: his
"*fundamental insight*" is that "there is no pre-established harmony between
the furtherance of truth and the well-being of mankind" (HH 517). He
also notes that the pursuit of culture by means of truth might undermine
culture itself: "we belong to an age whose culture is in danger of perishing
through the means to culture" (HH 520). In short, Nietzsche hints at
some fundamental tensions within the free spirit project and the difficulty
of grounding culture in the quest for truth.

The final aphorisms of the chapter are some of the most important for
both the chapter and the book. These aphorisms focus on truth, conviction, knowledge, and science, and they reaffirm a number of the positions
articulated throughout *Human*. In "Of Conviction and Justice," Nietzsche
considers whether there is a duty to be faithful to convictions and causes to
which one has sworn an oath in a state of passion even if such faith injures
our higher self. The position he eventually takes is that "there exists no law,
no obligation, of this kind; we *have* to become traitors, be unfaithful, again
and again abandon our ideals." The revision of beliefs is necessary in order
to advance to higher stages of life. Although people often despise someone
who leaves behind such convictions because they believe such betrayal is
motivated by personal advantage, Nietzsche insists that such convictions
have no "*intellectual significance*" and so one should change one's convictions when they are shown to be false (HH 629).

Nietzsche begins the next aphorism by defining conviction: it is "the
belief that on some particular point of knowledge one is in possession of
the unqualified truth" (HH 630). He then notes a series of assumptions
upon which convictions are based: (1) such unqualified truths exist; (2) we
have discovered the proper methods of finding these truths; (3) we are in
possession of these methods. Each of these assumptions, Nietzsche claims,
reveals that the "man of convictions" is not the "man of science." Indeed,
the "man of convictions" lived in childlike naivety prior to the rise of
science, and this naivety led many to sacrifice themselves and others for
their convictions. As Nietzsche notes, convictions, not mere opinions, have
led to a great number of wars, and so he speculates on just how peaceful
human history would have been if people had inquired into the truth of
their convictions (HH 630).

Nietzsche continues to address the importance the scientific spirit has
for the maturity of humanity in subsequent aphorisms. Although a certain
skepticism and relativism regarding knowledge can always cause displeasure by forcing us to resist the convictions of authority figures, the scientific
spirit brings a *cautious reserve* necessary to maturity (HH 631). Also

necessary to both culture and maturation is the ability to pass through different convictions so that we do not remain stuck in a set of beliefs. Such an individual represents a *"retarded"* culture and a lack of "cultivation [*Bildung*]" (HH 632). Similarly, Nietzsche claims that the distrust and caution that the scientific spirit has propagated marks "anyone who advocates opinions with violent word and deed" as an "enemy of our present-day culture" or at least a member of a "retarded" culture (HH 633).

Although he appeals to the results of the natural sciences to undermine commonsense and metaphysical beliefs in chapter 1, Nietzsche notes in the concluding stages of chapter 9 that, "the procedures of science are at least as important a product of inquiry as any other outcome." The scientific spirit is not a spirit that assiduously learns the facts that scientific procedures discover. Instead, the scientific spirit is an "instinctive mistrust of devious thinking." Nietzsche contrasts those who want convictions from a thinker with the small minority that "want *certainty*" in opinions. The former want to be carried away to experience an increase in power, and this is why they are attracted to a thinker who takes himself to be a genius, maintains the "fire of convictions," and arouses "distrust of the modesty and circumspection of science." In contrast, the latter have an "objective interest that ignores personal advantage" and the corresponding feeling of strength (HH 635). For this reason, Nietzsche suggests that they long for a different sort of genius: a genius of justice who stands as an *"opponent of convictions"* (HH 636).

In the penultimate aphorism, Nietzsche presents the free spirit as one who does not let his opinions stiffen into convictions. Instead, he is continuously alive and undergoing change. Thus, the free spirit advances "from opinion to opinion" as a *noble traitor* that serves the god of justice and so feels no sense of guilt for leaving behind the opinions of his family, culture, country, and time (HH 637). For this reason, the free spirit will also feel like "a wanderer on earth" without a destination. In this condition, the wanderer observes the events of human life but does not "let his heart adhere too firmly to any individual thing." As a wanderer who lacks both a cultural and cosmological home, the free spirit will undoubtedly suffer hard nights as an exile. At the same time, there will come "joyful mornings" in which "the Muses come dancing by him in the mist of the mountains." Here, he will enjoy "the gifts of all those free spirits who are at home in mountain, wood and solitude and who, like him, are, in their now joyful, now thoughtful way, wanderers and philosophers." Here the free spirit will seek "the *philosophy of the morning*" (HH 638).

The final aphorism makes clear that Nietzsche does not conceive of the final chapter of *Human* as the end of the narrative and so the end of the free spirit's quest for truth and self-cultivation. Because the work ends with the free spirit seeking something, *Human* cannot be a complete and self-sufficient project. Instead, Nietzsche's characterization of the free spirit as a wanderer foreshadows *The Wanderer* – even though Nietzsche considered publishing *The Wanderer* under the title "Thought-Paths of St. Moritz" (KSA 8: 43[Title]) – and so a subsequent work in the free spirit progression. Similarly, the fact that the wanderer is seeking "the *philosophy of the morning*" (HH 638) points forward to a work like *Daybreak*, even if Nietzsche only adopted the title at a late stage in the composition of the text.

Indeed, prolepsis is present even in the aphorism that Nietzsche had, for a time, considered to be the conclusion of *Human*. As D'Iorio has shown (2016: 107ff.), Nietzsche originally planned to end *Human* with the aphorism that is now "Seriousness in Play." The aphorism is important because it connects the title of the book, *Human, All Too Human*, with Plato's judgment in the *Republic* that human things are not worthy of great seriousness. It is also significant because the aphorism ends with a "*trotz-dem*" or a "nonetheless" (HH 628). The idea is that although he agrees with Plato's assessment of the vanity of all human things – a sentiment expressed throughout the text – Nietzsche nevertheless wants to render an alternative judgment about existence. What this alternative judgment is remains unexplained. All we can surmise is that the two em dashes that end the aphorism in its original and current form suggest that there is more to the story. Thus, like the conclusions to *The Wanderer*, *Daybreak*, and even *The Gay Science*, *Human* ends with aphorisms that indicate to the reader that there is more to the story that needs to be told.

Concluding Remarks

It should be evident from this relatively brief account of the central themes of *Human* that the work is structured as a narrative that begins with a commitment to finding truth in all matters and ends with a free spirit detached from any relationship that might hinder this quest. In so doing, Nietzsche articulates a tragic worldview that bears important similarities to the factual pessimism of his earliest works, even though he refrains from rendering any evaluative judgment about life based on these insights. Although Nietzsche will advance the free spirit project in ways that will ultimately conflict with the asceticism adopted in the work, a number of the insights expressed here will become permanent pieces of Nietzsche's philosophy that will be rearticulated at later junctures in his published works. Like the opening stages of Descartes' *Meditations*, there is no going back on the project Nietzsche has initiated in *Human*, and so the free spirit cannot return to the comforts offered by either metaphysical speculation or social life.

Nevertheless, my reading of *Human*'s relationship to subsequent free spirit works conflicts with Cohen's claims that, for Nietzsche, "the individual book" is the "legitimate unit of interpretation" and that *Human* exemplifies this very point (2010: 16). By this, Cohen means that *Human* is a complete, standalone product that can be read independently of the other free spirit works, even though Cohen rightly emphasizes that the placement of *Human* within Nietzsche's larger oeuvre is significant (2010: 176). The problem that the final aphorism causes for Cohen's reading is that it clearly points to something beyond the narrative of *Human*. So although Cohen is right to highlight the literary integrity of the work in the sense that the ordering of the aphorisms and the structure of the chapters matter for the interpretation of the work, he is wrong about the literary integrity of *Human* insofar as he claims that it is a self-contained unit.

Cohen recognizes this problem toward the end of his work. However, the problem, in Cohen's view, is not so much the reference to the philosophy of the morning in the final aphorism, but the fact that Nietzsche decided to republish *Assorted Opinions* and *The Wanderer* as volume two of *Human* in 1886. According to Cohen, Nietzsche's republication of these texts in a two-volume set suggests one of two things: either (1) *Assorted Opinions* and *The Wanderer* retrospectively undermine the literary integrity of *Human* or (2) *Human* never had any integrity in the first place (2010: 196). Cohen responds by arguing that *Assorted Opinions* and *The Wanderer* should be read as supplements to *Human* just as Schopenhauer's second volume of *The World as Will and Representation* is a supplement to the first. That is, they are parasitic on the structure and dialectical flow of *Human* and so further elaborate on the content of the original nine chapters (2010: 201).

Cohen's argument faces a number of challenges, and I end this chapter by highlighting two. First, Cohen seems to be unaware of the fact that Nietzsche did not just republish *Assorted Opinions* and *The Wanderer* as appendices in 1886, but, as I documented in the previous chapter, originally composed these works as continuations of *Human*. So understood, Nietzsche never intended *Human* to be a discrete work separate from these two appendices. Second, Cohen's claim that *Assorted Opinions* and *The Wanderer* have the same function as Schopenhauer's second volume of *The World as Will and Representation* is highly dubious. Nietzsche presents opinions in both works that are not found in, and even conflict with, *Human*. As I explain in the next chapter, *Assorted Opinions* begins to resuscitate the value of art given the critique of metaphysics in *Human*. In *The Wanderer*, Nietzsche turns his attention to what he calls the "closest things" and so turns away from the "first and last things" of the opening chapters of *Human*. In both cases, Nietzsche is not supplementing the content of *Human*. Instead, he is moving beyond the positions of *Human* in a way that advances the dialectical *Bildungsprogramm* of the free spirit works.

CHAPTER 4

An Epicurean in Exile
Assorted Opinions and Maxims *and*
The Wanderer and His Shadow

The subject matter of this chapter is the two appendices to *Human* that Nietzsche would later publish as one volume under the title *Human, All Too Human II*: *Assorted Opinions and Maxims* and *The Wanderer and His Shadow*. The purpose of this chapter is not, however, to rehearse or summarize the contents of these two works. Instead, it is to explain how these works are best read in a dialectical relationship to *Human* and the subsequent free spirit works. In other words, the purpose is to show how these two volumes presuppose the ideas of *Human* by addressing some of the implicit tensions in the work and so further advance the education of the free spirit.

Assorted Opinions and *The Wanderer* lack the kind of structure readily identifiable in *Human*. Unlike *Human*, there are no distinct chapters and so there are no aphorisms that present an introduction to or a concluding summary of a given topic. Instead, *Assorted Opinions* reads like a collection of aphorisms on different topics that were thrown together without any plan or organization and so can be read in any order or combination. The same is largely true of *The Wanderer*. In this sense, these works largely conform to Danto's understanding of Nietzsche's oeuvre more generally, and they may provide support for a postmodern reading of Nietzsche's corpus insofar as this lack of order may be understood as implicitly attacking systematic philosophy.

Nevertheless, there is nothing here that speaks decisively in favor of or against any one particular reading. Instead, each reading is based on an inference about the reason for this apparent lack of order. Whereas the Danto approach holds that Nietzsche simply lacks the talent for organizing his thoughts, the postmodern or anti-systematic reading holds that Nietzsche has designed these texts as a subtle attack on systematic philosophy. However, in each case, there is no explicit evidence for either reading in the form of a note, letter, or passages from the texts. In contrast, there are aphorisms from *Assorted Opinions* that speak directly against such a

reading. Thus, Nietzsche writes: "Do you think this work must be fragmentary because I give it to you (and have to give it to you) in fragments?"
(AOM 128). The opposite of a fragmentary work is a work that constitutes
a whole, and Nietzsche suggests that the aphorisms of *Assorted Opinions*
constitute a whole: "The worst readers are those who behave like plundering troops: they take away a few things they can use, dirty and confound
the remainder, and revile the whole" (AOM 137).

The reading I provide here shows how distinctive themes emerge in
each text that are important to the dialectic of the free spirit works. In my
account of *Assorted Opinions*, I point to Nietzsche's frequent discussion of
art and contrast the views of art he presents in the text with those he
articulates in *Human*. In particular, *Assorted Opinions* gradually resuscitates
the importance of an art that is now detached from any metaphysical
principles. In my account of *The Wanderer*, I follow Brusotti in emphasizing the significance of Nietzsche's turn to the "closest things," a theme that
contrasts sharply with the free spirit's interest in the first and last things in
the opening chapter of *Human*. Taken together, we can see that Nietzsche
is not further explicating the ideas of *Human*. Instead, he is gradually
moving beyond them, and in so doing, he is moving toward the eventual
position of the final chapter of *The Gay Science* in which the quest for truth
will ultimately be subordinated to art and the affirmation of life.

Assorted Opinions and Maxims

Nietzsche began writing *Assorted Opinions* relatively soon after the appearance of *Human* in May of 1878, and he intended the work to be a
continuation of *Human*. Although it is the least structured of all the free
spirit works, *Assorted Opinions* begins with aphorisms that depend on the
ideas of *Human*. This is evidenced by the very first aphorism, "To the
Disappointed of Philosophy." Here, Nietzsche asks whether those who
previously thought that life had the highest value must now reduce it to
"the lowest possible price" (AOM 1).

The aphorism is significant for a number of reasons. First, Nietzsche
asks about the value of life "now" that something has happened. Nothing
here is explicit, but he seems to be referring to the insights of *Human*. This
is because *Human* presents a series of reflections that undercut the idea
that life has some inherent meaning, purpose, or value, and so it would
only follow that someone might be disappointed in such a philosophy. So
understood, the first aphorism assumes the conclusions of *Human* as a
starting point and, in turn, continues a process in which the free spirit is

driven forward. If this is right, then the Danto approach to this aphorism must be wrong. It could not have been placed anywhere in Nietzsche's corpus or even anywhere else in the works of the free spirit and still retain its meaning. Instead, the aphorism has the meaning it does because it follows directly upon the pessimistic insights of *Human*.

That *Assorted Opinions* further develops the free spirit project is also evinced by the fourth aphorism. There, Nietzsche speaks about the difference between an older understanding of the free spirit and the current understanding of the free spirit. The difference has to do with the differing attitudes each adopts toward Voltaire's proposition that error also has its merits. Whereas previous generations had to summon their intrepidity to recognize this view, the current generation of free spirits judges this to be "a piece of involuntary naivety" and so recognizes the benefits of error as almost obvious (AOM 4). Although a literal reading indicates that Nietzsche is comparing his own free spirit project to an understanding that predated his efforts, it seems that Nietzsche is contrasting the attitude of the free spirit in *Assorted Opinions* with the attitude expressed in *Human*. Nietzsche dedicated *Human* to Voltaire and presented the free spirit as a figure committed to the absolute value of truth and so resistant to the idea that error could have any merit. If this is right, then the attitude Nietzsche is now adopting toward error in *Assorted Opinions* represents "progress" in his own free spirit project.

In line with the argument of *Human*, Nietzsche solidifies the connection between the free spirit and uncomfortable truths in the eleventh aphorism of *Assorted Opinions*. Here, Nietzsche insists that freedom of thought characterizes the free spirit, but also notes that this means the free spirit "will not dissemble over certain dreadful elements in its origin and tendency." For this reason, Nietzsche frets that others might accuse the free spirit of being a "pessimist of the intellect" (AOM 11).[1] As we have seen, Nietzsche's reflections in *Human* place his work within a tradition of pessimism that highlights the general incompatibility between the desire for meaning and knowledge and what nature has to offer (factual pessimism). At the same time, Nietzsche wants to resist the pessimistic attempt to condemn life for this very reason (evaluative pessimism).

In contrast to such pessimists, Nietzsche claims in a subsequent aphorism that the utility of the pursuit of wisdom outweighs the costs. Thus, he points to the way in which "the utility of the unconditional search for the

---

[1] Nietzsche later refers to *Assorted Opinions* under the heading, "pessimist of the intellect" (KSA 12: 2 [124]).

true is continually being demonstrated," and it is for this reason that we can accept the occasions in which this search causes harm to the individual. According to Nietzsche, the harm caused by the search for truth is like a chemist who occasionally poisons or burns himself during experiments. The means can be painful, but the end justifies the pain involved (AOM 13). Indeed, Nietzsche reaffirms the free spirit's commitment to truth, as well as the Cartesian method of obtaining it, in the aphorism, "Truth Will Have No Other Gods Beside It" (AOM 20).

So although Nietzsche confirms the free spirit's commitment to truth in the opening aphorisms of *Assorted Opinions*, he also notes that error has its merits and that this commitment can have negative consequences for the individual. Nietzsche also appeals to his previous considerations about the utility of knowledge in the aphorism, "From the Thinker's Innermost Experience," to question the idea that there is a "drive to knowledge in and for itself" – a theme that recalls Nietzsche's early reflections in "On Truth and Lies." Nietzsche notes that the production of ideas is often tied to the power, honor, and fame of the producer: In the "glitter" of the idea the thinker "glitters" too. There is a "*secret*" struggle for power and fame in the production of ideas, and the true and untrue contribute to this struggle because we have habitually associated the true with the useful. Thus, Nietzsche claims that power and fame cannot be erected on error and lies, and so the demand for truth is here united with the quest for personal immortality and its hidden thought: Let the world perish so long as I am safe! Consequently, it is the vice of arrogance that has inflated the respect we accord to truth and has ultimately led to the development of what Nietzsche calls an "intellectual conscience" (AOM 26).

Nietzsche advances this line of reflection a number of aphorisms later in "Honesty and Play-Acting Among Unbelievers." Although the aphorism begins with a discussion of the profound influence of the Bible, it gradually moves toward a discussion of science and the related pursuit of truth and knowledge. Specifically, Nietzsche rejects "the monk's cowl of renunciation" as the reason for pursuing science. Instead, the real reason the free spirit pursues science is "the *joy* of knowledge and the *utility* of what is known." Thus, if science did not produce these, there would be no reason to engage in the activity. As the aphorism unfolds, Nietzsche argues that even though the practice of science demands an impersonal standpoint and so depersonalization, the achievements of scientists are bound up with the ego in the form of respect, fame, and "a modest personal immortality." Nietzsche claims that without this unscientific concern for our own status, the pursuit of knowledge through science "*would be a matter of indifference.*" Thus, the depersonalization of science requires that we remain *"unscientific"* in that we still care about ourselves. In short, there is no purely impersonal or self-sacrificing drive for knowledge (AOM 98), and so the purely theoretical standpoint adopted in *Human* can no longer be sustained.

These two aphorisms can be situated within a dialectical process that moves from the impersonal asceticism of *Human* toward the outright rejection of asceticism in Nietzsche's post-*Zarathustra* works. Nietzsche's concern with asceticism is implied in these aphorisms: he not only speaks of the depersonalization necessary for science, but also connects this to monkish renunciation. Given that Nietzsche later characterizes *Human* as an exercise in asceticism and that he presents himself in the work as a figure pursuing truth at all costs, the position adopted in these aphorisms should be read as a gradual departure from the strict asceticism and theoretical standpoint of *Human* toward a greater emphasis on passion and life in subsequent works. In this way, Nietzsche's questioning of the drive to truth harkens back to the view he already adopted in "On Truth and Lies" and points forward to his questioning of the will to truth at the beginning of *Beyond Good and Evil.*

Just as Nietzsche is moving away, in *Assorted Opinions*, from the strict asceticism and the unconditional commitment to science and truth that characterizes the opening stages of *Human*, he is also moving away from the sharp rejection of art found in the fourth chapter of *Human*. The *Nachlass* from the time indicates that the subjects of art and poetry are central to *Assorted Opinions*. The most substantive evidence for this reading is found in what are likely titles and fragments of introductions for *Assorted Opinions*. In one note, we find a proposed title for the work: "On the Causes of Poetry. Prejudices about the Poets. Aphorisms" (KSA 8: 30[2]). In the same set of notes, Nietzsche writes: "Introduction. I could have titled this book: From the Souls of Artists and Writers; in fact, it is a continuation of the fifth section, which carries this title" (KSA 8: 30[95]).[2] In another note, Nietzsche mentions art in connection with the Greeks: "Introduction. Stance of the wise toward art. The Greeks more refined than we: The wise man, the man of taste" (KSA 8: 30[93]).

Reflections on art and poetry run throughout *Assorted Opinions*. In the first aphorism in which art is mentioned, Nietzsche continues the line of attack in *Human* by identifying "metaphysical-mystical philosophy" as the means by which art is corrupted (AOM 28). A few aphorisms later, in

---

[2] Nietzsche likely means the fourth section of *Human*.

"Alleged 'Real Reality'," he is critical of the poet as well. Presumably borrowing from Plato's critique of art in the *Ion*, Nietzsche claims that the poet poses as someone who knows something about the things he describes. In this sense, he is a deceiver, and he practices his deception before those who "*do not know.*" Because the ignorant praise the poet for his wisdom, the poet begins to believe that he "possesses a *higher* truth and veracity." For poets who are conscious of their power to deceive, Nietzsche claims that they then set out to discredit reality with doses of skepticism. In this way, they can then present the spectator with a "path to 'true truth', or 'real reality'" (AOM 32).

This seemingly critical attitude toward art diminishes as *Assorted Opinions* unfolds, and Nietzsche sketches a conception of poetry in sync with the Enlightenment principles of calm rationality that the free spirit embraces at this stage of the project. This occurs in an aphorism entitled "The Poet as Signpost to the Future." Nietzsche claims that the poetic power not used up in depicting contemporary life should be used in "signposting the future." The poet should do this by emulating artists of previous eras to develop "a fair image of man," thereby showing the way in which "the great and beautiful soul is still possible" in the modern world. Nevertheless, these poets must be protected from "the fire and breath of the *passions*" – a point that clearly differentiates the poet here from the "passion for knowledge" at work in *Daybreak* and the poetry of the Troubadour that Nietzsche embraces in *The Gay Science*. Instead, the image they paint will be "harmonious and well-proportioned," and their characters will exhibit "strength, goodness, mildness, purity" and "moderation." According to Nietzsche, the path to "this poetry of the future starts out from *Goethe*," but it requires a power greater than present-day poets possess (AOM 99).

In two subsequent aphorisms, Nietzsche returns to Goethe and the poet of the future. In the first, Nietzsche mentions Goethe's view that Laurence Sterne, the author of *Tristram Shandy*, was the "most liberated spirit of the century." Nietzsche praises Sterne as the master of ambiguity, and he claims that "such an ambiguousness" became "flesh and soul" in Sterne and so his "free-spiritedness" went through "every fibre and muscle of his body" (AOM 113).[3] In the next aphorism, Nietzsche attributes a different capacity to the "poet of the future." Specifically, this poet strives to depict reality and is even in love with reality (AOM 135). However, she won't

---

[3] See Vivarelli (1998: Ch. 3) for an extended analysis of Nietzsche's interest in Sterne during this period. As Blue (2016: 144) notes, Nietzsche was also taken with *Tristram Shandy* in his youth.

strive to depict all of reality. Instead, she will ignore much and so only "depict a select reality" (AOM 114).

The description of the "poet of the future" can again be understood as pointing back to Nietzsche's critique of art in *Human* and pointing forward to his understanding of the function of poetry in *The Gay Science*. The aphorism rests on the insights of *Human* because it develops a conception of art that is now divorced from metaphysical speculation and is instead committed to the depiction of empirical reality. Thus, the conception of art presented here is tied to the free spirit's continued concern with representing reality and so truth. At the same time, it points forward to the conception of art in *The Gay Science* because it advocates a depiction and arrangement of only select features of this reality, and so the aim of art is not a perfect mirroring of reality.

A similar intermediary position can also be found in Nietzsche's assessment of the need for art. In "Origins of the Taste for Works of Art," Nietzsche provides a list of various hypotheses as to why different peoples take an initial interest in art: It is an attempt to understand each other; it can be used to memorialize pleasurable events in the past; in more advanced forms, it can be used as a cure for boredom. However, he concludes the aphorism by noting that there is a certain kind of hypothesis that is being avoided on principle (AOM 119). Although not explicit, it seems that Nietzsche is avoiding metaphysical explanations. If this is right, then Nietzsche is presupposing *Human*'s critique of metaphysics and yet advancing beyond it by offering alternative explanations of art.

Near the middle of *Assorted Opinions*, Nietzsche again addresses the need for and interest in art. At one level, Nietzsche claims that everyday people have a need for art, but "it is small and cheap to satisfy." There is, however, "an artistic need of an *exalted kind*," and this can be found in the upper echelons of society where "a seriously intentioned artistic community" is still possible. The problem is that even this community is still "*second rank*." This is because these more refined people are nevertheless "discontented" and "unable to take any real pleasure in themselves." Thus, these individuals look to art to "scare away their discontent." According to Nietzsche, the ancient Greeks provide a different model: "Their art was an outflowing and overflowing of their own healthiness and wellbeing," and they loved to see their own perfection "*repeated* outside themselves" (AOM 169).

In two further aphorisms, Nietzsche weaves together the idea of art emanating from an exemplary individual with the previous idea of art as the process of transfiguring reality through selection. In the first aphorism,

Nietzsche speaks of the art of Homer, Sophocles, Racine, and Goethe as emerging from "the *surplus* of a wise and harmonious conduct of life" (AOM 173). The underlying idea is that only a person with a certain psychic disposition can create great art. In the subsequent aphorism, Nietzsche argues that genuine art is not found in the work of art, but rather in the labor and so the *Bildung* that goes on within an individual who, in turn, externalizes the inner artwork of the self. Art is supposed to beautify life and so make us bearable and even pleasing to others, and art does this by *concealing* and *reinterpreting* everything ugly, painful, dreadful, and disgusting. However, this art of concealing, reinterpreting, and selecting is first and foremost directed at one's self, and only once this art is successfully applied to the self can a work of art emerge as an *appendage* or, to use the language above, an externalized repetition of the self (AOM 174).

In "Poets No Longer Teachers," Nietzsche again looks to the ancient Greeks as exemplars who reveal the poverty of modernity. Echoing themes from Plato's *Republic*, Nietzsche notes that the Greeks thought of the poet as a teacher of adults. According to Nietzsche, placing such a demand on a modern poet would cause embarrassment. For a poet to teach others, he must first *educate himself* and so make *himself* into a fine poem or a fair statute (AOM 172). In another aphorism, Nietzsche praises Goethe for having achieved just this: his person exudes a "*spirituality* in *wellbeing and well-wishing!*" Goethe achieved this because he was "educated by antiquity." The aphorism concludes with Nietzsche praising the Greeks for their fine sense of taste and wisdom. For the Greeks, wisdom or *sophia* simply was the sense of aesthetic taste (AOM 170; also see KSA 8: 30[93]).

As *Assorted Opinions* unfolds, Nietzsche praises the ancient Greeks in another cluster of aphorisms, and the themes he addresses recall some of the central motifs of *The Birth of Tragedy*. In "Joy in the Ancient World," Nietzsche claims that the difference between the moderns and the ancient Greeks is that whereas the moderns know how to suffer less, the Greeks knew how to rejoice more. This follows Nietzsche's argument in *The Birth of Tragedy* because the central question was not how to avoid suffering, but rather how to redeem, justify, and affirm it, and Nietzsche praised the ancient Greeks because they were cheerful even in the face of suffering. In this aphorism, Nietzsche speaks of their ability to create "new occasions for happiness and celebration," and so he sees in them a model for how "men of the future" might again "erect the temple of joy" (AOM 187).

In another cluster of aphorisms, Nietzsche explains how the ancient Greeks "made as it were a festival of all their passions and evil natural inclinations and even instituted a kind of official order of proceedings in the celebration of what was all-too-human in them." Similar to both *The Birth of Tragedy* and his later writings, Nietzsche contrasts this attitude with Christianity's hatred of the passions and the related attempt to combat them "with the greatest severity." He then claims that this celebration of the "all-too-human" was "the root of all the moral free-mindedness of antiquity," and in asking where the Greeks might have acquired this freedom and sense for the actual, Nietzsche points to poets like Homer: such poets "possess by way of compensation a joy in the actual and active *of every kind* and have no desire to deny even evil altogether" (AOM 220).

In addition to advancing key ideas from *The Birth of Tragedy*, Nietzsche also appeals to Heraclitus, the central figure of *Philosophy in the Tragic Age*. Whereas Heraclitus' philosophy implicitly forms the basis for Nietzsche's attacks on the metaphysical tradition in *Human*, Nietzsche explicitly endorses the so-called radical flux theory of Heraclitus in *Assorted Opinions*. In "Whither We Have to Travel," Nietzsche writes that Heraclitus' dictum that "we cannot step into the same river twice" is a piece of wisdom that "has gradually grown stale, but it has nonetheless remained as true and valid as it ever was" (AOM 223). Nietzsche's continued commitment to Heraclitus' ontology could not be more explicit.

The larger point of the aphorism, however, is not ontology. Instead, the issue is the all-important topic of self-knowledge. Similar to his call for a historical philosophy at the beginning of *Human*, Nietzsche argues that we need history and travel in order to understand ourselves. However, this does not just mean movement from place to place. Such history can be discovered in those individuals, families, and cultures next to us, and this sort of travel connects the discoveries of history with the discoveries of the ego. Here, "self-knowledge will become universal knowledge with regard to all that is past," just as "self-determination and self-education could, in the freest and most far-sighted spirits, one day become universal determination with regard to all future humanity" (AOS 223). The language Nietzsche employs here not only harkens back to the guiding theme of *Schopenhauer as Educator*, but also the end of *History for Life* in which Nietzsche refers to the Delphic oracle of "know thyself" and the need to organize the chaos in oneself (HL 10).[4]

Just as he praises the ancient Greeks in *Assorted Opinions*, Nietzsche also criticizes Christianity and the views associated with it, and Nietzsche's

---

[4] This again recalls Scheffler's encounter with Nietzsche in 1876 in which he emphasizes the Delphic theme of self-knowledge in relation to Heraclitus' philosophy (Gilman and Parent 1984: 73).

preference for the former and rejection of the latter can be understood through his critique of sin and his continued commitment to the fatalism of ancient Greek tragedy. This is most evident in the aphorism "The Desire to be Just and the Desire to be a Judge." Here, Nietzsche praises Schopenhauer for emphasizing the strict necessity of all human actions, but then chides him for turning to metaphysics to escape the ethical implications of this doctrine. One of the consequences that opponents of such a doctrine fear is that no one can be held accountable for their actions. There must be someone accountable and so a sinner, and this doctrine abolishes human sin. Nietzsche offers two responses to such concerns. First, if we insist on holding someone or something accountable, we could hold the "necessary wave-play of becoming" responsible. This would stand Christianity on its head by making God – the creator of this wave play – the sinner. The second response, which Nietzsche prefers, is to give up the idea that someone or something must be held responsible. That is, to be just, we should give up the desire to be judge (AOM 33).

Although there is no explicit mention of the (tragic) Greeks in the passage, Nietzsche's commitment to the necessity of all actions, as well as the Heraclitean phrase of the "necessary wave-play of becoming," is a central feature of his tragic worldview and so tragedy. Indeed, an unpublished note from the time of *Assorted Opinions* substantiates the claim that Nietzsche understands the text to be a contribution to the revitalization of this ancient Greek way of thinking. Specifically, Nietzsche writes: "Restore the ancient worldview! Truly moira above everything, the gods representative of real powers! Become ancient!" (KSA 8: 28[40]).

Nietzsche's interest in the ancient Greeks, however, is not limited to the period in which tragedy blossomed. Not only does this become evident in *The Wanderer*, in which Nietzsche turns to Epicurus as his most prized philosopher from antiquity, Nietzsche writes in another note from this time: "I need the salve cans and medicine bottles of *all* ancient philosophers" (KSA 8: 28[41]). This is reflected in the final aphorism of *Assorted Opinions*, "Descent into Hades" (AOM 408). There, Nietzsche compares himself, *qua* free spirit, to Odysseus venturing to the underworld. Specifically, Nietzsche claims to have "wandered long alone" and conversed with the likes of "Epicurus and Montaigne, Goethe and Spinoza, Plato and Rousseau, Pascal and Schopenhauer." The people of today, Nietzsche claims, appear to be mere shadows that lust for life. In contrast, these figures, now *after* death, seem to exhibit an "eternal liveliness," and so these are his real conversation partners, the ones to whom Nietzsche will "listen" and "accept judgment" (AOM 408).

Although the meaning of this final aphorism is far from clear, the themes of wandering, death, and life refer back to *Human* and look forward to *The Wanderer* and *Daybreak*. Similar to the end of *Human*, which concludes with the aphorism "The Wanderer" (HH 638), Nietzsche again presents himself as someone who has wandered far from home at the end of *Assorted Opinions*. The quasi-death experience presented at the end of *Assorted Opinions* also corresponds to Nietzsche's retrospective claims that he is operating at a minimum of life during this time (HH II P 5). At the same time, Nietzsche's trip to Hades seems to set the stage for the free spirit's turn toward life in *The Wanderer*. As we will see, Nietzsche turns his attention to the most fundamental matters of maintaining life such as food, clothing, and shelter, and this turn toward life in *The Wanderer* then paves the way for the emergence of a philosophy of morning in *Daybreak* (EH "Books" HH:4).

The Wanderer and His Shadow

When Nietzsche sent *The Wanderer and His Shadow* to his publisher on October 5, 1879, he referred to it as the second and last supplement to *Human* (KSB 5: 890). He also wrote the text as he was leaving his position at the university, and so the title seems to reflect the events of his own life. The contents of *The Wanderer* show that Nietzsche has abandoned the interest in metaphysical speculations that characterizes the opening chapters of *Human*. The final aphorism of *The Wanderer* shows that Nietzsche considers himself, *qua* free spirit, to be in the *process* of removing the chains of metaphysical, religious, and moral errors. Like the conclusion of *Human*, the conclusion of *The Wanderer* thus points to additional stages of the free spirit and so indicates that Nietzsche does not plan to end the project at this point.

The Wanderer both opens and concludes with a dialogue between the wanderer and his shadow. Just exactly who the wanderer is and what his or her shadow represents are far from clear, and Nietzsche largely leaves the reader to speculate (even the *Nachlass* offers little help). From what we can surmise, the wanderer is the same figure found at the end of *Human*, a figure whose quest for knowledge has detached him from home and society (HH 638). What the shadow represents is murkier. All we know for certain is that the sun produces the shadow, and the sun represents the knowledge of the wanderer. We also know from the initial dialogue that the wanderer and his shadow have reached a certain agreement, and the concluding dialogue indicates that the wanderer wants "to become a good neighbor to the closest things." As Brusotti (1997: Ch. 1.7) explains, becoming good neighbors to the closest things is the central theme of the text, and it stands in sharp contrast to the free spirit's interest in first and last things at the beginning of *Human*.[5]

Nevertheless, the aphorisms of *The Wanderer* clearly continue the "chain of thought" initiated in *Human* and developed in *Assorted Opinions*. In the first aphorism, Nietzsche draws our attention to the distinction between "the tree of knowledge" and "the tree of life." To highlight this distinction, he points to two truths. The first runs throughout *Human* and *The Wanderer*: "the appearance of freedom, but no freedom." Because this repeats Nietzsche's critique of intelligible freedom in chapter 2 of *Human* and his commitment to a fatalistic, "necessary wave-play of becoming" in *Assorted Opinions*, the first aphorism of *The Wanderer* presupposes that the reader is familiar with the preceding free spirit works. The second truth is that we only have probability, not truth (WS 1). Although this is puzzling given the series of tragic truths that Nietzsche has unpacked in the previous works, what he likely has in mind is that there are no fixed or eternal truths to which we can anchor our lives. Instead, it is true, as Nietzsche declares in the second aphorism of *Human*, that everything has become (HH 2), and this is why, as the first aphorisms of *Assorted Opinions* and *The Wanderer* make clear, there is a radical disjunction between the pursuit of truth and the flourishing of life.

Familiar themes from the first two books of the free spirit are also expressed in the next two aphorisms of *The Wanderer*. In the second, Nietzsche commits himself to a certain form of skepticism and highlights the irrationality of the world. Although we cannot know much of the world, the part we do know, our own rationality, is not that rational, and insofar as we are part of the world, we can therefore infer the irrationality of the world from our own irrationality (WS 2). In the third aphorism of *The Wanderer*, Nietzsche implicitly refers back to the opening aphorism of *Human*. Specifically, it explains how we glorify the historical origin of a thing as a result of our previously held metaphysical beliefs, and this implies that the free spirit has effectively replaced metaphysical beliefs with the idea that everything has a history of coming to be (WS 3).

The fourth aphorism is also important for the dialectical reading because it foreshadows the question that takes center stage at the beginning of

---

[5] In *Ecce Homo*, Nietzsche refers, positively, to the concern for "these small things" as a "casuistry of selfishness" and claims that these are "inconceivably more important than everything one has taken to be important so far" (EH "Clever" 10).

Beyond Good and Evil: what is the value of truth? The argument in the fourth aphorism of *The Wanderer* is that we should not be deceived into thinking that truth has a high value simply because of the difficulty involved in attaining it through the rigors of science. The difficulty of attaining a thing does not indicate its value. Although he does not conclude that truth lacks any value, Nietzsche casts doubt on the assumption that truth has some intrinsic and extraordinary value such that we should pursue it at all costs (WS 4).

Thus, the first four aphorisms effectively presuppose and, in some cases, extend the line of thought already established in *Human* and *Assorted Opinions*. This, of course, is precisely what we would expect from a work written as a second appendix to *Human*. At the same time, *The Wanderer* represents a decisive break from *Human* and an advance in terms of the free spirit's progress. It is a break because Nietzsche begins to direct the drive for truth away from the ultimate questions of metaphysics and toward questions having to do with everyday life. It is an advance because it moves the free spirit a step closer to the standpoint ultimately adopted in *Beyond Good and Evil* regarding the relationship between life and truth. Although Nietzsche does not present truth as having a purely instrumental value in *The Wanderer*, the quest for truth should be directed toward things that matter for life.

The theme that highlights this shift in attention is what Nietzsche calls the *closest things* [*nächsten Dinge*]. Nietzsche introduces this theme in the fifth and sixth aphorisms, refers to it again in the eighth, discusses it at length in the sixteenth, and then mentions it in the concluding dialogue between the wanderer and his shadow. In the *Nachlass* from this time, Nietzsche refers to the closest things in multiple notes (KSA 8: 40[16], [22], [23], and [31]). In the first appearance of the concept in the *Nachlass*, Nietzsche presents "the doctrine of the closest things [*die Lehre von den nächsten Dingen*]" as the heading of a list of topics for simple and healthy living: food, social intercourse, nature, solitude, sleep, earning a living, weather, and health (KSA 8: 40[16]).

In *The Wanderer*, Nietzsche's discussion of the closest things follows the ideas in the *Nachlass*. In the fifth aphorism, Nietzsche points to a feigned disrespect "*for all things closest*" and a corresponding lack of genuineness about the esteem with which the most serious things of the priests and metaphysicians are held. The problem with "this twofold hypocrisy" is that "the closest things" such as "eating, housing, clothing, social intercourse" are "not made the object of constant impartial and *general* reflection and reform." This lack of reflection on such things, however, puts us in a disgraceful state of "dependence and bondage" to "physicians, teachers and curers of the soul." The implication is that if we want to free ourselves from this bondage, we need to pay attention to the closest things (WS 5).

The need to pay attention to the closest things is echoed in the next aphorism. Nietzsche gives a number of examples of knowledge regarding the closest things: longer eggs taste best; thunderstorms are beneficial to the bowels; pleasant odors are even more pleasant in the cold; the moon affects our sense of taste. His point is that most people fail to pay attention to these facts (even if some seem a bit far-fetched), and this is lamentable because "*almost all the physical and psychical frailties* of the individual derive from this lack" of knowledge about the closest things (WS 6). This, of course, is a strong claim, but it can be understood as following from the reductionist program unpacked in *Human*. If there is nothing other than motions (HH 19), then this is true of ourselves, and if we are wholly part of nature, then the care of the body will be paramount for psychic health. Indeed, Nietzsche explains in the last half of the aphorism that the lack of knowledge about "*the smallest and most everyday things*" has transformed "the earth for so many into a 'vale of tears'." In other words, many have flocked to the evaluative pessimism of Schopenhauer and apocalyptic thought of Christianity because they have not paid enough attention to the closest things (WS 6).

In the eighth aphorism, Nietzsche explicitly links attention to the closest things to the kind of philosophy one produces. The aphorism begins with Nietzsche noticing the effect that night has on perception. The aphorism ends with Nietzsche speculating about the sort of philosophy that would emerge were darkness a permanent feature of our existence. His unsurprising conclusion is that it would surely render philosophy dark and gloomy (WS 8). Nietzsche makes a similar remark in a subsequent aphorism. In the "Origin of the Pessimists," he claims that food "makes all the difference to whether we look into the future hopefully or hollow-eyed." The present generation is so gloomy because they have inherited the hunger of previous generations. This is in contrast to the Greeks, whose thought and action were "bathed in fair sunlight" because they ate more simply and so better. Thus, the attitude one takes toward life, according to Nietzsche, depends on what one eats and so the closest things (WS 184).

The sixteenth aphorism is the most important section regarding Nietzsche's turn to the closest things in *The Wanderer* and his corresponding rejection of the interest he takes in the first and last things from *Human*. Specifically, Nietzsche counsels himself and his readers to adopt an attitude of indifference toward grand metaphysical questions and so first and last things: What is the purpose of man? What happens after death? How can we be reconciled with God? This is because, "just as the ant has no need of them to be a good ant," we can get on perfectly well in life without answering such questions. To think that we require such answers is to fall prey to Schopenhauer's "metaphysical need," but this metaphysical need is an after-effect of a long tradition of metaphysical thinking. To counter this after-effect, we need to remind ourselves of the historical development of ethical and religious sensations – as articulated in chapters 2 and 3 of *Human* – and adopt an attitude of skeptical indifference about knowledge and faith claims in these areas. In other words, we need to get over the metaphysical need and "again become *good neighbours to the closest things*" (WS 16).

One of the ways in which metaphysical concepts have shaped the way we think and feel about ourselves is through notions of guilt and punishment. This theme runs consistently throughout all stages of the free spirit works, and it is very much present in *The Wanderer*. Not only does Nietzsche mention guilt and punishment in adopting an attitude of indifference in the sixteenth aphorism, he discusses the concept in the surrounding aphorisms. Nietzsche first discusses the complex of ideas surrounding this theme in aphorism nine, where he explains how "freedom of the will" was an *invention* of the ruling classes (WS 9).

In the eleventh aphorism, Nietzsche implicitly appeals to the Heraclitean understanding of nature he unpacked in the first section of *Human* to attack the notion of free will. Nietzsche's claim is that our conception of free will requires the isolation of facts. The problem is that there are no isolated facts in reality. This is because "all our doing and knowing is not a succession of facts and empty spaces but a continuous flux." In other words, our "belief in freedom of will is incompatible precisely with the idea of a continuous, homogeneous, undivided, indivisible flowing." Instead, free will requires an "*atomism* in the domain of willing and knowing." Although Nietzsche identifies the cause of our false belief in atomism – it is the familiar claim from *Human* that words and concepts generate this "philosophical mythology" – he does not make explicit *why* free will is incompatible with "continuous flux" in the aphorism itself. The closest thing he offers to such an explanation is that praise and blame require us to isolate and then classify actions so that they can be evaluated, and since everything is a continuous flux, the isolation and classification of actions is impossible (WS 11).

In two subsequent aphorisms, Nietzsche explains how the false belief in free will has given humanity a false sense of its own significance. In particular, Nietzsche claims that humans take themselves to be the only free beings in a world of unfreedom, and so we take ourselves to be eternal miracle workers, the meaning of creation, "the solution to the cosmic riddle," and "the creature which calls *its* history *world* history." All of this is the vanity of vanities (WS 12). In the other aphorism, Nietzsche reflects on how the belief in the cosmic significance of humanity would be a source of laughter for the gods. Making points that echo the opening lines of "On Truth and Lies," Nietzsche highlights the way in which astronomers help us understand that "the drop of *life* in the universe is without significance for the total character of the tremendous ocean of becoming and passing away" (WS 13), and just as the ant might imagine itself as the goal and purpose of the forest, we imagine ourselves as the goal and purpose of the cosmos (WS 14).

In a later aphorism, Nietzsche connects his critique of free will to a belief in fatalism. However, he distinguishes this belief with what he calls "Mohammedan fatalism." The problem with Mohammedan fatalism is that it effectively pits man against fate. On this view, fate is an external force controlling human beings. Thus, the only question for the Mohammedan fatalist is whether to engage in futile resistance or simply resign oneself to fate. Nietzsche, however, contends that this is the wrong way to think about fate. Foreshadowing the final section of *Ecce Homo*, Nietzsche claims that "every man is himself a piece of fate," and so whatever we do, whether it be resistance, resignation, or acceptance, is itself a fulfillment of this very fate. Referring back to the Greek concept of fate that already played a central role in *Assorted Opinions*, Nietzsche writes: "You yourself, poor fearful man, are the implacable *moira* enthroned even above the gods that governs all that happens; [. . .] in you the whole future of the world of man is predetermined: it is of no use for you to shudder when you look upon yourself" (WS 61).

Nietzsche's critique of free will is intimately bound up with what he thinks is our false belief in sin and punishment, and the latter theme takes on increased significance as *The Wanderer* unfolds. In the twenty-third aphorism, Nietzsche attacks the idea that free will can justify the right to punish, and this line of attack continues in the next aphorism. There, Nietzsche claims that those who condemn an act often find the act more astonishing than the person who performed it. This, however, is due to a lack of knowledge about the conditions that led up to the act. If we had complete knowledge of all the circumstances that led up to a particular deed, every wrongdoer would be absolved of guilt. Knowledge of such circumstances would show that the wrongdoer *had* to act this way, and so punishing him would be punishing necessity. This, however, conflicts with the idea of fairness (WS 24).

In a subsequent aphorism, Nietzsche returns to a point he made in the eleventh aphorism about the way in which freedom of the will requires the isolation of events from each other to attack the notion of free will and punishment. Specifically, Nietzsche argues that wrongdoing often occurs within a context of habitual wrongdoing, and so if we look at the history of a particular offense, we must return to when the offender first engaged in the activity, and in so doing, we find that the initial cause of the activity were individuals like "parents, educators, society, etc." Thus, the punishment of a particular deed must involve the punishment of an entire society, as it would be capricious to limit blame to the criminal alone. To do so presupposes that we can isolate guilt from its larger web of associations (WS 28), and this is something we cannot do (WS 11).

Nietzsche's critique of punishment is tied to concerns about the formation of bad conscience. Although this theme is central to his later works, Nietzsche is already critical of the sting of conscience in *The Wanderer*: "the sting of conscience is, like a snake stinging a stone, a piece of stupidity" (WS 38). If we have a better understanding of ourselves and the nature of guilt and punishment, we will not feel the sting of punishment in the form of conscience. Nietzsche argues in another aphorism that our moral conscience is formed early on by repeated demands that lack any justification for them. We internalize these demands and punish ourselves when we fail to act accordingly. Thus, "the voice of God in the heart of man" is really "the voice of some men in man" (WS 52).

Nietzsche's critique of punishment and conscience is also part of a broader critique of morality in the first half of *The Wanderer*. In "Stages of Morality," Nietzsche explains how morality, as "a means of preserving the community," progresses from being inculcated through "*fear* and *hope*" to "commands of a god" and eventually to "the concept of unconditional duty with its 'thou shalt'." The aphorism concludes, somewhat cryptically, with a discussion of a morality based on inclination, taste, and insight that transcends the illusory motivations behind morality (WS 44). However, Nietzsche picks up the thread of discussing the "thou shalt" in a subsequent aphorism. There, he claims that the person thirsty for knowledge will put any prohibition "whose reason we do not understand" to the test. For instance, prohibitions found in the Decalogue cut against the free spirit's ethic of putting everything to the test. They are commands without reasons, and commands without reasons are no longer suitable to the free spirit (WS 48).

In an aphorism important for the dialectical reading, Nietzsche flirts with the idea that this same demand for reasons should be applied to the duty we have toward truth. Specifically, Nietzsche highlights the incompatibility between feeling a duty toward something and the recognition that everything has an origin. Feeling a duty toward something means making it "undiscussable" and so setting aside questions of origin. Nietzsche then wonders what would happen if we applied this thought to our duty toward the truth. However, he doesn't answer his own question. Instead, he points to the fact that it might cause the "thinker's machine" to breakdown, noting that a hypothetical adoption of the duty toward truth seems contradictory (WS 43). Thus, the reader is left wondering about the origins of the drive toward truth at this point in the free spirit project.

That Nietzsche still feels a commitment, even a duty, to pursue truth in *The Wanderer* is evidenced by his praise of Socrates at the beginning (WS 72) and the end (WS 86) of a series of aphorisms that deal with religious belief and provide Nietzsche's *first* presentation of the death of God in the free spirit works. In the first of these aphorisms, Nietzsche praises Socrates for his attitude toward the divine. Although Socrates presents himself – or is presented by Plato in the *Apology* – as a divine missionary, Nietzsche claims that Socrates nevertheless does this with a "touch of Attic irony and sense of humour." Indeed, Socrates' real mission is to put "*the god to the test in a hundred ways* to see *whether* he has told the truth." In this sense, Socrates occupies a middle ground between piety and the commitment to truth. Nietzsche, however, concludes the aphorism by remarking that the free spirit no longer needs to strike such a compromise (WS 72).

In the aphorisms that follow, Nietzsche puts god and religion to the test by discussing faith, prayer, the apostles, and the soul. He then returns to the theme of sin six aphorisms after the reference to Socrates in "Belief in the Sickness as Sickness." Specifically, Nietzsche claims that Christianity created sin by painting "the Devil on the world's wall." According to Nietzsche, Christianity then offered a cure for the sickness of sin. However, the belief in the cure is no longer viable, and so the real problem is that "*belief in the sickness*" continues to exist (WS 78).

The theme of sin is picked up again only three aphorisms later in "Secular Justice." There, Nietzsche begins by rearticulating the familiar idea from *Human* that "everyone is wholly unaccountable and innocent" and noting how this view would "lift secular justice off its hinges." Nietzsche's point, however, is that the founder of Christianity did largely the same thing by removing "judging and punishing from the world." He did so by recasting all injustice as "an offence against *God* and *not* as an offence against the world." So understood, he "regarded everyone as being in the greatest measure and in almost every respect a sinner." This is why no human could take on the role of judge. Instead, this task was left for himself (or God) alone (WS 81).

Two aphorisms later, Nietzsche challenges the therapeutic function of Jesus as savior. Nietzsche presents Jesus as a "physician of the soul devoted to that infamous and untutored faith in a universal medicine." However, Nietzsche also claims that Jesus suffered from some grave shortcomings and prejudices in his knowledge of the human soul. For instance, he compares Jesus to a dentist whose only cure is to pull teeth. The problem is that rooting out sensuality never completely succeeds. Instead, "it lives on in an uncanny vampire form and torments him in repulsive disguises" (WS 83).

The climax of this group of aphorisms is Nietzsche's first portrayal of the death of God in the free spirit works.[6] The title of the aphorism is "The Prisoners," and the purpose of the aphorism is to show how the free spirit responds to the death of God at this stage in the free spirit project. The scene is one of bondage, and the bondsman is the prison warder or God. The prison is a metaphor for the judgment that God threatens to pass on his prisoners, and this is what keeps them working each day.

The aphorism begins with the claim that the warder has gone missing, and the prisoners don't know how to react. The action progresses when one of the prisoners declares that even though the warder is gone, the warder is still watching the prisoners, and he will one day pass judgment on them. This same prisoner then declares that he is the son of the prison warder and that he can save the prisoners on one condition: that they believe he is the son of the prison warder. The prisoners respond with irony, doubt, and indifference. Whereas one prisoner doubts the claims outright, another prisoner wonders why it should matter that they believe he is the son of the prison warder. The aphorism concludes with another prisoner announcing that the prison warder has died. Nevertheless, the self-proclaimed son of the prison warder still insists that the other prisoners believe in him. The prisoners respond by shrugging their shoulders and walking away (WS 84). In other words, the aphorism presents a thoroughgoing indifference to the death of God and so metaphysical questions, and

---

[6] My reading of this aphorism has been shaped by both Brusotti (1997: Ch. 4.1) and Hödl (2009: Ch. 4.2.1.2).

this fits with *The Wanderer*'s emphasis on the "closest things" and contrasts sharply with Nietzsche's portrayal of the death of God in *The Gay Science*.

The set of aphorisms concludes with a second discussion of Socrates in an aphorism named after the Greek philosopher (WS 86). The aphorism contrasts Socrates with Jesus and presents Socrates as a better educator and physician of the soul. Thus, the aphorism begins with the claim that a time will come when the memorabilia of Socrates will supplant the Bible as a guide to morals and life.[7] Specifically, Socrates is hailed as the founding father of various philosophical modes of existence that are all "directed toward joy in living and in one's own self." In this sense, "Socrates excels the founder of Christianity in being able to be serious cheerfully and in possessing that *wisdom full of roguishness* that constitutes the finest state of the human soul" (WS 86).

Nietzsche's view of Socrates here is strikingly out of step with what he says about him elsewhere in his corpus. Rather than criticizing Socrates for killing tragedy in *The Birth of Tragedy* or subjecting him to *ad hominem* attacks in the style of Aristophanes in *Twilight of the Idols*, Nietzsche is embracing aspects of Socrates and the Socratic project. Just as we have reason to understand *Human* as an exercise in asceticism, we have reason to think of the free spirit project as working *within* the confines of the Socratic tradition, and as we will see, this will make Nietzsche's discussion of the death of Socrates at the end of the 1882 edition of *The Gay Science* all the more significant (GS 340).

That Nietzsche is working within the Socratic tradition in the free spirit project is evidenced by his appreciation for various sects of Hellenic philosophy in *The Wanderer*. The three schools of Hellenic philosophy that occur most frequently are the Cynics, the Skeptics, and the Epicureans (the Stoics will appear in *Daybreak*), and what is common to all three schools is that they, like the wanderer, exist outside of society and convention (*nomos*). The subtlest mention of Hellenic philosophers comes in the final dialogue between the wanderer and his shadow. The shadow asks the wanderer what he might do for him. The wanderer replies that the shadow can do nothing "except perhaps that which the philosophical 'dog' desired of the great Alexander: that you should move a little out of the sunlight" (WS: pp. 394–395). Talk of the philosophical dog and

---

[7] Here, Nietzsche has Xenophon's *Memorabilia* in mind. As Brusotti has noted (1997: 135–136), Nietzsche's interest in the *Memorabilia* can be found in the *Nachlass* from this time (KSA 8: 41[2]) and can be traced back to a letter to Carl von Gersdorff from May 1876 in which Nietzsche points to the Greek philosophers as models and explains that he is reading Xenophon's *Memorabilia* with great interest (KSB 5: 529).

Alexander moving out of the sunlight are clear references to the Cynic, Diogenes of Sinope, and what they suggest is that the free spirit, like Diogenes himself, is someone living outside of convention and society, only interested in the sunlight of knowledge. As Branham (2004: 174) has noted, this is confirmed by Nietzsche's reference to Cynicism in the later preface to the work (HH II P 5).[8]

Nietzsche also expresses an interest in ancient skepticism and one of its modern proponents, Montaigne. Indeed, Nietzsche mentions Montaigne, along with Horace, in the same aphorism in which he praises Socrates for being able to live cheerfully (WS 86). This is important because Berry (2004; 2010) has emphasized Nietzsche's connection to Montaigne, and she has, in turn, used this connection to argue that Nietzsche is a Pyrrhonian skeptic.[9] At the end of *Assorted Opinions*, Montaigne is listed as one of the great spirits in history with whom Nietzsche wishes to converse (AOM 408), and in another aphorism from *The Wanderer*, Nietzsche praises him and other French moralists for continuing a tradition of the Renaissance that harkens back to the ancient Greeks (WS 214).

Interestingly, Nietzsche refers to Pyrrho in the preceding aphorism. The aphorism presents a dialogue between Pyrrho, "the fanatic of mistrust," and an old man, and the dialogue moves through various stages of Pyrrhic doubt. It begins with Pyrrho insisting that others ought to mistrust him. It ends with Pyrrho embracing a philosophy of laughing and staying silent. In between, Nietzsche has Pyrrho advocate the mistrust of truth. Paradoxically, Nietzsche's Pyrrho argues that such mistrust is the only path to truth. This means – and Nietzsche seems to be re-emphasizing the tragic discord between truth and happiness – that we should not believe that truth will lead us to "fruit-trees and fair meadows." Instead, we will find "hard little grains of corn upon it." Although these grains of corn, if sown and buried, may lead to a harvest, Nietzsche's Pyrrho cannot promise this either (WS 213).

In the concluding aphorism of *Assorted Opinions*, Nietzsche pairs Montaigne with Epicurus, and some have argued that the philosophy of *The Wanderer* is decidedly Epicurean.[10] Evidence for this, however, is far from explicit. This is because his name is only mentioned on a few

---

[8] See also Jensen (2004) for a discussion of Nietzsche's relationship to Cynicism.
[9] To my knowledge, Berry (2011) never discusses the role that Montaigne and Pyrrho play in either *Assorted Opinions* or *The Wanderer*. In contrast, see Donnellan (1982: 18) and Vivarelli (1994).
[10] See Ansell-Pearson (2018) for his most recent statement of this position. Young (2010: 298) also emphasizes the Epicurean themes in both *The Wanderer* and *Daybreak*. However, he denies that there is a contradiction between Epicurean *ataraxia* and the passion of *Daybreak* (2010: 308).

occasions in the text. Nevertheless, in his letters from 1879, Nietzsche compares his lifestyle to that of Epicurus (KSB 5: 799), and he speaks of renewing the garden of Epicurus (KSB 5: 826; also see KSB 5: 899). Moreover, Nietzsche links Epicurus' philosophy to the central theme of *The Wanderer*, namely, establishing a better relation to the closest things and maintaining a corresponding attitude of indifference to the first and last things discussed at the beginning of *Human*.

This is most evident in the seventh aphorism in which Nietzsche praises Epicurus for adopting the attitude of indifference toward metaphysical speculations exhibited in "The Prisoners" (WS 84). Similar to his assessment of Socrates, Nietzsche points to the therapeutic function of Epicurus' philosophy and how it can help those tormented by fear of the gods. Specifically, Epicurus' philosophy offers two potential treatments. First, we can remind ourselves that if gods exist, they do not concern themselves with us. Second, we can admit that gods exist and that the hypothesis of their existence might explain certain phenomena, but remind ourselves that there are other possible explanations for these same phenomena. According to Nietzsche, both points should relieve us of any fear we might feel vis-à-vis a potential god and the threat of punishment in the afterlife (WS 7).

In other aphorisms, Nietzsche also speaks positively of Epicurus. In "The Philosopher of Sensual Pleasure," he endorses Epicurus' concern for closest things such as a good garden, good food, and a few good friends (WS 192), and in "Eternal Epicurus," Nietzsche claims that the spirit of Epicurus' philosophy is alive and well (WS 227). Finally, in "Et in Arcadia Ego," Nietzsche talks of inserting Hellenic heroes into Poussin's idyllic painting of Arcadia, thereby producing a heroic-idyllic effect, and the aphorism ends with the claim that Epicurus is the inventor of a heroic-idyllic mode of philosophizing (WS 295).

These are not the first mentions of Epicurus in the free spirit project. Not only does he appear among the eight interlocutors Nietzsche identifies throughout history (WS 408), Nietzsche refers to Epicurus in the second chapter of *Human*. There, Nietzsche claims that the natural sciences have not only aligned themselves point by point with Epicurus' philosophy, they have taken sides against Christianity in the same way (HH 68). Nevertheless, Brusotti (1997: 387n.12) has noted that Nietzsche's characterization of Epicurus' medicine against Christianity has close affiliations with ancient skepticism, and he claims that the concluding portion of the seventh aphorism in *The Wanderer*, in which Nietzsche emphasizes that things can always be otherwise, is more skeptical than Epicurean.

Perhaps the one feature that binds the Epicurean and skeptical philosophies together and links both of them to the project of *The Wanderer* is *ataraxia* or the understanding of happiness as a lack of disturbance, and this seems to be the psychic or spiritual ideal that Nietzsche erects in *The Wanderer*. That Nietzsche praises this condition is evidenced by the aphorism, "The Three Good Things." The three good things are tranquility [*Ruhe*], greatness [*Grösse*], and sunlight [*Sonnenlicht*] (WS 332).[11] As Brusotti (1997: 94n.147) explains, these three correspond to the "trinity of joy" – elevation [*Erhebung*], illumination [*Erhellung*], tranquility [*Ruhe*] – that Nietzsche identifies in the *Nachlass* fragment in which he introduces "the doctrine of the closest things" (KSA 8: 40[16]). In the published aphorism, Nietzsche speaks of elevating [*erhebend*], illuminating [*aufhellend*], and tranquil [*beruhigend*] thoughts, and he claims that everything "earthly" is transfigured in this "*trinity of joy*" (WS 332).

If the works of the free spirit were to stop here, Nietzsche's project would culminate in the belief that the Hellenic philosophers he derided for their superficiality in *The Birth of Tragedy* (BT 15) now provide the key to life affirmation, and so the free spirit project would represent a turn away from the Dionysian arts of his first work. This is because the goal of the free spirit at this stage is to calm the passions and live simply, detached from the conventions and commotion of society, and Nietzsche turns to Epicurus and other Hellenistic philosophers for techniques to transfigure – a key term from *The Birth of Tragedy* – all earthly things with the sunlight of knowledge. What is striking about the pose Nietzsche adopts here is not only that it ignores some of the more "terrifying" aspects of existence such as suffering and death that Nietzsche praises the tragic Greeks for confronting, but also that he will quickly leave behind the "tranquility" of *The Wanderer* for a passionate quest for knowledge in *Daybreak* and *The Gay Science*.

A close look at two aphorisms near the end of *The Wanderer* reveals the instability of the position Nietzsche sketches in the text and therefore suggests that the free spirit project is by no means complete. In "At Noon," the instability of transfiguring life through the sunlight of knowledge is subtly intimated. The imagery of noon is central to *Zarathustra*, and it is associated with the aforementioned trinity of joy. Here, Nietzsche speaks of a noontime of life and a long repose that can last for years. The light of knowledge shines down on the thinker and all things have fallen asleep, and in this sense, it represents a "death with open eyes." Everything is

---

[11] My translation.

enmeshed in a net of light, and the thinker experiences happiness in his gaze. This happiness, however, is "heavy." It is heavy because the wind eventually blows in the trees, and "life" pulls the thinker away from this transcendent state and brings along with it "desire, deception, forgetfulness, destruction, transience." The implicit idea is that although the life-transfiguring strategy sketched in *The Wanderer* may offer a better form of therapy than the sin-and-redemption scheme of Christianity, it cannot cope with – and even tries to ignore – the realities of desire, change, and death (WS 308).[12]

The other aphorism indicating that Nietzsche, at the time of writing *The Wanderer*, thinks that the free spirit project is unfinished and so requires further development is the final aphorism of the text, "The Golden Watchword." In the aphorism, Nietzsche refers to the chains that have kept us in bondage for so long. As he makes clear, these chains represent the "errors contained in the conceptions of morality, religion and metaphysics." Although these chains have made us gentler, more spiritual, more joyful, and more reflective than other animals, we now suffer "from being deprived for so long of clear air and free movement." The task of the free spirit is not only to remove these chains – a process that began in the opening sections of *Human* – but also to overcome the *sickness* that these chains have caused. In a line indicating that there is still more work for the free spirit to do, Nietzsche claims that "we stand now in the midst of our work of removing these chains, and we need to proceed with the greatest caution." Only an ennobled type of individual can cure herself of this sickness and "*be given freedom of spirit*." This noble individual is one who "lives for the sake of *joy*" and "no further goal" and who wishes "*peace*" and "*goodwill*" to "*all things closest*" (WS 350). In short, only a free spirit who has reached the ideal of *The Wanderer* can continue to remove the chains of unfreedom and overcome the sickness they have caused.

Concluding Remarks

Because we are coming to the end of the second section of the book, it would be helpful to take stock of where we are at and where we will be going. The reason for grouping Chapters 3 and 4 together into a single

---

[12] In contrast, Ansell-Pearson claims that, "it is a striking feature of Nietzsche's texts how little there is in them on the subject of death" (2017: 134). Although this may be true of *The Wanderer*, even a cursory reading of *The Birth of Tragedy* shows that this is not the case, and as Loeb (2010) has shown, the theme of death permeates *Zarathustra* and so Nietzsche's own tragedy.

section is because they treat three texts – *Human, Assorted Opinions*, and *The Wanderer* – that Nietzsche composes as a single unit. Although Cohen (2010) has argued that *Assorted Opinions* and *The Wanderer* should be understood as supplements to *Human*, the positions Nietzsche adopts in these works presuppose but then also move beyond *Human*. Both *Assorted Opinions* and *The Wanderer* presuppose the critique of metaphysics executed in *Human*, and in this sense, there is no backtracking on those positions. At the same time, they revise the views that the free spirit holds toward art, life, and metaphysics. In *Assorted Opinions*, we are presented with a poet who is a signpost to the future. In this sense, Nietzsche is relaxing his sharp rejection of art in *Human* and, instead, sketching an understanding of art compatible with his critique of metaphysics. In *The Wanderer*, Nietzsche moves away from the cheerfulness of the theoretical man sketched at the end of the first chapter of *Human* and moves toward an Epicurean attitude of indifference toward metaphysical speculations and a corresponding interest in the closest things. In this way, *The Wanderer* takes a renewed interest in life even though the commitment to truth from *Human* remains largely intact.

As I stressed in the opening chapters, the fact that Nietzsche wrote these two texts as continuations of *Human* shows that he composed these works not as mere collections of statements on various philosophical matters, but rather as an unfolding narrative that both builds upon but then transforms various stances taken at earlier stages in the narrative. I have also emphasized the way in which both *Human* and *The Wanderer* end with aphorisms that point beyond themselves and so indicate that the free spirit project has not come to its conclusion with the completion of either of these works. What this means is that at the time he composed these texts, Nietzsche was at the very least planning further installments of the free spirit works.

The concluding section of *The Wanderer* is therefore particularly important for my project. As noted in the opening chapters of this book, if there is any point in the free spirit project in which there is a potential break, it occurs between *The Wanderer* – and so the final appendix of *Human* – and *Daybreak*, a work clearly linked to both *The Gay Science* and *Zarathustra* by way of its compositional history and Nietzsche's retrospective claims. The concluding aphorism indicates, however, that Nietzsche does not, at the time he was composing the work, consider *The Wanderer* to be the final work of the free spirit project.

For this reason, it is unlikely that Nietzsche understood the positions he adopts in *The Wanderer* to be his final views at this time. Instead, it is more likely that Nietzsche, *qua* free spirit, has turned to Hellenistic philosophers such as Epicurus, Pyrrho, and Diogenes in this work to help the free spirit cope with existence without appealing to metaphysical principles. As I argue in subsequent chapters, Nietzsche will soon reveal the inadequacy of these therapies, and his continued search for more adequate ways of confronting suffering, death, and despair without appealing to metaphysical principles will drive the dialectic of the free spirit works toward the "*incipit tragoedia*" that ends the 1882 edition of *The Gay Science* and marks the beginning of Nietzsche's tragedy in *Thus Spoke Zarathustra*.

PART II

The Dragon-Slaying Lion

CHAPTER 5

Undermining the Prejudices of Morality
Daybreak

Thus far, we have traversed three works of the free spirit that Nietzsche both composed and later republished as a single unit. At the same time, we have witnessed the dialectical shifts that take place within those works. Whereas he focuses on the first and last things of metaphysics and proceeds to undermine the metaphysical basis for various beliefs about morality, religion, and art in the opening chapters of *Human*, Nietzsche turns his attention to the closest things such as food, clothing, and shelter and adopts an Epicurean attitude of indifference toward metaphysical questions in *The Wanderer*. Along with this shift in attention, there is a corresponding shift in the therapeutic strategy that the free spirit employs to avoid the threat of despair identified at the end of the first chapter of *Human*. Whereas the free spirit takes on the role of the contemplative who enjoys discovering and reflecting on deep truths about the universe in *Human*, the free spirit turns toward a life of spiritual peace or *ataraxia* outside the customs of society in *The Wanderer*.

Nietzsche thinks of *Daybreak* as a "decisive book" (KSB 6: 102) that begins his "campaign against morality" and so a *"revaluation of all values"* (EH "Books" D:1).[1] Specifically, Nietzsche claims that with *Daybreak* he "first took up the fight against morality that would unself man" (EH "Books" D:2). In this sense, *Daybreak* moves beyond the project of *Human* of merely "unlearning" old values and moves toward a project of creating new ones.[2] Nietzsche started work on the book just after the publication of *The Wanderer* in the winter of 1880, and *Daybreak* was eventually published in July of 1881. He wrote a number of initial notes for the work in Venice with Köselitz under the title of *L'Ombra di Venezia*

---

[1] This point is often made by commentators (e.g., Clark and Leiter (1997: viii) and Bamford (2012: 139)). See Owen (2003) for a reading of how *Daybreak* relates to Nietzsche's later revaluation of values.

[2] As Brusotti (1997: 56) notes, Nietzsche speaks of the task of a "revision of all evaluations [*Revision aller Werthschätzungen*]" in an 1880 note (KSA 9: 3[158]).

(KSA 9: 3[Title]), and he completed the work in Genoa in the winter of 1880–1881. The proposed title of the work at this time was "The Plough-share: Thoughts on the Prejudices of Morality" (KSA 9: 9[Title]).[3] How-ever, upon the suggestion of Köselitz, Nietzsche then changed the title to *Daybreak: Thoughts on the Prejudices of Morality* (KSB 6: 80) and added a corresponding epigraph from the *Rig Veda*: "There are so many days that have not yet broken."

Despite the decisive nature of the text, *Daybreak* can be understood as a further step in the free spirit progression that builds upon the insights of the previous works and yet develops a new conception of the free spirit that resolves some of the difficulties inherent in previous conceptions. In dialectical fashion, *Daybreak* builds on the previous ideas of the free spirit because the critique of morality that Nietzsche initiates in the work presupposes the insight from *Human* that morality has no metaphysical basis. In contrast to his attack on our beliefs in a metaphysical world in *Human*, *Daybreak* now takes aim at the habitual and customary evalu-ations that persist in our feelings, values, and judgments after the rational basis for these evaluations has been undermined. In other words, whereas *Human* purges the free spirit of the false belief in God, *Daybreak* begins to eliminate the "shadow" of God by attacking what are now "prejudices of morality" that remain in our collective psyches.

As both the end of *The Wanderer* and the whole of *Daybreak* make clear, Nietzsche believes that morality has made the world appear so dark and gloomy and much of humanity sick. This, of course, recalls the basic concern with morality that Nietzsche articulated as early as *The Birth of Tragedy*. In agreement with Schopenhauer, Nietzsche believes that moral-ity is aligned with a life- and world-denying response (evaluative pessimism) to the tragic truths that a figure like Silenus articulates (factual pessimism). Because Nietzsche rejects the life-denying response to these tragic truths, he must attack the morality that leads us to condemn the world. At the same time, this liberation from morality – a morality that subordinates the individual to the community and even demands a form of selflessness[4] – opens up the possibility for a life-affirming response that Nietzsche associates with the education, cultivation, and aestheticization of the very self that morality enjoins us to deny.[5]

---

[3] As Franco (2011: 57) remarks, the "ploughshare" appears twice in *Daybreak* (D 146 and 202).
[4] See Janaway (2007: Ch. 4) for an extended treatment of Nietzsche's later critique of selflessness.
[5] Aesthetic self-shaping is a central theme in Brusotti (1997). Franco (2011: Ch. 2) discusses it at length, and both Bamford (2012; 2015) and Ansell-Pearson (2011a) emphasize self-cultivation in *Daybreak*.

Applied to the free spirit works, *Daybreak* moves the free spirit beyond the simple, life-preserving strategy of *The Wanderer* in response to the Silenus-like truths articulated in *Human* toward the robust aestheticism of *The Gay Science,* and Nietzsche advances this movement in *Daybreak* by taking aim at a morality that places constraints on or even opposes this very project. Indeed, Nietzsche is very concerned that the moral evaluations that persist even after the death of God in *The Wanderer* will eventually turn humanity into what he repeatedly calls "sand" (D 174, D 429; KSA 9: 6[163], 8[16], 8[47], and 8[103]), and this fear of what can be associated with the "last man" of *Zarathustra* or even what Nietzsche later calls nihilism drives the critique of moral prejudices in *Daybreak.*

Such a reading of *Daybreak* explains why a book that bears the subtitle, "Thoughts on the Prejudices of Morality," also amounts to a "philosophy of the morning" (HH 638) and so a "daybreak." As Nietzsche remarks in *Ecce Homo,* the "liberation from all moral values" that have hitherto darkened existence makes for a "Yes-saying book" that "pours its light, its love, its tenderness upon ever so many wicked things; it gives back to them their 'soul,' a good conscience, the lofty right and privilege of existence" (EH "Books" D:1). In this sense, *Daybreak* both continues the project of *The Wanderer* of curing the "sickness" that the chains of moral beliefs have caused (WS 350) and prepares the way for the "*convalescence*" and the "gratitude of a convalescent" that runs throughout *The Gay Science* (GS P 1).

Daybreak is also the work in which Nietzsche moves from the affect-free condition of the good temperament in *Human* (HH 34) and the Epicurean *ataraxia* or peace of soul that characterizes *The Wanderer* (WS 332) to a passionate quest for knowledge. Based on an analysis of Nietzsche's *Nachlass* from this time, Brusotti (1997: 34) has shown how this passionate condition emerges from Nietzsche's view, adopted from J. J. Baumann's *Handbuch der Moral,* that life is spontaneous and purposeless activity (see KSA 9: 1[70]). It is this continuous movement of the soul – a point implicit in the Heracliteanism of *Human* – that makes the goal of tranquility impossible, and it sets the stage for the emergence of a "Passio nova" or a new passion in *Daybreak.* As Nietzsche's notes reveal, this is a passion for honesty (KSA 9: 6[461]), and this passion for honesty is a precursor to the passion for knowledge (KSA 9: 7[171]). This latter concept first appears in the final book of *Daybreak* (D 429 and 482) and reappears at crucial moments in *The Gay Science* (GS 3, 107, and 123). Indeed, this passionate quest for knowledge drives the free spirit toward the sacrilege of killing God in *The Gay Science* and ultimately prepares the way for "going under" in the tragedy of *Zarathustra* (KSA 9: 7[302]).

The willingness of the free spirit to "perish of this passion for know-ledge" (D 429) is something Nietzsche associates with the hero, and it is the heroic quality of this phase of the free spirit, one that continues into *The Gay Science*, that connects it to the second metamorphoses of Zar-athustra's speech, "On the Three Metamorphoses." The second metamor-phosis describes a lion-like spirit that slays the dragon of all created values. The lion is traditionally a symbol for courage and pride, and the free spirit of *Daybreak* and *The Gay Science* embodies these traits. Not only does Nietzsche claim in a note that pride will make us heroes (KSA 9: 7[220]), a notebook from this time bears the title, "Religion of Courage" (KSA 9: 8 [1]). Moreover, Nietzsche refers to Tristan in his discussion of the pas-sionate hero willing to perish of a raging ambition (D 240), and Tristan is known as a dragon-slayer. Thus, there are reasons to think that the passionate, courageous, and heroic features Nietzsche attributes to the free spirit at the end of *Daybreak* lay the groundwork for slaying the dragon of the "thou shalt" and so the elimination of God's shadow in *The Gay Science*.

On a strict reading and application of the three metamorphoses to the free spirit works, Nietzsche's transformation into the artistic child is supposed to occur after the second stage of the lion is complete. That is, Nietzsche will be free to pursue an aesthetic affirmation of life once the shadow of God has been eliminated in *The Gay Science*. However, it is better to understand these changes as a gradual process in which the more Nietzsche's critique of morality advances, the more his interest in and discussion of art and aesthetics increases. As Brusotti (1997: Ch.1.7) has argued, even Nietzsche's turn to the closest things in *The Wanderer* constitutes a type of aesthetic self-formation, and readers of *Daybreak* have pointed to the increasing role that aesthetic themes play as the text unfolds.[6]

So understood, *Daybreak* is a transitional work in the free spirit project. Whereas it emerges from the truth-seeking program initiated in *Human* and continued in *The Wanderer*, the book closes with an inconclusive "Or" (D 585) and so points to the continuation of the narrative in *The Gay Science*. Indeed, it is the transitional character of *Daybreak* – similar to the transitional character of *Assorted Opinions* and *The Wanderer* – that may

---

[6] See Bamford (2012).

explain its relative neglect in the secondary literature.[7] Although one can find a number of insights scattered throughout the work that have value in their own right, *Daybreak*, like *Assorted Opinions* and *The Wanderer*, is really a work that further develops a storyline first introduced in *Human* and only reaches its climax in *The Gay Science*. So understood, trying to read *Daybreak* as a standalone text is akin to reading the second book of *Zarathustra* without any knowledge of its connection to the other books.

Nevertheless, Nietzsche does think of *Daybreak* as a whole, and he emphasizes this in his letters from this time. Thus, he writes to Köselitz in the summer of 1881 that he should try to make sense of the book as a whole and to see if it communicates "a passionate condition" (KSA 6: 119). In another letter to his sister from this time, he encourages her to read between the lines, especially the fifth chapter, to see if she can make sense of the work as an expression of what her brother most wants and needs (KSB 6: 131). Thus, Julian Young is right to claim that "there is a structure" to *Daybreak*, "but one has to *work* to find it" (2010: 297). In what follows, I will do my best to make sense of the work as a whole and do so in relation to the unfolding dialectic in the free spirit works.

Chapter I: Eliminating the Shadows of God

Nietzsche begins *Daybreak* with a claim that repeats the idea embedded within the first aphorism of *Human*: Rationality comes from its opposite, irrationality, and over time, the irrational origins are hidden or sublated in the emergence of rationality (D 1). Although not explicit, the claim suggests the task of *Daybreak*: To reveal the irrational origins of a seemingly rational morality and to show that our moral beliefs are mere prejudices. The very next aphorism picks up on the theme of prejudice announced in the subtitle of the book. There, Nietzsche argues that even though the learned correctly claim that all ages believed they discovered the nature of good and evil, they still fail to see that they suffer from the same lack of self-knowledge that plagued previous generations (D 2).

The third aphorism also refers to a theme central to *Human*: our tendency to anthropomorphize reality. Here, however, Nietzsche's critique is focused on moral prejudices. Just as humans have falsely projected gender onto reality through language, we have falsely "laid an *ethical significance* on the world's back." According to Nietzsche, "one day this

---

[7] Although the situation has improved, Clark and Leiter (1997: vii) highlight this point in their introduction to the text. More recently, Ansell-Pearson (2011b: 365) has echoed this.

will have as much value, and no more, as the belief in the masculinity or femininity of the sun has today" (D 3). In the subsequent aphorism, Nietzsche implies that the denial of the ethical significance of reality derives from a sense of justice. This is important because, as Brusotti (1997: 104) shows, our sense of justice and honesty (KSA 9: 6[67]) forces us to see the world as it really is (KSA 9: 3[172]), and so justice and honesty force us to "rid the world of much *false* grandeur" (D 4). Insofar as ridding the world of its false grandeur includes ridding the world of moral prejudices, Nietzsche's critique of morality derives from his commitment to justice and honesty and so morality. So understood, *Daybreak* is initiating the *Selbstaufhebung* of morality (D P 4), a process by which morality – justice and honesty – eliminates the moral or ethical significance of the world.

The fifth aphorism "Be Grateful!" also follows upon and likely refers to the previous accomplishments of the free spirit. Although he explicitly speaks of "the greatest accomplishment of past mankind," Nietzsche's claim that we no longer live in fear of gods implicitly points to the Epicureanism of *The Wanderer* and the scientific attitude adopted in *Human* (D 5). Nietzsche intimates his continued commitment to the scientific attitude in the next two aphorisms and so emphasizes the continuity between *Human* and *Daybreak*. In the first, he contrasts science with the art of the conjurer, noting that unlike the latter, science often compels us to see a complicated causal mechanism where we might only think there is a simple one (D 6). In the second, Nietzsche claims that science gives us a different sense of space, both in terms of the solar system and of the difference between the highest happiness and the deepest unhappiness (D 7).

In "Towards the Re-education of the Human Race," we again see that Nietzsche's critique of moral prejudices in *Daybreak* is continuous with his other writings. Nietzsche claims that there is no more noxious weed than a concept of punishment that makes "our very existence" a punishment, and so people of good will must root out this weed and restore "innocence" to the "purely chance character of events" (D 13). The concepts of cosmic punishment and innocence can be traced back to Nietzsche's respective accounts of the philosophies of Anaximander and Heraclitus in the central chapters of *Philosophy in the Tragic Age* and point forward to the "innocence of becoming" in *Twilight of the Idols* (TI "Errors" 8). In *Daybreak* and the other free spirit works, Nietzsche is not just speaking about the liberation of becoming from the shadow of God. Instead, he is engaged in this process of liberation, and it is the overcoming of moral prejudices that will eliminate punishment from our understanding of the world.

Nietzsche's critique of moral prejudices begins in the ninth aphorism, "Concept of Morality of Customs." As the title suggests, Nietzsche is no longer concerned with the metaphysical basis of morality. The aphorism starts from the fact – established in *Human* – that morality lacks any metaphysical basis. Instead, Nietzsche focuses on the way in which morality is grounded in custom or "the *traditional* way of behaving and evaluating," and he claims that tradition is a necessary condition for morality: "morality is nothing other (and therefore *no more!*) than obedience to customs," and therefore "in things in which no tradition commands there is no morality." Tradition is understood as a commanding authority that stands over the individual. It is, to use the language of Zarathustra's speech on the three metamorphoses, a simple "thou shalt," and what the morality of custom commands is the sacrifice of the individual for the sake of the community (D 9).

This aphorism reveals a deep tension between the morality of custom and the free spirit's quest for personal freedom and the related task of educating oneself as an individual (D 19). According to Nietzsche, the morality of custom sees everything, including education, as demanding the sacrifice of the individual (D 9). Reminiscent of the argument from "On Truth and Lies," Nietzsche claims that civilization needs customs or so-called "truths" by which to live, and so the community believes that "any custom is better than no custom" (D 16). Individuals who break customs arouse dread, and so such individuals are dubbed evil and dangerous. In this way, "originality of every kind has acquired a bad conscience" (D 10). According to Nietzsche, anyone who wanted to break with the dominant customs of a community had to become a "lawgiver and medicine man and a kind of demi-god: that is to say, he had to *make customs*" (D 9). In a passage that foreshadows the madman in *The Gay Science* and possibly his own fate, Nietzsche claims that madness can prepare the way for a new idea that conflicts with inherited customs: "all superior men who were irresistibly drawn to throw off the yoke of any kind of morality and to frame new laws had, *if they were not actually mad*, no alternative but to make themselves pretend to be mad" (D 14).

In other aphorisms, Nietzsche returns to the irrational basis for morality by exploring our moral feelings and valuations. This is important because Nietzsche knows that the force of custom operates at both cognitive and affective levels and that delusional and nonsensical beliefs can often nourish "*higher feelings*" that exalt mankind. Nietzsche, however, presents the free spirit as a "man of science" who must be suspicious of such higher feelings even though the ultimate goal is their purification rather than their elimination (D 33). Nietzsche explains in the next two aphorisms that we cannot trust our feelings (D 35). Because feelings are saturated with value judgments we form as children by observing our parents (D 34), obeying our feelings in these matters amounts to a blind obedience to the morality of custom (D 35).

In his analysis of moral judgments, Nietzsche often speaks of passion, drives, and the feeling of power, and this sort of analysis not only marks a notable advance over the analysis provided in *Human*, it also foreshadows the psychology of the will to power that becomes pervasive in the later works. In "The Morality of Voluntary Suffering," Nietzsche opposes pity to cruelty and analyzes the latter in terms of enjoying "the highest gratification of the feeling of power" (D 18). A few aphorisms later, he claims that the history of culture can be analyzed in terms of the subtle evolution of the feeling of power (D 23). In "The Value of Belief in Suprahuman Passions" – an aphorism that seems to foreshadow the *Uebermensch* in *Zarathustra* – Nietzsche explains how potentially shameful passions can be enhanced and even elevate humans to a suprahuman level through institutions, such as marriage, that sanctify them (D 27). In "Drives Transformed by Moral Judgments," Nietzsche introduces the important language of drives into his analysis,[8] and he argues that the praise or blame attached to a custom can transform a drive from the painful feeling of cowardice into the pleasant feeling of humility. According to Nietzsche, this means that no inherent good or evil can be attached to any particular drive. Instead, such evaluations depend on the customs and so the conditions under which a drive expresses itself (D 38).

In an aphorism that seemingly divides the first chapter into two parts, Nietzsche begins to focus on suffering and sickness, themes essential to the account of the free spirit's transformations in the 1886–1887 prefaces to these works. The title of the aphorism is "Where Are the New Physicians of the Soul?" (D 52), and Nietzsche explains how the comforts for our psychic sickness "have bestowed upon life that fundamental character of suffering it is now believed to possess." Nietzsche argues that the cures offered thus far, for example, anesthetization and intoxication, have not been cures at all. Instead, they have made us worse, and we now need a physician capable of curing us of the damage these so-called cures have

[8] Katsafanas (2016: Ch. 4) has made this a centerpiece of his interpretation of Nietzsche's moral psychology.

done. As Brusotti (1997: 231n.41) has argued, Nietzsche counts himself among these new doctors of the soul, and as a number of commentators have noted, *Daybreak*, like *The Wanderer* before it, has this therapeutic function.[9]

The aphorism effectively divides the first book in half because Nietzsche dedicates many of the remaining aphorisms to launching a critique of Christianity, and so it initiates his cure of the so-called cure that has made the sick even sicker. The idea is that Christianity is a pseudo-cure for suffering that has made the sickness worse, and in the next aphorism, Nietzsche notes the "superfluous cruelty and vivisection" that "have proceeded from those religions which invented sin" (D 53). He also contrasts the Christian system of comfort with that of the ancient philosophers by noting the way in which Christianity wanted to restore, rather than calm, the affects (D 58). Even though it freed "men from the burden of the demands of morality," the comfort Christianity offered to "the exhausted and despairing" was nevertheless based on error (D 59).

Nietzsche's subterranean (D P 1) analysis continues in the next aphorism in which he explains the psychological dynamics of Christianity in terms of the feelings of power and surrender (D 60), and this line of thought is continued five aphorisms later in "Brahminism and Christianity." Nietzsche argues that both operate with the feeling of power, but there are two different types of this feeling. Whereas Brahmanism arouses the feeling of power through self-control, Christianity produces the feeling of power through the feeling of surrender in those who have no experience controlling themselves (D 65).

The feeling of power also plays an important role in Nietzsche's account of "The First Christian." The first Christian is Paul, and Nietzsche claims that the Bible really tells the story of Paul's confrontation with the Jewish law. Possessed by an extravagant lust for power, Paul was continually on watch for violators of the law. However, he soon discovered that he could not fulfill the law, and so, like Luther, he set out to destroy it. Christ provided him with a way to do this. According to Nietzsche, this idea took Paul to intoxicating heights, and the "intractable lust for power" revealed itself "as an anticipatory reveling in *divine* glories" and a mystical union with Christ (D 68).

According to Nietzsche, Christianity heightens the intensity of the feeling that the believer experiences by first creating the depths of despair. One way it does this is by making the passion so central to the later stages

---

[9] Ure (2008: Ch. 4) makes this a central theme of his reading of the free spirit.

of *Daybreak* into a diabolical force within the soul (D 76). It also does this by elevating the standard of virtue so high that no one can achieve it. This creates a feeling of *despair* – Nietzsche claims that Pascal tried to bring everyone to despair (D 64) – and Christianity promises to overcome such despair through a "breakthrough of grace" and so a "moral miracle." This "moral miracle" is taken to be God at work within the human soul, and it is understood as a rebirth of the Christian believer. Thus, Christianity first makes us sick by convincing us of our sinful natures and then provides a pseudo-cure by elevating us above sin through God's grace (D 87).

In the final aphorisms of the chapter, Nietzsche articulates the free spirit's rejection of Christianity in language that foreshadows the death of God in *The Gay Science*. In "Historical Refutation as the Definitive Refutation," Nietzsche explains his new strategy for refuting the existence of God. Rather than proving the non-existence of God or knocking down all available proofs for God's existence, the way for atheists to "make a clean sweep" is to show how the belief in God arose and "acquired its weight and importance." Although many will be concerned that he is committing the genetic fallacy here, Nietzsche nevertheless claims that this sort of refutation is a "definitive refutation" (D 95).

In "At the Deathbed of Christianity," Nietzsche also bids farewell to any hold Christianity might have on the free spirit. He claims that even though "really active people are now inwardly without Christianity," Christianity has "crossed over into a gentle *moralism*" in the form of "benevolence and decency of disposition" for most people. However, Nietzsche argues – presumably because it eliminates the entire drama of sin and redemption central to the theology of Pascal and Paul – that this understanding amounts to "the *euthanasia* of Christianity" (D 92), and this is why Christianity is on its deathbed.

Nietzsche makes subtle references throughout the chapter to alternative ways of combating the despair Christianity claims to cure. Some of these are references to familiar ideas from previous free spirit works. Thus, Nietzsche claims that science has relieved us of our fear of death and hell, and in this way "Epicurus triumphs anew!" (D 72). Similarly, Nietzsche points to the ancient Greek notion of innocent misfortune that resisted transforming everything into punishment (D 78). Other claims, however, are new and anticipate the views Nietzsche adopts in subsequent works. In one aphorism, Nietzsche claims that rather than joining Pascal in hating the self only to have it loved by God, we should go a step further by loving ourselves as an act of clemency. In this way, we will no longer need God because the drama of fall and redemption can be played out in ourselves (D 79).

The theme of self-redemption is echoed in the final aphorism of the chapter. There, Nietzsche refers to the Buddha as "the teacher of the *religion of self-redemption*," and he places the idea of "self-redemption" at a stage of culture that Europe has yet to reach – even though he knows that Schopenhauer advocated this kind of self-redemption. This stage of culture will come when "all the observances and customs upon which the power of the gods and of the priests and redeemers depends will have been abolished" (D 96). In short, Nietzsche suggests that Europe will reach this stage through the critique he is executing in the free spirit works.

It would, however, be a mistake to think that Nietzsche's call for a religion of self-redemption is, at the same time, an endorsement of Buddhism. Nietzsche associates Buddhism with Schopenhauer's ethics of life denial and so nihilism both in his early (BT 7) and later works (GM P 5). Instead, Nietzsche praises the Buddha for encouraging individuals to pursue enlightenment and take upon themselves the project of self-redemption, and it is a mark of high culture because this form of redemption does not rely on some metaphysical solution to the problem of suffering. Nevertheless, we know from *The Birth of Tragedy* that Nietzsche had already differentiated his project from the quasi-Buddhism of Schopenhauer by offering an alternative form of self-redemption. As we learn in *The Gay Science*, the one thing needful is that we learn to love ourselves by becoming poets of our lives (GS 299). Thus, it is through art and the aesthetic formation of the self, not Buddhism, that we can affirm suffering and so redeem life, and this aesthetic form of self-redemption takes on increasing prominence in the free spirit works as Nietzsche unpacks his critique of the prejudices of morality.

Chapter II: Feeling Differently

The second chapter of *Daybreak* begins with a summary statement of what has been accomplished in the first: subjection to morality is anything but moral because morality emerges from non-moral drives like vanity, servility, and despair (D 97). In the third aphorism, Nietzsche then pivots to the central topic of the second chapter. The problem is that although the free spirit no longer believes in a number of presumably moral teachings and so asserts that morality is founded on error, the feelings of the free spirit still compel her to draw false conclusions (D 99). Thus, the free spirit must not only learn to *"think differently"* but also to *"feel differently"* (D 103), and this is the project Nietzsche undertakes in chapter 2 of *Daybreak* and beyond. Nietzsche claims that when this project is complete, "wise and noble men" will no longer believe in "the moral significance of existence" just as such wise individuals no longer believe in the music of the cosmos (D 100).

In "The Oldest Moral Judgments," Nietzsche appeals to a principle that links morality to individual valuations and becomes more prominent as his works unfold. Specifically, he introduces the idea that the origin of morality can be traced back to personal valuations: whatever harms me is evil; whatever benefits me is good. Although he initially presents this discovery as revealing the *"pudenda origo"* of morality, the aphorism concludes by noting that there might be a principle underlying this claim that is "the most immodest of all secret thoughts: that because good and evil are measured according to our reactions, we ourselves must constitute the principle of the good?" (D 102).

Even though the aphorism ends with a question mark, such reflections foreshadow some of Nietzsche's later views in which certain individuals are presented as standards of value (BGE 260), and so Nietzsche is suggesting here that we are going to replace God as the measure of good and bad. In *Daybreak*, the shift from an objective standard of value to a subjective standard of value is developed two aphorisms later in "Our Evaluations [*Werthschätzungen*]." Nietzsche argues that all action can be traced back to values, and he distinguishes between two types of values: original and adopted. In this aphorism, Nietzsche notes that most of our values are adopted, and fear and cowardice compel us to remain committed to values that are not genuinely our own. We adopt these values early in childhood, and most of us never think to revise these values and so return to ourselves as we mature (D 104). In short, most of us fail to educate ourselves in the way that Nietzsche outlines in *Schopenhauer as Educator* and is now doing in the free spirit works.

This theme continues in the next aphorism, "Pseudo-Egoism." The problem Nietzsche discusses here is that "the great majority [. . .] do nothing for their ego their whole life long." Most people have a phantom ego that exists in the opinions of others. It is this ego, that is, how we appear in the eyes of others, that we care for, and this is why we remain "unknown" to ourselves. In contrast, Nietzsche implies that we ought to know our real selves and so attend to our genuine wants and needs. In so doing, we might become individuals capable of setting up a real ego that opposes and ultimately vanquishes the pseudo ego (D 105). In short, we need to become the type of individuals Nietzsche celebrates in *Schopenhauer as Educator*.

In subsequent aphorisms of *Daybreak*, we get hints of who these sorts of individuals might be. After highlighting the tension between the needs of the individual and the demands of morality (D 106), Nietzsche turns to a critique of the moral law. The problem, according to Nietzsche, is that there is no common or universal goal – a point already stated in *Human* (HH 33) – and so it would be irrational to *impose* a moral law, from above, upon the likes and dislikes of humans. This, however, ignores the possibility that humans should actually want "to *impose* this law" upon themselves (D 108). Although not explicit or even fully articulated, the aphorism is clearly reminiscent of the ideas of *Schopenhauer as Educator* and foreshadows the project of becoming oneself through self-legislation expressed in the fourth chapter of *The Gay Science* (GS 335).

The theme of self-legislation is continued in the next aphorism in which Nietzsche analyzes different ways of preserving self-mastery through moderation. Although most of the aphorism discusses different ways in which one can combat "the vehemence of a drive," the aphorism is important for two reasons. First, Nietzsche begins to deconstruct the ego as a simple, unified entity by analyzing it in terms of a multiplicity of drives.[10] Second, Nietzsche makes a claim that rejects a tradition dating back to Plato's *Republic* IV and Aristotle's *Nicomachean Ethics* in which reason or the intellect is the means by which one combats desires, emotions, and drives. In contrast, Nietzsche argues that it is another drive that combats a drive (D 109), and this claim paves the way for his later analysis of the subject entirely in terms of non-rational drives, instincts, and affects (GS 333; BGE 12). As noted above, this marks a key advance over the position stated in *Human*, and it goes hand in hand with Nietzsche's move away from a contemplative pose in which the free spirit hovers above the world she contemplates (HH 34).

The analysis of self-mastery in terms of drives also lays the groundwork for explaining the life of the ascetic in terms of a lust for power – a strategy Nietzsche used to explain the saint in *Human* (HH 142) and pursues in the final essay of the *Genealogy*. Nietzsche begins with the claim that the striving for distinction is designed to make others suffer

---

[10] Franco (2011: 69ff.) makes this a central theme of his interpretation of chapter 2.

from us, and this drive reaches its apex in the ascetic and the martyr. This is because the ascetic rejoices in the pleasure he takes in watching himself (as spectator) suffer (as embodied human being), and so he rejoices at the "*sight of* [his own] *torment*" because it gives him the liveliest feeling of power (D 113).

Two aphorisms later, Nietzsche continues to employ the language of drives. On the one hand, he claims that these drives outstrip the realm of linguistic expression and conscious observation. On the other hand, these drives "weave the web of our character and our destiny." Because of this, we often "*misunderstand* ourselves" (D 116), and Nietzsche emphasizes our lack of self-knowledge in subsequent aphorisms. Thus, Nietzsche writes: "that which [. . .] men have found so hard to understand is their ignorance of themselves" (D 116), and "however far a man may go in self-knowledge, nothing however can be more incomplete than his image of the totality of *drives* which constitute his being" (D 119). Nevertheless, Nietzsche notes that "*our opinion of ourself,*" one that is formed through inadequate and even erroneous observation, is "a fellow worker in the construction of our character and our destiny" (D 115).

In subsequent aphorisms, Nietzsche continues to address the themes of destiny and the concepts opposed to destiny: purpose and free will. Having rejected the contrast typically drawn between dreams and reality (D 119), Nietzsche argues that just as Oedipus – a central figure in *The Birth of Tragedy* – did not feel responsible for his dreams, we are "just as little" responsible "for our waking life" (D 128). Two aphorisms later, Nietzsche again refers to the ancient Greeks and their concept of *moira*, a notion central to both *Assorted Opinions* and *The Wanderer*. *Moira* is what the Greeks called the "realm of the incalculable and of sublime eternal narrow-mindedness" (D 130). This vision of reality is opposed to the providential Christian God who guides the world to "bring all to glory," and Nietzsche claims that we are returning to the ancient Greek view that there may be neither will nor purposes, but only the "iron hands of necessity which shake the dice-box of chance" and "play their game for an infinite length of time" (D 130). This view is already in Nietzsche's early portrayal of Heraclitus' philosophy (PTAG 7), and it foreshadows Nietzsche's characterization of the cosmos – itself a forerunner to the eternal recurrence (GS 341) – in the third chapter of *The Gay Science* (GS 109).

In the next aphorism, Nietzsche again appeals to the ancient Greeks, and although one might expect him to turn to tragedy given his previous discussion of *moira*, he instead turns to another sect of ancient philosophers who play a prominent role at this stage of the free spirit project: the Stoics.[11] The first reference to the Stoics is by way of Nietzsche's discussion of Epictetus (D 131),[12] and the second aphorism explicitly refers to the Stoics as a group (D 139). In both aphorisms, Nietzsche contrasts the Stoic attempt to make themselves immune to pain and suffering with the view championed by the likes of Schopenhauer that makes concern for others the essence of morality (D 131).

It is therefore no surprise that between these two aphorisms Nietzsche issues a series of critical reflections on pity, the centerpiece of Schopenhauer's life-denying morality. Nietzsche not only mentions Schopenhauer's name in the aphorism immediately following the discussion of Epictetus, he also adopts Schopenhauer's view that the morality of sympathy is an after-effect of Christianity. In "The Echo of Christianity in Morality," Nietzsche argues that once the concern for "eternal *personal* salvation" subsided, the "love of one's neighbor" took center stage in modern moral theory. Nietzsche claims that the more one distanced oneself from Christian dogma, "the more one sought as it were a *justification* of this liberation in a cult of philanthropy." In this way, modern moralists like Schopenhauer and John Stuart Mill have tried to "outchristian Christianity" (D 132).

Nietzsche's reflections on the roughly synonymous terms of pity, neighbor love, and altruism continue through the end of the chapter, and similar to the concluding aphorisms of each of the chapters of *Human*, the final aphorism of the second chapter summarizes the conclusions of the previous aphorisms and their significance for the free spirit project. In particular, Nietzsche claims that there are neither

[11] Nussbaum (1994) identifies the Stoics as Nietzsche's positive alternative to pity and bases much of her argument on passages from *Daybreak*. Nussbaum, however, overlooks the significance of the tragic Greeks as Nietzsche's alternative to the morality of pity, and on my reading, Nietzsche will leave behind the Stoics for the arts of Dionysus as the dialectic of the free spirit advances. Nietzsche's commitment to the Stoics is tenuous because the *passion* for knowledge that characterizes the free spirit at this stage conflicts with the tranquility of mind that the Stoics seek to achieve. Moreover, Nietzsche is explicitly critical of the Stoics in *Beyond Good and Evil* (BGE 9). Thus, it is better to agree with Groff (2004: 152) that there is an "awkward kinship" between Nietzsche and the Stoics.

[12] See Brobjer (2003) for more on Nietzsche's engagement with Epictetus. Brobjer also refers back to Nietzsche's appeal to Epictetus in *Assorted Opinions* as an example of the self-sufficiency of the sage (AOM 386). At the same time, Brobjer also notes that Nietzsche soon became critical of Epictetus in the period just after composing *Daybreak* (see KSA 9: 15[55] and KSA 10: 17[42]). In my view, the fact that Nietzsche is criticizing, in his notes, the Stoics only months after publishing a book (*Daybreak*) in which he appropriates their therapeutic techniques indicates that Nietzsche is consciously adopting Stoicism only as a temporary strategy that will soon be abandoned as the dialectic of the free spirit unfolds.

actions performed for the sake of others nor actions that result from the exercise of free will, and so if these are markers of the moral, then there are no moral actions. Instead, belief in such actions is the result of "certain intellectual mistakes." However, these mistakes still inform our value judgments, and this is why we still look down upon "egoistic" and "unfree" actions. Nevertheless, the purpose of the reflections in this chapter has been to "restore to men their goodwill towards the actions decried as egoistic and restore to these actions their *value*." In so doing, Nietzsche claims that, "*we shall deprive them of their bad conscience!*" (D 148). Although nothing is explicit, we see the way in which the set of reflections Nietzsche offers in the second chapter of *Daybreak* begin what he later calls a revaluation of values.

Chapter III: Learning How to Command

In the third chapter, Nietzsche attributes to the free spirit a variety of heroic features that seemingly prepare the way for the death of God and the elimination of his shadow in *The Gay Science*: self-mastery, individualism, rebelliousness, passion, risk-taking, boldness, nobility, and the ability to command. Nietzsche begins the chapter by advocating what he calls "deviant" acts (D 149). The idea is that it is not enough for the free spirit to think or even feel differently from what is customary and so to live outside of society like a wanderer, Epicurean, or Cynic. Instead, the free spirit is now called upon to act in ways that openly deviate from and so undermine unjustified customs. Thus, atheists should not have their children baptized for the sole reason of going along with the dominant custom. This is because the free spirit has shown that such customs are mere prejudices, and so acting in accordance with custom lends legitimacy to these irrational practices (D 149).

In the aphorisms that immediately follow, Nietzsche discusses a variety of themes that are arguably linked to the chivalry of the Troubadours – a prominent feature of *The Gay Science*. Thus, he discusses love and marriage in the next two aphorisms (D 150 and 151), the significance of the oath (D 152), a brave man who loves honors, plundering, and beautiful women (D 153), and finally the bold and daring undertakings of the Middle Ages (D 155). In another aphorism, Nietzsche attacks Rousseau for the softness of his morality. Whereas Rousseau blamed civilization for its corrupt morality, Nietzsche argues that it is the "unmanly" morality of thinkers like Rousseau who have corrupted society and "finally weakened all bodies and souls and snapped the self-reliant, independent, unprejudiced men," thereby destroying the "pillars of a *strong* civilization" (D 163).

In "Perhaps Premature," Nietzsche refers to those free spirits who no longer feel themselves bound to "existing laws and customs." Hitherto, such "free-thinkers" were denounced as criminals, immoral persons, and villains "under the ban of outlawry and bad conscience." However, they are now starting "to create for themselves a *right*" to function as a counter-force to such laws and customs and to "deviate from morality, either in deed or thought." This right is justified because "there is no such thing as a morality with an exclusive monopoly of the moral, and every morality that affirms itself alone destroys too much valuable strength and is bought too dear." This right allows for "numerous novel experiments [. . .] in ways of life and modes of society" and "a tremendous burden of bad conscience shall be expelled from the world" (D 164). Thus, Nietzsche's call for deviant acts in the first aphorism of the chapter is bound up with the need to lend a good conscience to such deeds as well as his call for an experimental philosophy that will become more prominent as the free spirit works unfold.

Having carved out a space for the free spirit to pursue this antinomian project, Nietzsche then directs his disdain against those who fail to heed this call and instead make themselves into a cog of a larger system. The problem is that being a cog in a system is directly inimical to the task of becoming a genuine individual, and this tension between the demand to be useful to the community and becoming a genuine individual underlies Nietzsche's reflections on the ills of commercial society in the chapter. Thus, Nietzsche claims that the command to work hides a covert fear of the genuine individual (D 173), and he explains how modern individuals are "worn out daily" through excessive work (D 178). In another aphorism, he laments the "tyranny of timidity" that runs throughout commercial society and how it is "turning mankind into *sand*" (D 174).

As we have seen throughout the free spirit works, the ancient Greeks function as a point of contrast for Nietzsche's complaints about contemporary society, and this, again, shows the way in which he remains committed to the general framework of his earliest writings. After referring to the ancient Greeks in multiple aphorisms (D 154, 156, 161, and 165), Nietzsche devotes an aphorism to explaining why Thucydides is his model.[13] In the Greek historian, the "*culture of the most impartial*

---

[13] See Mann and Lustila (2011) for more on this point. Clark and Leiter (1997: ix–x) also emphasize Nietzsche's relationship to the pre-Socratic Greeks.

knowledge of the world finds its last glorious flower." This culture had Sophocles as its poet, Pericles as its statesman, Hippocrates as its physician, and Democritus as its natural philosopher. According to Nietzsche, this culture deserves to be baptized with the name of its teachers, the sophists, even though this might suggest that it was "a very immoral culture" (D 168).

Nietzsche's praise, here, is not of the ancient Greeks as such, but of the very period he praised in *The Birth of Tragedy* and opposed to the declining culture initiated by Socrates and furthered by Plato, and so Nietzsche is taking a step away from the post-Socratic thinkers he admired in *The Wanderer*,[14] even though the Stoics also permeate his reflections here. In a subsequent aphorism, Nietzsche thus turns to what he calls the "age of Aeschylus" – the leading tragedian in *The Birth of Tragedy* – to highlight the "bravery and manliness" of this "fundamentally warlike" culture. Nietzsche's point is that, like the Stoics, the tragic Greeks were not soft and tender and so not easily susceptible to something like fear and pity, that is, the two affects Aristotle associates with tragedy. Although Nietzsche acknowledges that the time is not right for such tragedies, he speculates – in contrast to his dismissive attitude toward art in *Human* – that "an age full of danger," such as the one now commencing, may "have need of tragic poets" (D 173).

The ancient Greeks are again the topic of the aphorism "So-Called Classical Education," and here we get some sense of the tragic nature of the "passion for knowledge" that is central to Brusotti's account of this period. The tragic nature of this passion is first evident in the Stoic line that Nietzsche quotes in the beginning of the aphorism: "Destiny, I follow thee! And if I would not that I should have to nonetheless, though sighing as I did so" (D 195).[15] Although attributed to the Stoic Cleanthes, the notion of tragedy is implicit in the concept of fate introduced here. It is further implied by the aphorism insofar as Nietzsche speaks of the free spirit's life being "*consecrated* to knowledge." On the one hand, such remarks point back to the aphorism, "A Tragic Ending for Knowledge," in which Nietzsche speaks of a humankind ready to sacrifice itself for "knowledge of the truth" (D 45). On the other hand, the aphorism points forward to the aphorism, "The New Passion," in which Nietzsche explains that the quest for knowledge has been transformed into a passion and that

---

[14] In "Greek Ideal," Nietzsche also speaks positively of the Greeks' admiration for Odysseus and his ability to lie (D 306).

[15] See Brusotti (1997: 206–209) for a more extensive discussion of this notion.

"perhaps mankind will even perish of this passion for knowledge" (D 429). Again, these aphorisms recall Nietzsche's claim in *Wagner in Bayreuth* that the meaning of tragedy is "the individual must be consecrated to something higher than himself" (RWB 4), and so they seem to be foreshadowing his own tragedy of *Zarathustra*.

As an aphorism from the fourth chapter indicates, there is a certain nobility attached to a tragic hero like Tristan who perishes of his passion (D 240), and it is therefore not surprising that Nietzsche devotes subsequent aphorisms in chapter 3 to discussing nobility and aristocracy. In "We are Nobler," Nietzsche argues that moderns have the ability to be even nobler than the Greeks he generally reveres. The aristocracy is still chivalrous in nature and so has inherited an "adventurousness and desire for self-sacrifice." What Nietzsche wants, therefore, is not for the free spirit to abandon the noble virtues of "loyalty, magnanimity, and care for one's reputation," but rather to "see to it that this precious inherited drive is applied to new objects" (D 199). Although not explicit, the surrounding aphorisms suggest that these new objects are the objects of knowledge, and here again we see a foreshadowing of the Troubadours in *The Gay Science* insofar as Nietzsche is attributing a heroic quality to the quest for knowledge.

Although he criticizes the ancient Greeks for their ranging lust for power (D 199), Nietzsche thinks that the feeling of power is a central feature of the new nobility. This is made clear in "Future of the Aristocracy." There, Nietzsche writes: "The demeanour adopted by the nobility is an expression of the fact that the consciousness of power is constantly playing its charming game in their limbs." In this sense, the aristocracy breathes power, and Nietzsche now wants to connect this feeling of power to the free spirit's quest for knowledge: "thanks to the work of our free-spirits, it is now no longer reprehensible for those born and raised in the aristocracy to enter the orders of knowledge and there to obtain more intellectual ordinations, learn higher knightly duties, than any heretofore, and to raise their eyes to the idea of *victorious wisdom* which no previous age has been free to erect for itself with so good a conscience as the age now about to arrive" (D 201).

The need for a good conscience is also a central motif in the chapter. Nietzsche not only talks about aristocrats of the future, but also criminals of the future, and this is because his new nobility consists of those willing to violate the very customs that restrain the quest for knowledge and self-realization. Thus, Nietzsche begins the aphorism immediately following "Future of the Aristocracy" with a discussion of the similarities between

criminals and the insane. The criminal, Nietzsche claims, needs a physician and should be treated as a patient, and the purpose of this treatment
is to "wipe the pangs of conscience from his soul." Just as the invalid
should not feel guilty for inadvertently harming the community, the
criminal should also have this same sense of innocence. Thus, Nietzsche
looks to a time when we can do away not only with revenge, but also the
sin, guilt, and punishment that are all associated with the bad conscience
(D 202).

The most notable aphorism about the criminal in the third chapter is
"From a Possible Future." Here, Nietzsche speaks of a future criminal who
willingly punishes himself. This, however, is not because the criminal
wants to reassure the community of his obedience to laws that have been
dictated to him. Instead, the criminal will do so on the condition that the
laws to which he submits are laws that he has made.[16] In this sense, the
criminal will punish himself for violating the law because it reasserts his
status as an autonomous agent. Thus, Nietzsche's "criminal of a possible
future" is founded on the idea that "I submit to the law which I myself
have given, in great things and in small" (D 187). One cannot miss the
connections between this "criminal of a possible future" and the notion of
self-legislation in *Schopenhauer as Educator* and *The Gay Science* (GS 335).

The willingness to obey only a law that one creates for oneself – and so
the willingness to obey only in those cases in which one is also master –
stands in sharp contrast to the willingness to obey *simpliciter*, and the
contrast Nietzsche draws here can be mapped onto the contrast he draws
between emerging free spirits, who largely look back to ancient Greece and
the chivalry of the Middle Ages for their models, and his fellow Germans,
whom Nietzsche criticizes throughout the chapter. This is evident in the
title of the aphorism in which Nietzsche first criticizes the Germans,
"Unconditional Homage." There, Nietzsche speaks of the unconditional
homage paid to the likes of Schopenhauer, Wagner, and Bismarck, but
then notes the impossibility of giving unconditional respect to three men
who oppose each other. Thus, Nietzsche concludes the aphorism by
noting the ludicrous nature of such "unconditional homage" (D 167).

After noting the loss of any semblance of culture that may have been
achieved through the efforts of Schiller, Wilhelm von Humboldt,
Schleiermacher, Hegel, and Schelling (D 190), Nietzsche returns to a
central idea of *Human* in critiquing the Germans for their hostility to

---

[16] See Sachs (2008) for an account of autonomy in *Daybreak* that he claims foreshadows Nietzsche's
later disassociation of morality from autonomy in the *Genealogy*.

the Enlightenment. Specifically, Nietzsche attacks the likes of Goethe and Schopenhauer for fighting against the spirit of Newton and Voltaire and for seeking "to restore the idea of a divine or diabolical nature suffused with ethical and symbolic significance." This obscurantism erected a "cult of feeling" in place of a "cult of reason." However, Nietzsche takes comfort not only in that this latter age has passed, but that it has also aroused a "passion for feeling and knowledge" that will "now fly on the broadest wings above and beyond their former conjurers as new and stronger genii of *that very Enlightenment* against which they were first conjured up" (D 197). Similar to his exhortations at the beginning of *Human* (HH 26), Nietzsche again claims that, "this Enlightenment we must now carry further forward" (D 197), and thereby reinforces the idea that his own free spirit works are advancing the dialectic of the Enlightenment.

Nietzsche concludes the chapter with an extended reflection on German morality. He begins the aphorism by claiming that although a German is capable of great things, it is unlikely he will ever do them because he "obeys *whenever he can.*" Although there are some instances in which a German has obeyed himself, Nietzsche claims that, "he is afraid of depending *on himself alone.*" Given this general inclination toward obedience, Nietzsche says that we should expect this in matters of morality. Thus, the German sensation is that "man has to have something which he can *obey unconditionally,*" and, according to Nietzsche, this need animated both Luther and Kant, and so they both conjured up something everyone had to obey (D 207).

Similar to what we have seen in the free spirit works thus far, Nietzsche contrasts this German attitude toward obedience with the ancient Greeks and Romans. For the latter, life was about attaining individual distinction. They had what Nietzsche calls a "southerly freedom" that was skeptical about unconditional trust. Thus, the philosophy of antiquity can be summed up in Horace's Stoical phrase: "Nil admirari" or "respect nothing."[17] Although not explicit, the underlying idea is that Germans need to learn from the ancients how to command, and they can begin to do this by learning how to command themselves (D 207). As noted above, the emphasis on autonomy is a much different stance than the Epicurean indifference and tranquility that Nietzsche adopts in *The Wanderer*, and it will become an increasingly important theme as the free spirit works unfold.

---

[17] As Brusotti (1997: 103) notes, Nietzsche also expresses this idea in *The Wanderer* (WS 313).

Chapter IV: Power, Passion, and Art

Nietzsche's attack on the prejudices of morality largely comes to a conclusion in chapter 3, and he dedicates chapters 4 and 5 to a series of reflections that articulate what the free spirit must become given the critique of morality executed in the previous chapters. Chapter 4 contains the most aphorisms of the chapters in *Daybreak* but has the least identifiable structure, and in this sense, it resembles a work like *Assorted Opinions*. It begins with a call to overcome the bad conscience and ends with a call to make joyful, and so it seems to be shifting away from countering the darkening effects of morality to the more affirmative attitude of *The Gay Science*. In between, the aphorisms cover a wide range of issues, but largely continue the discussion, initiated in chapter 3, of topics such as power, passion, pride, and heroism.

Despite the relative (or apparent) lack of structure, the first aphorism summarizes a key lesson from the preceding three chapters. It begins by asking what, "in *summa*," the free spirit wants changed. The answer is that the free spirit wants to stop "making causes into sinners and consequences into executioners." In other words, the free spirit wants to put an end to the bad conscience and the Christian moral framework (D 208). The first three chapters of *Daybreak* have taken significant steps toward this goal, and this task will continue driving the free spirit project toward the elimination of God's shadow in *The Gay Science*.

The third aphorism of the chapter also seems to summarize a conclusion that has been reached through the previous free spirit works and is even implicit in the first aphorism of *Human*: "There is nothing good, nothing beautiful, nothing sublime, nothing evil in itself, but that there are states of soul in which we impose such words upon things external to and within us." Of course, this claim entails the denial of the Christian God and Plato's Form of the Good, and, according to Nietzsche, this is why the free spirit investigates – following the historical method of the first aphorism of *Human* – how these values originated. Here, we seek to *remember* – and so overcome the forgetting that is central to "On Truth and Lies" and *History for Life* – that we have lent these qualities to reality, and, in so doing, we realize that we have the capacity to engage, consciously, in this activity (D 210).

A central theme that emerges in these diverse aphorisms is Nietzsche's continued appeal to the "feeling of power" as an explanatory mechanism. The idea first appears in the aphorism, "Morality of Sacrificial Beasts," where Nietzsche analyzes those who are enthusiastically devoted to a morality of self-sacrifice. According to Nietzsche, the enthusiasm for such a morality is actually driven by a subtle lust for power and the feeling of power. This is because the sacrifice of oneself is often combined with the imaginary communion with some powerful deity. So understood, this is not self-sacrifice. Instead, the real purpose is to become a god (D 215).

In addition to explaining Napoleon's desire to speak worse than he actually could in terms of a subtle feeling of power (D 245), Nietzsche explains Stoicism in a similar fashion without explicitly referring to the feeling of power. Thus, Nietzsche writes that, "there is a cheerfulness peculiar to the Stoic," and he experiences this whenever he feels constrained by rules that he has prescribed to himself. According to Nietzsche, it is here that "he then enjoys the sensation of himself as dominator" (D 251).

Again, the language of power is not explicit, but we know from a contemporaneous note that Nietzsche understands Stoicism in terms of a feeling of power. On the one hand, Nietzsche compares the Stoic to the ascetic: Both achieve a tremendous feeling of power. On the other hand, Nietzsche differentiates the Stoic from the Epicurean. The Epicurean, claims Nietzsche, does not experience a feeling of power. Instead, Epicurean joy is bound up with the feeling of fearlessness vis-à-vis the gods and nature, and so the happiness the Epicurean feels has a negative quality (KSA 9: 4[204]). Nietzsche's analysis of the Stoics in terms of the feeling of power marks a shift away from the Epicurean quest for tranquility in *The Wanderer*, and so his analysis in *Daybreak* can again be understood as advancing the dialectic of the free spirit works.

We can also detect a clear shift away from *The Wanderer* in another aphorism in which Nietzsche speaks of power. In "The Demon of Power," Nietzsche claims that even if humans have all they need with regard to health, food, shelter, and entertainment, they will still "remain unhappy and low-spirited." This is because there is a demon in the form of a desire for power that waits to be satisfied. In contrast, one could take away all of the aforementioned things and so long as this demon is satisfied, people will be happy. As an example of this, Nietzsche points to Luther's willingness to give up everything only to have his *Reich* (D 262). Thus, just as the city of pigs fails to satisfy the ambitions of Glaucon in the second book of Plato's *Republic*, the free spirit is no longer content with the simple life of Epicurus that Nietzsche sketches in *The Wanderer*.

In other aphorisms, Nietzsche speaks of the feeling of power as a dominant drive in certain human psyches. In "Feeling of Power," he differentiates between one who strives with all his might to get the feeling of power and one who already enjoys this feeling. Whereas the former will do anything to get it, the latter becomes "very fastidious and noble in his tastes" (D 348). Elsewhere, Nietzsche casts the *"feeling of power"* as an effect of happiness and claims that it expresses itself to others through bestowal, mockery, and destruction (D 356). Finally, Nietzsche argues that the ancient Greeks "valued the feeling of power more highly than any kind of utility or good name" (D 360).

In "The Festive Mood," Nietzsche contends that certain people "who strive most hotly after power" occasionally like to be overcome. In this state, they become "a plaything of primeval forces," and just as a climber might dream about falling off the very mountain she is trying to scale, these individuals take delight in this occasional feeling of powerlessness. Thus, this feeling functions as a reprieve from their primary occupation, and so once they have experienced this festive mood and the feeling of being overcome, they resume their relentless quest for power (D 271).

Nietzsche's reflections on power in "The Festive Mood" can be tied to his reflections on passion and art. A connection between art and passion is suggested in "The Artist," as Nietzsche speaks of Germans who seek to achieve an "imagined passion" through artists and Italians who "want to rest from their real passions" (D 217). In "On the Morality of the Stage," the relationship between ambition, passion, and tragic art plays a central role. Reminiscent of *The Birth of Tragedy*, Nietzsche denies that tragic art is supposed to have a moral effect as thinkers from Aristotle to Schopenhauer claimed. Instead, the true effect of tragedy is the pleasure we take in a hero so possessed by a passion that he is willing to perish. According to Nietzsche, the poets "are enamoured of the passions," even of "their *death-welcoming* moods." Such passion, adventure, and danger function as "the stimulants of stimulants," and this is what the poets represent through their tragedies (D 240).

The treatment of tragedy here not only recalls the argument of *The Birth of Tragedy*, it stands in sharp contrast to the assessment of art in *Human*. A shift from *Human* to *Daybreak* is also noticeable in the positive assessment Nietzsche gives of passion and pleasure in this and other passages in chapter 4 (see D 339). In particular, Nietzsche advances the idea that passion and even the desire for conquest are now driving the free spirit's quest for knowledge. In an aphorism that recalls the idea from *The Birth of Tragedy* that we enjoy the search for truth more than its discovery (BT 15), Nietzsche claims that even the pursuit of pleasant truths is more pleasant than their acquisition (D 396). A similar idea is also found in "A Fable." There, Nietzsche speaks of "the Don Juan of knowledge," an individual who does not love knowledge but rather the chase for knowledge. The chase is so appealing that this Don Juan begins to pursue knowledge that is even "*detrimental.*" In this way, the lover of knowledge can begin to lust "after Hell" (D 327).

Although he emphasizes the tragic dimension of the quest for knowledge, Nietzsche nevertheless ends the chapter by speaking of joy. In "Making Others Joyful," he claims that making joyful is the greatest of all joys precisely "because we thereby give joy to our fifty separate drives all at once." Taken separately, our drives experience "very little joys." Taken together, our heart can be filled with joy (D 422). In the next chapter, joy takes on an even more prominent role, and this prepares the way for Nietzsche's joyous or gay science in further developments of the free spirit.

Chapter V: New Seas

The final chapter begins and ends with an image of the sea. The sea is significant in Nietzsche's writings and can often represent the realm of the unconsciousness or the flux of Heraclitean becoming. Here, it has another meaning: Like the desert, the sea can mean a place where the city is left behind, and so it is the realm of freedom in which the customs that place restraints on its citizens are no longer applicable. Understood in the context of *Daybreak*, the image of the sea Nietzsche introduces at the beginning and places at the end of chapter 5 symbolizes that the free spirit is now moving beyond the customs of the city for some unknown adventure (D 423).

The second aphorism takes up a theme that reoccurs throughout the free spirit works and is subject to the dialectical transformations that I have been tracing throughout this book: the free spirit's attitude toward truth, science, and knowledge. Here, it is recognized that unlike errors, truth may not console. However, this does not mean that there are not truths. Instead, it means that only certain types of individuals are capable of taking pleasure in science. Specifically, anyone looking for a cure and consolation from science will turn away from it. In contrast, souls who are powerful and full of peace and joy will be able to engage in a genuine pursuit of truth and find "real pleasure in science." In short, science is only for the healthy, and so only for the type of free spirit who is now recovering from the sickness of morality (D 424).

The conception of science presented in the opening sections of this chapter contrasts sharply with the cold rigor of the science pursued in *Human.* In "The Beautification of Science," Nietzsche assigns a new role to philosophy that anticipates the union of poetry and the quest for wisdom expressed in the motto of *The Gay Science* (KSA 3: p. 343). Specifically, Nietzsche speaks of a philosophy that can beautify a science that is otherwise "ugly, dry, cheerless, difficult, laborious." This, of course, is much different from Nietzsche's embrace of this type of science and his corresponding rejection of philosophy as the "mischief-maker in science" in *Human* (HH 7). Rather than opposing science, philosophy is now said to work with science to make it a cheerful enterprise and so a gay science (D 427).

These reflections segue to what is, for Brusotti's account, one of the most important aphorisms in *Daybreak*. In "The New Passion," Nietzsche explicitly discusses the notion of a "passion for knowledge," a concept quickly glossed in an earlier aphorism in which Nietzsche called on free spirits to carry the Enlightenment forward (D 197). Continuing to develop the emphasis on passion in the previous chapter, we are told that the free spirit is now possessed of a passion or drive for knowledge that is so strong that happiness can only be conceived in relation to the satisfaction of this drive (D 429). For this reason, everything else can be sacrificed to this drive. Although this sounds like a recipe for tragedy, Nietzsche concludes by noting that it is either a matter of mankind consecrating itself to something higher – as explained in "So-Called Classical Education" (D 195) – or perishing in the sand – a worry already raised in "Moral Fashion of a Commercial Society" (D 174).

Nietzsche also makes clear that this passionate quest for knowledge will bring science and art closer together. In one aphorism, he remarks that because the connection between happiness and knowledge of reality is so strong, artists have now become "glorifiers of the 'delights' of science" (D 434). In another aphorism, he notes that science has such an effect on passionate spirits that it will likely turn them into poets, "so vehement is their craving for the happiness of those with knowledge" (D 450). Finally, Nietzsche claims that although reality might not be beautiful in itself, it is nevertheless the case that "knowledge of even the ugliest reality is itself beautiful" (D 550).

Nietzsche also employs the idea of a passionate quest for knowledge to differentiate the likes of Kant and Schopenhauer from philosophers such as Plato, Spinoza, Pascal, Rousseau, and Goethe (the latter are all names Nietzsche mentions in the final aphorism of *Assorted Opinions* (AOM 408)). The distinction Nietzsche draws is between philosophers whose thoughts constitute "a passionate history of the soul" and "an involuntary biography" and those thinkers for whom this is not the case. According to

Nietzsche, Kant is excluded from the former group because his philosophy is a "biography of a *head*," as he lacked the inner experiences that would give his philosophy breadth and power. Similarly, Schopenhauer's philosophy is "the description and mirroring of a *character*," and as such, it lacks any sort of "development" and "history" (D 481). Thus, Nietzsche's remarks suggest that the problem with Kant's and Schopenhauer's philosophies is that they do not take the form of the kind of *Bildungsroman* that Nietzsche is composing in the free spirit works.

Although Nietzsche thinks a passionate history of the soul is essential to the philosophical project, the passionate quest for knowledge pushes the free spirit beyond and so outside herself, and this is expressed in the phrase, "what do I matter [*was liegt an mir*]." This concept not only appears twice in the fifth chapter of *Daybreak* (D 494 and 547) and once in *The Gay Science* (GS 332), it also runs throughout Nietzsche's *Nachlass* and his letters from this time. According to Brusotti (1997: 207–208), "what do I matter" is bound up with courage and passion. In *Daybreak*, it is introduced in the aphorism, "Final Argument of the Brave" (D 494), and Nietzsche speaks of the willingness of the free spirit to be a sacrifice in the pursuit of knowledge. It is linked to passion by its proximity to aphorisms about passion in chapter 5 of *Daybreak* and then explicitly in the *Nachlass*. There, Nietzsche claims that "what do I matter" is the "expression of the true passion" and the most extreme degree of being outside of oneself (KSA 9: 7[45]).

Similar to Nietzsche's willingness to follow destiny in "So-Called Classical Education," Brusotti has also shown that "what do I matter" can be traced back to the Stoics. This is made explicit in a *Nachlass* note written just after the publication of *Daybreak* in which Nietzsche claims that he learned from the Stoics to ask "what do I matter" in the midst of stress and necessity (KSA 9: 15[59]). It is also implicit in Nietzsche's praise of Epictetus' bravery and his lack of fear before God (D 546). In short, Epictetus seems to be the model for the "religion of courage" that Nietzsche sketches in his notes from this time (KSA 9: 9[1]) and the courage that Nietzsche identifies as one of the future virtues (D 551).

At the same time, Brusotti (1997: 206–209) explains how Nietzsche combines Stoic bravery with a passionate condition that differs from Stoical *apathia* and effectively expresses a willingness to have one's life consecrated to knowledge. The consecration of one's life to knowledge, however, is not a flight from a hated self that Nietzsche associates with Pascal, but rather comes from a self well disposed toward itself. Similar to the call for a religion of self-redemption at the end of chapter 1 (D 96),

Nietzsche warns against the wrath and revenge of those who hate themselves (D 517), and he calls upon us to be benevolently inclined toward ourselves before we express such benevolence to others (D 516).

The opposite of hating oneself is loving oneself, and the term that expresses such self-love is *Selbstsucht*. Because Nietzsche gives a decidedly positive valence to a term that normally implies an illness – it can mean an addiction [*Sucht*] to the self – and has had a correspondingly bad reputation in German philosophy,[18] there is reason to think it lies at the heart of Nietzsche's later revaluation project.[19] In *Daybreak*, *Selbstsucht* appears on four occasions, and three times in the final chapter. In its first appearance in chapter 2, Nietzsche contrasts *Selbstsucht* to the selfless love of altruism (D 147). In its first appearance in chapter 5, Nietzsche speaks positively of "selfishness and self-enjoyment" (D 449). After employing the term in a discussion of friendship (D 489), Nietzsche then returns to the topic in "The Ideal Selfishness [*Selbstsucht*]." Much like Diotima's account of *eros* in Plato's *Symposium*, the discussion begins with pregnancy, but then moves to the realm of ideas. In both cases, Nietzsche calls on the free spirit to live in a "*state of consecration*." That is, we should continually watch over and tend to the self so that "our fruitfulness shall *come to a happy fulfillment*" (D 552). In this way, the care of the self ultimately allows one to live for something beyond the self, and for the free spirit, this means the pursuit of knowledge.

Part of consecrating one's life to knowledge is the willingness to experiment with life, and *Daybreak* is the work in which Nietzsche introduces his notion of experimental philosophy. Following upon the free spirit's liberation from custom in earlier stages of *Daybreak*, the idea takes on a prominent role in chapter 5. In the aphorism, "Moral Interregnum," Nietzsche explains that this experimental philosophy emerges from the critique of moral prejudices that has been executed in *Daybreak*. The aphorism begins with a reference to a day when "moral feelings and judgments" are eliminated. Because the foundations of moral judgments are defective and "their superstructure is beyond repair," Nietzsche claims it is time "to construct anew the laws of life and action." Because the sciences of physiology, medicine, and sociology are not yet up to this task,

---

[18] In this sense, I disagree with Acampora's (2013b: 370) attempt to translate *Selbstsucht* as "self-seeking." As Sommer (2013: 349) makes clear, *Selbstsucht* is largely synonymous with egoism both in Nietzsche and in the tradition against which he is rebelling.

[19] For instance, the term appears in important passages throughout *The Gay Science* (GS 21, 28, 55, 99, 143, 291, 328, and 335) and *Ecce Homo* (EH "Clever" 9; EH "Clever" 10; and EH "Destiny" 7).

we need, in the meantime, to create "little *experimental states"* and make ourselves into experiments to lay the foundations for new ideals (D 453).

In these aphorisms, Nietzsche is connecting this experimental philosophy to what he calls in the *Nachlass* from this time a "revision of all evaluations" (KSA 9: 3[158]), and so he is going beyond a mere rejection of old values toward the construction of new laws of life and action. Nietzsche also links the emergence of experimental philosophy to another position that has been implicitly developed in the free spirit works. In "Mortal Souls," Nietzsche explains that the rejection of the immortal soul is a great achievement for the promotion of knowledge. In the past, thinkers rushed to this or that theory in order to make a decision about something that could have consequences for the salvation of their soul. Now, however, we no longer have this concern, and so "we may experiment with ourselves" and even offer ourselves as a sacrifice to knowledge (D 501).

In addition to this experimental attitude, Nietzsche speaks of the free spirit's willingness to undergo change. This is expressed most prominently in the antepenultimate aphorism of *Daybreak*: "Sloughing one's skin. – The snake that cannot slough its skin, perishes. Likewise, spirits which are prevented from changing their opinions; they cease to be spirits" (D 573). The image of a snake sloughing its skin is also employed a few aphorisms earlier in "First Nature." There, Nietzsche recalls the idea from chapter 2 (D 104) of needing to remove an acquired second nature in order to discover one's own first nature under the skin, one that has hopefully matured rather than dried up (D 455). In "Small Doses," Nietzsche reminds us, however, that any change in our values must be gradual. Thus, he writes, "let us take care not to exchange the state of morality to which we are accustomed for a new evaluation of things head over heels and amid acts of violence." Instead, we must slowly become aware that a "*new evaluation* has acquired predominance within us and that the little doses of it *to which we must from now on accustom ourselves* have laid down a new nature within us" (D 534).

In chapter 5, Nietzsche also notes that thinkers need to be willing to throw off their virtues (D 510), and honesty (*Redlichkeit*) is one of the virtues central to the free spirit project that nevertheless undergoes change.[20] *Redlichkeit* only occurs once in Nietzsche's writings prior to composing *Daybreak* (KSA 8: 5[1]), but it occurs repeatedly in a notebook from the fall of 1880. As noted above, the term occurs in a variant to the

---

[20] See Lane (2007) for more on honesty in *Daybreak* and its relationship to Stoic and Epicurean strategies of self-shaping.

"passion for knowledge" as the "passion for honesty" (KSA 9: 8[1]), and it appears in important aphorisms in both *The Gay Science* and *Beyond Good and Evil*. Indeed, the shifting positions regarding *Redlichkeit* that Nietzsche adopts from *Daybreak* to *The Gay Science* and even into *Beyond Good and Evil* provide a microcosm for exploring the dialectical shifts that take place over the course of the free spirit works and beyond.

The fact that *Redlichkeit* is a cardinal virtue for the free spirit is made clear by its inclusion in the list of cardinal virtues Nietzsche identifies in "The Good Four" (D 556). The fact that it is undergoing dialectical shifts is evinced by the title of the aphorism "A Virtue in the Process of Becoming." There, Nietzsche argues that honesty is "the youngest virtue" that is in a "process of becoming" and "still hardly aware of itself." To illustrate this point, Nietzsche argues that the alleged unity of virtue and happiness so often asserted in antiquity and the Christian claim that righteousness will be rewarded have never been put forward "with total honesty." And yet, these claims were made with a good conscience. This is because they stood at a "level of truthfulness" in which these thinkers no longer had to trouble themselves about truth so long as they felt themselves to be selfless, and it is this level of truthfulness that the free spirit will eventually have to transcend (D 456).

As Brusotti (1997: Ch. 1.6) explains, passionate honesty and the quest for knowledge does not, in *Daybreak*, emanate from a moral command to be honest. Instead, honesty is tied to a non-intellectual drive that, as a passion, becomes dominant in the psychic economy of the free spirit. What Nietzsche also emphasizes in *Daybreak* is the way in which the thinker is at liberty to cultivate and dispose of the drives of anger, pity, and curiosity just like a gardener tending to her garden (D 560). The cultivation of drives has an aesthetic quality to it, and as Rebecca Bamford (2015: 88) explains, this can be tied to notions of self-fashioning that foreshadow Nietzsche's call for self-creation in *The Gay Science*. Rather than disappearing into sand, the free spirit should look to create "something out of oneself that the other can behold with pleasure: a beautiful, restful, self-enclosed garden perhaps, with high walls against storms and the dust of the roadway but also a hospitable gate" (D 174).

Just as honesty is a virtue in the process of becoming, so too is the free spirit's attitude toward art and the notion of self-fashioning. Such an interpretation is substantiated by the aphorism "A Different Feeling for Art." The idea articulated in the aphorism – one also present in previous drafts (KSA 14: p. 226) – is that Nietzsche has changed his opinion of art now that he is more solitary and lives "in the company of profound fruitful ideas" (D 531). As Franco (2011: 96ff.) has noted, the theme of solitude runs throughout the final aphorisms of *Daybreak*, and solitude is essential to the self-education of the free spirit. Nietzsche makes this explicit in "On Education," an aphorism that gives expression to the *Bildungsprogramm* Nietzsche is executing in these works. There, he writes: "I have gradually seen the light as to the most universal deficiency in our kind of cultivation and education: no one learns, no one strives after, no one teaches – *the endurance of solitude*" (D 443).

The theme of solitude is also implicit in the closing aphorisms of *Daybreak*. Nietzsche employs the imagery of a bird flying up to heights at which it no longer can be seen and out to distant lands that have never been reached before. Although "our greatest teachers and predecessors" have flown their farthest, this does not mean we cannot fly farther. Here, Nietzsche suggests that the free spirit will vie with his predecessors to fly into a distance "where everything is sea, sea, sea!" The free spirit is pushed by a "mighty longing," but there is little sense of where this longing will lead. It may be in the direction of India, but it may be the free spirit's fate to be "wrecked against infinity" (D 575).

The fate of the free spirit, however, remains to be seen, and the book closes with an "Or" (D 575), a clear indication that there are more developments to come. Indeed, the language of the "sea" and "infinity" foreshadows the death of God and the elimination of his shadow in *The Gay Science*. This is because such language appears in the aphorism just prior to the announcement of God's death (GS 124), and it reoccurs in Nietzsche's description of the death of God in the first aphorism of the fifth chapter of *The Gay Science* (GS 343). Of course, this confirms what we already know from the compositional history of *The Gay Science*: The first three chapters of *The Gay Science* continue the project of *Daybreak*.

Concluding Remarks

In this chapter, I have endeavored to read *Daybreak* as a whole. Although my reading is selective and only touches on a small portion of the aphorisms, it shows that the work has a narrative structure that moves from a critique of moral prejudices in the opening chapters to the beginnings of Nietzsche's project of revaluing values. In chapter 1, Nietzsche undermines the authority of custom and rejects Christian strategies of redemption in favor of a religion of self-redemption. In chapter 2, Nietzsche presents a free spirit interested not only in thinking differently but also feeling differently, and so he analyzes and critiques the moral sentiments that remain as aftereffects of Christianity. In chapter 3, Nietzsche portrays a free spirit who is now willing to engage in deviant acts that contravene reigning custom, and in this spirit, he replaces the German morality of obedience with a heroic free spirit able to command. In the final two chapters, Nietzsche focuses on themes such as power, passion, and art, and here the free spirit's quest for knowledge transitions from the gray asceticism of *Human* to a form of knowledge seeking that is both experimental and joyous. In this sense, *Daybreak* moves from the project at the end of *The Wanderer* of removing the chains of morality and curing the sickness they have caused to a passionate knowledge seeking that takes center stage in *The Gay Science*. So understood, the primary purpose of *Daybreak* is to advance the narrative of Nietzsche's dialectical *Bildungsroman* by undermining the prejudices of morality that will then make possible an aesthetic justification of existence in subsequent works.

CHAPTER 6

The Selbstaufhebung *of the Will to Truth*
The Gay Science I–III

In the final three chapters of this book, I discuss the five chapters that make up the 1887 edition of *The Gay Science*. However, I do so by dividing the first three chapters from the rest of the work and treating the fourth and fifth chapters separately and in relation to the works that follow upon the 1882 edition of *The Gay Science*. This division is based on the genesis of the text. Whereas the first three chapters were written separately from the final two chapters and as continuations of *Daybreak* (KSB 6: 190), the fourth and final chapter of the 1882 edition, "Sanctus Januarius," is importantly different from the first three. The fifth chapter, which was added, along with a preface, a new motto, and poetry, "Songs of Prince Vogelfrei," to the 1887 edition, is even more distinct from the first four. Not only is it written from the standpoint of a *freed* spirit, it ends with both "*incipit parodia*" as well as "*incipit tragoedia*" and so effectively creates a double ending to the book.[1]

Another reason for placing my treatment of the first three chapters of *The Gay Science* in the same section as my treatment of *Daybreak* is that I think the death of God and the elimination of his shadow should be read as the culmination of the critique of moral prejudices that Nietzsche initiates in *Daybreak*. There is much in *Daybreak* – from Nietzsche's call for little deviant acts in chapter 3 to his characterization of the free spirit as a passionate hero ready to violate conventions and suffer the consequences – that prepares the way for this event. So although there are noticeable differences between the first three chapters of *The Gay Science* and *Daybreak*, there are also important continuities that encourage us to read these chapters as chapters 6, 7, and 8 of *Daybreak*.

There is also an important shift that takes place from *Daybreak* to *The Gay Science*. Nietzsche not only begins to speak more about poetry and art,

---

[1] I am echoing here a point that Groddeck (1997) made some time ago and has been repeated more recently by Georg (2015: 28).

he himself takes a renewed interest in music during this time and composes his own poetry. As he explains in *Ecce Homo*, Nietzsche returned to music – something he had largely eschewed after fleeing Bayreuth in 1876 – when he met with Köselitz in Recoaro, Italy, to go over the proofs of *Daybreak* in the spring of 1881. There, Nietzsche claims that he and Köselitz were "reborn" as "the phoenix of music flew past [them] with lighter and more brilliant feathers than it had ever displayed before" (EH "Books" Z:1).

Nietzsche's interest in music and poetry only intensified after his rendezvous with Köselitz. Not only does he repeatedly refer to Bizet's opera *Carmen* in his letters toward the end of 1881 (KSB 6: 172, 174, and 177), he also takes a serious interest in Köselitz's work as a musician. He tries to help Köselitz get his opera, "Joke, Cunning, and Revenge [*Scherz, List, und Rache*]," staged (KSB 6: 307), and he uses the title of Köselitz's opera for his own set of poems that he adds, with the subtitle, "Prelude in German Rhymes," to the beginning of *The Gay Science*. Moreover, Nietzsche composes *Idylls from Messina* just prior to the publication of *The Gay Science* in the spring of 1882, and although initially published separately in the *Internationale Monatschrift*, these eventually form the basis for the "Songs of Prince Vogelfrei" that were added to the 1887 edition of the work.

The title page of the 1882 edition also gives two hints about the poetic nature of *The Gay Science*. The first is the motto from Ralph Waldo Emerson that implies the union of poetry and philosophy: "To the poet and the wise man, all things are friendly and sacred, all experiences useful, all days holy, all humans divine" (KSA 3: p. 343).[2] The other comes from the title. As he explains in an 1882 letter to Rohde, Nietzsche has in mind the "gaya scienza" – a phrase Nietzsche later adds to the title of the 1887 edition – of the Troubadour (KSB 6: 345). According to Kathleen Higgins (2000: 16), the Troubadours were known for their "music, poetry, and gallant expression," and their particular theme was love, a topic central to *The Gay Science* and closely associated to "the passion for knowledge" that animates this phase of the free spirit.

The significance of Nietzsche's return to poetry in *The Gay Science* for my dialectical reading cannot be overestimated. Nietzsche has moved away from the strict asceticism of *Human* and the corresponding rejection of art and is moving toward the aestheticism characteristic of both his earlier project and his later writings. As I have argued elsewhere (Meyer 2002),

[2] My translation.

the fact that Nietzsche takes a renewed interest in music and opera just prior to beginning work on his own tragedy follows, in striking fashion, the argument of *The Birth of Tragedy Out of the Spirit of Music*. Specifically, it is a musical mood (Nietzsche's rendezvous with Köselitz in 1881) that gives birth to lyric poetry (*Idylls from Messina* and "Joke, Cunning, and Revenge") and then tragedy (*Zarathustra*).

The argument of *The Birth of Tragedy* is also helpful for understanding the dialectical interplay between morality and art that takes place in the shift from *Daybreak* to *The Gay Science*. As I explained in the last chapter, the more Nietzsche's critique of morality advances, the more his interest in art and the aesthetic justification of existence increases. Indeed, this dialectic between art and morality can even be found within the 1882 edition of *The Gay Science*, and part of what I will be doing in these chapters is explaining how this dialectic unfolds in the work. Central to this reading are the divergent treatments of art found in the second and fourth chapters of *The Gay Science*. In the second chapter, Nietzsche provides a more positive assessment of art than he did in *Human*. Nevertheless, this positive assessment is still restrained, and this is evidenced by Nietzsche's puzzling claim at the end of the second chapter that "as an aesthetic phenomenon existence is still *bearable* for us" (GS 107). It is puzzling not only because it is an obvious modification of the leitmotif of *The Birth of Tragedy* (BT 5 and 24), but also because Nietzsche returns to the view of *The Birth of Tragedy* that art can justify and affirm existence in the fourth chapter of *The Gay Science*.

In order to make sense of this contradiction, I argue that the difference between the second and fourth chapters is due to the death of God and the elimination of his shadow in the third chapter of *The Gay Science*. The idea is that Nietzsche can only return to the position of *The Birth of Tragedy* once the free spirit has overcome the ascetic commitment to the absolute value of truth, and as Nietzsche's retrospective reflections make clear (GS 344), the death of God in the third chapter marks the free spirit's recognition that truth does not have absolute value and so the overcoming of the asceticism that characterizes the opening phases of the free spirit project. Because the overcoming of the ascetic ideal results from the quest for truth, *The Gay Science* can be said to enact a *Selbstaufhebung* of the morality of truth that makes possible the rebirth of tragedy in *Zarathustra*.

The Gay Science is also significant for my reading of the free spirit works because Nietzsche is clearly employing prolepticism in the text. As I detailed in Chapter 2, Nietzsche composed *The Gay Science* with central features of *Zarathustra* already in view. Not only does he sketch his ideas for the eternal recurrence in 1881 under the title "the new weight" (KSA 9: 11[141]), he also pens a version of the opening lines of *Zarathustra* in this same notebook (KSA 9: 11[195]). Moreover, initial drafts of *The Gay Science* included frequent mentions of Zarathustra that Nietzsche removed in the final version. For instance, he planned to have Zarathustra announce the death of God (GS 125; KSA 14: pp. 256–257) and to call the final chapter, "Zarathustra's Leisure" (KSA 9: 12[225]). Finally, Brusotti (2016: 213) notes that the third chapter of the handwritten manuscript ended with aphorism 268, rather than 275, and the former originally included an appearance of Zarathustra (see KSA 9: 15[50]). Thus, it is clear that Nietzsche has consciously constructed *The Gay Science* so that it foreshadows his next work, *Thus Spoke Zarathustra*.

It has been argued that the lyrical poetry of "Joke, Cunning, and Revenge" also foreshadows the emergence of the tragedy of *Zarathustra*. According to Christian Benne (2015: 29–30), the lyrical poems should be understood as "epigrams in verse" (KSB 6: 224), and as such, they provide a stylistic bridge between the aphorisms of the free spirit works and the poetry of *Zarathustra*. The contents of these poems also point back to the previous free spirit works, and this is most evident in "Human, All Too Human: A Book." Taken together, these poems function, in both style and content, as a bridge between the previous free spirit works and Nietzsche's eventual turn toward tragic and even comic poetry in his later works.

My proleptic reading of *The Gay Science* contrasts with recent interpretations by Higgins (2000) and Monika Langer (2010) that apply the dynamic of tragedy and comedy to *The Gay Science* itself. Even Franco (2011: 139), who situates *The Gay Science* between the earlier free spirit works and Nietzsche's subsequent publications, follows Higgins in holding that there is a dialectical ebb and flow between tragedy and comedy in the work. In contrast, I argue that *The Gay Science* is a work in "media vita" (GS 324),[3] and so rather than applying Nietzsche's references to tragedy and comedy to *The Gay Science*, we should understand these as proleptic references to *Zarathustra* and the possibility of a subsequent comedy in which the waves of laughter overwhelm even the tragedians (GS 1).

There is, however, one point on which I agree with Higgins, Langer, and Franco: Like other free spirit works, *The Gay Science* consists of a series of interconnected aphorisms that reveal a coherent structure upon closer

---

[3] Salaquarda (1997: 171) emphasizes this point and refers to an 1888 letter in which Nietzsche calls it his "most middle" book (KSB 8: 1075).

examination, and so the task of the interpreter is to decipher these interconnections in reading the work as a whole. In this spirit, Franco (2011: 107) has pointed to a *Nachlass* note that provides possible titles for each of the chapters in the 1882 edition of *The Gay Science*. Among the five titles given in the note, we know two of their corresponding chapters: "Sanctus Januarius" is the title of chapter 4, and "Joke, Cunning, and Revenge" is the title of the poetic prelude. Thus, there are three titles remaining that need to be associated with their corresponding chapters in *The Gay Science*. Because it is obvious that "Thoughts of a Godless One" is the title of chapter 3 and chapter 2 seems to correspond to "On Artists and Women," "From the 'Moral Diary'" must be the planned title for the first chapter (KSA 9: 19[12]). So understood, there is a unifying theme to each chapter, and, in what follows, I highlight the structure of the work and discuss the various ways in which *The Gay Science* can be seen as emerging from the free spirit works that precede it and as pointing to the works that follow it.

Chapter 1: From the 'Moral Diary'

The first aphorism of *The Gay Science*, "The Teachers of the Purpose of Existence," is important for understanding the arc of *The Gay Science* and central to my interpretation of Nietzsche's oeuvre. The opening of the aphorism continues and even radicalizes the treatment of morality central to *Daybreak*. We are, claims Nietzsche, all hardwired "to do what is good for the preservation of the species." Nietzsche, however, goes on to claim that in contrast to what many myopic people think, harmful and even evil inclinations may belong "to the most amazing economy of the preservation of the species" (GS 1). The passage takes an interesting turn when Nietzsche claims that it may be impossible to live in a way that damages the species. No matter how we live, we will always find some eulogist. However, we may never find someone who can mock us as an individual. Even the best and most gifted so far have not had enough genius to be able "to laugh" at themselves as they would "have to laugh in order to laugh *out of the whole truth*." Nevertheless, Nietzsche claims that this laughter "may yet have a future." Once we accept that "the species is everything, *one* is always none" and so make accessible to everyone "this ultimate liberation and irresponsibility," laughter and wisdom may unite to form a "gay science" (GS 1).

As the passage unfolds, Nietzsche claims that the present age is much different from this future in which wisdom and laughter will unite. This means that *The Gay Science* begins with the claim that a "gay science" is only a future possibility, not something now being practiced, and so if we are going to find a gay science in Nietzsche's works, we are not, paradoxically, going to find it in *The Gay Science*. Instead, we must wait until "the comedy of existence" becomes "conscious of itself." For now, "we still live in the age of tragedy, the age of moralities and religions." That is, we still live in an age in which "the teacher of the purpose of existence" convinces mankind that life is worth living *because* of some grander purpose, and this teacher "wants to make sure that we do not *laugh* at existence, or at ourselves" by insisting that "there is something at which it is absolutely forbidden henceforth to laugh" (GS 1).

Nevertheless, Nietzsche also claims that, "*in the long run* every one of these great teachers of a purpose was vanquished by laughter, reason, and nature" as "the short tragedy always gave way again and returned into the eternal comedy of existence" (GS 1), and the aphorism concludes with the claim that both tragedy and comedy are necessary for the preservation of the species. In terms of the free spirit works, this is a striking claim. Although he has gradually softened his initial rejection of art as the free spirit works have unfolded, at no point has Nietzsche used aesthetic categories to characterize entire ages or even existence itself and claimed that certain forms of poetry are necessary for the preservation of the species. Instead, this is a return to the views Nietzsche expressed in his earliest writings in which he spoke of "tragic wisdom," a "tragic world-view," and a "tragic age" and argued that the "*retention of the sense for the tragic*" constitutes the only hope for "the future of humanity" (RWB 4).

What is also new in the progression of the free spirit works but commonplace in his earliest writings is the emphasis on life and the idea that poets "promote the life of the species, *by promoting the faith in life*" (GS 1). The resonance of this claim with the argument of *The Birth of Tragedy* should be obvious. However, Nietzsche goes beyond the argument of *The Birth of Tragedy* by introducing comedy into the economy of life-preservation and affirmation. Indeed, this seems to be the primary criticism that Nietzsche issues in the preface of the 1886 edition of his first work: Other than a brief reference to the comic discharge of the absurdity of existence (BT 7), there is no extended discussion of the this-worldly comfort of laughter, and this is why the work runs the risk of falling into the trap of an other-worldly romanticism (BT "Attempt" 7).

Not only does the first aphorism draw on themes from his earliest writings, Nietzsche is clearly foreshadowing some of his future projects, so much so that the real question is the extent to which he is doing this.

The claim that we now live in the age of tragedy points to the ending of the 1882 edition with "*incipit tragoedia*" and so the tragedy of *Zarathustra* that follows. Nietzsche also associates tragedy with the teachers of the purpose of existence, and so he may be referring to Zarathustra's teaching of the *Uebermensch* in this passage. This is because the *Uebermensch* provides a purpose for human existence in light of the death of God, and within the context of *Zarathustra* I, the *Uebermensch* is a figure about which one should not laugh. Nevertheless, Nietzsche insists that "the short tragedy always gave way again and returned into the eternal comedy of existence: and 'the waves of uncountable laughter' – to cite Aeschylus – must in the end overwhelm even the greatest of these tragedians" (GS 1). Applied to Nietzsche's own writings, some work or set of works must follow upon the tragedy of *Zarathustra* that returns to the eternal comedy of existence.

Whereas the first aphorism signals a significant shift in tenor and topic from *Daybreak*, the second aphorism, "The Intellectual Conscience," develops the unfolding argument of the free spirit project. The intellectual conscience explores, among other things, how valuations about good and evil – and so the moral conscience – were formed and inquires into the truth of these valuations. Nietzsche's reference to the intellectual conscience is a reference to the truth-seeking activity initiated in *Human*, and Nietzsche's application of this intellectual conscience to the moral conscience is precisely the subterranean project that *Daybreak* initiates and the opening of *The Gay Science* continues.

At the same time, the aphorism represents an advance on *Daybreak* in at least two respects. First, it speaks from the standpoint of one who has already started this project, and so it looks down with *contempt* upon those who do not feel the pull of the intellectual conscience. Indeed, the aphorism seems to foreshadow the contempt the madman expresses toward those in the marketplace who fail to understand the consequences of God's death and so those who look at the madman "with strange eyes" and go "right on handling his scales, calling this good and that evil" (GS 2). Second, the aphorism also expresses a coming-to-awareness of the singularity and uniqueness of the passion, that is, the passion for knowledge, that now drives the free spirit. Although Nietzsche wants to convince himself that everyone else shares his contempt for those who "stand in the midst of this *rerum concordia discors* and the whole marvelous uncertainty and rich ambiguity of existence *without questioning*," he knows that this is a projection of his idiosyncratic longings onto the rest of humanity (GS 2).

In the next aphorism, "Noble and Common," Nietzsche connects this injustice to the "passion for knowledge," and he argues that such passion is the marker of the noble. Here, the common man is portrayed much like the last man of *Zarathustra*: there is nothing that motivates him other than self-directed, short-term advantage. By contrast, the noble individual is motivated by passion that posits a "singular value standard" and so makes him willing to sacrifice other things – including his own advantage – for the sake of this passion. The injustice of this higher type arises because he rarely recognizes the idiosyncrasy of this taste and so posits "its values and disvalues as generally valid" (GS 3).

In the fourth aphorism, Nietzsche continues his discussion of passion and combines it with claims about "evil" from the first aphorism. Part of what makes "evil" good, on Nietzsche's account, is that it awakens the passions among individuals and the corresponding interest in doing things that are new, daring, and untried. Indeed, Nietzsche defines the "wicked" or "evil" in this passage as that which is new and so that which violates reigning convention: "what is new, however, is always *evil*, being that which wants to conquer and overthrow the old boundary markers and the old pieties; and only what is old is good." Although the so-called good defend reigning convention, Nietzsche claims that, "the ploughshare of evil must come again and again" (GS 4).

Nietzsche's critique of modern morality continues in the next aphorism. There, he takes aim at "unconditional duties" in general and Kant's "categorical imperative" in particular. Similar to his attacks on morality elsewhere, Nietzsche provides an account of the amoral motivation for adopting moral principles. Specifically, he claims that unconditional moral principles like the categorical imperative are invented, first, to justify some "great pathos" and inspire confidence in others and, second, to provide justification for the subordination of oneself to another. In both cases, Nietzsche casts those who espouse such moral principles as "opponents of moral enlightenment and skepticism" (GS 5).

As we have seen, Nietzsche increasingly emphasizes the experimental character of the quest for knowledge, and he often contrasts this experimental character with the unconditional duties he is critiquing. At the end of "Something for the Industrious," Nietzsche asks "whether science can furnish goals of action after it has proved that it can take such goals away and annihilate them." To answer this, Nietzsche appeals to an "experimentation" that "would allow every kind of heroism to find satisfaction" (GS 7).

Only a few aphorisms later, Nietzsche again takes up the topic of science and the aim of science, and he argues that science itself furnishes no goal. In this case, he challenges the idea that science should provide as much pleasure as possible, and he does so by making the Stoic – and even Heraclitean – point that it may be impossible to separate pleasure and pain. However, Nietzsche explicitly opens the possibility of departing from the Stoic position – and implicitly the Epicurean and Christian (see KSA 14: p. 240) – that we therefore ought to avoid pleasure because of its inherent connection to displeasure. By choosing to avoid pain, we also undermine our capacity to experience joy, and so Nietzsche suggests that we should embrace pain in order to experience great joy (GS 12). According to Nietzsche, science can actually promote both goals, and although not explicit, Nietzsche seems to be directly pointing to a "gay science" that can make "new galaxies of joy flare up" but must also be a "*great dispenser of pain*" (GS 12). Nietzsche says in a related *Nachlass* note that, in order to avoid the pessimistic conclusion that the predominance of pain proves that life is not worth living, we need to recognize that many good things come from pain and so "we must increase the pain in the world if we want to increase pleasure and wisdom" (KSA 9: 13[4]; see also KSA 9: 15[16]).

It is worth pausing to reflect on the relationship between the position Nietzsche is articulating here and the positions he has articulated in his previous works. Nietzsche's insistence on the unity of pain (suffering) and pleasure (joy) and on the corresponding need to embrace pain and suffering marks a clear departure from the Epicurean stance he adopts in *The Wanderer* that focuses on calming the passions and enjoying the simple pleasures of existence. At the same time, the position Nietzsche is adopting in *The Gay Science* marks a return to a central idea of *The Birth of Tragedy*. Specifically, Nietzsche argues that at the core of the aesthetic justification of existence is the idea that musical dissonance and so tragedy reveals the way in which we can embrace the pleasure and pain, suffering and joy that are essential features of the cycle of life and death (BT 24).

In between his remarks about science are a series of aphorisms that deal with the unconscious and introduce Nietzsche's views about the superficiality of consciousness. Nietzsche begins by distinguishing between conscious and what he calls "unconscious virtues" in an aphorism that bears this name (GS 8). In the next two aphorisms, he explains how past habits and evaluations concealed in the unconscious can "erupt" into something extraordinary (GS 9–10). In the aphorism, "Consciousness," Nietzsche then rejects the idea that consciousness constitutes "the *kernel* of man;

what is abiding, eternal, ultimate, and most original." Instead, consciousness develops latest in the organism and gives rise to countless errors
(GS 11).

Nietzsche continues to focus on the non-rational elements of the human
psyche by discussing two themes, power and love, central to his later
revaluation project. In "On the Doctrine of the Feeling of Power,"
Nietzsche again employs a strategy familiar from *Daybreak* to critique
benevolence and pity. Although not yet couched in the language of the
will to power, Nietzsche claims that we want to help people because it
strengthens our own power. By merely witnessing the effect we have in
helping others, we directly experience the power we have over them. We
also enhance our power indirectly because those we help will want to help
us in turn. The aphorism concludes with a similar analysis of pity: Pity for
others gives those who have nothing great to achieve a feeling of power
over those they help (GS 13). In short, feelings of benevolence, sympathy,
and pity can be analyzed in terms of the feeling of power.

The next aphorism is about love, and the point is to re-conceive of what
are often thought of as selfless forms of love, such as neighbor love and the
love of truth, in terms of a self-regarding desire for possession. Here again,
Nietzsche claims that the supposed selflessness embedded within Christian
neighbor love is really a self-regarding desire for possession. According to
Nietzsche, this lust for possession is an attempt to take pleasure in oneself
by changing something that does not belong to the self into something
that does. Sexual love is one example of this lust for possession. This can
also be applied to the love of knowledge. This is implied both by
Nietzsche's explicit reference to *Eros* and so implicitly Plato's *Symposium*
in the aphorism[4] and by the unfolding passion for knowledge that is
central to this stage of the free spirit. In this sense, Nietzsche no longer
understands the quest for knowledge in terms of a selfless contemplation of
an objective order. Instead, it is a quest for possession that is ultimately
selfish (GS 14).

Nietzsche continues to analyze selflessness in terms of an underlying
selfishness a few aphorisms later. He repeats concerns, already raised in
Daybreak, about the way in which society's praise of selfless actions
effectively transforms individuals into self-sacrificial instruments for the
common good. According to Nietzsche, society praises what he calls
virtues because virtues are instincts that dominate the individual to the

---

[4] Pippin (2010: 35) emphasizes the erotic dimension of *The Gay Science* and claims that, "the gay
science is, then, knowledge of erotics." For more on these themes, see Babich (2006).

detriment of that individual, and so virtues show that an individual is prepared to sacrifice his own interests for something greater. In this sense, the praise of virtue is meant to deprive human beings of what Nietzsche calls their "noblest selfishness [*Selbstsucht*]." The contradiction within this sort of morality, according to Nietzsche, is that it does not arise from selflessness. Instead, the selfishness of the community requires others to develop virtues that make them into instruments for the common good and so deprives them of their noble selfishness (GS 21).

As Nietzsche remarks in a draft for "To the Teachers of Selflessness [*Selbstlosigkeit*],"⁵ preaching selflessness only makes sense for someone like the Buddha who teaches "pessimistic nihilism" and the depravity of existence (KSA 14: p. 242). That is, selfless behavior is good only if the renunciation of the self is the ultimate good. Nietzsche, however, subjects such renunciation to a similar critique in a subsequent aphorism. Although most people see in the so-called man of renunciation his willingness to renounce his possessions as an act of self-sacrifice, Nietzsche claims that this renunciation is really a form of selfishness. The man of renunciation gives up his things for a higher reality and, in so doing, he secretly takes pride in his belief that he is soaring above us. In this sense, the man of renunciation is really a man of affirmation in the sense that his so-called renunciations are really designed to feed his sense of superiority (GS 27).

Toward the end of the chapter, Nietzsche emphasizes the role that suffering plays in the human psyche and, in this respect, he returns to the pessimistic framework of *The Birth of Tragedy*. To recap, Nietzsche divided the tragic Greeks from the post-Socratic Greeks along the lines of pessimism and optimism and so along the lines of whether one believed that suffering was an ineluctable feature of existence (factual pessimism) or that suffering could be cured or eliminated (optimism). Nietzsche criticized post-Socratic philosophy for holding the optimistic belief that knowledge represented a kind of panacea or cure for suffering (BT 15). In contrast, we have seen throughout the free spirit works the interest Nietzsche takes in Hellenic philosophy and the therapeutic strategies they have to offer.

The Gay Science marks a return to a number of positions that Nietzsche held in his earliest works, and his view of Hellenic philosophy is no different. For instance, we have already seen Nietzsche diverging from the Stoic interest in minimizing both suffering and joy in "The Aim of Science" (GS 12). In "Epicurus," Nietzsche now explicitly casts the

---

⁵ Kaufmann (1974: 92) mistranslates "*Selbstlosigkeit*" as "selfishness."

happiness of Epicurus – and implicitly the Epicurean solution to the problem of suffering offered in *The Wanderer* – as something superficial. In the aphorism, Nietzsche recalls the imagery of *The Wanderer* by associating Epicurus with "the happiness of the afternoon of antiquity." However, Nietzsche then asserts that, "such happiness could be invented only by a man who was suffering continually." In other words, the happiness of Epicurus, and so the happiness on display in *The Wanderer*, was mere surface – an invention – and beneath this sunlight was a sea of suffering that forced Epicurus to become inventive (GS 45).[6]

Nietzsche addresses topics of pain and suffering as well as the related question of the value of life only three aphorisms later in "Knowledge of Misery." The point of the aphorism is to critique "the emergence of pessimistic philosophies," and similar to his implicit critique of Schopenhauer in *The Birth of Tragedy*, Nietzsche's tactic is *not* to deny the presence of suffering in the economy of existence and so the description of existence that such philosophies provide (factual pessimism). Instead, his goal is to counter the valuation that such philosophers place on existence given the ineluctability of human suffering (evaluative pessimism). According to Nietzsche, pessimistic philosophers now condemn life because they have become so sensitive to physical pain and psychic suffering. Had they been educated like those of former ages to endure pain and suffering, they wouldn't suffer from what Nietzsche calls the "mosquito bites of the soul." Thus, Nietzsche concludes that the best recipe against the idea that "existence is evil" and so evaluative pessimism is greater exposure to misery (GS 48).

In the final aphorism of the chapter, "The Craving for Suffering," Nietzsche again discusses suffering in a way that recalls Schopenhauer's philosophy. Thus, he claims that many Europeans crave suffering as a way of avoiding boredom. The problem, however, is that they project this suffering outwards, thereby creating monsters in society that they then seek to vanquish. Nietzsche, in contrast, counsels such individuals to create their own internal distress. The idea seems to be that through such distress a legitimate response to suffering can emerge, one in which genuine happiness can be painted on the wall of existence (GS 56).

Nietzsche's talk of creating one's own distress could be a reference to the free spirit project. On the one hand, *Human* seems to be dedicated to creating the kind of internal distress Nietzsche mentions here. On the other hand, this distress could relate to the passionate condition that

---

[6] See Ansell-Pearson (2017: 136–138) for an alternative reading of the aphorism.

emerges in the later phases of *Daybreak*, and the penultimate aphorism of the first chapter of *The Gay Science* explicitly connects passion to nobility. The topic of the aphorism is the question of what makes a person noble, and after rejecting a series of possible answers, including the willingness to do something for others, Nietzsche claims that the noble soul is attacked by a peculiar passion that uses "a rare and singular standard and almost a madness." It is this passion that creates "a self-sufficiency that overflows and gives to men and things" (GS 55). It also permits the noble soul to live differently from conventions and so withstand the solitude that results from such "madness" (GS 50). Although nothing is explicit, aphorisms like these seem to be preparing for the emergence of a self-determining individual that Nietzsche sketches in chapter 4 (GS 335).

Before moving on, there is one final aphorism in the first chapter that needs to be discussed. This is both because of the role it has played in a larger discussion of Nietzsche's views on truth and because of the way in which it transitions to topics of the second chapter. The title of the aphorism is "The Consciousness of Appearance," and the aphorism is important because Nietzsche rejects the distinction between appearance and reality. This, it has been argued, marks an advance in the understanding of reality Nietzsche articulates in *Human*, where he still grants the possible existence of a metaphysical world (HH 9). Now, however, Nietzsche seems to be rejecting the metaphysical world, even though he does not yet fully appreciate the consequences of doing so (Clark 1990: Ch. 4).

On the reading I am defending here, Nietzsche *qua* author fully understands the consequences of rejecting the appearance-reality distinction – something he did via his interpretation of Heraclitus as early as 1873 in *Philosophy in the Tragic Age* (PTAG 5). However, he is slowly unpacking the consequences of this theory as the free spirit project develops. Thus, Nietzsche's rejection of opposites in the first aphorism of *Human* implies a corresponding rejection of the distinction between appearance and reality in the form of the thing in itself. Nevertheless, Nietzsche takes pains to walk himself and his readers through a progression in which we are slowly detached from the metaphysical world. Indeed, even with the assertion that appearance is not the opposite of some essence in *The Gay Science*, Nietzsche is still not claiming, as he does in a work like *Twilight of the Idols*, that appearances *are* reality. Instead, Nietzsche compares the apparent world to a dream world, and although he, as a knower, is aware of the dream-like character of this world, he claims that the task for such knowers is "*the continuation of the dream*" (GS 54). As we will see in the next section, this denial of the metaphysical world along with the emphasis on the dreamlike character of experience goes hand in hand with Nietzsche's turn to art in the subsequent chapters of *The Gay Science*.

Chapter 2: On Artists and Women

Chapter 2 of *The Gay Science* is an important moment for my interpretation for two reasons. First, and less controversially, the chapter marks a clear departure from the rejection of art that Nietzsche authored in *Human* and an ever-closer approximation of the position he articulated in *The Birth of Tragedy*. Although some might argue that Nietzsche has simply changed his mind – again! – on such matters and so returned to a version of his earlier views, the fact that he is returning to a version of the position he held in his earlier works suggests that he never embraced, *qua* author, a wholesale rejection of art in *Human*. Second, this chapter nevertheless presents a more tempered view of art in comparison to *The Birth of Tragedy*, and I argue that this is because Nietzsche's praise of art is still restrained by the high value he places on honesty and truth and so is still under the shadow of God. However, once God's shadow is eliminated in the third chapter, Nietzsche is free to endorse a more robust view of art in the fourth chapter of *The Gay Science* and so promote views that fall more in line with his earliest writings, now stripped of any metaphysical commitments.

The second chapter begins roughly where the first chapter left off: discussing the distinction between appearance and reality. The aphorism "To the Realists," is addressed to a self-described (and self-deceived) realist. Realists, in the aphorism, are those who believe that the way the world appears to them is the way the world is in itself. Nietzsche, however, makes two points that contradict the realist's self-understanding. First, these so-called realists are not as sober as they take themselves to be. Instead, their sobriety contains a hidden and unacknowledged passion and even drunkenness. Second, Nietzsche doubts that these realists can ever reach an intelligible reality. On the one hand, Nietzsche's skepticism here – reminiscent of the argument from "On Truth and Lies" – seems to be based on the claim that there is a reality we cannot know because we can never get beyond appearances. On the other hand, Nietzsche seems to endorse the stronger claim – one that resonates more with the position in "The Consciousness of Appearance" (GS 54) – that there is no reality that transcends appearance. Thus, he not only doubts that we can "subtract the phantasm and every human *contribution*" from the appearance of a cloud or a mountain, he also asserts that, "there is no 'reality' for us – not for you either, my sober friends" (GS 57).

The next aphorism, "Only as Creators!" continues this line of inquiry and again recalls the argument of "On Truth and Lies." Although the general point is to emphasize the significance of appearances over reality, the aphorism, like "On Truth and Lies," curiously seems to imply the very appearance-reality distinction that Nietzsche just called into question. Thus, he begins by claiming that what things are called is much more important than what they really are. This implies that there is a distinction between opinions about things and what things are independently of those opinions, and Nietzsche's subsequent claim implies this, too. This is because he claims that opinions about things "are almost always wrong and arbitrary, thrown over things like a dress and altogether foreign to their nature and even to their skin," and so this implies that there is a real nature underlying the reputation attached to a thing (GS 58).

Despite the potential inconsistency here, Nietzsche nevertheless concludes the aphorism with two points that again suggest the denial of the appearance-reality distinction. First, because things are what they are called or what they are taken to be, we can destroy the "so called 'reality'" of these things by revealing their origins. Second, just as we can destroy things by pointing to their origins, "it is enough to create new names and estimations and probabilities in order to create in the long run new 'things'" (GS 58). In this latter sense, Nietzsche seems to be endorsing the view that reality is constituted by appearances, and this means that a strong poet can effectively "create" our lived realities by creating new names and estimations of things.

In the next aphorism, Nietzsche relates the previous discussion of appearance to art. He begins by highlighting the way in which lovers prefer a selection of appearances to reality. Just as a lover does not think about the natural functions of the beloved, a lover of God in previous ages did not want to know about the workings of nature from science. Thus, when the worshipper was told that nature functioned according to laws rather than the will of God, he simply ignored the science and lived in a dream as best he could. In this sense, he lived in a dream while awake. Nietzsche, however, goes on to remark that "we" artists of today are much like the lover of God. This is because we "ignore what is natural" and so we are "somnambulists of the day!" (GS 59).

The position adopted here is again striking in the context of Nietzsche's larger free spirit project. Although we have seen the gradual introduction of non-rational elements of the human psyche such as the passions and the feeling of power as well as more positive remarks about art, nowhere, until now, has Nietzsche referred to himself or "we free spirits" as artists and nowhere has he embraced appearance rather than truth to such an extent. Nevertheless, there are aphorisms in chapter 2 of *The Gay Science* which show that Nietzsche's praise of art is nevertheless more restrained than we find either in *The Birth of Tragedy* or in the fourth chapter of *The Gay Science*.

As we have seen, the ancient Greeks are never far from Nietzsche's mind. In chapter 2 of *The Gay Science*, however, Nietzsche makes some claims about the Greeks that are quite at odds with the position he articulates in *The Birth of Tragedy*. In "Art and Nature," Nietzsche begins by claiming that the Athenians "liked to hear people speak well. Nothing distinguishes them so thoroughly from non-Greeks as does this truly greedy craving." They also demanded that passion speak well on stage, even though passion can hardly articulate itself when it occurs naturally. Based on such claims, Nietzsche rejects Aristotle's theory of tragedy: Rather than experiencing a catharsis of pity and fear, the ancient Greeks, Nietzsche now claims, went to tragedies "*in order to hear beautiful speeches*" (GS 80).

The emphasis on speech along with reason giving in the passage is worlds away from the theory of tragedy that Nietzsche articulated in his first work. Indeed, this understanding of tragedy seems to fall under what Nietzsche criticized in *The Birth of Tragedy* as "aesthetic Socratism" (BT 12). To recall, Nietzsche argued that genuine tragedy emerged from two art drives, the Apollonian and the Dionysian, that symbolized the imagination and the will, respectively, and he not only downplayed any significant role that speech and reason had in epic, lyric, and tragic poetry, he also argued that the emergence of the logo-centrism of Socrates put an end to the music-driven tragedies of Aeschylus and Sophocles.

What is striking about each of the points above, then, is that they stand in direct contradiction to *The Birth of Tragedy*. Here again, one could argue that Nietzsche's remarks in *The Gay Science* constitute a shift in his understanding of tragedy and that he has therefore left behind the theory of *The Birth of Tragedy* for an understanding of tragedy that is more rationalistic than Aristotle's. The problem is that Nietzsche provides an understanding of tragedy in the 1888 *Twilight of the Idols* that criticizes Aristotle by emphasizing the non-rational, vitalistic forces at work in the genre and so corresponds to the understanding of tragedy articulated in his first work (TI "What I Owe" 5). Thus, if Nietzsche has changed his mind in *The Gay Science* about the nature of tragedy, then he must have changed his mind again by 1888 so as to return to the view of *The Birth of Tragedy*. Because this makes his thoughts about tragedy strangely circular, even schizophrenic, I think we should read this aphorism as part of an unfolding dialectic between truth and art in the free spirit works. That is, the view of tragedy articulated here is that of Nietzsche *qua* free spirit, not Nietzsche *qua* author, and so it is not a view that Nietzsche himself holds at this time.

In further aphorisms, Nietzsche continues to adopt positions that seem out of keeping with both his earlier and later works. In "Esprit as un-Greek," he claims that "the Greeks were exceedingly logical and plain in all of their thinking and so they differed from the French and their esprit" (GS 82). Although this may characterize the Greeks after the Socratic turn, it is certainly out of step with Nietzsche's praise of pre-Socratic poetry and culture in *The Birth of Tragedy* and the re-emergence of Dionysus in his later writings. In "Of the Theater," Nietzsche argues that whoever is capable of tragedy and comedy in himself does best to stay away from the theater and the music of intoxication (GS 86) and so the *Rausch* that he associates with Dionysus. In "Prose and Poetry," Nietzsche continues to praise more rationalized forms of artistic expression in a way that diverges from the music-centered account of poetry in *The Birth of Tragedy*. Whereas he attacks the novel as a degenerate art form in his first work (BT 14), he now claims that the great masters of prose – such as Giacomo Leopardi and Ralph Waldo Emerson – have "almost always been poets" (GS 92).

In "On the Origin of Poetry," Nietzsche uncharacteristically defends a utilitarian account of poetry. Specifically, he claims that the rhythmic force of poetic language performed very specific functions in ancient times. On the one hand, because it moved and impressed itself on humans so easily, it was believed that poetic language could "*compel* the gods by using rhythm and to force their hand: poetry was thrown at them like a magical snare" (GS 84). On the other hand, it was used by the likes of the Pythagoreans and Empedocles to cleanse the soul of unwanted emotions and so-called demons. Indeed, Nietzsche claims that, "by means of verse one almost became a god," and he notes that even today, philosophers are still swayed by verse because they cite poets to support their claims, thereby forgetting Homer's remark that poets tell many lies (GS 84).

As the motto from Emerson suggests, *The Gay Science* is a work in which poetry and wisdom merge, and the relationship between philosophy and art plays a central role in one of the most important aphorisms in the second chapter of *The Gay Science*: "Schopenhauer's Followers" (GS 99).

It not only deals with some of the central themes of *The Gay Science*, but also refers back to Nietzsche's relationship to Schopenhauer and Wagner. In the aphorism, Nietzsche divides the real or cultured Schopenhauer from the excesses of Schopenhauer that were appropriated by "barbaric" followers like Wagner. On the one hand, there is a Schopenhauer endowed with a strong "intellectual conscience" who, according to Nietzsche, "lived and died 'as a Voltairian'," that is, the figure to whom Nietzsche dedicated *Human* (see KSA 8: 27[43]). This Schopenhauer wrote with a clarity that was almost English, not German, and with a cleanliness regarding matters of the Church, and he defended doctrines such as the "instrumental character of the intellect and the unfreedom of the will." On the other hand, there is the more mystical thinker who abandoned the aforementioned cleanliness. This Schopenhauer propounded doctrines such as the existence of one will, was ecstatic about genius, believed that pity could break through the principle of individuation, and claimed that dying is the real purpose of existence (GS 99).

It was the more mystical Schopenhauer to which the barbaric Wagner was attracted, and just as he did with Hegel's philosophy, Wagner began to read his own views into Schopenhauer's philosophy. However, Nietzsche claims that Schopenhauer's philosophy was completely at odds with Wagner and Wagner's heroes. Heroes like Siegfried exhibit an "innocence of the utmost selfishness [*Selbstsucht*], the faith in great passion as the good in itself" (GS 99). This, according to Nietzsche, smells much more like Spinoza than Schopenhauer, and this description of the hero is very much in keeping with the kind of free-spiritedness Nietzsche is pursuing in *The Gay Science*.

After listing the ways in which Wagner is Schopenhauerian, Nietzsche concludes the aphorism on a conciliatory note vis-à-vis Wagner that explains his own turn toward the free spirit project. Similar to the argument of *Richard Wagner in Bayreuth*, Nietzsche claims that we ought to remain committed disciples of the true and authentic Wagner, and being a true disciple of the authentic Wagner means being authentic and true to ourselves. For Wagner's life shouts: "Be a man and do not follow me – but yourself! But yourself!" Nietzsche concludes the aphorism by quoting a passage from *Richard Wagner in Bayreuth* that emphasizes the importance of freedom, in contrast to obedience to custom, and the need for each individual to undertake this project himself (GS 99). On my reading, this is precisely the prescription that Nietzsche has been following in the free spirit works since fleeing Wagner's festival in Bayreuth in 1876, and it is an idea that takes on ever-greater significance as the free spirit project unfolds.

Although the contents of "Schopenhauer's Followers" largely resonate with some of Nietzsche's earlier writings and many of his later ideas, the final aphorism of chapter 2, "Our Ultimate Gratitude to Art," presents a view of art in which Nietzsche seems to move consciously between his celebration of art in *The Birth of Tragedy* and his rejection of art in *Human*. On the one hand, the aphorism casts art as a cure for the otherwise depressing discoveries that Nietzsche unpacked via the natural sciences in *Human*. On the other hand, Nietzsche opposes the intellectual virtue of honesty to art and so claims that art can only make existence bearable for us. All of this – including the latter half of the aphorism in which tragedy and comedy again come to the fore – is worth a closer look, especially because the aphorism has received some attention in the secondary literature.

The aphorism begins with a striking claim: If there were no art, which Nietzsche defines as a "kind of cult of the untrue," then we would find the truth science reveals, namely, that "delusion and error are conditions of human knowledge," utterly unbearable. The virtue of honesty or *Redlichkeit*, which is central to the free spirit project and closely related to the "passion for knowledge," "would lead to nausea and suicide." There is, however, "a counterforce against our honesty," and this is "art as the *good* will to appearance." What makes life bearable, then, is art. Thus, Nietzsche writes, "as an aesthetic phenomenon existence is still *bearable* for us," and this is why – and here Nietzsche echoes the themes of tragedy and comedy from the first aphorism – we "must discover the *hero* no less than the *fool* in our passion for knowledge" (GS 107).[7]

What is striking about the opening lines is not that Nietzsche thinks that truth is unbearable or even that the natural sciences reveal such unbearable truths. This idea is a central feature of the tragic philosophy in *The Birth of Tragedy*, and we have seen how Nietzsche turns to the natural sciences in *Human* to unpack such pessimistic truths. What is striking is that, in contrast to the anti-art ethos of *Human*, Nietzsche now identifies art as providing a life-preserving strategy, and in this sense, Nietzsche is adopting a position much closer to *The Birth of Tragedy*. This is because art prevents nausea and suicide, and these are two terms Nietzsche employs in his first work (BT 7). At the same time, art does not – as Nietzsche claims in *The Birth of Tragedy* – make life into an object

---

[7] See Brusotti (2016) for a detailed analysis of this aphorism along with the revisions that Nietzsche made in the final stages of the editing process.

of intense longing and affirmation. Instead, art simply allows us to get by, bearing the suffering and misery essential to life.

For Aaron Ridley, these reflections provide a statement of Nietzsche's mature view about the relationship between art and truth. According to this reading, Nietzsche thinks we must face the ugly truth about our existence and the world. However, because this truth may push us to nausea and suicide, we need art to soften the blow of truth by "rounding off something and, as it were, finishing the poem." Thus, according to Ridley, we need "to cultivate and value the false, but to do so to the minimum extent necessary to ward off 'nausea and suicide'" (2007: 82). So understood, Nietzsche endorses an alteration between pursuing truth to the greatest extent possible and embracing an art that mollifies some of the deadly effects that this pursuit can have.[8]

As Christopher Janaway has pointed out, one problem with Ridley's reading is that it presents Nietzsche as employing art in service of the truth. On Ridley's reading, the goal is maximal truth or honesty, and art helps us out when the truth becomes unbearable. This, however, does not resonate with the concerns about truth that Nietzsche raises in later works. Specifically, Janaway claims that, "Nietzsche paints the value of truth as poignantly troubling and problematic," and he cites passages from both the *Genealogy* and the late *Nachlass* to show that Nietzsche problematizes the value of truth as well as the relationship between truth and art (2013: 266–267). So understood, there are reasons to think that Nietzsche abandons in his later works the position Ridley extracts from GS 107.

On the dialectical reading of the free spirit, Ridley is right to argue that Nietzsche expresses the view in GS 107 that art is a means by which a lover of truth can bear existence. However, Ridley is wrong to infer that Nietzsche *qua* author embraces this position. This is not simply because Nietzsche eventually questions the value of truth in his later writings. Indeed, we have seen that Nietzsche questioned the value of truth in his earlier writings as well. Instead, it is because the view articulated in GS 107 conflicts with the view Nietzsche articulates in the fourth chapter of *The Gay Science* about the relationship between art, science, and honesty (GS 335). There, Nietzsche claims that science and honesty are subordinate to an artistic project of justifying existence as an aesthetic phenomenon.

Because GS 107 and GS 335 conflict, they cannot both express Nietzsche's considered views on this topic at the time *The Gay Science*

---

[8] Siemens and Hay (2015: 119) also endorse this "alteration model," based in part on a reading of GS 107.

was published. Thus, there are reasons for abandoning the assumption that these passages provide a straightforward expression of Nietzsche's views at this time. Instead, we can make better sense of these passages if we read them as part of a consciously constructed dialectic between truth-seeking and science, on the one hand, and art and life affirmation, on the other. Specifically, we should understand GS 107 as the expression of a free spirit still beholden to the idea that truth has an absolute value and so operating under the shadow of God, and so even though the free spirit gives a prominent role to art in making life bearable in the second chapter of *The Gay Science*, the significance of art is nevertheless bound by these constraints. However, once this shadow is eliminated in the third chapter of *The Gay Science*, Nietzsche *qua* free spirit will finally be free to adopt the view that art is capable of justifying existence and that science should play a subordinate, instrumental role in this larger task. In so doing, Nietzsche will then be able to present a view, in the fourth chapter of *The Gay Science*, that resonates with what he says in both his early and later writings and so a view that we can infer is genuinely his own.

Chapter 3: Thoughts of a Godless One

Because of the compositional history of *The Gay Science* and the special position Nietzsche gives to "Sanctus Januarius," the third chapter of *The Gay Science* is best understood as the culmination of the quest Nietzsche initiated in *Daybreak* to undermine the moral prejudices that are remnants of the metaphysical tradition. The apex of this project occurs with the pronouncement of God's death – the end of metaphysics – and the elimination of his shadows – the end of morality in the third chapter of *The Gay Science*. Because the will to truth has driven the free spirit to kill God and the elimination of God's shadow includes the elimination of the moral obligation to pursue truth at all costs, this chapter executes a *Selbstaufhebung* of the ascetic ideal and the related will to truth, and the self-overcoming of the ascetic ideal lays the foundation for both an artistic solution to the death of God (GS 153) and the project of becoming who one is (GS 270).

That the third chapter is about the elimination of God's shadow, and not simply the death of God, is indicated by the first aphorism. Nietzsche begins by declaring that "God is dead" (GS 108), and the task that now faces the free spirit is vanquishing his shadow. To those familiar with the preceding free spirit works, the pronouncement of God's death should come as no surprise. The belief in God was already deemed false in the first chapter of *Human*, and Nietzsche has already provided one portrayal of the death of God in *The Wanderer*. In this sense, Nietzsche's claim that "God is dead" at the beginning of the chapter presupposes the insights won over the course of the free spirit project, and the task Nietzsche now sets for himself is to complete the elimination of his shadow and so the moral prejudices that he began to critique in *Daybreak*.

The dialectical reading of the third chapter is supported by a number of aphorisms that precede the madman's declaration of the death of God. This is because they repeat and consolidate a number of the "tragic truths" about the world that Nietzsche unpacked in *Human*. However, these aphorisms – with their rejection of anthropomorphism in all its forms – still operate under the ascetic ideal that is undone once God's shadow is vanquished. In this sense, they function as a final recapitulation of the free spirit's de-anthropomorphized view of nature. At the same time, this understanding of nature allows the madman to announce the death of God and to eliminate his shadow in subsequent aphorisms, and in this way, this view of nature undermines the very ban on anthropomorphism that led to the discovery of these truths.

The most prominent of these aphorisms is "Let Us Beware." At stake in the aphorism is nothing less than the complete de-anthropomorphization of an otherwise all-too-human world, and the title indicates that we need to beware of and so resist our tendency to anthropomorphize the cosmos – a central idea in *Human*. Thus, the aphorism provides a list of anthropomorphic projections we need to eliminate: (1) The world is an organic being; (2) The universe is a machine; (3) The universe is elegant; (4) The universe is heartless and unreasonable or their opposites; (5) There are laws in nature; (6) Life and death are opposed; and (7) The world eternally creates new things (GS 109).

In the aphorism, Nietzsche also gives a positive description of nature in non-anthropomorphic terms. For instance, Paul Loeb (2013: 656) has argued that the aphorism gives expression to a cosmological version of the eternal recurrence, and *Nachlass* notes from this time support this reading. In the text, Nietzsche speaks of a "musical box" that "repeats eternally its tune" (GS 109). In the *Nachlass*, Nietzsche employs the phrase "let us beware" on at least two occasions in which he also speaks of a cyclical conception of the cosmos (KSA 9: 11[157] and [202]). In one of the fragments, Nietzsche also speaks of an "eternal chaos" (KSA 9: 11 [157]), and this language appears in the published text: "the total character of the world, however, is in all eternity chaos – in the sense not of a lack of necessity but of a lack of order, arrangement, form, beauty, wisdom, and whatever other names there are for our aesthetic anthropomorphisms." For this reason, Nietzsche concludes that, "none of our aesthetic and moral judgments apply to it" (GS 109).

Read as an isolated aphorism independently of the other free spirit works, we might wonder about the justification behind Nietzsche's proclamations about the true nature of the world. Understood, however, within the unfolding dialectic of the free spirit, we simply need to recall the basic insights of *Human*. There, Nietzsche appealed to the natural sciences and the scientific method to strip the world of its various aesthetic anthropomorphisms. Indeed, in the first chapter of *Human* Nietzsche claimed that good and evil have no basis in nature (HH 28), and in subsequent texts of the free spirit, Nietzsche proceeded to show, in systematic fashion, how this is true.

In the next three aphorisms, we find claims that repeat some of the central features of the argument of *Human*. In "Origin of the Logical," Nietzsche asserts that the logical came from the illogical, by which he means that logical thinking emerged from the non-logical quest for survival, and this repeats the governing idea of *Human* that everything comes from its opposite (HH 1). Given such origins, there is no reason to think that forms of logical thinking have a neat correspondence to reality (GS 111), and Nietzsche claims that such correspondence does not, in fact, exist (see KSA 9: 11[153]). For logical thinking to apply to reality, there need to be substances or self-identical things. However, we know from *Human* that there are no such things (HH 19). This is because everything is in "flux" (GS 111). Thus, both logic and so-called substances that correspond to logic have their origin in the non-logical quest for survival.

Similar claims are also found in "Cause and Effect." Nietzsche argues that we have better descriptions than previous ages, presumably because science now gives us a better description of nature in terms of flux or a continuum. However, he denies that such descriptions provide better explanations. Claims about cause and effect simply tell us that one thing follows another, and Nietzsche argues that we cannot explain anything because our explanations presuppose things that do not, in fact, exist: "lines, planes, bodies, atoms, divisible time spans, divisible spaces." As Nietzsche explains in the *Nachlass*, such entities presuppose that there are things, substances, something persistent. These, however, do not exist (KSA 9: 11[151] and [235]). Even when we try to describe how one thing follows another, we are isolating a piece of reality in a way that falsifies the continuum confronting us – a point already made in WS 11 – and so if we could see the continuum as a continuum, we "would repudiate the concept of cause and effect" altogether (GS 112).

In "Origin of Knowledge," Nietzsche largely repeats and summarizes what is sometimes called the "falsification thesis" that runs throughout the first chapter of *Human*.[9] The simple idea is that the mind is hardwired, through evolutionary processes, for error. These errors include: "that there are enduring things; that there are equal things; that there are things, substances, bodies; that a thing is what it appears to be; that our will is free; that what is good for me is also good in itself" (GS 110). In order to claim that these are errors in the sense of not corresponding to reality, Nietzsche must have some understanding of what reality is like. In the *Nachlass* from this time, we know that Nietzsche thinks the "final truth" is the "flux of things" (KSA 9: 11[162]), and this repeats the point from *Human* that the natural sciences show that all things can be reduced to motion (HH 19).

In "Origin of Knowledge," Nietzsche's discussion of how we are hard-wired for error leads to a central theme in the dialectic of the free spirit project: the tragic tension between life and knowledge. Although he claims that any sort of tension between the two would result in the victory of life over knowledge, Nietzsche points to Parmenides' school of the Eleactics as a group of philosophers who tried to make life conform to their knowledge of the "One and All." To do this, however, they had to "*deceive* themselves about their own state." That is, they had to invent a conception of themselves in which they stood above change and desire and so a conception of reason as "completely free and spontaneous activity" (GS 110).

In the later stages of the aphorism, Nietzsche claims that a "subtler honesty [*Redlichkeit*] and skepticism" has made the Eleactic understanding of the knowing subject and the world impossible (GS 110). Nietzsche then explains how honesty itself came into being from a non-rational struggle between opinions and "lust for power." At the present stage, there is now a fight between the impulse for truth and "those life-preserving errors," and the question – "to what extent can truth endure incorporation?" – can only be answered by experimentation (GS 110). Although Nietzsche's remarks here are highly cryptic, we know from both earlier writings such as *History for Life* and the *Nachlass* from the time of *The Gay Science* that he thinks the truth cannot be fully incorporated. This is because the "ultimate truth" is the "flux of things," and so the incorporation of truth must also include

---

[9] See Meyer (2012b) for a treatment of this topic.

the incorporation of error (KSA 9: 11[162]; also see KSA 9: 11[141]).[10] As we will see, the most important result of the elimination of God's shadow is that the free spirit will be permitted to incorporate error into life and even knowledge, a point to which Nietzsche returns in the opening stages of *Beyond Good and Evil* (BGE 4 and 24).

As the opening aphorisms of the third chapter unfold, Nietzsche shifts from cosmological and ontological speculations to matters of value and morality, and much like the opening aphorisms of the chapter that summarize the views articulated at length in *Human*, the views he expresses on morality repeat a number of insights from *Daybreak*. Thus, in the next two aphorisms, Nietzsche attacks what he calls the "herd instinct" and "herd remorse." First, Nietzsche claims that morality derives from the needs and values of the community or "herd," and so "morality is herd instinct in the individual" (GS 116). He then contrasts the way we now think about individuality with the way societies used to think about individuality. In the past, to be an individual "was not a pleasure but a punishment," and so any inclination "to be a self and to esteem oneself according to one's own weight and measure" would have been a piece of "madness." Nietzsche, however, claims that we now think much differently (GS 117), and this "now" seems to be a reference to the program of self-education that Nietzsche has undertaken in the free spirit works. That is, we now think differently about the individual after the free spirit's critique of morality in *Daybreak*.

In subsequent aphorisms, we hear the drumbeat of anticipation as Nietzsche continues his attack on morality. Thus, he analyzes benevolence in terms of a necessary pattern of impulses among weaker and stronger organisms to appropriate and submit (GS 118). In "No Altruism!" Nietzsche suggests that altruistic activity is really a manifestation of the desire to make oneself into a function of some higher or more dominant person (GS 119). In "Health of the Soul," he rejects the idea of a singular standard of health that applies to all individuals (GS 120). In "Life No Argument," Nietzsche again asserts that, "the conditions of life might include error" (GS 121). Finally, in "Moral Skepticism in Christianity," Nietzsche argues, first, that Christianity taught us to be skeptical of ancient paragons of virtue and, second, that we have now applied this same skepticism to "all *religious* states and processes," including Christianity itself (GS 122).

---

[10] Franco (2011: 113–115) makes this point central to his interpretation of *The Gay Science*. For more on the incorporation of truth, see Mitcheson (2015).

Nietzsche's claims in "Moral Skepticism in Christianity" not only build upon the insights already presented in *Daybreak*, they lend credence to the idea that Nietzsche understands the overcoming of morality as a self-overcoming or a *Selbstaufhebung* of Christian morality. Nietzsche argues that Christianity taught us the very form of skepticism that is now being applied to Christianity, and a similar argument can be found in the next aphorism, "Knowledge as More Than a Mere Means." In modern times, Nietzsche claims that science has become an "ethos" in which people have "faith," and so science would be promoted even without the "passion for knowledge" now driving the free spirit project. Nevertheless, it is only now, with the emergence of this new *pathos*, that "knowledge wants to be more than a mere means" (GS 123), and so although this *pathos* emerges from a Christian *ethos*, we know from *Daybreak* that the passion for knowledge is ready to make sacrifices to satisfy its quest, and Christianity is one of the things that will be sacrificed for its sake.

This brings us to the aphorism just preceding the announcement of the death of God. The title of the aphorism is "In the Horizon of the Infinite," and Nietzsche begins by explaining how free spirits have left land and burned the bridges behind them. They are now departing on the sea, and what stands before them is "nothing more awesome than infinity" (GS 124). Notably, the first aphorism of the fifth chapter of the 1887 edition of *The Gay Science* also refers to the open sea that stands before the free spirit with "the news that 'the old god is dead'" (GS 343). Whereas the news expressed in the 1887 edition is met with "happiness, relief, exhilaration, encouragement, dawn" (GS 343), the tone in the third chapter is much less auspicious. Similar to the dramatic conclusion of *Daybreak* (D 585), there is a sense that the free spirit may suffer from homesickness for a land that no longer exists (GS 124).

According to the dialectical reading, such remarks must be read in the context of the free spirit progression. There is no going back to the safety of land precisely because the insights the free spirit has acquired through this program of self-education make this impossible. The metaphysical-moral interpretation of existence is now coming to an end, and this offers the free spirit an incomprehensible and awe-inspiring freedom. At the same time, the free spirit is not yet the "fearless one" of the fifth chapter, and so the impending death of God and the elimination of his shadow are still presented with a sense of anxiety about where this project will lead.

It is also important to note the contrast between the announcement of God's death in *The Gay Science* and the announcement of God's death in *The Wanderer*. In the latter, there is no mention of the shadow of God and the corresponding need to eliminate it. Instead, God's death is announced, and the prisoners simply shrug their shoulders and walk away, indifferent to the consequences this event might have. As I explained in Chapter 4, this goes along with the Epicurean stance that Nietzsche consciously cultivates in *The Wanderer* that includes three positions: (1) an indifference to metaphysical questions and their consequences; (2) a willingness to leave customs untouched in order to carve out a private garden in which one can attend to the "closest things"; (3) a striving for tranquility that takes pleasure in the sunlight of knowledge.

What we have seen in the free spirit progression is that the care of the soul initially developed in *The Wanderer* inevitably requires the removal of the chains of the metaphysical tradition and a treatment of the sickness they have caused (WS 350), and this has forced the free spirit to confront the "moral prejudices" that remain embedded within customary evaluations. Nietzsche initiated this project in *Daybreak*, and along with this project, a new passion emerged, one that leaves behind the tranquility of *The Wanderer* and prepares the free spirit to challenge reigning conventions in much the same way that a passion between two lovers drives them to violate convention to consummate their love. In this sense, it is the passion for knowledge that leads Nietzsche to slay the so-called dragon of created values and ultimately vanquish the shadow of God in *The Gay Science*.

The death of God passage in *The Gay Science* bears the title, "The Madman," and it begins with a madman holding a lantern in the daylight – a scene reminiscent of Diogenes the Cynic[11] – storming the marketplace in search of God. Those standing in the marketplace quickly ridicule and mock the madman. They all realize that God is "dead," but those in the marketplace – much like the prisoners from *The Wanderer* – do not think that the death of God has any significant consequences. It is against this idea that the madman directs his scorn. Like Pascal and in contrast to Epicurus, Nietzsche now thinks that whether one believes in God makes a great deal of difference, and this attitude is expressed quite vividly throughout the aphorism. The death of God now means that there is no horizon for human activity and culture and that the earth has lost its center of gravity. As Reginster puts it, the death of God results in a general disorientation and loss of meaning, and so it raises the specter of nihilism (Reginster 2006: 44).

---

[11] As Brusotti (1997: 413–414) explains, like Diogenes, the madman's use of the lantern ironizes the very idea that he is searching for God. Simply put, he knows that God does not exist.

The madman also makes clear that the death of God is the result of human activity and developments in thought and culture. Thus, the madman claims: "God is dead. God remains dead. And we have killed him" (GS 125). Although not explicit, the "we" Nietzsche employs here seems to refer to "we free spirits," and so it is free spirits like Nietzsche who have killed God. So understood, Nietzsche's claim that God is dead and we have killed him is not something that refers to events in European culture happening independently of the free spirit project.[12] Instead, Nietzsche is thinking primarily in terms of the progression of thought carried out in the free spirit works. In short, it is the uncompromising quest for truth via the natural sciences in *Human* and the subsequent rejection of moral preju- dices in *Daybreak* that has led to the death of God and the elimination of his shadow.

Just as there are analeptic references in "The Madman," there are also potentially proleptic references that point to a future project. Specifically, Nietzsche has the madman emphasize that we must atone for this deed, and so he asks whether we must become gods "simply to appear worthy of it" (GS 125). Although he does not elaborate on this idea, we know from the *Nachlass* that Nietzsche ends a variant of the passage by asking if we must not become the most powerful and most holy poet to atone for this deed (KSA 9: 12[77]). As subsequent aphorisms show, Nietzsche is think- ing in precisely these terms.

Nietzsche's return to poetry in *The Gay Science* also means a return to the central theme and the general framework of *The Birth of Tragedy*, and a number of the aphorisms following the death of God support such a reading. In the "Origin of Sin," Nietzsche argues that "sin" is a Jewish invention and that the purpose of Christianity was to Judaize the world in this respect. In contrast, Greek antiquity was "a world without feelings of sin." According to Nietzsche, the Greeks would have found Christian exhortations for repentance to be "ridiculous and annoying," attributing such a feeling to slaves (GS 135). Rather than repenting, the Greeks attributed nobility to sacrilege, and the story of Prometheus – Nietzsche is repeating a central point from *The Birth of Tragedy* (BT 9) – provides evidence of this. Here, Nietzsche claims that the Greeks created tragedy "to invent some dignity for sacrilege and to incorporate nobility in it" (GS 135). Applied to the free spirit works, the idea is that because Nietzsche

---

[12] Owen (2003: 252) seems to sketch such an account to explain the shift in Nietzsche's strategy from *Daybreak* to *The Gay Science*.

has just committed sacrilege by pronouncing the death of God, he must now turn to tragedy in order to lend dignity and nobility to this deed.

In "*Homo Poeta*," we find the most explicit evidence in the third chapter of *The Gay Science* that the death of God and the elimination of his shadow amounts to a *Selbstaufhebung* of the morality of truth and a corresponding turn to poetry. As I noted in Chapter 2 of this book, support for this reading comes from a combination of interconnected passages from the end of the *Genealogy* (GM III 27) and the fifth chapter of *The Gay Science* (GS 344 and GS 357) that explain the death of God in terms of a *Selbstaufhebung* of morality and the will to truth. One reason for thinking that Nietzsche is not retrospectively projecting this meaning onto the 1882 edition of the text is that we have a series of *Nachlass* notes from the time he was composing *The Gay Science* in which he articulates various versions of "the suicide of morality" (KSA 9: 15[15]). Finally, the reason for thinking that Nietzsche may have planned, from the beginning, for the free spirit project to enact this *Selbstaufhebung* is that he had already described such a dynamic as early as *The Birth of Tragedy* (BT 15) and other *Nachlass* notes from that time (KSA 7: 19[35]).

Such evidence, therefore, gives us reason to look for this dynamic in *The Gay Science*, and because "*Homo Poeta*" provides the most explicit evidence for this interpretation, the aphorism is worth quoting in full:

> I myself, having made this tragedy of tragedies all by myself, insofar as it is finished – I, having first tied the knot of morality into existence before I drew it so tight that only a god could untie it (which is what Horace demands) – I myself have now slain all gods in the fourth act, for the sake of morality [*aus Moralität*]! Now, what is to become of the fifth act? From where am I to take the tragic solution? – Should I begin to think about a comic solution? (GS 153)

The aphorism begins with a mention of "this tragedy of tragedies," and this is a reference to the tragedy of Christian morality and the related death of God. In this sense, it is Nietzsche, *qua* free spirit, who has "slain all gods in the fourth act," and he has done so through his efforts in works like *Human* and *Daybreak*. The aphorism provides evidence for a *Selbstaufhebung* of Christian morality because Nietzsche claims that morality has driven the free spirit to slay these gods. That is, the free spirit has done this "*aus Moralität*," and by this we know that Nietzsche means the morality of "truth and honesty" (KSA 9: 15[15]). Since Nietzsche believes the death of these gods is also the death of morality, it is morality that has driven the free spirit to eliminate the very "thou shalt" of truth and honesty that animates the free spirit project. This amounts to a *Selbstaufhebung* or a "suicide of morality" precisely because the free spirit has killed God and so morality "for the sake of morality" (GS 153).

As the concluding lines of the aphorism make clear, this *Selbstaufhebung* of morality allows for a return to poetry, and in this sense, "*Homo Poeta*" expresses the very idea that we must become most powerful and holy poets to atone for the death of God (KSA 9: 12[77]). The idea is that since the free spirit is liberated from the morality of truth, she can now fully embrace the art that Nietzsche typically associates with lies and a "*will to deception*" (GM III 25). In *The Gay Science*, Nietzsche specifically refers to the two most important genres associated with Dionysus: tragedy and comedy. Thus, Nietzsche first speaks of a "tragic solution" to this tragedy of Christian morality and then speculates about a comic solution. In this way, Nietzsche not only links the death of God to his reflections on the tragic and the comic in previous aphorisms of *The Gay Science* (GS 1 and 107), he also points forward to the "*incipit tragoedia*" that ends the 1882 edition of the text (GS 342) and to a possible comedy and so a "*incipit parodia*" in his subsequent works.

The concluding aphorisms of chapter 3 are also significant for the dialectical reading. This is because they announce a project of becoming who one is that points beyond *The Gay Science*. In this sense, the final aphorisms of chapter 3, much like the whole of chapter 4, mark a "turning point [*Wendekreis*]" in Nietzsche's larger philosophical project (KSB 6: 301). They constitute a "turning point" because they move from the project of using the ploughshare to clear away any false and foreign beliefs, which has been the primary goal of the free spirit project thus far, toward a positive project of fashioning a self based on one's true needs. This aesthetic self-shaping is nowhere more evident than in *Ecce Homo*, and not only does *Ecce Homo* have a variant of Pindar's call to become who you are as its subtitle, Nietzsche also refers to the final eight aphorisms of the third chapter of *The Gay Science* as the "granite words in which a destiny finds for the first time a formula for itself, for *all* time" (EH "Books" GS:1).[13] So understood, the free spirit project is not – as he stresses in an 1882 letter to Salomé – Nietzsche's ideal or final resting place, but rather just a "phase" in a now larger project that seems to extend well beyond the free spirit works (KSB 6: 335).[14]

---

[13] As Brusotti (2016) explains, Nietzsche added these aphorisms toward the end of the editing process, and so there is reason to think that he saw these as very significant at the time he composed them.

[14] See Franco (2011: 159–160) for a discussion of this point.

In *The Gay Science*, Nietzsche returns to the leitmotif of *Schopenhauer as Educator* in an aphorism that reads as follows: "*What does your conscience say?* – You shall become the person you are" (GS 270). The fact that Nietzsche refers to "conscience" suggests that this now functions as an ethical command that replaces the "thou shalt" of the Christian moral tradition, and it is not a coincidence that Nietzsche places this new command at the end of the book in which he announces the death of God and the elimination of his shadow. This is because the latter amounts to the elimination of a morality that commands us to be other than we are, for example, like a self-sacrificial God, and so the elimination of God's shadow means that the free spirit is now free to pursue the project of becoming precisely who one is.

That Nietzsche is developing a new ethic that foreshadows his revaluation project is also suggested by the three aphorisms that precede the command to become the person you are. In "What Makes One Heroic?" Nietzsche refers to the very heroism he developed in *Daybreak* and led to the elimination of God's shadow in *The Gay Science* (GS 268). In "With a Great Goal," Nietzsche claims that, "one is superior even to justice," and so he suggests that his project of slaying God is justified by some larger task (GS 267). And in "In What Do You Believe?" Nietzsche claims that, "the weights of all things must be determined anew" (GS 269). Taken together, we find a heroic willingness to suffer in order to determine anew the weights of all things, and this is an idea that points back to the claim in *Schopenhauer as Educator* that the philosopher "wants to determine" the value of existence anew (SE 3) and points forward to a philosopher of the future who creates tables of good (GS 335) and legislates values (BGE 211).

In the final five aphorisms of the chapter, Nietzsche seems to be initiating the revaluation to which he just alluded. In an aphorism that foreshadows the central theme of *Zarathustra* IV, Nietzsche claims that pity constitutes his greatest danger (GS 271). To understand why pity constitutes such a great danger to the project of becoming who one is, we need to recall that Schopenhauer connects pity to an overall ethic of selflessness, and this ethic of selflessness commands us to disregard ourselves. In the next aphorism, Nietzsche re-enforces the idea that we need to care for ourselves before we care for others. This is because he claims that what he loves in others are his own hopes (GS 272), and so any concern for others must ultimately be tied to a concern for this self-regarding project.

The final three aphorisms also relate to the task of becoming who one is. This is because the goal of becoming who one is requires that we resist the demands of others to become something we are not. One thing that can tempt us to become something we are not is shame, and the final three aphorisms all deal with shame. Thus, we learn that "bad" people are precisely those who want to put others to shame (GS 273), and so bad people are those who make us want to be something other than we are. In the next aphorism, we are told that being humane consists of sparing someone shame (GS 274), and so again, being humane consists of letting others be who they are.

In the final aphorism, we find a new understanding of the meaning of liberation, one that goes hand in hand with the project of becoming who one is. Specifically, the seal of liberation consists in "no longer being ashamed in front of oneself" (GS 275), and this recalls the conclusion of chapter 2: "And as long as you are in any way *ashamed* before yourselves, you do not yet belong with us" (GS 107). Taken together, we can say that the task of becoming oneself goes hand in hand with the task of finding satisfaction with oneself. So understood, this seems to be the very self that Nietzsche presents in *Ecce Homo*, one that cannot but be grateful for its entire life and so a self that no longer feels a sense of shame before itself.

Concluding Remarks

In many ways, the free spirit project is now complete, as the purpose of chapter 4 of *The Gay Science* is to transition from the free spirit project to a new project of affirming existence through the tragic poetry of *Zarathustra*. Nietzsche began the free spirit project in *Human* with an uncompromising quest for truth that led to the destruction of the metaphysical tradition. After detaching himself from friends, family, and the state, Nietzsche found himself alone in the desert of knowledge. To counter the threat of despair that emerged from the destruction of the metaphysical tradition, he turned to "the salve cans and medicine bottles of *all* ancient philosophers," most notably those of Epicurus and the Stoics.

Although these provided temporary therapy, Nietzsche *qua* free spirit soon realized that countering the threat of despair meant eliminating the moral prejudices that remained even after the destruction of the metaphysical tradition, and in the last two chapters, I have detailed how this project unfolds in *Daybreak* and the first three chapters of *The Gay Science*. This began with Nietzsche's rejection of the morality of custom and the sin-and-redemption framework of Christianity and ended with the death of God and the elimination of his shadow. Along the way, we saw the emergence of a heroic free spirit who is not only willing to commit deviant acts, but also ready to be the murderer of all murderers.

As both *Nachlass* notes and the aphorisms of the third chapter of *The Gay Science* make clear, the death of God still needs to be justified, and Nietzsche thinks that only the arts associated with Dionysus can do this. Fortunately, the destruction of the metaphysical-moral tradition now means that the free spirit is liberated from the ascetic ethos of *Human*, and so the free spirit can now pursue an aesthetic justification of a thoroughly naturalized world by means of both tragic and comic art.

PART III

The Dionysian Child

CHAPTER 7

Incipit Tragoedia
From The Gay Science IV *to*
Thus Spoke Zarathustra

The purpose of the final two chapters of this book is to provide some explanation of the last two chapters of *The Gay Science* and their potential relationship to the works that follow the free spirit project. In this chapter, I explain how the fourth chapter of *The Gay Science* transitions to *Zarathustra* and give a brief account of why *Zarathustra* should be read as a tragedy (the first three parts) and a satyr play (the final part). In Chapter 8, I turn to Nietzsche's remarks on the free spirit in both *Beyond Good and Evil* and the final book of the 1887 edition of *The Gay Science*, and I claim that both texts point to a philosophy of the future that can be understood as a Dionysian comedy. In this way, *The Gay Science* and so the free spirit project as a whole can be said to have a double ending that corresponds to the first aphorism of the text. Whereas the 1882 version flows directly into the tragedy of *Zarathustra*, the 1887 version points to a genre in which the "comedy of existence" becomes conscious of itself and the waves of laughter "overwhelm even the greatest of tragedians" (GS 1).

In the previous chapter, I claimed that *The Gay Science* is a book "in media vita" or "in mid-life," and as Nietzsche's 1882 letter to Overbeck indicates, this characterization is perhaps even more true of the fourth and final chapter of the 1882 edition, "Sanctus Januarius" (KSB 6: 301). It follows upon the death of God and is clearly designed to present, for the first time, the doctrine of the eternal recurrence that is the fundamental conception of *Zarathustra* (EH "Books" Z:1). It also contains much discussion of the relationship between philosophy and poetry, and so it seems to be the chapter in which the poet and the wise man, foreshadowed in the motto at the beginning of the 1882 edition, merge. At the same time, Nietzsche is still writing aphorisms, not poetry, and so although he is now adopting positions that place poetry at the center of his project, he is still not writing as a Dionysian poet. In this sense, "Sanctus Januarius" stands at the end of a free spirit project in which Nietzsche has liberated

himself from God and his shadow and at the beginning of a new project
that turns to poetry to affirm a completely naturalized world.

It is for these reasons that "Sanctus Januarius" deserves to be treated in a
separate chapter, and I will explain how the aphorisms in "Sanctus Januarius" depend on the preceding free spirit works and point forward to
Nietzsche's future endeavors. On the one hand, I highlight, first, the
significant differences between the positions Nietzsche is now adopting
in "Sanctus Januarius" and the positions he adopted only four years earlier
in *Human*. On the other hand, I emphasize the way in which "Sanctus
Januarius" flows into the tragedy of *Zarathustra*. In short, I will unpack the
analeptic and proleptic references in "Sanctus Januarius" that are a crucial
feature of the dialectical reading.

Chapter 4: Sanctus Januarius

Nietzsche began *Human* and so the free spirit project by quoting a passage
from Descartes in which he promised to devote his life to finding the truth.
He then turned to the methods of science to strip life of its significance by
revealing the errors of various ethical, religious, and aesthetic conceptions
and sensations. Although he noted the despairing effect that such investigations can have, he nevertheless suspended judgment about the value of
existence. To combat the feeling of despair, he adopted the good
temperament of the theoretical individual, a figure who is divorced from
life but nevertheless takes pleasure in discovery and observation. Because
he was committed to pursuing truth at all costs, Nietzsche's vitalistic forces
were at a minimum in these works.

The contrast between the sober method of *Human* and the motto from
Sanctus Januarius could not be more striking: "With a flaming spear you
crushed / All its ice until my soul / Roaring toward the ocean rushed / Of
its highest hope and goal. / Even healthier it swells, / Lovingly compelled
but free: / Thus it lauds your miracles, / Fairest month of January!" As
Kaufmann notes,[1] the poem celebrates the miracle of St. Januarius in
which it is said that a vial of his blood would become liquid on festival
days. The fact that Nietzsche appeals to a fourteenth-century miracle is far
removed from the scientific ethos of *Human*. The motto also signals
Nietzsche's turn away from the ascetic attempt to suppress the forces of
life in a quest to find a non-anthropomorphic conception of the world and
a turn toward a life-affirming conception of philosophy that is united with

[1] See Kaufmann's translation (1974: 221).

aesthetic affirmation. Thus, we see how Nietzsche has moved, through a continuous chain of aphorisms that stretches from *Human* to *The Gay Science*, from the rigors of the scientific method to the re-emergence of life and a celebration of art.

The fact that Nietzsche is turning away from the life-denying asceticism of *Human* to a life-affirming aestheticism in "Sanctus Januarius" is evinced by the first aphorism of the chapter, "For the New Year." The aphorism begins with a modification of the Cartesian *cogito*: "I still live, I still think: I still have to live, for I still have to think. *Sum, ergo cogito: cogito, ergo sum*" (GS 276). The claim asserts the unity of life and thought and so rejects a conception of thinking that stands above life and tries to observe it objectively. This is something that Nietzsche explicitly criticizes in referring to the Eleactics in the third chapter (GS 110) and a point to which he returns later in this chapter (GS 333). Important here, however, is that this aphorism rejects a model of thinking presupposed in *Human* and the corresponding attempt to divorce thinking from life.

The aphorism also rejects the attempt in *Human* to suspend judgment about the value of life. To recall, *Human* laid out a tragic conception of the world that emphasizes the ineluctability of suffering and so corresponds to what I have called the factual pessimism of Silenus and Schopenhauer. Factual pessimism, however, raises the evaluative question of whether existence is preferable to non-existence, and although Schopenhauer thought that a desire for non-existence simply follows from the truth of factual pessimism, Nietzsche denied such an inference. Instead, Nietzsche dedicates his first book, *The Birth of Tragedy*, to articulating a life-affirming response to meaningless suffering. Because he concludes "For the New Year" with the claim that he wishes "to be only a Yes-Sayer" (GS 276), Nietzsche is returning to the central issue of *The Birth of Tragedy*, "to be or not to be" (BT 7), and the affirmative position he defends in that work.

At the same time – and here we see an instance of the dialectical nature of the free spirit project – the task that Nietzsche sets before himself is nothing less than "*amor fati*" or love of fate, which Nietzsche understands as wanting "to learn more and more to see as beautiful what is necessary in things" (GS 276).[2] This points to the dialectical structure of the free spirit because the concept of fate is something that Nietzsche claimed to discover via the uncompromising methods of science in the second chapter of *Human* and repeated throughout the subsequent works of the free spirit. So even though the premium placed on truth and the discovery of truth via

---

[2] For alternative accounts of *amor fati*, see Han-Pile (2009) and Stern (2013).

the natural sciences is slowly being overcome as the free spirit project advances, Nietzsche is nevertheless preserving truths that the free spirit has discovered in this process, and there is no idea more central to the genre of tragedy and so the tragic worldview than the fate that the free spirit is now supposed to love.

To make it an object of love, fate nevertheless needs to be made beautiful, and Nietzsche claims that he can make things beautiful by seeing them as beautiful. This claim recalls the discussions of both art and the appearance-reality distinction in earlier chapters of *The Gay Science*. Although art and poetry are not explicitly mentioned in this aphorism, the notion of *making* beautiful is associated with art and the transformation of the world into an aesthetic phenomenon. Nietzsche's earlier rejection of the appearance-reality distinction is at work in the aphorism because it implies that we can make something beautiful by seeing it as beautiful. In other words, by modifying how we experience the world, we modify how the world appears to us, and since there is no fundamental distinction between appearance and reality, the world actually becomes beautiful insofar as it appears beautiful to us. So understood, the task that Nietzsche sets for himself is to experience fate or necessity as something beautiful, and in those cases that he cannot incorporate and transfigure necessity, he will learn to look away (GS 276).

This, then, is the recipe that he now proposes for the new task of affirming life, and this task points directly to the "*incipit tragoedia*" that concludes the chapter. For even though "For a New Year" lays out a program of affirming and so loving fate, it is something that Nietzsche will try to achieve through his own poetry. For now, Nietzsche's task is to articulate these new ideas and so transition to the tragedy of *Zarathustra*, and Nietzsche does this in the subsequent aphorism, "Personal Providence." Although it begins by expressing the free spirit's newfound sense of health and exuberance after denying the "beautiful chaos of existence" all "providential reason and goodness," the point of the aphorism is to remind the free spirit not to fall into the trap of attributing such moments to a deity. Instead, Nietzsche claims that these are due to the fact that "our own practical and theoretical skill in interpreting and arranging events has now reached its high point" (GS 277). At the same time, we also need to recognize that "good old chance" – again a key feature of Nietzsche's tragic worldview (PTAG 7) – guides our hands and that "the wisest providence could not think up a more beautiful music than that which our foolish hand produces then" (GS 277).

It goes without saying that this passage presupposes the free spirit's rejection of metaphysics in *Human*, and it even references the Epicurean stance adopted toward the divine in *The Wanderer*. In this sense, the aphorism builds on the insights of the previous free spirit works. Such connections can also be found in "Excelsior." The title is borrowed from Longfellow's poem by the same name, and Nietzsche's familiarity with the poem dates back to the time he was developing the free spirit project. Mathilde Trampedach first introduced Nietzsche to the poem in April of 1876, and Nietzsche was so taken with both the poem and Mathilde that he sent a subsequent letter to her with a marriage proposal (KSB 5: 517). As Julian Young explains (2010: 217), Nietzsche was likely attracted to Mathilde because he saw in her a "convention-defying 'free spirit'" with whom he could "bypass normal social conventions." However, she turned down the proposal, and Nietzsche soon took on the free spirit project in the company of Malwida von Meysenbug.

In the aphorism itself, Nietzsche is writing from the standpoint of a free spirit who is liberated from the shadow of God. Thus, he writes of a second-person "you" who will not "stop before any ultimate wisdom, ultimate goodness, ultimate power," and he claims that there is no "avenger for you any more nor any final improver." At the same time, Nietzsche points to someone who wills "the eternal recurrence of war and peace" and so foreshadows the eternal recurrence at the end of the chapter. Indeed, the aphorism ends with Nietzsche wondering, first, if the "man of renunciation" could renounce all this and, second, whether through such renunciation "man will rise ever higher as soon as he ceases to *flow out* into a god." Although not explicit, these remarks may be a subtle foreshadowing of the idea from *Zarathustra* that the *Uebermensch* will soon replace God (Salaquarda 1989: 322).

The foreshadowing of themes in *Zarathustra* continues in "Embark!" where Nietzsche speaks of a sun similar to the "great star" that shines for Zarathustra. In the aphorism, Nietzsche presents the sun as a "philosophical justification" for an individual's "way of living and thinking," and as such, the sun makes the individual "independent of praise and blame, self-sufficient, rich, liberal with happiness and good will" as it "refashions evil into good, leads all energies to bloom and ripen, and does not permit the petty weeds of grief and chagrin to come up at all." According to Nietzsche, this is what evil or unhappy or even exceptional human beings all need: not pity, confession, and forgiveness, but a new "*justice*" (GS 289). Indeed, Nietzsche claims in a subsequent aphorism that in this state of happiness Homer invented gods for himself (GS 302).

Nietzsche continues this line of reflection in "One Thing Is Needful," an aphorism that gives a clear statement of the free spirit's return to an aestheticism that resembles that of *The Birth of Tragedy* and points forward to central themes of *Ecce Homo*. The allusion to the Gospel of Luke in the title points to a contrast that runs throughout all three works: art, rather than faith in Christ, is the genuine means by which we can respond to an existence characterized by suffering and death. Here, the one thing needful is not faith or prayer, but "to give style to one's character," and this is achieved by placing all of one's strengths and weaknesses "into an artistic plan until every one of them appears as art and reason and even weaknesses delight the eye." Central to this aesthetic is a singular and unifying taste that provides a law of constraint that an individual imposes upon herself. In so doing, strong and domineering natures achieve the one thing needful: "that a human being should *attain* satisfaction with himself, whether it be by means of this or that poetry and art" (GS 290).

The theme of giving style to one's character continues in "What One Should Learn from Artists." The aphorism begins with a claim familiar from "Let Us Beware" and repeated two aphorisms later: Things are not inherently beautiful, attractive, or desirable. The question is how we make them such, and artists have a lot to teach in this respect. The problem is that artists often end their work where life begins, and so the "we" of the aphorism differs from typical artists. This is because Nietzsche claims that "we" want to apply these artistic techniques to life itself. In short, "we want to be the poets of our life – first of all in the smallest, most everyday matters" (GS 299). Of course, the position here could not be more opposed to the view of art in *Human*.

In the next two aphorisms, Nietzsche weaves together themes of self-satisfaction and artistic creation with themes of contemplation and knowledge. Developing the idea of a heroic quest for knowledge already expressed in *Daybreak* and the aphorism, "Preparatory Human Beings" (GS 283), Nietzsche now refers to "the whole tragic *Prometheia* of all seekers after knowledge."[3] The reference to Prometheus harkens back to both GS 135 and *The Birth of Tragedy* (BT 9), and the idea is that the lust for science emerged with the non-scientific promise of attaining something hidden and even forbidden.

Even more important is the claim that Nietzsche makes at the end of the aphorism. There, he suggests that religion may have been a means by which certain individuals can "enjoy the whole self-sufficiency of a god and

---

[3] Nietzsche also refers to Prometheus in the original version of GS 109 (see KSA 14: p. 254).

a whole power of self-redemption" by learning "to find satisfaction and fullness" in themselves. That is, we may have had to invent a god and then be punished for stealing from this god before we realize that both man and god are the work of our hands. In other words, we now realize that we are the makers of "the whole tragic *Prometheia* of all seekers after knowledge" (GS 300).

As Brusotti has argued (1997: 423), Nietzsche's discussion of the Promethean seekers after knowledge forms the basis for "The Fancy of Contemplatives." Nietzsche begins the aphorism by distinguishing between higher and lower human beings, arguing that higher human beings "see and hear immeasurably more, and see and hear thoughtfully." In this sense, Nietzsche's view is directly in line with the characterization of the free spirit in *Human*. However, Nietzsche now presents an idea that moves the free spirit from the asceticism of *Human* to the aestheticism of the final stages of the free spirit. According to Nietzsche, the contemplative assumes that "he is a *spectator* and *listener* who has been placed before the great visual and acoustic spectacle that is life." However, this contemplative fails to recognize that "he himself is really the poet who keeps creating this life," and in this sense, his *vis contemplativa* (theoretical gazing) is "also and above all *vis creative*" (poetic making) (GS 301). In the language of "On Truth and Lies," such contemplative individuals fail to recognize that they are essentially "artistically creating subjects" (TL 1).

Themes of experimentalism, honesty, and heroism continue into the later stages of the chapter. In "As Interpreters of Our Experiences," Nietzsche attacks the founders of religions for failing to apply the intellectual conscience to their own experiences. Rather than subjecting their experiences to the examination of conscience, they simply assumed a truth to their inner experiences and made them the foundation for their religion. In contrast to this, Nietzsche claims that there are others, presumably free spirits, who want to be their own "experiments and guinea pigs" (GS 319), and he expands on this experimentalism in the important aphorism "In Media Vita." Specifically, Nietzsche claims to be almost intoxicated with the mystery of life because it is an "experiment of the seeker for knowledge" (GS 324). Here, the quest for knowledge takes on a heroic character as life becomes "*a means to knowledge*," and "with this principle in one's heart one can live not only boldly but even gaily, and laugh gaily, too" (GS 324).

"In Media Vita" is a crucial aphorism for the dialectical reading because it establishes a position that is foreign to the framework of *Human* and yet gestures toward the notion of a "gay science." In *Human*, life and the principles of life – desire, affect, subjectivity, perspective, and so forth – were opposed to the quest for objective truth, and this is why the work is an exercise in asceticism. In contrast, Nietzsche now holds that life is a means to knowledge, and this view explicitly rejects the asceticism of *Human*. It is in reconciling life to knowledge that "science" becomes a playful and joyous exercise that allows one to laugh, and this, according to "Taking Seriously," is precisely what a "gay science" is. Contrary to the prejudice that seriousness is a necessary condition for all good thinking, Nietzsche claims that some of our best thinking is done in connection with life, laughter, and joy (GS 327).

Although these aphorisms are harbingers of a "gay science," Nietzsche also stresses that this project involves a tragic heroism that is willing to endure and even inflict pain. In "Wisdom in Pain," Nietzsche returns to the idea that pain belongs to the economy of existence and the preservation of the species, and he explains this point by referring to a seafarer at sea. Specifically, there are heroic types that welcome pain and so the storms at sea that give "them their greatest moments." Nietzsche refers to these heroic types as "the great *pain bringers of humanity*" (GS 318), and in a subsequent aphorism, he explains that greatness lies not so much in the ability to endure suffering, but rather in the ability to endure the internal distress that results from inflicting "great suffering" and hearing "the cry of this suffering." According to Nietzsche, "that is great, that belongs to greatness" (GS 325).

The dual emphasis on joy and suffering – along with the implicit rejection of pity or a suffering from suffering – is a common theme that runs throughout Nietzsche's works, and he continues his reflections on the remedy for pain and suffering in the next aphorism. He begins by criticizing preachers and theologians who "try to con men into believing that they are in a very bad way and need some ultimate, hard, radical, cure" for their pain and suffering. Everyone fails to overlook that we have multiple techniques to deal with pain. Recalling his analysis of musical dissonance in *The Birth of Tragedy* (BT 24), Nietzsche claims that, "we know quite well how to drip sweetness upon our bitterness, especially the bitterness of the soul." It is this sort of suffering that can lead to an "over-rich happiness," and this is why Nietzsche condemns the "*lies*" that have been told about the evil of passion and how "happiness only begins after the annihilation of passion and the silencing of the will." We do not need to exchange a life of passion for – and here we see Nietzsche rejecting the Stoicism in *Daybreak* – the Stoic petrification of life (GS 326).

In "The Meaning of Knowing," Nietzsche returns to the idea – prominent in the first aphorism of the chapter and essential to the notion of "gay science" – that knowing and understanding are bound to life and so our desires and affects. Nietzsche's point here is not simply that the understanding is influenced or colored by our drives and affects. Instead, understanding simply is a relation of these drives and affects. Thus, understanding is not tied to a faculty of knowledge that stands above these competing desires and instincts and adjudicates between them. Instead, understanding or "*intelligere*" is "nothing but a *certain behavior of the instincts toward one another*" (GS 333). The implication is that thinking is wholly embedded within the web of nature, life, and even fate, and so if there is going to be knowledge, it must be reconciled with these forces.

Nietzsche laid the foundations for this conception of the understanding in *Human* and advanced a drive-centered analysis in *Daybreak*, and he provides a similar analysis of the moral conscience at the beginning of "Long Live Physics!" A common theme in all these reflections is that we are unknown to ourselves. Whereas most people believe that conscience has the first and final say in matters of morality – "the voice of conscience is never immoral" because "it alone determines what is to be moral" – Nietzsche is committed to an intellectual conscience which shows that moral judgments have a "pre-history" in "instincts, likes, dislikes, experiences, and lack of experiences" (GS 335). Because of this, listening to conscience may be nothing more than listening to what one has been taught as a child and reaffirmed through the community. In this sense – and here Nietzsche is summarizing a central idea from *Daybreak* – it is the herd instinct internalized.

Although he simply seems to be revealing the origin of our moral conscience in non-moral sources – again, this is the leitmotif of *Human* – Nietzsche holds that once we do this, the moral conscience loses its moral authority. Here, Nietzsche takes aim at Kant's categorical imperative. Like "the thing in itself," the categorical imperative is a "very ridiculous thing," as it was the way Kant returned to those old ideas of "God," "soul," "freedom," and "immortality." Nietzsche's analysis, however, shows that the universal character of the categorical imperative is rooted in an unacknowledged self-love or *Selbstsucht* in which one naively experiences "one's own judgment as a universal law." According to Nietzsche, "anyone who still judges 'in this case everybody would have to act like this' has not yet taken five steps toward self-knowledge" (GS 335).

The most important part of "Long Live Physics!" comes toward the end of the aphorism. Nietzsche transitions from his critique of objective and universal morality to a new project that involves "the *creation of our own new tables of what is good.*" Just as he claims, after the death of God, that "what is now decisive against Christianity is our taste, no longer our reason" (GS 132), he now asserts that, "sitting in moral judgment should offend our taste." This is because the free spirit has advanced – in both thought and feeling – to a new project of becoming "*those we are* – human beings who are new, unique, incomparable, who give themselves laws, who create themselves." To this end, Nietzsche claims that, "we must become *physicists* in order to be able to be *creators* in this sense – while hitherto all valuations and ideals have been based on *ignorance* of physics or were constructed so as to *contradict* it. Therefore: long live physics! And even more so that which *compels* us to turn to physics – our honesty [*Redlichkeit*]!" (GS 335).

The final lines of the aphorism are filled with connections to Nietzsche's other works. The rejection of morality in the name of an aesthetic justification of existence is central to *The Birth of Tragedy*, and the very notion of making oneself into a unique and autonomous individual points back to *Schopenhauer as Educator* and forward to Nietzsche's self-presentation in *Ecce Homo*. Nietzsche also stresses the necessity of physics and the honesty that compels us toward physics, and in this sense, his view can be linked to *Human*. However, he now assigns to honesty, physics, and so the natural sciences a subordinate role in a project of becoming who one is. Thus, Nietzsche has moved beyond the ascetic ideal of *Human* precisely because truth-seeking via the natural sciences is no longer the aim of the free spirit project. Instead, science and honesty are useful tools for a new project: becoming who one is.

The union between the aesthetically constructed self and the forces of nature revealed by physics finds its parallel in Nietzsche's attempt to connect personal history to world history in "The 'Humaneness' of the Future," and it recalls Nietzsche's attempt to link self-knowledge with historical knowledge in "Whither We Have to Travel" from *Assorted Opinions* (AOM 223). Nietzsche begins the aphorism by speaking of the historical sense as both a "virtue and disease" of present-day humanity. The disease here seems to be the disease Nietzsche diagnosed in *History for Life*: The historical sense gives a feeling of old age and being an epigone. The historical sense that Nietzsche discusses in the aphorism, however, can also be a virtue and a glorious possibility. Thus, he speaks of an individual who "manages to experience the history of humanity as a whole as *his own history.*" If this can be endured, it makes possible a new day in which a hero could take the burden of this suffering and concentrate it into a single feeling that would "result in a happiness that humanity has not known so far; the happiness of a god full of power and love, full of tears and laughter." This "godlike feeling," Nietzsche claims, "would then be called – humaneness" (GS 337).

What is also significant about "The 'Humaneness' of the Future" is that Nietzsche refers to this heroic and even divine soul as being "full of tears and laughter." Such a reference immediately recalls the themes of tragedy and comedy that run throughout *The Gay Science*. This is because we are now presented with an individual who seems to be experiencing himself as a god, and there is reason to think that Nietzsche finds in the Dionysian arts of tragedy and comedy the human capacity to do this. That is, the poet engages in an act of self-redemption that is also the redemption of humanity, and this, again, is a central motif in *The Birth of Tragedy*. So understood, the free spirit project is now giving way to a new project in which Nietzsche will try to incorporate all the tears and laughter of humanity and, like the sun, bless this entire process. Although it might be tempting to identify this individual with the *Uebermensch*, Nietzsche refers to this as a form of "humaneness [*Menschlichkeit*]" (GS 337). In this sense, Nietzsche's atheism might not culminate in transhumanism, but the ultimate form of humanism.[4]

In *The Birth of Tragedy*, Nietzsche opposed the idea of an artistic justification of life to the sort of redemption Christianity offers through the cross, and in the very next aphorism of *The Gay Science*, Nietzsche returns to the topic of pity and so the form of redemption Christianity offers. The aphorism begins with a reflection on suffering, and Nietzsche again insists that our deepest happiness is linked to internal distress and so suffering. In other words, "the path to one's own heaven always leads through the voluptuousness of one's own hell" (GS 338). The problem with the religion of pity, according to Nietzsche, is that it judges "suffering and displeasure" as something "evil, hateful, worthy of annihilation," and it is this prejudice – one embedded in Schopenhauer's philosophy – that Nietzsche rejected as early as *The Birth of Tragedy*. Here, Nietzsche claims that it betrays a further prejudice that he finds contemptible: human happiness amounts to a "*religion of comfortableness*" that eschews suffering at all costs (GS 338).

In the final portion of the aphorism, Nietzsche points to two further criticisms of pity. The first is that pity diverts one from the fundamental task announced in *The Gay Science* of becoming who you are (GS 270 and

---

[4] Brusotti (1997: 477–478) argues that the ideas in this aphorism can be connected to *amor fati*.

335). The morality of pity is a command "to lose one's *own* way in order to come to the assistance of a neighbor," and this call seduces us from keeping our own way. At the same time, Nietzsche emphasizes both the distress that this project entails and the distress that he will indeed feel – as Zarathustra does in *Zarathustra* IV – when called to help others in distress. However, the help here will come not through forgetting oneself. Instead, it will come by first helping oneself. In this way, the free spirit will then be able to make others "bolder, more persevering, simpler, gayer," and so he will share not with their sufferings – as *Mitleid* suggests – but in their joys and so their *Mitfreude* (GS 338).

From the Free Spirit to the Tragedy of *Thus Spoke Zarathustra*

The final three aphorisms of the 1882 edition of *The Gay Science* are extremely significant for the dialectical reading of the free spirit works and their relationship to Nietzsche's earlier and later writings. They stand at the end of a thought-chain that stretches back to the beginning of *Human*, and all three aphorisms can be directly tied to central themes of *The Birth of Tragedy*. Whereas the first aphorism implicitly critiques the will to truth that has animated the free spirit since *Human* and so recalls Nietzsche's criticism of Socrates in his first work, the second and third can be linked to tragedy and a corresponding tragic worldview. Thus, these aphorisms not only recall the central argument of *The Birth of Tragedy*, they effectively transition from the free spirit project to Nietzsche's own tragedy in *Zarathustra*.

The antepenultimate aphorism, "The Dying Socrates," marks Nietzsche's final break with the Socratic tradition. In *The Birth of Tragedy*, Nietzsche identified two components of this tradition. First, he noted and even praised the uncompromising quest for truth that Socrates represented. Second, he identified an optimistic illusion that justified the unrelenting quest for truth by attributing to truth the capacity to cure suffering and promote human flourishing. At the beginning of the free spirit project, we saw how Nietzsche, driven by the will to truth, began to attack the optimistic myth in *Human*. At the end of the free spirit project, we now find Nietzsche critiquing the very will to truth that animated both Socrates and the free spirit project up to this point. Specifically, "The Dying Socrates" presents an implicit critique of the will to truth that Nietzsche makes explicit in his later writings. That is, "The Dying Socrates" shows us that the "will to truth" is really a "concealed will to death" (GS 344).

In the aphorism, Nietzsche does not explicitly refer to truth and the will to truth. Instead, he presents Socrates and so the Socratic project as hostile to life, and in this way, Nietzsche is claiming to unmask Socrates here as a pessimist in the evaluative sense. That is, Socrates is someone who instinctively said "no" to life and therefore sought to escape existence by seeking truth. According to Nietzsche, Socrates' hostility to life is evidenced by his final words. By owing Asclepius a cock, Socrates thanks Asclepius for giving him a cure for the disease of life (GS 340).

To be sure, Nietzsche's analysis is not much of an unmasking. This is because he is referring to Plato's dramatization of Socrates' death in the *Phaedo*,[5] and Plato argues in the work that philosophy is a preparation for death in the sense of separating the soul from the body. Plato argues that the body, through sense perception and the appetites, clouds the pure vision of the philosopher and so prevents the philosopher from perceiving reality with perfect clarity. Thus, if a philosopher is truly in love with wisdom, she will strive as much as possible to quell desire and turn away from sense perception, and in so doing, she will be preparing for the ultimate separation of the soul from the body and so death.

The argument of the *Phaedo*, however, depends on a commitment to a soul that can separate from the body and an intelligible reality that is known through pure reason. To establish this, Plato has Socrates confront alternative understandings of both reality and death that are relevant to Nietzsche's free spirit project. Central to the *Phaedo* is the very problem that stands at the beginning of Nietzsche's free spirit project, namely, the problem of opposites (HH 1), and Plato has Socrates reject a cyclical understanding of life and death in which one opposite comes from another. Specifically, Socrates separates life from death and then proceeds to argue that the soul is immortal because it is essentially alive. This, then, is why death is not to be feared and why one should not be overwhelmed with emotions – as tragic characters and tragic audiences often are – when confronting death. Far from being the ultimate necessity, death is the ultimate liberation from the bondage of the body, and this is why the *eros* of the philosopher and so the will to truth is ultimately a longing for *thanatos*. In this sense, Plato and Nietzsche agree: The will to truth is a will to death. Nevertheless, they disagree about whether the will to truth is something we should embrace because it leads to a better reality (as Plato suggests), or whether it is the great danger now confronting humanity

---

[5] Loeb (2010: Ch. 2) also highlights the connection.

because it amounts to a longing for nothingness and so nihilism (as Nietzsche claims) (GM P 5).

"The Dying Socrates" ends with the claim, "alas my friends, we must overcome even the Greeks" (GS 340), and this claim is a potential source of confusion. Some have read the aphorism as Nietzsche's final reckoning with his previous interest in Greek culture and so as a call to move beyond the Greeks *in toto* as an ideal.[6] Nothing, however, could be further from Nietzsche's intention here. The next two aphorisms – and so the final two aphorisms of the 1882 edition of *The Gay Science* – point to Nietzsche's interest in reviving both a tragic worldview and a tragic art that can be traced back to the pre-Socratic Greeks. So understood, Nietzsche's claim that "we must overcome even the Greeks" is really a claim that we must overcome a Socratic and post-Socratic tradition that rejected both the tragic worldview and the tragic poetry that flourished as a response to it.[7] In this way, the aphorism represents the free spirit's departure from the last remnants of Platonic philosophy and the beginning of Nietzsche's turn to the Dionysian arts that provide an alternative way to confront suffering and death.

In the next aphorism, "The Greatest Weight," Nietzsche presents his reader with the idea of the eternal recurrence. We know that Nietzsche first penned his ideas for the concept in the summer of 1881 while in Sils Maria, Switzerland (KSA 9: 11[141]), and that he provides an almost mystical explanation of how this idea came to him in *Ecce Homo* (EH "Books" Z:1). This means that Nietzsche composed the whole of *The Gay Science* with this idea in mind, and he drops hints of its eventual appearance at the end of the text in at least two of the preceding aphorisms. Whereas he refers to a "musical box" that "repeats eternally its tune" in "Let Us Beware" (GS 109), Nietzsche speaks of "the eternal recurrence of war and peace" in "Excelsior" (GS 285).

In the aphorism itself, there is no explicit mention of its connection to the ancient Greeks or the potential role it might have in Nietzsche's tragic philosophy. There is, however, evidence from Nietzsche's later discussions of the doctrine in which he associates it with Dionysus and the tragedies performed in his honor. To recall, Nietzsche argued in *The Birth of Tragedy* that the tragedies of Aeschylus and Sophocles were intimately connected to the mystery religions of ancient Greece and those associated

---

[6] See Strong (1975: 184) and Borsche (1985: 85).
[7] See Halliwell (1996) for the claim that Plato not only attacked poetry but also a corresponding tragic worldview.

with Dionysus Zagreus (BT 10), and Nietzsche links the eternal recurrence to the mystery teachings of antiquity in an 1883 *Nachlass* note: "I have discovered the Hellenic: they believed in the eternal recurrence! That is the mystery-faith" (KSA 10: 8[15]).[8]

In *The Twilight of the Idols*, Nietzsche also connects the eternal recurrence to the mysteries associated with Dionysus and the genre of tragedy. Specifically, he explains why even Goethe – whom Nietzsche praises for creating himself and affirming existence (TI "What the Germans Lack" 49) – did not understand the Greeks. The reason is that he did not understand the Dionysian, and Nietzsche explains what the Dionysian means: "For it is only in the Dionysian mysteries, in the psychology of the Dionysian state, that the *basic fact* of the Hellenic instinct finds expression – its 'will to life'." In these mysteries the Hellene guaranteed "*eternal* life, the eternal return of life; the future promised and hallowed in the past; the triumphant Yes to life beyond all death and change" (TI "What I Owe" 4).

Nietzsche also claims that in these mysteries "*pain* is pronounced holy" (TI "What I Owe" 4), and this transitions to the final section of the *Twilight of the Idols* in which Nietzsche links the discussion of Dionysus to the tragic effect and so *The Birth of Tragedy*. Specifically, Nietzsche argues that both Schopenhauer and Aristotle misunderstood tragedy and the tragic effect. Rather than producing pity and fear (Aristotle) or even life-negation (Schopenhauer), Nietzsche claims that the Dionysian, and so the "psychology of the *tragic* poet," amounts to "a saying Yes to life even in its strangest and hardest problems, the will to life rejoicing over its own inexhaustibility even in the very sacrifice of its highest types." This is all so that one can "be *oneself* the eternal joy of becoming, beyond all terror and pity – that joy which included even joy in destroying." The section then concludes with Nietzsche claiming to be "the last disciple of the philosopher Dionysus" and "the teacher of the eternal recurrence" (TI "What I Owe" 5).

We can further substantiate these connections by noting that Nietzsche also links the eternal recurrence to *amor fati* and so the fatalism essential to tragedy.[9] In *Ecce Homo*, Nietzsche claims that his "formula for greatness in a human being is *amor fati*," and he explains that *amor fati* means wanting

---

[8] Loeb (2010: 3) also makes this point. Also see KSA 13: 14[89].
[9] See Ridley (1997) and Domino (2012) for a rejection of this connection.

"nothing to be different, not forward, not backward, not in all eternity" such that we do "not merely bear what is necessary" but even "*love* it" (EH "Clever" 10). The language of "eternity" suggests the idea of the eternal recurrence and so a connection between the eternal recurrence and *amor fati*, and a *Nachlass* note from 1888 substantiates this connection. There, Nietzsche speaks of a "Dionysian affirmation of the world, as it is, without subtraction, exception, and selection – it wants the eternal circularity – the same things, the same logic and unlogic of knots," and he claims that his formula for this "Dionysian" stance toward existence is "*amor fati*" (KSA 13: 16[32]).

There are further connections Nietzsche makes between the eternal recurrence and Greek tragedy as well as tragic philosophy. In his account of *The Birth of Tragedy* in *Ecce Homo*, Nietzsche refers to himself as "the first *tragic philosopher*" because he transposed "the Dionysian into a philosophical pathos." However, he acknowledges that Heraclitus might deserve such a title, and this is why Nietzsche "feels warmer and better than anywhere else" in his proximity. Heraclitus held a doctrine of becoming that involved both a "radical repudiation of the very concept of *being*" and a Dionysian notion of philosophy that affirms "passing away *and destroying*." Nietzsche also acknowledges that Heraclitus – and to a lesser extent the Stoics – *might* have taught "the doctrine of the 'eternal recurrence,' that is, of the unconditional and infinitely repeated circular course of all things" (EH "Books" BT:3).

The idea that Heraclitus is, in some sense, a tragic philosopher is by no means a novel idea in Nietzsche's writings. As I have argued elsewhere (Meyer 2014a: Ch. 1), Heraclitus' philosophy is important for Nietzsche because it allows him to replace the metaphysical principles of Schopenhauer he used in *The Birth of Tragedy* to express his understanding of a tragic worldview with principles that reject metaphysics in the name of a thoroughgoing naturalism. I argued in Chapter 3 of this work that Nietzsche begins the free spirit works with a denial of opposites and a corresponding commitment to Heraclitean becoming – ideas that point back to Nietzsche's exposition of Heraclitus' philosophy in *Philosophy in the Tragic Age*. What the connection between Heraclitus and the eternal recurrence means is that Nietzsche concludes the free spirit works with another Heraclitean teaching that complements and even completes this naturalistic project.

There is much debate in the secondary literature about whether Nietzsche understood the eternal recurrence as a cosmological principle or merely as an existential or ethical test of some sort.[10] Construed as a cosmological principle, Nietzsche thinks that the eternal recurrence accurately describes the events of the cosmos and so he thinks that there is an "unconditional and infinitely repeated circular course of all things" (EH "Books" BT:3). Construed as an existential or ethical principle, the idea is a thought experiment to test whether one has lived such that one would want to repeat this same life over and over.[11] Because defenders of the cosmological version also think that the principle has existential or ethical import, the real debate is whether the principle is merely an existential test or whether Nietzsche also thought that it accurately describes the cosmos.

Although I think there is enough evidence to show that the eternal recurrence should be construed in cosmological terms, the presentation of the doctrine at the end of the fourth chapter of *The Gay Science* focuses primarily on its existential impact. That is, it focuses on the central question of *The Birth of Tragedy*: Should we affirm or deny existence? In "The Greatest Weight," Nietzsche's poetic powers are in full effect as he poses this question to the reader. He dramatizes the situation by having a demon "steal into" our "loneliest loneliness" and reveal to us that we will have to live this life as we now live it "innumerable times more" and that "there will be nothing new in it." Even the smallest details will return "all in the same succession and same sequence" and so "the eternal hourglass of existence is turned upside down again and again" and we specks of dust will be with it (GS 341).[12]

Given this understanding, Nietzsche then raises the question as to how we might respond to this idea. On the one hand, we might throw ourselves down, gnash our teeth, and curse the demon that speaks thus. On the other hand, we might, upon experiencing "a tremendous moment [*eine ungeheure Augenblick*]" welcome the demon's message as something most divine. In either case, Nietzsche claims that if this thought were to gain possession of us, it would certainly change us, and perhaps even crush us. This is because a great weight would lie on all our actions as to whether we would desire this innumerable times more. Alternatively, we may become so well disposed toward ourselves and life that we end up craving "*nothing more fervently* then this ultimate eternal confirmation and seal" (GS 341).

---

[10] See Loeb (2013) for a comprehensive treatment of this topic and links to the relevant literature. See Soll (1973) for a classic treatment.

[11] Clark's (1990: 269) famous example is: "If you had it to do all over, would you marry me again?"

[12] See Salaquarda (1989) as well as Loeb (2018) for detailed analyses of this aphorism.

The eternal recurrence plays roughly the same role in *The Gay Science* that Silenic wisdom plays in *The Birth of Tragedy*. That is, it presents the reader with what seems to be, at least initially, a rather bleak characterization of existence and so a form of factual pessimism. That the eternal recurrence can be experienced as something bleak is suggested by the way in which we are characterized as "specks of dust" in an eternal hourglass, and so it is reminiscent of Nietzsche's portrayal of human existence at the beginning of "On Truth and Lies." The doctrine also undermines any hope for some essential or permanent change in the human condition (even though we might hope that things will get better within a given cycle) and so the achievement of some ultimate or final goal. Thus, like Silenic wisdom, it is a terrifying thought, so much so that one might long to escape a world so understood. This seems to be why Nietzsche, in his later *Nachlass*, refers to the eternal recurrence as the thought of meaninglessness "in its most terrible form: existence as it is, without meaning or goal, but inevitably recurring without a finale into nothingness" (KSA 12: 5[71]).

According to *The Birth of Tragedy*, the ancient Greeks turned to art – first Homeric epic but then eventually tragedy – as a life-affirming response to the wisdom of Silenus, and Nietzsche's turn to tragedy in the next and final aphorism of the 1882 edition of *The Gay Science* follows this logic. That is, confronted with the potentially terrifying thought of the eternal recurrence, Nietzsche turns to the very art form that he claimed, in his first work, could both confront and affirm a tragic worldview. Thus, the final aphorism – an aphorism that completes the dialectical transition from ascetic truth-seeking through the natural sciences to the aesthetic affirmation of life through the art forms associated with Dionysus – introduces Nietzsche's own tragedy, *Thus Spoke Zarathustra*, under the title, "*incipit tragoedia*" (GS 342).

That *Zarathustra* should be understood as Nietzsche's own tragedy has not been obvious to everyone.[13] However, there are a handful of commentators who have made this claim,[14] and the fact that Nietzsche introduces the work under the title of "*incipit tragoedia*" at the end of *The Gay Science* places the burden of proof on anyone who denies this approach to the

---

[13] Schacht (2015: 101) acknowledges Nietzsche's invitation to read *Zarathustra* as a tragedy, but claims it is not easy to do so.

[14] As noted in the first chapter, this claim can be found in Higgins (1987), Loeb (1998), and Reginster (2006). I also made this argument in Meyer (2002). See Loeb (2010) for an extended treatment.

work. Moreover, Nietzsche thinks that the eternal recurrence is a form of "fatalism" (KSA 11: 25[214]), and since fatalism is central to ancient Greek tragedy and the eternal recurrence is the fundamental conception of *Zarathustra*, there are good reasons to think that *Zarathustra* centers on the task of affirming tragic fate. So unless it can be shown otherwise, the question is not whether *Zarathustra* is a tragedy, but rather in what respect it should be understood as such.

I have argued elsewhere (Meyer 2002) that *The Birth of Tragedy* is essential to understanding *Zarathustra* as a tragedy. The basic idea is that reading *Zarathustra* as a tragedy means reading the work with Nietzsche's understanding of tragedy – not Aristotle's, Hegel's, or even our own – in mind, and this means turning to early works like *The Birth of Tragedy* and *Richard Wagner in Bayreuth* to develop this interpretive framework.[15] Using the opening sections of *The Birth of Tragedy* as a sort of blueprint for understanding *Zarathustra*, I have argued that the character of Zarathustra is an ecstatic creation of Nietzsche, the tragic poet, and so a second self or "son" (KSB 6: 407), and that the *Uebermensch* is the Apollonian vision of Zarathustra that provides an idealized and heroic conception of humanity whose beauty contributes to the aesthetic justification of existence.

According to *The Birth of Tragedy*, tragedy requires that the hero be sacrificed, and it is through the sacrifice of this godlike individual that one reunites with an eternally creative nature. Applied to *Zarathustra*, I have argued that there is a deep tension between the *Uebermensch*, which represents a future goal for human striving, and the eternal recurrence, a doctrine that undermines any sort of goal-directed and future-oriented striving (Meyer 2002).[16] Thus, I have claimed that Zarathustra must ultimately sacrifice the *Uebermensch* in order to become the teacher of the eternal recurrence, and it is in sacrificing the *Uebermensch* – or the highest type (TI "What I Owe" 5) – that Zarathustra also "goes under" and experiences a ritual death similar to the old-man, new-man dynamic in Christianity. By teaching and so incorporating the eternal recurrence, Zarathustra is effectively reborn not as the *Uebermensch*, but as the Heraclitean-Dionysian child that experiences fate or necessity as play and revels in the "innocence of becoming." In this way, the third book of *Zarathustra* completes the

---

[15] Hollinrake (1982) also emphasizes the operas of Wagner.
[16] Stern (2008: 301–302) has also argued this.

final transformation of the spirit that Nietzsche has Zarathustra describe in his first speech, "On the Three Metamorphoses."[17]

Such an interpretation not only resonates with the three metamorphoses of Zarathustra's first speech, it also finds support in Nietzsche's initial presentation of the eternal recurrence in his 1881 notebooks. There, Nietzsche associates the incorporation of the eternal recurrence with what he calls a "philosophy of indifference [*Philosophie der Gleichgültigkeit*]." In his explanation of this idea, Nietzsche claims that everything will be experienced like a "game" that will be "enjoyed aesthetically." As such, we will feel ourselves like children in relation to what we previously took so seriously (KSA 9: 11[141]), and in a subsequent note, Nietzsche associates this "game of life" with both "necessity and innocence" (KSA 9: 11[144]).

These notions of aesthetic enjoyment, innocence, and the play of children can also be linked to Nietzsche's early understanding of Heraclitus' philosophy and Greek tragedy. In his account of Heraclitus' philosophy in *Philosophy in the Tragic Age*, he describes Heraclitus' vision of the world as one in which the play of artists and children "exhibits coming-to-be and passing away, structuring and destroying, without any moral additive, in forever equal innocence" (PTAG 7). In *The Birth of Tragedy*, Nietzsche appeals to Heraclitus' philosophy in order to explain the leitmotif of the work, namely, that only as an aesthetic phenomenon is existence eternally justified (BT 5 and 24). Specifically, Nietzsche refers to a Heraclitean child that "places stones here and there and builds sand hills only to overthrow them again." Just as we can find primordial joy in pain, we can take pleasure in both creation and destruction, and tragedy is so significant because it reflects, embraces, and ultimately justifies a natural world constituted by this cycle of creation and destruction (BT 24).

One potential problem with claiming that Zarathustra completes the third metamorphosis by becoming a Dionysian child at the end of the third book is that it leaves the fourth and final book of *Zarathustra* unexplained, and the presence of this book, one that Nietzsche distributed only privately during his lifetime, has posed a number of interpretive difficulties.[18] Although I disagree with his analeptic reading of the text, I follow Loeb (2010) in reading the fourth book as a satyr play and so a literary form of the ancient genre that gave expression to this childlike, playful attitude that I claim Zarathustra has achieved by teaching the

---

[17] See Wohlfart (1991) for an extended analysis of the role of the child in Heraclitus' philosophy and Nietzsche's *Zarathustra*.

[18] Providing a response to this problem is central to Loeb's (2000; 2010) reading.

eternal recurrence. Here, the spirit of gravity has been overcome, and Nietzsche seems to engage in a parody of the very distress that Zarathustra experienced throughout the first three books. Thus, the satyr play climaxes in an ass festival in which a number of so-called higher men engage in the worship of an ass that parodies the reverence one might accord to Christ or even the *Uebermensch*.

It is important to note, however, that a satyr play is not the same as comedy. Instead, the satyr play is best understood as a genre that transitions from tragedy to comedy, and I think that *Zarathustra* IV plays this role in Nietzsche's works, evidenced by his later claim that *Zarathustra* IV is an interlude or "*Zwischenspiel*" (KSB 8: 974 and 1075). Thus, Nietzsche has Zarathustra exhort his higher men to learn what he calls in the 1886 preface to *The Birth of Tragedy* the "this-worldly" comfort of laughter (BT "Attempt" 7), and such a command points beyond *Zarathustra* IV toward Nietzsche's post-*Zarathustra* writings, which I argue culminate in the Dionysian comedy of his 1888 works. So understood, Nietzsche's works fulfill the claim that he makes at the very beginning of *The Gay Science* that "the short tragedy always gave way again and returned into the eternal comedy of existence" (GS 1). It is to some concluding remarks about these post-*Zarathustra* works that I now turn.

CHAPTER 8

Incipit Parodia
From the Free Spirit to the Philosophy of the Future?

To begin this final chapter, I want to note that the central argument of the book is now complete. After outlining and justifying the dialectical approach in the first two chapters, I then applied this interpretive approach to the free spirit works in Chapters 3 through 7. In those chapters, I provided an account of how the free spirit moved from an ascetic quest for truth via the natural sciences in *Human* to an aesthetic justification of existence through the tragedy of *Zarathustra* by way of a *Selbstaufhebung* of the will to truth with the death of God and the elimination of his shadow. Taken together, the first seven chapters have developed substantive evidence for thinking that Nietzsche's free spirit works from *Human* (1878) to the first edition of *The Gay Science* (1882) are best understood as a consciously constructed dialectical *Bildungsroman*.

In this final chapter, I venture beyond the confines of the free spirit works into Nietzsche's post-*Zarathustra* writings. Although he thinks of the free spirit works as a discrete project that runs from 1876 to 1882, Nietzsche understands his subsequent writings as related to and even following from the free spirit project. As we have seen, Nietzsche ends the free spirit works by transitioning to the tragedy of *Zarathustra*, and as we move to his subsequent works, Nietzsche continues to draw upon and refer back to the free spirit project. Thus, I want to bring some closure to this book by discussing the appearance of the free spirit in some of Nietzsche's post-*Zarathustra* writings and the various ways in which central themes from the free spirit project continue into Nietzsche's later writings.

This chapter focuses on two texts that are linked to the free spirit project: the second chapter from *Beyond Good and Evil* that bears the title, "The Free Spirit," and the fifth chapter of *The Gay Science* that Nietzsche added to the 1887 edition of the work. Whereas the purpose of the free spirit chapter from *Beyond Good and Evil* is to transition from the free spirit to what Nietzsche calls the philosopher of the future, the fifth chapter of *The Gay Science* can be read as a retrospective reflection upon the free spirit project and a statement of where a now *freed* spirit stands given the developments that take place in the free spirit works.[1]

Both of these texts include frequent references to laughter and comedy, and so both develop a theme already announced in the first aphorism of the 1882 edition of *The Gay Science* (GS 1). I have argued elsewhere that Nietzsche's 1888 works should be understood as a Dionysian comedy (Meyer 2012a; 2018), and so there are reasons for thinking that Nietzsche's praise of Aristophanes in the second chapter of *Beyond Good and Evil* and his talk of "*incipit parodia*" in the 1887 edition of *The Gay Science* (GS P 1) are proleptically foreshadowing his 1888 works just as "*incipit tragoedia*" foreshadows the tragedy of *Zarathustra*. Because Nietzsche speaks of laughter and the future of laughter on important occasions in *Beyond Good and Evil* and other texts from this time period, I conclude this chapter by giving some reasons why we should think that Nietzsche's philosophy of the future is the Dionysian comedy of his 1888 works.

To be sure, such claims will strike skeptical readers as highly speculative and even dubious.[2] In response to such concerns, it must be said that I do not propose to defend such ideas here. Instead, my purpose is simply to sketch an understanding of how Nietzsche's free spirit project continues to animate his post-*Zarathustra* works in a way that makes sense of the dual emphasis on tragedy and comedy that emerges in *The Gay Science*. Although what I say here has no immediate bearing on the truth or falsity of the central thesis of the book, reading the free spirit works as an unfolding dialectic that transitions to the tragedy of *Zarathustra* encourages us to begin looking for these kinds of connections in Nietzsche's later writings, and in what follows, I will do just this.

From the Free Spirit to the Philosophy of the Future in *Beyond Good and Evil*

According to the dialectical reading, the most significant event in the free spirit works is the *Selbstaufhebung* of the will to truth that takes place with

---

[1] See Sommer (2015: 259–262) for the claim that Nietzsche speaks of *freed* spirits in his 1888 works (A 37).

[2] There is much debate about the philosophy of the future, whether Nietzsche considers himself to be such a philosopher, and whether *Beyond Good and Evil* is an exercise in just such a philosophy. See Nehamas (1988) for a defense of the latter view. See Loeb (2019) for the view that Nietzsche is not a future philosopher.

the death of God in the third chapter of *The Gay Science*, and the opening aphorisms of *Beyond Good and Evil* indicate that Nietzsche is writing as a free spirit liberated from the ascetic ideal and the corresponding false belief that truth has an absolute value. It is here that the relationship between *Human* and *Beyond Good and Evil* takes on great significance. We know that the idea for *Beyond Good and Evil* emerged from Nietzsche's interest in producing a revised version of *Human* (Prange 2012: 232), and the parallels between the two works are notable. Both have nine chapters, both are written in the same style, both cover many of the same topics, and both begin (roughly) with the problem of opposites (HH 1 and BGE 2).

There is, however, an important difference between the two works. Whereas *Human* is driven by an ascetic commitment to truth that demands the suppression of human subjectivity and reveals truths hostile to life, Nietzsche opens *Beyond Good and Evil* by questioning both the nature of truth (BGE P) and the will to truth (BGE 1) and making life, rather than truth, the standard for assessing judgments (BGE 4). As Nietzsche remarks, it is "in this respect that our new language may sound strangest" (BGE 4), and this language is new precisely because he is abandoning the old language of truth-seeking in *Human* and the other free spirit works.

What this suggests is that going beyond good and evil means, first and foremost, going beyond what I have called the morality of truth or the idea that we have an obligation to pursue truth at all costs, and we see here that the position Nietzsche adopts at the beginning of *Beyond Good and Evil* is a result of the labors that he undertook in the free spirit works. This attitude toward truth continues in the second chapter of *Beyond Good and Evil* that bears the title "The Free Spirit." There, Nietzsche exhorts philosophers and friends of knowledge to "beware of martyrdom" and suffering for the sake of truth (BGE 25), and so he counsels against some of the most extreme forms of the ascetic ideal. Similarly, he begins the first aphorism of the chapter with the claim, "O *sancta simplicitas*," and this is followed by the assertion that we live in such "strange simplification and falsification." Indeed, it is through this process of falsification and our corresponding superficiality that we now enjoy "an almost inconceivable freedom, lack of scruple and caution, heartiness, and gaiety of life" (BGE 24).

The mention of "gaiety of life" points to the title and overall ethos of *The Gay Science*, and as the aphorism continues, Nietzsche also wants to link this newfound openness toward falsification to both knowledge and science. Although this will strike most contemporary philosophers as absurd, we know that Nietzsche, as early as 1881, was claiming that we must first falsify and so construct a life-world so as to make it intelligible to human consciousness. For this reason, Nietzsche claims that "error" is the "womb of knowledge" and that art is the curator of such error (KSA 9: 11 [162]).[3] In the second chapter of *Beyond Good and Evil*, Nietzsche unpacks this idea. Thus, he claims that knowledge emerged from "a far more powerful will: the will to ignorance, to the uncertain, to the untrue! Not as its opposite, but – as its refinement!" He then concludes the aphorism by claiming that "science [*Wissenschaft*] at its best seeks most to keep us in this *simplified*, thoroughly artificial, suitably constructed and suitably falsified world – at the way in which, willy-nilly, it loves error, because, being alive, it loves life" (BGE 24).

Both the 1881 note and BGE 24 introduce a host of technical difficulties that I cannot hope to solve here. What I will say, however, is that Nietzsche's understanding of *Wissenschaft* in this passage is not the same thing as the kind of science, that is, the natural sciences and their methods, that Nietzsche embraced and associated with historical philosophy in *Human* (HH 1). Whereas the latter can be understood as a skeptical method that carefully observes, identifies, and describes patterns found in the empirical world, the former has to do with generating a body of knowledge that conforms to our cognitive apparatus and provides systematic explanations of a wide variety of phenomena. In terms of ancient philosophy, whereas the science that Nietzsche pursues in *Human* can be understood as a form of *empeiria*, the science – and so a gay science – that Nietzsche is discussing in *Beyond Good and Evil* is a form of *epistêmê* and so a systematic body of knowledge. As I have argued elsewhere (Meyer 2012b; 2014a), Nietzsche believes that we can never achieve an objective, non-anthropomorphic, and non-falsifying *epistêmê* precisely because (1) all explanations must be in human terms and (2) the natural world does not neatly conform to human cognition, and so by a gay science Nietzsche has in mind a *Wissenschaft* or an *epistêmê* that openly embraces anthropomorphism and allows for falsification.

If this is right, then the upshot of BGE 24 is that if we are going to have science or knowledge in the sense of *epistêmê*, it will have to embrace the quasi-Kantian idea that we must first shape, even create, the object of knowledge so that it conforms to the demands of our cognition. So understood, philosophy can no longer be a quest for objectivity that attempts to make the soul into a mirror of the world. Instead, the philosopher of the future must shape the world in his or her own image

---

[3] See Siemens and Hay (2015: 116–117) for an extended discussion of this note in relation to GS 110.

such that the world mirrors the philosopher. In a later aphorism, Nietzsche thus speaks of "*genuine philosophers*," in contradistinction to philosophical laborers, who will be "*commanders and legislators*" for whom "'knowing' is *creating*" and "creating is a legislating" (BGE 211).

Nietzsche ends the aphorism by claiming that such legislation is not a manifestation of the will to truth, but rather a will to power (BGE 211), and so we see how the philosopher of the future has moved beyond asceticism. However, some might find such a reading problematic because Nietzsche seems to criticize the Stoics for engaging in precisely this sort of activity: It was through their will to power that they projected their values onto nature and so created a world in their own image (BGE 9). This, however, would be a misreading of the aphorism. The problem with the Stoics is not that they cultivated "the most spiritual will to power" and so engaged in "the creation of the world." Instead, the problem is that they engaged in this creative activity without knowing they were doing this. In this sense, they were both "self-deceivers" (BGE 9) and dogmatists (BGE P) because they took themselves to be discovers of a value-laden cosmos and so overlooked the fact that they were the artistic creators of their life-worlds (see GS 301).

Returning to the second book of *Beyond Good and Evil*, we see that Nietzsche thinks of the free spirit as providing the conditions for this sort of philosophy of the future.[4] This is because he devotes the final three aphorisms of the chapter to discussing future philosophers and their relationship to the free spirit. In the first of these aphorisms, Nietzsche refers to these philosophers of the future as "attempters" (BGE 42), and we have seen the way in which Nietzsche unpacks an experimental philosophy in the latter part of the free spirit project that makes life a means to knowledge. In the next aphorism, he claims that such philosophers will be friends of truths that are nevertheless non-dogmatic, that is, they will present "truths" – and here Nietzsche likely means the sort of "truths" he discusses in "On Truth and Lies" – that will not necessarily be valid for everyone (BGE 43). In the final aphorism, Nietzsche presents the future philosopher as a further development of the free spirit. Thus, he claims that, "these philosophers of the future" will be "free, *very* free spirits." At the same time, they will not just be free spirits. Instead, they will be

---

[4] As Mullin (2000: 384) rightly argues, we cannot simply equate free spirits with philosophers of the future, as Nehamas (1985) does. Instead, the former provide the conditions for the emergence of the latter.

"something more, higher, greater, and thoroughly different that does not want to be misunderstood and mistaken for something else" (BGE 44).[5]

Given the dialectical reading of the free spirit project as well as Nietzsche's remarks in *Beyond Good and Evil*, we can piece together the relationship between the free spirit and the philosopher of the future as follows. Although the free spirit is initially driven by the will to truth, the mature and so *freed* spirit has enacted a *Selbstaufhebung* of the will to truth and therefore is now liberated from the corresponding idea that truth has an absolute value. As such, the free spirit can now embrace a conception of philosophy that is self-consciously driven by the will to power and creates a life-world in the image of the philosopher. Because this philosophy will be a voluntary and conscious memoir and bear decided witness to who the philosopher fundamentally is (BGE 6), the philosophy of the future will be self-consciously autobiographical. So understood, there is reason to think that the centerpiece of Nietzsche's philosophy of the future is *Ecce Homo*, the work in which he tells us who he is.

What should also be clear is that the philosophy of the future is a form of art and so the philosopher of the future is a type of artist. This is because Nietzsche explicitly links the title, "Beyond Good and Evil," to both "the lawgiver of the *future*" and "the philosopher as artist" (KSA 11: 34[201]). Moreover, Nietzsche describes the philosophy of the future in terms of creation. This is not only the case when he speaks of philosophy as the "creation of the world" and so the highest form of the will to power (BGE 9), but also when he presents the future philosopher's knowing as a form of creating (BGE 211).

Because the aforementioned note also includes a reference to "Dionysus" (KSA 11: 34[201]), there are reasons for thinking that Nietzsche's new conception of philosophy will be a form of Dionysian art. Moreover, the second chapter of *Beyond Good and Evil* provides evidence for thinking that the philosophy of the future is a Dionysian comedy. There, Nietzsche speaks of laughter and comedy on a number of occasions. In the second aphorism of the chapter, Nietzsche claims that, "moral indignation" is a sign that a philosopher has lost his "philosophical sense of humor." In the same aphorism, Nietzsche also speaks of a "satyr play" or an "epilogue farce" in which the long philosophical tragedy has come to an end (BGE 25). In the next aphorism, he refers to the buffoonish Abbé Galiani and a "laughing and self-satisfied satyr"

---

[5] The idea of not being mistaken for something else is central to *Ecce Homo*: "*Hear me! For I am such and such a person. Above all, do not mistake me for someone else*" (EH P 1).

(BGE 26), and the subsequent aphorism concludes with two references to laughter (BGE 27).

The next aphorism is important for my argument because Nietzsche provides an extended discussion of Aristophanes. Specifically, Nietzsche praises the style of Petronius and Aristophanes in the context of discussing how Germans are incapable of *presto*, which is the style "of many of the most delightful and daring *nuances* of free, free-spirited thought." In the final portion of the passage, Nietzsche then praises Aristophanes and suggests that he had a deep influence on Plato. Thus, he describes Aristophanes as "that transfiguring, complementary spirit for whose sake one *forgives* everything Hellenic for having existed." According to Nietzsche, Plato could not have endured Greek life without Aristophanes, and this is why Plato kept a copy of Aristophanes under his pillow (BGE 28).

The implication of this aphorism is that the free spirit is now liberated to engage in an art form and so a philosophy of the future that involves mockery and laughter,[6] and this reading finds further support in subsequent aphorisms of *Beyond Good and Evil*. In the seventh chapter, Nietzsche again mentions Aristophanes in a passage that begins with remarks on history and "the hybrid European." Specifically, Nietzsche claims that in contrast to the past, we now specialize in studying the costumes of moralities, faiths, aesthetic tastes, and religions, and this has, in turn, set the stage for "a carnival in the grand style, for the laughter and high spirits of the most spiritual revelry, for the transcendental heights of the highest nonsense and Aristophanean derision of the world." As the aphorism continues, Nietzsche indicates that he is thinking of the philosophy of the future in terms of this Aristophanic derision. Thus, he writes: "Perhaps this is where we shall still discover the realm of our *invention*, that realm in which we, too, can still be original, say, as parodists of world history and God's buffoons [*Hanswürste Gottes*] – perhaps even if nothing else today has any future, our *laughter* may yet have a future" (BGE 223).

This call for a laughter of the future echoes the call for laughter that Zarathustra issues in *Zarathustra* IV and Nietzsche repeats in the 1886 preface to *The Birth of Tragedy* (BT "Attempt" 7), and Nietzsche ends *Beyond Good and Evil* with references to both laughter and Dionysus. In the antepenultimate aphorism, Nietzsche chides Hobbes for trying to

---

[6] Siemens and Hay (2015) rightly argue that Nietzsche's self-critique of *Redlichkeit* transitions to a philosophy associated with laughter. However, they do not then connect this transition to Nietzsche's post-*Zarathustra* writings.

"bring laughter into ill repute among all thinking men." In contrast, Nietzsche finds laughter so important for life and even philosophy that he is going to "risk an order of rank among philosophers depending on the rank of their laughter," and Nietzsche ends the aphorism by claiming that gods not only philosophize but "they also know how to laugh the while in a superhuman and new way" (BGE 294).

In the penultimate aphorism of *Beyond Good and Evil*, we encounter Nietzsche presenting himself, for the first time in his post-1876 works, as a disciple of the Greek god Dionysus (BGE 295), a claim he repeats in both *Twilight of the Idols* (TI "What I Owe" 5) and *Ecce Homo* (EH P 2). Although there is no mention of comedy, we know that Dionysus is the god of both tragedy and comedy, and so the close proximity of Nietzsche's self-declared discipleship to his discussion of divine laughter suggests an interest in the latter genre. For these reasons, we can infer that Nietzsche has a Dionysian comedy in mind at the end of *Beyond Good and Evil*, and since *Beyond Good and Evil* is also a "Prelude to a Philosophy of the Future," there are reasons to think that the philosophy of the future is a Dionysian comedy. If this is right, then Nietzsche's discussion of the free spirit in chapter 2 of *Beyond Good and Evil* transitions to a philosophy of the future that is a Dionysian comedy.

From the Free Spirit to *Incipit Parodia* in *The Gay Science* V

Whereas the chapter title explicitly links the second chapter of *Beyond Good and Evil* to the free spirit project, the fifth chapter of *The Gay Science* is linked to the free spirit project by virtue of its relationship to the first four chapters of the 1882 edition. The title of the chapter is "We Fearless Ones," and so the chapter seems to continue the heroic attitude of a free spirit willing to defy convention and remain fearless in the face of death. There are at least two functions that the fifth chapter to the 1887 edition fulfills. First, it provides a retrospective account of what the free spirit project means from the perspective of a fully matured and so freed spirit. Second, the chapter – along with a new motto, the 1887 preface, and the appendix of poems, "Songs of Prince Vogelfrei" – develops the theme of comedy that appears in crucial aphorisms throughout the first three books of the text (GS 1, 107, and 153) but subsides in a fourth chapter that ends with "*incipit tragoedia*." In this way, the fifth chapter provides a double ending to the text and so the free spirit project as a whole.

That Nietzsche regards the fifth chapter of *The Gay Science* as both a continuation of and a retrospective reflection on the events that take place in the free spirit works is evidenced by the opening five aphorisms that start with remarks on the death of God (GS 343) and end with an explicit reference to the free spirit (GS 347). In the first two aphorisms, Nietzsche speaks of God's death as an event that has already taken place and so assumes the events of the third chapter. Whereas "The Meaning of Our Cheerfulness" presents the originally disorienting announcement of the death of God now with a message of excitement and cheerfulness (GS 343), "How We, Too, Are Still Pious" explains the connection between the death of God and the value of truth (GS 344).

The first aphorism begins with a reflection on the death of God, and the idea that runs throughout the aphorism is that this event could not have greater significance. Nietzsche claims that the consequences of this event are just beginning to cast their "shadows over Europe," but there is still much to come. This is because everything built upon this faith, including "European morality," will gradually begin to collapse, and this will lead to a "monstrous logic of terror" and a "sequence of breakdown, destruction, ruin, and cataclysm." Nevertheless, Nietzsche stresses that "we philosophers and 'free spirits'" – a phrase that suggests a link between the free spirit and future philosophers – will experience this event quite differently. The initial consequences of this event are "not at all sad and gloomy but rather like a new and scarcely describable kind of light, happiness, relief, exhilaration, encouragement, dawn." As a fearless one, the free spirit is ready to face any danger, and in language that recalls the final aphorism of *Daybreak* (D 575), Nietzsche claims that "perhaps there has never yet been such an open sea" (GS 343).

As I argued in the previous two chapters, the ultimate liberation that takes place in the free spirit works is the liberation from the morality of truth, and this occurs through the free spirit's proclamation of the death of God and the elimination of his shadow in chapter 3 of *The Gay Science*. A substantive piece of retrospective evidence for this reading can be found in the second aphorism of chapter 5, "How We, Too, Are Still Pious." Nietzsche claims that the ascetic will to truth is bound up with the idea that we have a moral obligation to pursue the truth and to be truthful, and this is based on the idea that truth has some absolute or overriding value. Although it is more complex than I can explain here,[7] the essential argument of the passage is that the project of science itself rests on an unscientific faith. The faith identified here is *not* that there is truth or that

---

[7] See Jenkins (2012) for a more detailed analysis that presents an alternative account to the one offered here.

truth can be found, but rather the faith that "truth is *needed*," so much so that "*nothing* is needed more than truth, and in relation to it everything else has only second-rate *value*" (GS 344).

Nietzsche characterizes the high premium placed on truth as a faith because he does not think that science or anything else can justify it. This is because it rests on the moral principle that one should not deceive, not even oneself. This cannot be justified by science because Nietzsche thinks – and this is a point he has been making since *Human* – that our mundane existence and so nature, history, and even life itself rest on "error, decep-tion, simulation, delusion, self-delusion." Thus, the idea that truth is a supreme value and deception should be avoided at all costs must be grounded in another, metaphysical world, and since the value of science rests on the ultimate value of truth, Nietzsche claims that, "it is still a metaphysical faith upon which our faith in science rests" (GS 344).

In typical fashion, Nietzsche concludes the aphorism by raising ques-tions about this faith: What if it turns out that nothing is more divine than error, blindness, and the lie? What if God turns out to be "our most enduring lie"? Although we should hesitate to answer these hyperbolic questions affirmatively, we know that Nietzsche has already adopted some version of these ideas in *Beyond Good and Evil*. Even though error might not be most divine, we know that Nietzsche rejects the idea that there is nothing more divine than truth. Similarly, even though it might not be that God is our "most" enduring lie, Nietzsche calls "Plato's invention of the pure spirit and the good as such" "the worst, most durable, and most dangerous of all errors so far" (BGE P). So understood, the questions Nietzsche poses here – similar to the questions at the beginning of *Beyond Good and Evil* – are questions that he has already answered affirmatively.

In the next aphorism, Nietzsche attacks the value of morality and the value of selflessness that such a morality demands (GS 345). Although not explicit, we know from Nietzsche's other writings – most notably the conclusion of the *Genealogy* – that there is a close connection between the search for truth and the morality of selflessness. This is because the demand for objectivity is a demand for a certain sort of selflessness vis-à-vis the world (BGE 207). In this sense, the will to truth is a project of un-selfing (*Entselbstung*), and this is why it can be understood as a secret will to death (GS 344).

In the aphorism itself, Nietzsche contrasts this ethic of selflessness, which he insists has "no value either in heaven or on earth," with a "*great love*" that is demanded to solve great problems (GS 345). Although far from clear, the reference to strong, secure, and even *round* spirits might be a reference to the kind of love or *eros* that Plato has Aristophanes articulate in the *Symposium*. Because all love for Plato's Aristophanes is essentially self-love, that is, what we really want is our other halves and so ourselves, the kind of love that such problems demand would be a kind of selfishness or *Selbstsucht* and so the opposite of the selflessness demanded by scientific objectivity. In short, this sort of love would be the opposite of a Platonic *eros* that bears a close resemblance to what Nietzsche calls the will to truth.

The point of the aphorism is to highlight the need to make the morality of selflessness into a problem. Nietzsche claims that he is the first to recognize this morality as a problem and so "ventured a critique of moral evaluations," and much of the aphorism foreshadows the very critique he puts forward in the *Genealogy*. Thus, he refers to the prejudices of the English historians of morality who assume that "selflessness, self-sacrifice, or sympathy and pity" are essential characteristics of moral actions. Similarly, the critique he ventures here does not aim at the truth (or error) of this sort of morality. Instead, the real question is "the *value* of that most famous of all medicines which is called morality" (GS 345), and based on the opening sections of *Beyond Good and Evil*, we can say that Nietzsche wants to examine the value of this morality in terms of life (BGE 4).

In the following aphorism, "Our Question Mark," Nietzsche brings together his reflections in the previous three aphorisms, effectively identifying the standpoint from which he is now writing as well as pointing toward some future project. Thus, he begins by stating that he is not merely godless or an unbeliever or even an immoralist. He has advanced beyond the stage of feeling any bitterness and so he is beyond the stage of turning his new unbelief into a cause or even a martyrdom. Instead, he is used to the fact that "the world in which we live is ungodly, immoral, 'inhuman'" and that "we have interpreted it far too long in a false and mendacious way, in accordance with the wishes of our reverence, which is to say, according to our *needs*" (GS 346).

The concluding portion of the aphorism is significant and yet highly cryptic. It begins with Nietzsche questioning the opposition of "man *against* the world." It ends with Nietzsche claiming that this opposition might lead to a terrifying either-or. Either we are forced to abolish our reverences or ourselves. The latter, Nietzsche tells us, would be nihilism,[8] as we would dissolve the self into the world. Nietzsche, however, remarks that the former might be nihilism, too, even though his reasons are not

---

[8] Stegmaier (2012: 204) claims that this is the first substantive discussion of nihilism in Nietzsche's published works.

stated. Presumably, abolishing our reverences would lead to a valueless world, and a valueless world is one we could not endure. Hence, this is also a form of nihilism. So if we want to avoid nihilism, we need to overcome the very opposition between man and world that creates these two unwanted alternatives (GS 346). In short, the suggestion seems to be that in order to overcome nihilism, we must translate man back into nature (BGE 230).

Such a reading of this question mark would help link Nietzsche's comments to the next aphorism. There, Nietzsche turns to a central theme of the free spirit, namely, the need for religious belief and so Schopenhauer's metaphysical need that Nietzsche targeted in the opening four chapters of *Human*. Nietzsche begins "Believers and Their Need to Believe" with the claim that faith is ultimately an expression of human need. Thus, the reason why people have faith in Christianity is because they need to believe in Christianity. This is why intellectual or argumentative refutations do not matter. In contrast, the need for faith is often taken to be proof of faith. According to Nietzsche, this is also true of metaphysics and even the contemporary demand for certainty that takes "a scientific-positivistic form." In all cases, what is needed is "a faith, a support, backbone, something to fall back on" (GS 347).[9]

Nietzsche argues that the true root of this need for faith is the inability to will and so the inability to command. In other words, the need for an objective anchoring for one's life stems from the inability to experience oneself as an anchor and so a self-sufficient being. On this model, the rise of religions like Christianity and Buddhism can be explained by what Nietzsche calls "a tremendous collapse and *disease of the will*." When people cannot command or direct themselves, they need something to obey or something to direct them, and they turn to religions that offer them a "thou shalt." In this way, this sick, degenerate, and even decadent psychology gives rise to religious belief and a related need for something like a God to anchor the life of the individual.

Nietzsche devoted much of the free spirit works to undoing this ingrained psychology by first attacking the belief in metaphysical entities like God and then by subjecting the psychology of the believer to a critical analysis. With this in mind, we begin to see the significance of the end of

---

[9] Reginster (2013) relies on this aphorism to support his view that the marker of the free spirit is an open-mindedness characterized by curiosity. However, he also claims, at the end of the paper, that the chief benefit of this liberation is *not* a greater autonomy. As I explain in subsequent paragraphs, Nietzsche's discussion of "self-determination" in GS 347 suggests that overcoming the demand for certainty goes hand in hand with a greater sense of self-determination.

the aphorism. Nietzsche speaks of an individual who can take pleasure in the "power of self-determination" and so experience "a *freedom* of the will" (GS 347).[10] This recalls the ideal of giving laws to oneself that Nietzsche associates with the project of becoming who one is in "Long Live Physics!" (GS 335), and Nietzsche now calls such a self-determining individual "the *free spirit* par excellence." Specifically, Nietzsche claims that such a "spirit would take leave of all faith and every wish for certainty, being practiced in maintaining himself on insubstantial ropes and possibilities and dancing even near abysses." In short, such a self-sufficient, self-determining free spirit would no longer stand in need of metaphysics and so God (GS 347), and in this sense, such an individual will have completed the *Bildungspro- gramm* outlined in *Schopenhauer as Educator* and pursued in the free spirit works.

Thus far, we have covered the first five aphorisms of the fifth chapter of *The Gay Science*, and these aphorisms have provided a retrospective account of the free spirit and where Nietzsche now stands given the labors he has undertaken in the free spirit works. In this abbreviated account, I also want to show how the final aphorisms of the chapter point, either implicitly or explicitly, to the notion of "*incipit parodia*" found in the 1887 preface to the work. Before doing this, I want to touch on two well- known aphorisms that are important both for my purposes and in their own right. Whereas the first situates Nietzsche's project within the trajec- tory of modern German philosophy and gives an account of the self- overcoming of morality (GS 357), the second provides a critique of romanticism and a statement of Nietzsche's Dionysian pessimism (GS 370).

In "On the Old Problem: What Is German?" Nietzsche asks which philosophical discoveries in German thought are really German and which should be understood, in contrast, as European events. In so doing, he runs through a cast of individuals that appear frequently in his works. Goethe is pegged as a pagan; Bismarck is marked as Machiavellian. He then points to three important German discoveries: Leibniz's insight that not all experience is conscious experience; Kant's questioning of causality and – on Nietzsche's view – his doubts about the ultimate validity of science; and Hegel's rejection of being in favor of becoming and

---

[10] See Rutherford (2011) for analysis of a sort of freedom that is nevertheless compatible with the fatalism that runs throughout the free spirit works. Although Rutherford compares Nietzsche's understanding of freedom to the Stoics, I think that it is instead found in Dionysian comedy for the obvious reason that Nietzsche associates the "joyous and trusting fatalism" that Rutherford analyzes with Dionysus (TI "Skirmishes" 49).

development, without which, Nietzsche claims, there would have been no Darwin. The passage ends by discussing Schopenhauer and the German pessimists who came in his wake: Eduard von Hartmann, Julius Bahnsen, and Phillip Mainländer (GS 357).[11]

What stands out in the aphorism is how Nietzsche implicitly positions his own project in relation to Schopenhauer's philosophy, which Nietzsche claims is more of a European, rather than a merely German, event. Specifically, Nietzsche points to Schopenhauer's pessimism, which Nietzsche defines here in the evaluative sense as "the problem of the *value of existence*," and Schopenhauer's atheism, which Nietzsche claims is both the "locus of his whole integrity" and "the *presupposition* of the way he poses his problem." To explain the latter, Nietzsche gives an account of the self-overcoming of Christianity. Specifically, it was the Christian morality of truthfulness, which Schopenhauer embodied, that led to Schopenhauer's "honest atheism." Because of this, we cannot, as Hegel tried to do, interpret history as the manifestation of divine reason or interpret our experiences as having some providential significance. This now has "conscience" – and here Nietzsche likely means the "intellectual conscience" (GS 2) – against it (GS 357).

Nietzsche is not simply describing the consequences of Schopenhauer's philosophy, but also the results of his own free spirit project in which he subjected such beliefs to the honest examination he describes here. Indeed, Nietzsche's honest examination leads to the very same pessimistic question he attributes to Schopenhauer and declares to be a European event (GS 357). The question is this: Given we can no longer believe in a creator or find the world divine in any way, "*has existence any meaning at all?*" (GS 357). As we have seen, Nietzsche poses similar questions in central passages of the 1882 edition of *The Gay Science*: Will the death of God not create a sense of nauseating disorientation (GS 125)? Will a doctrine like the eternal recurrence not cause us to gnash our teeth and "curse the demon who spoke thus" (GS 341)?

Even though Nietzsche is summarizing the position he reaches through his endeavors in the free spirit works, he is nevertheless returning to the central question of *The Birth of Tragedy*: Given an honest assessment of nature and the human position within the cosmos, isn't non-existence ultimately preferable to existence (BT 3)? Again, the answer that Nietzsche gave in his first work was that existence could be justified as an aesthetic phenomenon (BT 5), and he argued that the arts of Dionysus could effect

---

[11] See Beiser (2016) for a treatment of these figures.

this aesthetic transfiguration and justification. Thus, we should not be surprised to find Nietzsche now returning to Dionysus and the arts associated with him to respond to the challenge that this sort of pessimism presents.

Perhaps one of the most striking features of the free spirit works is the absence of any reference to Dionysus in both the published works and unpublished notes and letters from this time (the only exception is a 1878 note (KSA 8: 29[1])). We know, however, that Nietzsche planned to introduce – almost like an unveiling – Dionysus as a title in the final section of the third part of *Zarathustra* (KSA 14: pp. 324–325). Moreover, we have seen that Nietzsche identifies himself as the last disciple and initiate of the god Dionysus at the end of *Beyond Good and Evil* (BGE 295), and the introduction of Dionysus in this aphorism reflects numerous *Nachlass* notes from this time in which Dionysus is mentioned as part of the title to *Beyond Good and Evil* (e.g., KSA 11: 34[182], 34[201], and 35 [26]).

In the fifth chapter of *The Gay Science*, we again find Nietzsche announcing his allegiance to Dionysus in "What is Romanticism?" Specifically, Nietzsche refers to a "pessimism of the future" – a phrase that recalls the "philosophy of the future" from *Beyond Good and Evil* – that he calls "Dionysian pessimism" (GS 370). Here, he differentiates his Dionysian pessimism from the kind of romantic pessimism he associates with Schopenhauer and Wagner. Nietzsche begins the aphorism by discussing how he mistakenly interpreted both German philosophy and music in *The Birth of Tragedy*. Although he thought they signified the "Dionysian power of the German soul," he soon realized their truly romantic character (GS 370).

To explain what romanticism is, Nietzsche launches into a broader explanation of art and philosophy. Specifically, he claims that "every art, every philosophy may be viewed as a remedy and an aid in the service of growing and struggling life; they always presuppose suffering and suffers." Such a claim emphasizes the significance of suffering in a way that recalls the pessimism of Schopenhauer's philosophy, the wisdom of Silenus in *The Birth of Tragedy*, and the insights of *Human*. Nietzsche, however, then distinguishes between two types of sufferers in a way that parallels the two possible responses to the wisdom of Silenus. According to Nietzsche, the first type suffers from "the *over-fullness of life*" and so "they want a Dionysian art and likewise a tragic view of life, a tragic insight." The second type, in contrast, are those who suffer "from the *impoverishment of life* and seek rest, stillness calm seas, redemption from themselves through art and knowledge, or intoxication, convulsions, anesthesia, and madness" (GS 370).

As the passage continues, Nietzsche explains this distinction in greater detail. On the one hand, he paints a picture of what he calls "the Dionysian god and man" that is largely consistent with his understanding of an aesthetic justification of existence in the penultimate section of *The Birth of Tragedy*. There, Nietzsche explained how musical dissonance, which lies at the heart of the tragic myth, can justify the ugly and disharmonic elements of existence (BT 24). In *The Gay Science*, Nietzsche claims that the Dionysian god and man "cannot only afford the sight of the terrible and questionable but even the terrible deed and any luxury of destruction, decomposition, and negation. In his case, what is evil, absurd, and ugly seems, as it were, permissible, owing to an excess of procreating, fertilizing energies that can still turn any desert into lush farmland." In contrast, the romantic who suffers from an impoverishment of life longs for "mildness, peacefulness, and goodness in thought as well as deed" and so a god who is a "healer and a savior" (GS 370).

Nietzsche then identifies two further types that stand opposed to the Dionysian pessimist and so can be dubbed "romantics": the Epicurean and the Christian. Although the critique of Christianity is largely consistent with his other works, Nietzsche now claims that the Epicurean solution to the problem of suffering – one that he endorsed *qua* free spirit in *The Wanderer* but then left behind in the first chapter of *The Gay Science* – is superficial. As he indicates in an 1888 *Nachlass* note, all of ancient philosophy after Socrates carries the stigma of *décadence*: They are all moralistic quests for happiness, and Nietzsche points to Pyrrho as the highpoint of this *décadence* and equates such skepticism with Buddhism.[12] He then mentions both Christianity and Epicureanism. The underlying idea is that the quest for happiness culminates in a longing for peace, tranquility, and an end to suffering, and this, according to Nietzsche, is a sign of exhaustion and so *décadence* (KSA 13: 14[87]).

In the aphorism, Nietzsche analyzes romanticism in psychological terms. Specifically, he claims that he has made a "backward inference" from the work to the creator (GS 370). This implies that philosophies or religions are not reflections of nature, but rather reflections of the authors themselves. This view is consistent with Nietzsche's claim in *Beyond Good and Evil* that all philosophy is a sort of involuntary and unconscious memoir (BGE 6), and this style of analysis follows directly from the

---

[12] This note speaks against the Pyrrhonian reading of Nietzsche proposed by Berry (2011).

insights of the free spirit project. Once we know that such philosophies and religions do not express the truth about nature, we can begin to explore the kind of psychology that created these systems as well as the psychology of those who are attracted to them.

The passage ends with two more important points. First, Nietzsche rejects the idea that this distinction should be mapped onto a desire to fix and immortalize, on the one hand, and the desire for change and becoming, on the other. According to Nietzsche, both of these can be associated with either the Dionysian or the romantic depending on the psychology that underlies them. Just as there can be a desire for destruction that emerges from the "hatred of the ill-constituted, disinherited, and underprivileged," there can be a will to immortalize that stems from a tormented soul that "revenges himself on all things by forcing his own image, the image of his torture" on others. Both cases, Nietzsche argues, are versions of "*romantic pessimism.*" In contrast, there is both a desire for destruction that is pregnant with the future and a will to immortalize that is "prompted, first, by gratitude and love" and "will always be an art of apotheoses, perhaps dithyrambic." These cases, according to Nietzsche, are a form of "*Dionysian* pessimism," and this form of pessimism is the "pessimism of the future" (GS 370).

In discussing his "*Dionysian* pessimism" that is a "pessimism of the future" in *The Gay Science*, there is no explicit connection to laughter or comedy. However, the contrast between romanticism and the Dionysian can be linked directly to Nietzsche's call for laughter in the 1886 preface to *The Birth of Tragedy*, written only months before the 1887 edition of *The Gay Science*. This is because Nietzsche addresses the question of whether *The Birth of Tragedy*, with the "*art of metaphysical comfort*" it offers, is itself a piece of romanticism that will end, as Wagner did, in Christianity. Here, Nietzsche criticizes his youthful work in this respect, and he goes on to claim that, instead, we need to learn "the art of *this-worldly* comfort" first. Specifically, we "ought to learn to laugh" if we are "hell-bent on remaining pessimists." It is through laughter that we may some day "dispatch all metaphysical comforts to the devil," and Nietzsche ends the preface by quoting a passage from *Zarathustra* IV in which Zarathustra, whom Nietzsche now calls a "Dionysian monster," exhorts higher men to laugh: "This crown of the laughter, the rose-wreath crown: to you, my brothers, I throw this crown. Laughter I have pronounced holy: you higher men, *learn* – to laugh!" (BT "Attempt" 7).

Although there is no mention of laughter or comedy in "What is Romanticism?," we find such references in the final two aphorisms of the fifth chapter of *The Gay Science*. In "The Great Health," Nietzsche speaks of a new health that is "stronger more seasoned, tougher, more audacious, and gayer than any previous health." This health, he claims, is necessary for a spirit who wants "to experience the whole range of values and desiderata to date" (GS 382) and so it recalls the ideal sketched in "The 'Humaneness' of the Future" (GS 337). Such a person will likely feel dissatisfaction with "*present-day man*." At the same time, such health points toward another ideal that is "strange, tempting, dangerous." This is an ideal spirit "who plays naively – that is, not deliberately but from overflowing power and abundance – with all that was hitherto called holy, good, untouchable, divine." Such an ideal spirit will even appear "*inhuman*" when "it confronts all earthly seriousness so far, all solemnity in gesture, word, tone, eye, morality, and task so far, as if it were their most incarnate and involuntary parody" (GS 382).

The aphorism nevertheless ends with the claim that such an individual might mark the beginning of a "*great seriousness*" in which "the real question mark is posed for the first time, that the destiny of the soul changes, the hand moves forward, the tragedy *begins*" (GS 382), and this juxtaposition of parody and tragedy marks the double ending of the 1887 edition of *The Gay Science*. Whereas "the tragedy *begins*" refers back to the "*incipit tragoedia*" that ended the 1882 edition of the work (GS 342), Nietzsche also points to parody in the 1887 preface: "Beware! Something downright wicked and malicious is announced here: *incipit parodia*, no doubt" (GS P 1). This not only seems to be a reference to the "involuntary parody" mentioned in "The Great Health" (GS 382), but also to the laughter that bursts forth in the "Epilogue." There, Nietzsche remarks on the "gloomy question mark" at the end of the previous aphorism, but then exclaims that he hears "all around [...] the most malicious, cheerful, and koboldish laughter." The spirits of his own book are supposedly attacking him, and they remind him that they are surrounded by "bright morning" and "the kingdom of dance," and so they ask if there is not a better "hour for gaiety" (GS 383).

The fifth chapter was not the only addition Nietzsche made to the 1887 edition of *The Gay Science*. He also added a preface, changed the motto of the book, and attached an appendix of songs. For my purposes, what is remarkable about each of these additions is that they all include references to parody and laughter. For instance, the first song in the appendix refers to a fool's game and an eternal foolishness (GS SPV: "To Goethe"), and the second song speaks of being "overcome by laughter" (GS SPV: "The Poet's Call"). In the new motto, Nietzsche writes: "I live in my own place, have never copied nobody even half, and at any master who lacks the grace to laugh at himself – I laugh."[13] Finally, Nietzsche concludes the 1887 preface by praising a superficiality of the ancient Greeks that is nevertheless born out of profundity – this echoes his praise of the Greeks in *The Birth of Tragedy* (BT 3) – and by referring to Baubo, a Greek goddess who moved a weeping Demeter to laughter by exposing her genitalia (GS P 4).

There is one final point that needs to be addressed in the preface to the 1887 edition of *The Gay Science*. Nietzsche not only refers to ancient Greek artists and the Greek goddess Baubo, he also explains how "this will to truth, to 'truth at any price'" has now lost its charm such that "today we consider it a matter of decency not to wish to see everything naked" (GS P 4). The juxtaposition between the critique of the will to truth and a figure known for producing laughter suggests that the *Selbstaufhebung* of the will to truth that Nietzsche executes in the free spirit works culminates in a comedy in which one laughs at oneself "*out of the whole truth*" (GS 1). If this is right, then we can see the way in which the emphasis on laughter and comedy in the 1887 edition picks up on themes already present in the 1882 edition and so creates a text that ends in both "*incipit tragoedia*" and "*incipit parodia.*" Whereas the former transitions to the tragedy of *Zarathustra*, I think the latter transitions to the Dionysian comedy of Nietzsche's 1888 works.

The Dionysian Comedy of Nietzsche's 1888 Works?

Thus far, I have claimed that the free spirit project transitions to a philosophy of the future, and I have pointed to evidence from *Beyond Good and Evil* to suggest that Nietzsche's philosophy of the future is a Dionysian comedy. Because this book is about Nietzsche's free spirit works, I will not try to demonstrate this here. However, I do want to end this work by giving a brief sketch of why Nietzsche's 1888 works might be a Dionysian comedy and so his philosophy of the future. In so doing, we can begin to ask whether Nietzsche realizes in his latest works a number of the themes that emerge in the 1882 edition of *The Gay Science*.

One reason for thinking that Nietzsche's 1888 works should be read as a comedy is that every work – with the exception of the prefaces to *Human*, *The Wanderer*, and *Daybreak* – that Nietzsche published between 1885 and 1887 concludes with some reference to comedy, parody, or

---

[13] See Kaufmann's translation (1974: 31).

laughter. *Zarathustra* IV (1885) ends with a call for laughing lions (Z IV: "The Sign"). *Beyond Good and Evil* (1886) ends with a discussion of philosophers ranked according to the rank of their laughter (BGE 294). The 1886 preface to *The Birth of Tragedy* ends with Nietzsche exhorting us to learn the this-worldly comfort of laughter (BT "Attempt" 7). The preface to the 1887 edition of *The Gay Science* ends with a mention of Baubo (GS P 4), and the final chapter added in 1887 ends with references to parody and laughter (GS 382 and 383). In the preface to the 1887 *Genealogy*, Nietzsche claims that "our old morality too is part *of the comedy*," and he speaks of a "grand old eternal comic poet of our existence" (GM P 7). Finally, the *Genealogy* ends with references to comedians of "the Christian-moral ideal" (GM III 26) and the ascetic ideal (GM III 27). Given that there is prolepticism at work in Nietzsche's free spirit project and we know that Nietzsche insists on the importance of the ordering of his published works, there is reason to read these references as setting the stage for his own Dionysian comedy in his subsequent works.

In other publications (Meyer 2012a; 2018), I have detailed the parallels between Nietzsche's 1888 works – *Twilight of the Idols*, *The Case of Wagner*, *Ecce Homo*, *The Antichrist*, and *Nietzsche contra Wagner* – and Aristophanic comedy and pointed to features of these works that indicate Nietzsche is thinking of himself as both a comic poet and a comic figure. For instance, Nietzsche presents himself as a *Hanswurst*, a stock figure from eighteenth-century Viennese comedy (Battersby 2013), in both *Ecce Homo* (EH "Destiny" 1) and his late letters (KSB 8: 1183 and 1240), and this is often accompanied by his self-presentation as both a satyr and a disciple of Dionysus (EH P 2). The latter, of course, is significant not only because Dionysus is the god of comedy, but also because Aristophanes presents himself in the *parabasis* of *The Clouds* as having been nurtured by Dionysus.

We have also seen that Nietzsche understands the philosopher of the future to be a legislator (BGE 211), and this idea can be linked to what he calls in his later writings, "great politics." Thus, in *Ecce Homo*, he writes: "it is only beginning with me that the earth knows *great politics*" (EH "Destiny" 1). As Sommer (2015: 262–264) has pointed out, Nietzsche not only takes on the role of this legislator by composing his *Laws against Christianity* in which he re-dates the calendar at the end of *The Antichrist* (KSA 6: p. 254), he also conceives of this legislative activity as an extension of the free spirit project. This sort of legislative activity and so great politics can be readily found in Aristophanic comedies such as the *Acharnians* and the *Birds*. In the former, a character named Dikaiopolis or "Just City" leaves behind a war-plagued Athens to create a one-man city-state. In the latter, a character named Peisetairos or "Persuader of Companions" initiates a war with the Greek gods only to become the new ruler and divinity of Greece at the end of the play. Not only are such characters driven by an insatiable desire for power, they exhibit the very kind of great politics that can be found in Nietzsche's 1888 works and letters.[14]

Although such associations are important, the crux of my reading of Nietzsche's 1888 works has to do with the presence of two structural elements common to early Aristophanic comedy, namely, the *agon* and the *parabasis*. The *agon* is not only representative of the competitive atmosphere that pervades Aristophanic comedy as a genre, it is also a formal element in the play that enacts a contest, struggle, or debate between the comic hero and some opposing character or force. The *parabasis* is also a formal element of Aristophanic comedy that usually occurs in the middle of the play, and it is a moment in which the dramatic action stops and the chorus leader, along with the chorus, turns and addresses the audience either in the name or on behalf of the comic poet. In so doing, the chorus leader speaks of the success and failure of the poet's previous plays and presents the poet's standing and accomplishments in rhetorically exaggerated terms, while denigrating the poet's personal rivals.

The primary reason I think Nietzsche's 1888 works constitute a Dionysian comedy is because they resemble these two formal features of ancient comedy. That Nietzsche's 1888 works, such as *The Twilight of the Idols*, *The Case of Wagner*, *The Antichrist*, and *Nietzsche contra Wagner*, enact an *agon* with the likes of Socrates, Wagner, and Paul, has been well-documented by Christa Davis Acampora (2013a). What is lacking in her treatment, however, is any substantive discussion of the potential relationship between the agonistic spirit that pervades Nietzsche's later works and Nietzsche's claim to be a disciple of Dionysus. In my mind, Dionysian comedy is the genre that makes this connection. Just as Aristophanes mocks Socrates in *The Clouds*, Nietzsche ridicules Socrates in *The Twilight of the Idols*. Just as Aristophanes mocks his poetic rivals, Nietzsche mocks Wagner in *The Case of Wagner* (and *Nietzsche contra Wagner*), and just as Aristophanes subjects even the gods to mockery, Nietzsche mocks the Christianity of Paul in *The Antichrist*.

---

[14] Drochon (2016: 162) is right to connect Nietzsche's great politics to the revaluation of values, and although he links this project to Dionysus, he only mentions the genre of tragedy (2016: 176). There is no significant mention of comedy or Aristophanes in the book, and so no thought that Nietzsche's great politics might be part of his Dionysian comedy.

Just as Nietzsche enacts a comic *agon* in these works, he provides us with a comic *parabasis* in *Ecce Homo*, and just as the comic *parabasis* forms the dramatic centerpiece of ancient comedy, it forms the centerpiece of Nietzsche's own comedy and so his 1888 works. That *Ecce Homo* has a comic dimension has been noted by other scholars (Conway 1993; More 2014). However, I have argued that we can make best sense of the comic nature of *Ecce Homo* by understanding it through the lens of the *parabasis* of Dionysian comedy. This not only helps explain the bombastic chapter titles of "Why I Am So Wise," "Why I Am So Clever," "Why I Write Such Good Books," and "Why I Am a Destiny," it also weds Nietzsche's discipleship to Dionysus to the theme of aesthetic self-making. As recent scholarship has shown (Bakola 2010; Biles 2011), the *parabasis* of ancient comedy provided poets with the freedom to shape, self-consciously, the details of their own lives into aesthetic phenomena, and this is precisely what Nietzsche is doing in *Ecce Homo*.

What these remarks on the *parabasis* indicate, however, is that Nietzsche's project of becoming who one is takes the form of a Dionysian comedy, and this means that the project Nietzsche initially sketched in *Schopenhauer as Educator* and developed through the *Bildungsroman* of the free spirit works comes to final fruition in the *parabasis* of his own comedy, *Ecce Homo*. Because I have argued that Nietzsche is best understood as having plans for a free spirit project that executes a dialectical novel of self-education which culminates in the tragedy of *Zarathustra* at the time of writing *Human*, some might now conclude that I also believe that Nietzsche had plans, as early as 1876, for a comedy that projects well beyond the tragedy of *Zarathustra*.

Although I am not aware of any evidence that speaks against such a reading, there is little that speaks in favor of it. To recall, one of the primary reasons for thinking that the free spirit works are best understood as a consciously constructed dialectical *Bildungsroman* that unfolds into Nietzsche's own tragedy is that his earliest writings provide ample evidence that he had been thinking of such ideas prior to composing the free spirit works. In contrast, there is very little, if anything, about laughter and comedy in his earliest works. Instead, his interest in laughter and comedy largely emerges in the 1882 edition of *The Gay Science*. Thus, it is best to reject the idea that Nietzsche was already thinking of a comedy that follows upon a tragedy like *Zarathustra* as early as 1876.

Nevertheless, *The Gay Science* provides some evidence that Nietzsche was already thinking of a comic autobiography like *Ecce Homo* as early as 1882. However, showing that he had plans for such a work in 1882 would be difficult, perhaps impossible, to prove, and I am not going to attempt it here. We do know, however, that Nietzsche was already thinking in terms of a "revision of all values" as he was writing *Daybreak* (KSA 9: 3[158]), and so he was already thinking, in 1881, of the project that reaches its apex in the 1888 *The Antichrist*. Indeed, Nietzsche first refers to himself as the "Antichrist" in an 1883 letter to Malwida von Meysenbug, and in so doing, he also refers to laughter: "Do you want a name for me? The language of the church has one: I am – – – – – – – – – the Antichrist. Let us not forget laughter" (KSB 6: 400).

Regardless of what one makes of such remarks and whether they provide evidence for plans for a revaluation project like the one we find in *The Antichrist*, there is one thing that does emerge from this study. Once we begin to notice the interconnections between Nietzsche's free spirit works and the way in which they should be read in the order in which they were written, we can begin to explore these sorts of questions and examine whether Nietzsche brings to fruition in his later works the ideas and plans he sketches in his earlier writings. Indeed, if there is one thing I hope to accomplish by defending the idea that Nietzsche's free spirit works are best understood as a consciously constructed dialectical *Bildungsroman*, it is to draw attention to the fact that his post-1876 publications are structured both internally and in relation to each other. In short, I hope to move scholarship beyond the idea that Nietzsche's published works "consist chiefly in assemblages of rather loosely connected notes" (Schacht 1983: ix) from which the interpreter should extract a coherent set of philosophical theories. Instead, the post-1876 works should be read as telling a story that begins with an ascetic quest for truth and liberation, that then moves through a dialectical process in which unrestrained truth-seeking undergoes a *Selbstaufhebung*, and that eventually transitions to the Dionysian art forms of tragedy, comedy, satyr play, and dithyramb.

Bibliography

PRIMARY SOURCES FOR NIETZSCHE'S PUBLISHED WORKS

For Nietzsche's German texts, I use the Colli-Montinari critical edition with the following abbreviations. Unless otherwise noted, all translations of Nietzsche's *Nachlass* notes are my own and based on the German edition found in KSA.

KSA = *Sämtliche Werke: Kritische Studienausgabe*, ed. G. Colli and M. Montinari, 15 vols. Berlin, Munich: DTV, De Gruyter (1999) (references include volume and note or page number).
KSB = *Sämtliche Briefe: Kritische Studienausgabe*, ed. G. Colli and M. Montinari, 8 vols. Berlin, Munich: DTV, De Gruyter (1986) (references include volume and letter number).

WORKS CITED

The following is a list of the secondary sources used in the text. Unless noted otherwise, all works are cited by date and page number.

Abbey, Ruth (2000). *Nietzsche's Middle Period*. Oxford: Oxford University Press.
  (2015). "Skilled Marksman and Strict Self-Examination: Nietzsche on La Rochefoucauld." In *Nietzsche's Free Spirit Philosophy*, ed. R. Bamford, 11–32. New York: Rowman & Littlefield.
Acampora, Christa Davis (2013a). *Contesting Nietzsche*. Chicago: Chicago University Press.
  (2013b). "Beholding Nietzsche: *Ecce Homo*, Fate, and Freedom." In *The Oxford Handbook of Nietzsche*, ed. K. Gemes and J. Richardson, 363–385. Oxford: Oxford University Press.
Allison, David B. (2001). *Reading the New Nietzsche*. Lanham, MD: Rowman & Littlefield.
Ansell-Pearson, Keith (2011a). "Beyond Compassion: On Nietzsche's Moral Therapy in *Dawn*." *Continental Philosophy Review* 44(2): 179–204.
  (2011b). "Editor's Afterword." In *Dawn: Thoughts on the Presumptions of Morality*, trans. Brittain Smith, 363–408. Stanford, CA: Stanford University Press.

(2017). "Nietzsche and Epicurus: In Search of the Heroic-Idyllic." In *Nietzsche and the Philosophers*, ed. M. Conard, 121–145. London: Routledge.

(2018). *Nietzsche's Search for Philosophy: On the Middle Writings*. London: Bloomsbury Academic.

Babich, Babette (2006). "Nietzsche's 'Gay' Science." In *A Companion to Nietzsche*, ed. K. Ansell-Pearson, 97–114. Oxford: Blackwell.

Bakola, Emmanuela (2010). *Cratinus and the Art of Comedy*. Oxford: Oxford University Press.

Bamford, Rebecca (2012). "*Daybreak*." In *A Companion to Friedrich Nietzsche*, ed. P. Bishop, 139–157. Rochester, NY: Camden House.

(2015). "Health and Self-Cultivation in *Dawn*." In *Nietzsche's Free Spirit Philosophy*, ed. R. Bamford, 85–110. New York: Rowman & Littlefield.

Battersby, Christine (2013). "'Behold the Buffoon': Dada, Nietzsche's Ecce Homo and the Sublime." In *Tate Papers, no. 13, Spring 2010*, www.tate .org.uk/art/research-publications/the-sublime/christine-battersby-behold-the-buffoon-dada-nietzsches-ecce-homo-and-the-sublime-r1136833.

Beiser, Frederick (2016). *Weltschmerz*. Oxford: Oxford University Press.

Benne, Christian (2015). "'Scherz, List und Rache': Vorspiel in deutschen Reimen." In Friedrich Nietzsche: *Die fröhliche Wissenschaft*, ed. C. Benne and J. Georg, 29–51. Berlin: De Gruyter.

Berry, Jessica N. (2004). "The Pyrrhonian Revival in Montaigne and Nietzsche." *Journal of the History of Ideas* 65(3): 497–514.

(2011). *Nietzsche and the Ancient Skeptical Tradition*. Oxford: Oxford University Press.

(2013). "Nietzsche and the Greeks." In *The Oxford Handbook of Nietzsche*, ed. K. Gemes and J. Richardson, 83–107. Oxford: Oxford University Press.

Biles, Zachary (2011). *Aristophanes and the Poetics of Competition*. Cambridge: Cambridge University Press.

Blue, Daniel (2016). *The Making of Friedrich Nietzsche: The Quest for Identity, 1844–1869*. Cambridge: Cambridge University Press.

Boes, Tobias (2006). "Modernist Studies and the *Bildungsroman*: A Historical Survey of Critical Trends." *Literature Compass* 3(2): 230–243.

Borsche, Tilman (1985). "Nietzsches Erfindung der Vorsokratiker." In *Nietzsche und die philosophische Tradition*, ed. J. Simon, 62–87. Würzburg: Königshausen & Neumann.

Branham, Bracht R. (2004). "Nietzsche's Cynicism: Uppercase or Lowercase?" In *Nietzsche and Antiquity: His Reaction and Response to the Classical Tradition*, ed. P. Bishop, 170–181. Rochester, NY: Camden House.

Brobjer, Thomas (2003). "Nietzsche's Reading of Epictetus." *Nietzsche Studien* 32: 429–434.

Brusotti, Marco (1997). *Die Leidenschaft der Erkenntnis: Philosophie und ästhetische Lebensgestaltung bei Nietzsche von* Morgenröthe *bis* Also sprach Zarathustra. Berlin: De Gruyter.

(2016). "Unsere letzte Dankbarkeit gegen die Kunst: Die Druckbogen der *Fröhlichen Wissenschaft* und Nietzsches Abschied von seiner 'Freigeisterei'."

In *Nietzsche zwischen Philosophie und Literatur*, ed. K. Grätz and S. Kaufmann, 199–220. Heidelberg: Winter.

Clark, Maudemarie (1990). *Nietzsche on Truth and Philosophy*. Cambridge: Cambridge University Press.

(1998). "On Knowledge, Truth, and Value: Nietzsche's Debt to Schopenhauer and the Development of His Empiricism." In *Willing and Nothingness: Schopenhauer as Nietzsche's Educator*, ed. C. Janaway, 37–78. Oxford: Clarendon Press.

Clark, Maudemarie and Brian Leiter (1997). "Introduction." In F. Nietzsche, *Daybreak: Thoughts on the Prejudices of Morality*, trans. R. Hollingdale. Cambridge: Cambridge University Press.

Clark, Maudemarie and David Dudrick (2012). *The Soul of Nietzsche's* Beyond Good and Evil. Cambridge: Cambridge University Press.

Cohen, Jonathan R. (2010). *Science, Culture, and Free Spirits: A Study of Nietzsche's* Human, All-Too-Human. Amherst, NY: Humanity Books.

Conway, Daniel (1993). "Nietzsche's *Doppelgänger*: Affirmation and Resentment in *Ecce Homo*." In *The Fate of the New Nietzsche*, ed. K. Ansell-Pearson and H. Caygill, 55–78. Aldershot: Avebury.

Danto, Arthur (1965). *Nietzsche as Philosopher*. New York: Columbia University Press.

(1988). "Nietzsche's *Daybreak: Thoughts on the Prejudices of Morality*." In *Reading Nietzsche*, ed. R. C. Solomon and K. M. Higgins, 186–191. Oxford: Oxford University Press.

Derrida, Jacques (1979). *Spurs: Nietzsche's Styles*, trans. B. Harlow. Chicago: Chicago University Press.

D'Iorio, Paulo (2016). *Nietzsche's Journey to Sorrento: Genesis of the Philosophy of the Free Spirit*, trans. S. M. Gorelick. Chicago: Chicago University Press.

Domino, Brian (2012). "Nietzsche's Use of *Amor Fati* in *Ecce Homo*." *Journal of Nietzsche Studies* 43(2): 283–303.

Donnellan, Brendan (1982). *Nietzsche and the French Moralists*. Bonn: Bouvier.

Drochon, Hugo (2016). *Nietzsche's Great Politics*. Princeton, NJ: Princeton University Press.

Forster, Michael (1993). "Hegel's Dialectical Method." In *The Cambridge Companion to Hegel*, ed. F. C. Beiser, 130–170. Cambridge: Cambridge University Press.

(1998). *Hegel's Idea of a "Phenomenology of Spirit."* Chicago: Chicago University Press.

Förster-Nietzsche, Elisabeth (1915). *The Lonely Nietzsche*, trans. P. V. Cohn. London: William Heinemann.

Franco, Paul (2011). *Nietzsche's Enlightenment: The Free-Spirit Trilogy of the Middle Period*. Chicago: University of Chicago Press.

Gemes, Ken and John Richardson (2013). *The Oxford Handbook of Nietzsche*. Oxford: Oxford University Press.

Georg, Jutta (2015). "Vorrede: Die Bedeutung der Zurückdatierung." In *Friedrich Nietzsche: Die fröhliche Wissenschaft*, ed. C. Benne and J. Georg, 19–28. Berlin: De Gruyter.

Gilman, Sander L. and David J. Parent (1984). *Conversations with Nietzsche.* Oxford: Oxford University Press.

Glatzeder, Britta M. (2000). *Perspektiven der Wünschbarkeit: Nietzsches frühe Metaphysikkritik.* Berlin: Philo.

Gooding-Williams, Robert (1990). "Zarathustra's Three Metamorphoses." In *Nietzsche as Postmodernist: Essays Pro and Contra*, ed. C. Koelb, 231–245. Albany, NY: SUNY Press.

(2001). *Zarathustra's Dionysian Modernism.* Stanford, CA: Stanford University Press.

Groddeck, Wolfram (1997). "Die 'Neue Ausgabe' der 'Fröhlichen Wissenschaft': Ueberlegungen zu Paratextualität und Werkkomposition in Nietzsches Schriften nach 'Zarathustra'." *Nietzsche Studien* 26: 184–198.

Groff, Peter (2004). "Al-Kindi and Nietzsche on the Stoic Art of Banishing Sorrow." *Journal of Nietzsche Studies* 28(1): 139–173.

Halliwell, Stephen (1996): "Plato's Repudiation of the Tragic." In *Tragedy and the Tragic*, ed. M. Silk, 332–349. Oxford: Clarendon Press.

Han-Pile, Béatrice (2009). "Nietzsche and Amor Fati." *European Journal of Philosophy* 19(2): 224–261.

Heller, Peter (1972). *Von den ersten und letzten Dingen.* Berlin: De Gruyter.

Higgins, Kathleen (1987). *Nietzsche's Zarathustra.* Philadelphia, PA: Temple University Press.

(2000). *Comic Relief: Nietzsche's* Gay Science. Oxford: Oxford University Press.

Hollinrake, Roger (1982). *Nietzsche, Wagner, and the Philosophy of Pessimism.* London: Routledge.

Horkheimer, Max and Theodor W. Adorno (1999). *Dialectic of Enlightenment.* New York: Continuum.

Janaway, Christopher (2007). *Beyond Selflessness: Reading Nietzsche's Genealogy.* Oxford: Oxford University Press.

(2013). "*The Gay Science.*" In *The Oxford Handbook of Nietzsche*, ed. K. Gemes and J. Richardson, 252–271. Oxford: Oxford University Press.

Jaspers, Karl (1997). *Nietzsche: An Introduction to the Understanding of His Philosophical Activity*, trans. C. F. Wallraff and F. J. Schmitz. Baltimore, MD: Johns Hopkins University Press.

Jenkins, Scott (2012). "Nietzsche's Questions Concerning the Will to Truth." *Journal of the History of Philosophy* 50(2): 265–289.

(2016). "Truthfulness as Nietzsche's Highest Virtue." *Journal of Value Inquiry* 50(1): 1–19.

(2018). "*The Gay Science.*" In *The Nietzschean Mind*, ed. P. Katsafanas, 41–53. London: Routledge.

Jensen, Anthony K. (2004). "Nietzsche's Unpublished Fragments on Ancient Cynicism: The First Night of Diogenes." In *Nietzsche and Antiquity: His Reaction and Response to the Classical Tradition*, ed. P. Bishop, 182–191. Rochester, NY: Camden House.

(2016). *An Interpretation of Nietzsche's* On the Uses and Disadvantages of History for Life. London: Routledge.

Katsafanas, Paul (2016). *The Nietzschean Self: Moral Psychology, Agency, and the Unconscious*. Oxford: Oxford University Press.

(ed.) (2018). *The Nietzschean Mind*. London: Routledge.

Kaufmann, Walter (1974). *Nietzsche: Philosopher, Psychologist, Antichrist*. Princeton, NJ: Princeton University Press.

Kirkland, Paul E. (2009). *Nietzsche's Noble Aims: Affirming Life, Contesting Modernity*. Lanham, MD: Lexington Books.

Kofman, Sarah (1993). *Nietzsche and Metaphor*, trans. D. Large. London: Athlone Press.

Lampert, Laurence (2017). *What a Philosopher Is: Becoming Nietzsche*. Chicago: Chicago University Press.

Lane, Melissa (2007). "Honesty as the Best Policy: Nietzsche on *Redlichkeit* and the Contrast between Stoic and Epicurean Strategies of the Self." In *Histories of Postmodernism*, ed. M. Bevir, J. Hargis, and S. Rushing, 25–51. New York: Routledge.

Langer, Monika M. (2010). *Nietzsche's* Gay Science. New York: Palgrave Macmillan.

Large, Duncan (1995). "Nietzsche and the Figure of Columbus." *Nietzsche Studien* 24: 162–183.

(1997). "Nietzsche's Helmbrecht, or: How to Philosophize with a Ploughshare." *Journal of Nietzsche Studies* 13: 3–22.

(2015). "The Free Spirit and Aesthetic Self-Re-Education." In *Nietzsche's Free Spirit Philosophy*, ed. R. Bamford, 69–84. New York: Rowman & Littlefield.

Leiter, Brian (2001). "The Paradox of Fatalism and Self-Creation in Nietzsche." In *Nietzsche*, eds. B. Leiter and J. Richardson, 281–321. Oxford: Oxford University Press.

(2002). *Routledge Philosophy Guidebook to Nietzsche on Morality*. London: Routledge.

Loeb, Paul (1998). "The Moment of Tragic Death in Nietzsche's Dionysian Doctrine of Eternal Recurrence: An Exegesis of Aphorism 341 in *The Gay Science*." *International Studies in Philosophy* 33(3): 131–143.

(2000). "The Conclusion of Nietzsche's *Zarathustra*." *International Studies in Philosophy* 32(3): 137–152.

(2004). "Zarathustra's Laughing Lions." In *A Nietzschean Bestiary: Becoming Animal Beyond Docile and Brutal*, ed. Christa Davis Acampora and Ralph R. Acampora, 121–139. Lanham, MD: Rowman & Littlefield.

(2010). *The Death of Nietzsche's Zarathustra*. Cambridge: Cambridge University Press.

(2013). "Eternal Recurrence." In *The Oxford Handbook of Nietszche*, ed. K. Gemes and J. Richardson, 645–671. Oxford: Oxford University Press.

(2018). "The Colossal Moment in Nietzsche's *Gay Science* 341." In *The Nietzschean Mind*, ed. P. Katsafanas, 428–447. London: Routledge.

(2019, forthcoming). "Genuine Philosophers, Value-Creation, and Will to Power: An Exegesis of Nietzsche's *Beyond Good and Evil* § 211." In *Nietzsche's Metaphilosophy: The Nature, Method, and Aims of Philosophy*, ed. P. Loeb and M. Meyer. Cambridge: Cambridge University Press.

Mann, Joel E. and Getty L. Lustila (2011). "A Model Sophist: Nietzsche on Protagoras and Thucydides." *Journal of Nietzsche Studies* 42: 51–72.

Martin, Nicholas (2008). "'Aufklärung und kein Ende': The Place of Enlightenment in Friedrich Nietzsche's Thought." *German Life and Letters* 61(1): 79–97.

Meyer, Matthew (2002). "The Tragic Nature of Zarathustra." *Nietzscheforschung* 9: 209–218.

(2004). "*Human, All Too Human* and the Socrates Who Plays Music." *International Studies in Philosophy* 36(3): 171–182.

(2006). "The Three Metamorphoses of the Free Spirit." *International Studies in Philosophy* 38(3): 49–63.

(2012a). "The Comic Nature of *Ecce Homo*." *Journal of Nietzsche Studies* 43(1): 32–43.

(2012b). "Nietzsche's Naturalism and the Falsification Thesis." In *Nietzsches Wissenschafts-Philosophie*, ed. H. Heit, G. Abel, and M. Brusotti, 135–148. Berlin: De Gruyter.

(2014a). *Reading Nietzsche through the Ancients*. Berlin: De Gruyter.

(2014b). "The Ancient Quarrel between Philosophy and Poetry in Nietzsche's Early Writings." In *Nietzsche's Value as a Scholar of Antiquity*, ed. A. Jensen and H. Heit, 197–214. New York: Bloomsbury Academic.

(2018). "The Divine Hanswurst: Nietzsche on Laughter and Comedy." In *Humor, Comedy, and Laughter in 19th-Century Philosophy*, ed. L. L. Moland, 153–173. New York: Springer.

Middleton, Christopher (1996). *Selected Letters of Friedrich Nietzsche*, ed. and trans. C. Middleton. Indianapolis, IN: Hackett.

Mitcheson, Katrina (2015). "The Experiment of Incorporating Unbounded Truth." In *Nietzsche's Free Spirit Philosophy*, ed. R. Bamford, 139–156. New York: Rowman & Littlefield.

Montinari, Mazzino (2003). *Reading Nietzsche*, trans. G. Whitlock. Urbana, IL: University of Illinois.

More, Nicholas (2014). *Nietzsche's Last Laugh:* Ecce Homo *as Satire*. Cambridge: Cambridge University Press.

Mullin, Amy (2000). "Nietzsche's Free Spirit." *Journal of the History of Philosophy* 38(3): 383–405.

Nehamas, Alexander (1985). *Nietzsche: Life as Literature*. Cambridge, MA: Harvard University Press.

(1988). "Who Are 'The Philosophers of the Future'?: A Reading of *Beyond Good and Evil*." In *Reading Nietzsche*, ed. R. C. Solomon and K. M. Higgins, 46–67. Oxford: Oxford University Press.

Nussbaum, Martha (1994). "Pity and Mercy: Nietzsche's Stoicism." In *Nietzsche, Genealogy, Morality*, ed. R. Schacht, 139–167. Berkeley, CA: University of California Press.

Owen, David (2003). "Nietzsche, Re-evaluation and the Turn to Genealogy." *European Journal of Philosophy* 11(3): 249–272.

Parkes, Graham (1994). *Composing the Soul: Reaches of Nietzsche's Psychology*. Chicago: The University of Chicago Press.

Pippin, Robert (2010). *Nietzsche, Psychology, and First Philosophy*. Chicago: The University of Chicago Press.

Poellner, Peter (1995). *Nietzsche and Metaphysics*. Oxford: Oxford University Press.

Prange, Martine (2012). "*Beyond Good and Evil*." In *A Companion to Friedrich Nietzsche*, ed. P. Bishop, 232–250. Rochester, NY: Camden House.

Reginster, Bernard (2006). *The Affirmation of Life: Nietzsche on the Overcoming of Nihilism*. Cambridge, MA: Harvard University Press.

(2013). "Honesty and Curiosity in Nietzsche's Free Spirits." *Journal of the History of Philosophy* 51(3): 441–463.

Rethy, Robert (1976). "The Descartes Motto to the First Edition of *Menschliches, Allzumenschliches*." *Nietzsche Studien* 5: 289–297.

Riccardi, Mattia (2009). *"Der Faule Fleck des Kantischen Kriticismus": Erscheinung und Ding an sich bei Nietzsche*. Basel: Schwabe Verlag.

Richardson, John (1996). *Nietzsche's System*. Oxford: Oxford University Press.

Ridley, Aaron (1997). "Nietzsche's Greatest Weight." *Journal of Nietzsche Studies* 14: 19–25.

(2007). *Nietzsche on Art*. London: Routledge.

Rutherford, Donald (2011). "Freedom as a Philosophical Ideal: Nietzsche and His Antecedents." *Inquiry* 54(5): 512–540.

Sachs, Carl B. (2008). "Nietzsche's *Daybreak*: Toward a Naturalized Theory of Autonomy." *Epoché* 13(1): 81–100.

Salaquarda, Jörg (1989). "Der ungeheure Augenblick." *Nietzsche Studien* 18: 91–136.

(1997). "Die fröhliche Wissenschaft: Zwischen Freigeisterei und neuer 'Lehre'." *Nietzsche Studien* 26: 165–183.

Salomé, Lou Andreas (1988). *Nietzsche*, trans. S. Mandel. Redding Ridge, CT: Black Swan Books.

Schaberg, William H. (1995). *The Nietzsche Canon*. Chicago: Chicago University Press.

Schacht, Richard (1983). *Nietzsche*. New York: Routledge & Kegan Paul.

(2015). "Nietzsche's 'Free Spirit'." In *Nietzsche's Free Spirit Philosophy*, ed. R. Bamford, 169–188. New York: Rowman & Littlefield.

Scheibenberger, Sarah (2016). *Kommentar zu Nietzsches Ueber Wahrheit und Lüge im aussermoralischen Sinne*. Berlin: De Gruyter.

Schopenhauer, Arthur (1966). *The World as Will and Representation*, trans. E. F. J. Payne. Volumes I and II. New York: Dover Publications.

Siemens, Herman and Katia Hay (2015). "Ridendo Dicere Severum: On Probity, Laughter and Self-Critique in Nietzsche's Figure of the Free Spirit." In *Nietzsche's Free Spirit Philosophy*, ed. R. Bamford, 111–136. New York: Rowman & Littlefield.

Small, Robin (2005). *Nietzsche and Rée: A Star Friendship.* Oxford: Oxford University Press.

(2016). *Friedrich Nietzsche: Reconciling Knowledge and Life.* Cham: Springer.

Soll, Ivan (1973). "Reflections on Recurrence: A Re-examination of Nietzsche's Doctrine, *Die Ewige Wiederkehr des Gleichen.*" In *Nietzsche: A Collection of Critical Essays*, ed. R. Solomon, 322–342. Notre Dame, IN: Notre Dame University Press.

Sommer, Andreas Urs (2013). *Kommentar zu Nietzsches – Der Antichrist, Ecce homo, Dionysos-Dithyramben, Nietzsche contra Wagner.* Berlin: De Gruyter.

(2015). "Is There a Free Spirit in Nietzsche's Late Writings?" In *Nietzsche's Free Spirit Philosophy*, ed. R. Bamford, 253–265. New York: Rowman & Littlefield.

(2016). "Das fünfte Buch. Zur philosophisch-literarischen Wechselwirtschaft der 'neuen Ausgabe' der *Fröhlichen Wissenschaft* und der Bücher von 1886/ 88." In *Nietzsche zwischen Philosophie und Literatur*, ed. K. Grätz and S. Kaufmann, 241–254. Heidelberg: Universitätsverlag Winter.

Speight, Allen (2001). *Hegel, Literature, and the Problem of Agency.* Cambridge: Cambridge University Press.

Stegmaier, Werner (2009). "After Montinari: On Nietzsche Philology." *Journal of Nietzsche Studies* 38: 5–19.

(2012). *Nietzsches Befreiung der Philosophie: Kontextuelle Interpretation des V. Buchs der 'Fröhlichen Wissenschaft'.* Berlin: De Gruyter.

Stern, Tom (2008). "Context and the Individual." *Nietzsche Forschung* 15: 299–315.

(2013). "Nietzsche, *Amor Fati*, and *The Gay Science.*" *Proceedings of the Aristotelian Society* 113(2): 145–162.

Strong, Tracy (1975). *Friedrich Nietzsche and the Politics of Transfiguration.* Berkeley, CA: University of California Press.

Swales, Martin (1978). *The German Bildungsroman from Wieland to Hesse.* Princeton, NJ: Princeton University Press.

Treiber, Hubert (1992). "Wahlverwandtschaften zwischen Nietzsches Idee eines 'Klosters fuer freiere Geister und Webers Idealtypus der puritanischen Sekte." *Nietzsche Studien* 21: 326–362.

Ure, Michael (2008). *Nietzsche's Therapy: Self-Cultivation in the Middle Works.* Lanham, MD: Lexington Books.

Vivarelli, Vivetta (1994). "Montaigne und der 'Freie Geist'." *Nietzsche Studien* 23: 79–101.

(1998). *Nietzsche und die Masken des freien Geistes: Montaigne, Pascal, und Sterne.* Würzburg: Königshausen & Neumann.

Westerdale, Joel (2013). *Nietzsche's Aphoristic Challenge.* Berlin: De Gruyter.

Wohlfart, Günter (1991). *Also sprach Herakleitos: Heraklits Fragment B 52 und Nietzsches Heraklit-Rezeption.* Freiburg/Munich: Karl Alber.

Young, Julian (1992). *Nietzsche's Philosophy of Art.* Cambridge: Cambridge University Press.

(2010). *Friedrich Nietzsche: A Philosophical Biography.* Cambridge: Cambridge University Press.

(2013). "Nietzsche and Women." In *The Oxford Handbook of Nietszche*, ed. K. Gemes and J. Richardson, 46–62. Oxford: Oxford University Press.

Zittel, Claus (1995). *Selbstaufhebungsfiguren bei Nietzsche.* Würzburg: Königshausen & Neumann.

Index

Abbey, Ruth, 35–36
Aeschylus, 66, 168, 189, 198, 232
affirmation, 56, 221
  Dionysian, 234
  of life, *see* life, affirmation of
  man of, 193
  practical world-, 96
agon, 260–261
altruism, 165, 178, 207, *see also* pity
amor fati, 221, 229, 233
analepsis, 49, 78–81
Ansell-Pearson, Keith, 46–47, 146
anthropomorphism, 88, 96, 155, 204–205,
  243
Antichrist, 262
aphorism, 9–10, 16, 28, 37–41
appearance, 56, 62, 93, 195–198, 201, 222
aristocracy, 169–170
Aristophanes, 241, 246, 250, 259–260,
  see also comedy
Aristotle, 29, 94, 103, 163, 168, 174, 198, 233,
  237
art, 5–8, 11, 15–16, 19, 29, 31, 33, 35,
  44, 46, 51–52, 54, 60–61, 85–86,
  88–89, 92, 96–97, 103, 105–109, 117,
  122, 124, 127–130, 147, 151, 154, 161,
  168, 174, 176, 180, 184–185, 188,
  196–203, 212, 222, 224, 236, 243,
  245–246, 254, 256
  Apollonian, 60, 198
  Dionysian, 12, 57, 145, 198, 229, 232, 245,
  254, 262
  tragic, *see* tragedy
artist, 14, 89, 105–109, 127–128, 174,
  176, 187, 196–203, 224, 238, 245,
  258
ascetic ideal, 58, 88, 185, 203–204, 228, 242,
  259
asceticism, 7, 46, 52, 56–58, 72, 85, 104, 120,
  127, 142, 164, 173, 182, 184–185, 221,
  225–226, 244

ataraxia, 46, 143, 145, 151, 153, *see also*
  tranquility
atheism, 229, 253
autobiography, 18, 261

Baubo, 54, 258–259
Bayreuth, 18, 65, 67, 69–70, 77, 184
  Festival, 16, 19, 50, 66–67, 106, 200
becoming, 44, 62, 89, 91, 93–94, 132, 134, 138,
  156, 175, 233–234, 252, 256,
  see also Heraclitus, *see also* ontology
  innocence of, 57, 156, 237
becoming who one is, 18–19, 24, 44, 50–51,
  64–66, 71, 79, 111, 163, 203, 228–229,
  252, 261
Bildung, 4, 18, 28–29, 31, 64, 111, 130, *see also*
  education
Bildungsroman, 3–6, 8–9, 18, 20–21, 26–29,
  31–35, 48, 64, 72, 80, 90, 177, 182, 203,
  240, 261–262
Brusotti, Marco, 22–23, 40, 56–58, 71, 75, 124,
  134, 142, 144–145, 151, 153–154, 156, 159,
  168, 176–177, 180, 186, 201, 209, 212, 225

camel, 7, 53, 56
categorical imperative, 190, 227
child, 7–8, 57, 62, 89, 154, 237–238
Christianity, 101–102, 104, 131, 136, 140, 142,
  144, 146, 159–160, 165, 182, 207–208, 210,
  214, 228–229, 237, 251, 253, 255–256, 260
  Laws Against, 259
Clark, Maudemarie, 10–13, 41, 55, 195
closest things, 44, 122, 124, 134–137, 142,
  144–145, 147, 151, 154, 209
cogito, 92, 221
Cohen, Jonathan, 40, 85–86, 89, 95, 121–122,
  147
comedy, 8, 20, 54, 57, 186–189, 199, 201, 212,
  219, 229, 239, 241, 245, 247, 252, 256,
  258–262, *see also* Dionysus, *see also*
  Aristophanes